THE
BICENTENNIAL
GUIDE TO
THE
AMERICAN
REVOLUTION

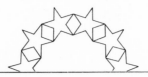

VOLUME ONE

THE BICENTENNIAL GUIDE TO THE AMERICAN REVOLUTION

THE WAR IN THE NORTH

Sol Stember

NEW YORK · 1974

SATURDAY REVIEW PRESS | E. P. DUTTON & CO., INC.

Library of Congress Cataloging in Publication Data

Stember, Sol.
The bicentennial guide to the American Revolution.

Includes bibliographies.
CONTENTS: *v. 1. The war in the North.—v. 2. The middle Colonies.—*
v. 3. The war in the South.
1. United States—History—Revolution—Campaigns and battles.
2. United States—History—Revolution—Museums.
3. United States—Description and travel—
1960–   —Guide-books. I. Title.
E230.S74   973.3'3   73-23108

Published simultaneously in Canada by Clarke, Irwin & Company Limited, Toronto and Vancouver
ISBN: 0-8415-0310-9 (cloth)
ISBN: 0-8415-0311-7 (paper)
Designed by The Etheredges

To my wife, Rosaline,
who packed the bags, made the reservations,
helped with the research,
typed the manuscript, read the maps,
and shared the driving and walking all the way
from Lexington to Yorktown.

PUBLISHER'S NOTE: Much of the detailed factual information in this book has been and is subject to change. Visitors to historical sites are urged to check locally on times of opening and closing and on admission charges. They should also remember that highway route numbers may have changed since the book was compiled, especially for county and municipal routes. In addition, speed limits may have been altered in the attempt to conserve fuel. In some cases, continuing restoration on sites may have altered the sites from the way they are described here.

Boldface type has been used to designate major features on the sites—named structures and the like. ***Boldface italics*** point out smaller landmarks, mostly those without particular names.

CONTENTS

III. MOVING SOUTH WITH BURGOYNE 48

IV. UP THE HUDSON WITH CLINTON AND OTHERS 115

LIST OF MAPS

ACKNOWLEDGMENTS
(For all three volumes of the Guide)

No man is an island, particularly when he is trailblazing through territory new to him and most particularly when he attempts to produce a work of this extent. Space does not permit me to acknowledge all the help and advice I received from numerous historical societies and their members who were in touch with me at one time or another during the preparation and writing of this book. A few names, I confess, I either neglected to record or lost along the way. I am thinking particularly of the Francis Marion National Forest ranger who took us to the site of the Wambaw fight and the gentleman at the courthouse in Calhoun County, South Carolina, who finally put us on the right track to Fort Motte. To you and to others whom I may have neglected to mention, my sincere apologies. I am most grateful for your help and for the help of all those persons and organizations listed below by state or agency.

FEDERAL GOVERNMENT: John V. Vosburgh, Chief, Branch of Features, U.S. Department of the Interior, National Park Service. CANADA: David Lee, National Historic Sites Service; Sergeant F. C. Ouellette, College Militaire Royal, Saint-Jean, Quebec; Jacques Seguin, Regional Director, National and Historic Parks, Department of Indian Affairs and Northern Development. CONNECTICUT: Susan C. Finlay, Wethersfield; Preston R. Bassett, Ridgefield; Daniel M. McKeon, Ridgebury; Herbert Barbee, Connecticut Historical Commission. GEORGIA: James G. Bogle, Georgia Historical Commission; William Cox and Josephine Martin, Liberty County Historical Society; Carroll Hart, Director, Department of Arhives and History; Lilla M. Hawes, Director, Georgia Historical Society; Billy Townsend, Georgia Historical Commission; A. Ray Rowland,

Richmond County Historical Society; Dixon Hollingsworth, Sylvania; Mary Gregory Jewett, Director, Georgia Historical Commission; Savannah Chamber of Commerce. MAINE: John W. Briggs, State Park and Recreation Commission; White Nichols, President, Arnold Expedition Historical Society; Ellenore Doudiet, Curator, Wilson Museum, Castine. MASSACHUSETTS: John P. McMorrow, Boston Redevelopment Authority; Mary V. Darcy, Executive Secretary, Revolutionary War Bicentennial Commission; Bernard Wax, Director, American Jewish Historical Society; Bay State Historic League. NEW HAMPSHIRE: Dr. J. Duane Squires, Chairman, New Hampshire American Revolution Bicentennial Commission; Enzo Serafini, Chairman, New Hampshire Historical Commission; Ralph H. Morse, Department of Resources and Economic Development, Division of Economic Development. NEW JERSEY: Dirk Van Dommlan, Superintendent, Washington Crossing State Park; Frank Ender, Acting Superintendent, Monmouth Battlefield State Park; Milicent Feltus, Monmouth County Historical Association; Margaret M. Toolen, Fort Lee; Mary T. Hewitt, Hancock House, Hancock's Bridge; Isabelle Brooks, Office of Historic Sites, Department of Environmental Protection. NEW YORK: Willa Skinner, Fishkill Town Historian; May M. MacMorris, Argyle; Wallace F. Workmaster, Old Fort Ontario; Dole F. Watts, Thousand Islands State Park Commission; Jean Saunders, Curator and Mrs. Charles Franklin, Historian, Putnam County Historical Society; John H. Mead, Curator, New Windsor Cantonment; Marie C. Preston, County Historian, Livingston County; Raymond Safford, Historian, Staten Island; Virginia Moskowitz, Eastchester; William H. Seeger, Curator, Old Stone Fort, Schoharie; William Meuse, Superintendent, Saratoga National Historical Park; Albert Cerak, Miller House; Leon Dunn, Curator, Oriskany Battlefield; Frank Pabst, Plattsburgh; Dean Sinclair, Cherry Valley; Lieutenant Colonel Merle Sheffield (Ret.), West Point Military Academy; Lieutenant Colonel Patrick H. Dionne, Public Information Officer, West Point Military Academy; Mark Lawton, Director, New York State Historic Trust; Scott Robinson, White Plains; Josephine Gardner, Suffern; John Focht, Garrison; Mrs. Jankovsky, Middleburgh; New-York Historical Society. NORTH CAROLINA: Hugh B. Johnston, Jr., Wilson; Sharon Kuhne, Ruth Little, and Elizabeth Wilborn, Division of Historic Sites and Museums, Department of Archives and History; Edenton Chamber of Commerce; Duke Power Company (Cowan's Ford Hydroelectric Station); Catherine Hoskins, Summerfield; Tryon Palace Commission. PENNSYLVANIA: Mr. and Mrs. O. W. June, Paoli; Wilbur C. Kriebel, Administrative Director, Chester County American Independence Bicentennial Committee; Robert

I. Alotta, President, Schackamaxon Society, Inc.; William A. Hunter, Chief, Division of History, Pennsylvania Historical and Museum Commission; Edward Seladones, Department of Forest and Water, Pennsylvania Historical and Museum Commission. RHODE ISLAND: Albert T. Klyberg, Director, Rhode Island Historical Society; Richard Alan Dow, Rhode Island Development Council; Leonard J. Panaggio, Chief, Tourist Promotion Division of the Development Council. SOUTH CAROLINA: David V. Rosdahl, U.S. Department of Agriculture Forest Service, Columbia; Virginia Richard Sauls, Clarendon County Historical Commission; Dr. Thomas Marion Davis, Manning; Terry W. Libscomb, South Carolina Archives Department; W. Bruce Ezell, Ninety-six; J. Percival Petit, Isle of Palms; John Morall, Beaufort; Thomas Thornhill and Harrington Bissell, The Old Provost, Charleston; Charles Duell, Middleton Gardens; Helen McCormick, Gibbes Art Gallery, Charleston; Jean Ulmer, Calhoun County Library; Dr. and Mrs. P. Jenkins of James Island; Charleston Chamber of Commerce; Georgetown Chamber of Commerce; Camden Chamber of Commerce; Beaufort Chamber of Commerce. VIRGINIA: Howard A. MacCord, Sr., Archaeological Society of Virginia; Elie Weeks, President, Goochland County Historical Society; Charles E. Hatch, Jr., Yorktown Battlefield, Colonial National Historical Park; Mrs. Ashton W. Clark, Yorktown; J. R. Fishburne, Assistant Director and H. Peter Pudner, Virginia Historic Landmarks Commission; Rufus Easter, Executive Director, Charles Long, Program Director, and Mrs. S. Evans, Hampton Association for the Arts and Humanities; Colonel and Mrs. Boris Polanski, Hampton; Alf J. Mapp, Jr., Chairman, Portsmouth Revolutionary Bicentennial Commission; Robert F. Selden, Mathews County Historical Society; Edward A. Wyatt, Petersburg; Mr. and Mrs. John H. Wright, Goochland County; Mr. and Mrs. J. W. Seigfried, Point of Fork; Captain and Mrs. Igor Moravsky, Goochland County; Mabel Bellwood, Red Hill; Mary R. M. Goodwin, Williamsburg; Emily N. Spong, Portsmouth; Park Rouse, Director, Virginia Bicentennial Commission and Jamestown Foundation; Hampton Information Center.

I also wish to express my thanks to my publishers for staying with me all the way and especially to the editors without whose guidance and help I would never have finished: Steve Frimmer who got me started, Stephanie Erickson who pronounced the book acceptable, and Tom Davis who saw it through to the end. I have a particular word of thanks and admiration for Judy Bentley who cast an appraising, critical eye over the finished manuscript and guided me through a polishing process that improved the book immensely. I owe a special debt of gratitude to Joy

Meisels, Director of the New City Library, and to her staff for searching out and providing many of the books and other reference works upon which my research was based.

There is a bibliography in the usual place which lists most of the books, pamphlets, magazines, and other materials I consulted and read. Since my purpose was to produce a readable, practical history-travel guide, I was under no compulsion to uncover new, hitherto unknown or forgotten material or even to go to primary sources, which I did, nevertheless, when they were readily available. I found the standard works on the Revolution more than suitable for my purposes. I especially recommend to any reader who may want to go deeper into this fascinating period of American history Christopher Ward's *War of the Revolution,* the first two volumes of James Thomas Flexner's four-volume biography of *George Washington,* E. B. Greene's *The Revolutionary Generation,* John C. Miller's *Origins of the Revolution,* and Carl Van Doren's *Secret History of the Revolution.* The Arno Press reprint series of eyewitness accounts makes for wonderful reading. Mark Boatner's *Encyclopedia of the American Revolution* is the best ready reference book I have ever used and an excellent distillation of Revolutionary War fact and lore.

A word about maps. As much as possible, I tried to lay out routes and tours according to the standard road maps issued by the American Automobile Association and the oil companies. I found most of them adequate for generally finding my way, but naturally inadequate once we left the well-traveled, well-beaten paths. Surprisingly, some of these maps contradict each other in specific details such as the locations of certain towns and the routes followed by certain roads. Therefore, it is always a good idea to use more than one map. County maps were indispensable once state routes were left behind for the more remote, back-country areas in which many sites are located. They are cheap and can be obtained by writing to or visiting state highway and transportation departments in state capitals.

PREFACE

(To all three volumes of the Guide)

I fell in love with Clio, the Muse of history, the day I sat in George Washington's chair. At the time I was writing a series of children's educational television programs, and I had been assigned scripts on Washington, Lincoln, Benjamin Franklin, Columbus, Thanksgiving, and the Constitutional Convention of 1789.

The very first of these scripts to go on the air was the one about the Constitutional Convention. This was *live* television and I had obtained permission to use a number of props connected with the actual event, some of them of great historical value, including the chair Washington had sat in while he presided over the convention. It was that chair that stole my heart for the Muse. The chair was the focal point of the set and the script. I had traveled to Philadelphia to get it and had sworn to the authorities in charge that I would protect and defend it with my life, my fortune, and my sacred honor. It had come from Philadelphia by station wagon, carefully crated and heavily insured. It was then placed in my special care for twenty-four hours, no more.

When the show was over, I stood amid the cables and discarded scripts, looking at the chair. It had been left for last while the rest of the props were repacked and sent on their way to their rightful owners. For the moment, it was deserted and forgotten. The bright lights were dimmed now and the cameras were off, but briefly it had regained a measure of its former glory in the eyes of a far larger audience spread out across a nation far greater than anything the man who had made it famous could possibly have imagined or foreseen.

There is a design of the rayed sun carved into it, just above where

Washington's head must have touched when he sat in it, for though he was a tall man, this chair has a very high back. At the end of the convention, after all the wrangling and arguing and bad feelings had been resolved, and old and tired Franklin, who had worked so hard on the side of reason and compromise, rose to remark that all through the weary sessions he had been looking at that sun on the chairman's chair, wondering if it represented a rising or a setting sun. Now he knew, he said, that it was indeed a rising sun.

I too had been looking at the chair during the long hours of rehearsal and repetition and exasperation and frustration over the little but important mistakes and delays that made live television so alive, and then through the final, tension-filled half hour of the performance. What would it feel like, I thought, to sit in the chair that Washington sat in while he was making history? No one was paying any attention, and—what the hell!—it was my life, my fortune, and my sacred honor, right? I crossed the studio, stood in front of the chair for a moment, then turned and sat down.

I cannot pretend that during the few seconds I sat where Washington had sat I was transported back in time to 1789. I cannot say that I felt his eyes staring at me accusingly or felt a well-placed boot on my rear end as I got up and stepped away, which is what I really deserved. The prop men took the chair to its waiting crate, and a few minutes later it was on its way back to Philadelphia; I did not see it again—much less resume my seat—until I visited Philadelphia for this book. I do know that in that moment I felt a sense of continuity of Time and of Man.

I have had in my hands the letter Washington wrote from Valley Forge to Congress asking for money and supplies for his starving, freezing soldiers, the purse he left behind in Jumel Mansion, Lincoln's traveling desk on which he may have written the Gettysburg Address, an astrolabe used by a sixteenth-century Spanish navigator, a hand-illuminated Bible from the twelfth century, Ben Franklin's glass harmonium and a pair of his spectacles, Robert E. Lee's personal copy of Grant's surrender terms, Aaron Burr's dueling pistols, and a set of "running irons" used by rustlers in the 1880s. I have walked on the field where Pickett led his famous charge (in fact, I slept in a motel on that field), stood on Jefferson Rock and looked at much the same view of Harpers Ferry that Jefferson saw long before John Brown made the place famous, touched the stones of the Roman Forum, and felt the pavement of Pompeii under my feet while I listened with my eyes closed for the lost sound of chariot wheels. Still waiting for me are the ruins of Luxor, the fortress on Masada, the climb up the sacred hill to the oracle at Delphi, and the descent into the caves of Lascaux.

This book is for everyone who feels that same sense of continuity, in an American context. This book is an invitation to walk where Washington, Lafayette, Alexander Hamilton, Benedict Arnold, Daniel Morgan, Benjamin Franklin, Thomas Jefferson, Ethan Allen, and Molly Pitcher and all that host of men and women walked who fought and died long before we were born, but who still live in the stones and buildings and hills and fields they touched and held in their eyes. This book is a guide and a passport to a far country in a time past that is in a sense still with us. I have been there myself, visiting all the places I describe in this book. I invite you to follow.

VOLUME ONE

THE
WAR IN THE NORTH

INTRODUCTION

The war came early to New York State. The echoes of "the shot heard round the world" fired in April, 1775, had scarcely died away before Ethan Allen and his Green Mountain Boys were storming the gates of Fort Ticonderoga. From then until the last British troops in New York City took ship for Canada in November, 1783, the Empire State loomed large in the developing story of the Revolution.

A great deal of military activity during the American Revolution took place in New York State. Armies and parts of armies marched and fought along its river valleys. Patriots, Tories, and Indians played a deadly game of foxes and hounds over its hills, down its valleys, and through its cities and towns. For almost eight years battles, skirmishes, massacres, raids, and intrigues were common occurrences, hardly surprising for a state encompassing within its borders both New York City, one of the principal seaports along the Atlantic coast, and the Hudson River, then a major artery of military traffic and communications linking New England with the Middle Atlantic states and the South. The city and the river were key factors in strategic planning for the British from the time Washington forced them out of Boston in 1775 until their final defeat at Yorktown.

For the convenience of you, the reader, as you travel from site to site, I have divided the state into five regions that roughly correspond to five periods in the history of the Revolution. This arrangement will lead you from one region to another on a north-south axis, with one long divergence westward to those sites in the interior where frontier warfare raged intermittently. Gradually the events of the Revolution will unfold and develop before you almost in calendar order, act by act, scene by scene, up to the demobilization of the Continental Army.

Volume I starts with Book I recounting the capture of Fort Ticonderoga and the raid on Crown Point, the opening phase of the war in New York. Book II traces the abortive Montgomery-Arnold invasion of Canada from Ile-aux-Noix to the assault on Quebec and the long retreat that followed. Book III follows British Generals Carleton and Burgoyne south from Canada, from the taking of Ticonderoga and its sister forts to the Battle of Saratoga, including the Battle of Valcour Island, the siege of Fort Stanwix, and the battles of Oriskany and Bennington. Book IV tells the story of the rebel fortifications in the Hudson Highlands and takes you north on Clinton's expedition from New York City to its high-water mark at Clermont. This section also covers the sites connected with Benedict Arnold's treason plot. Book V takes you to the few remaining Revolutionary War sites in New York City, then up into Westchester County to the sites in the city's environs, the Battle of White Plains and Washington's retreat into New Jersey. Books VI–X cover New England where it all began.

The British thought of New England as the head of the rebellious snake. Actually the fires that burned away the ties between the colonies and the mother country were lit in a hundred places from the rockbound coasts to rice paddy savannahs. Once the British evacuated Boston in the spring of 1776, the war shifted first to New York, then to Pennsylvania and New Jersey, and finally into the South.

In the winter of 1776, Sir Henry Clinton occupied Newport, Rhode Island, but when he went on to play a more important role in succeeding events, his men stayed behind, the only British garrison of any importance north of New York. In October, 1775, the town of Falmouth (today Portland in Maine) was bombarded by a small British naval force in retaliation for its acts of open rebellion. In July, 1777, the fields and hills near present-day Hubbardton, Vermont, were the scene of a small battle between a detachment of Burgoyne's army and the rear guard of the rebels they were hotly pursuing from Fort Ticonderoga. In 1778 an attempt was made to take Newport back from the British, very nearly at the expense of the newly formed French-American alliance. During this time, Connecticut was subjected to a series of hit-and-run raids.

New England is divided into five sections also. The first is a trip into Maine to cover a few coastal sites and the Arnold expedition's route through the state on its way to Quebec. The second section covers Massachusetts, the beginning of the war. After stopping in New Hampshire and Vermont in the third part, you will visit Rhode Island for the Battle of Rhode Island, and then wind up the New England tour along the Connecticut coast.

These sections correspond only approximately to the sequence of events in the years of the Revolution. Were you to attempt to follow a strict chronology, you would find yourself traveling back and forth through the original thirteen states, retracing your steps time and again until monotony and boredom replaced the eagerness and pleasure with which you started out. Nevertheless, you must expect to do some backtracking where events in widely separated areas were part of an overall design, if for no other reason than to avoid a certain amount of historical confusion. Where there is some geographical mingling of sites concerning events that occurred separately in time, the workaday history buff will find it a matter of small mental inconvenience to be taken in stride.

Are you ready to start? Good. Settle the kids in the back of the car, make sure someone has a nose firmly imbedded in the first road map, point your faithful family chariot in the right direction, and you're on your way.

I.

THE
FIRST NORTHERN
CAMPAIGN

FORT TICONDEROGA

Fort Ticonderoga takes its name from an Indian word meaning "land between waters." Idiomatically this refers to a portage, land over which it is possible to carry boats and supplies from one body of water to another. Two hundred years ago Fort Ticonderoga dominated such a portage, a vital connection between two links in a chain of waterways stretching from Montreal to New York City along one axis, and from the Hudson Valley west to the Great Lakes along another. The fort stands on a promontory overlooking southern Lake Champlain on the Montreal to New York City waterway. Around a hill to the south, called Mount Defiance, the waters of Lake George flow through two hundred feet of rapids into Champlain. Champlain stretches its narrow length north between Vermont and New York before emptying into the Richelieu River, which extends still farther north through Canada into the Saint Lawrence River to Montreal.

As you look at your New York State road map, notice that the New York State Thruway and the Adirondack Northway, Interstates 87 and 90, parallel the same system of rivers and lakes. Now, with a twist of the imagination, erase the present road system from the map, leaving the waterways, and you will clearly see why these rivers and lakes were worth the fighting and the dying. Colonial America was an almost impenetrable wilderness, a vast forest except for a narrow strip of settled land along its eastern edge, no wider in most places than the distance between the Atlantic beaches and the Appalachian mountain ranges. Through this

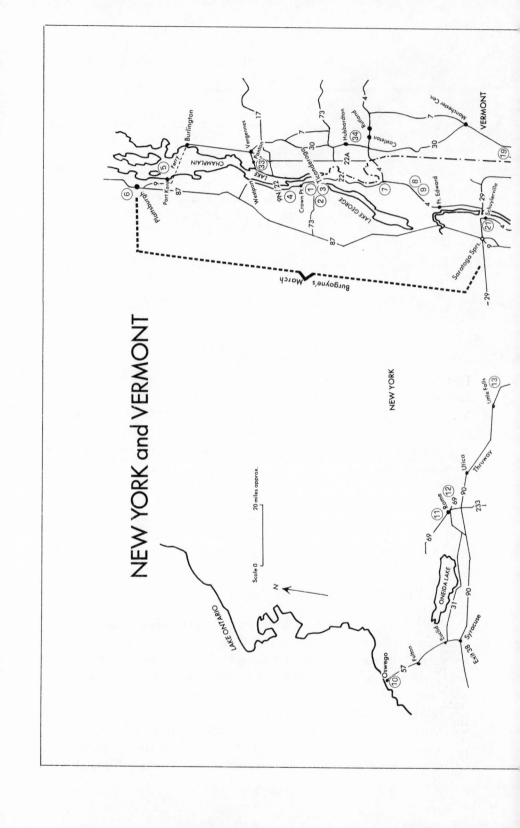

NEW YORK and VERMONT

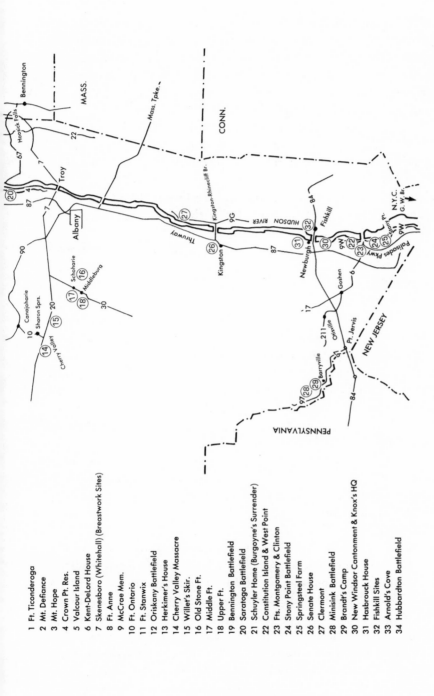

1 Ft. Ticonderoga
2 Mt. Defiance
3 Mt. Hope
4 Crown Pt. Res.
5 Valcour Island
6 Kent-DeLord House
7 Skenesboro (Whitehall) (Breastwork Sites)
8 Ft. Anne
9 McCrae Mem.
10 Ft. Ontario
11 Ft. Stanwix
12 Oriskany Battlefield
13 Herkimer's House
14 Cherry Valley Massacre
15 Willer's Skir.
16 Old Stone Ft.
17 Middle Ft.
18 Upper Ft.
19 Bennington Battlefield
20 Saratoga Battlefield
21 Schuyler Home (Burgoyne's Surrender)
22 Constitution Island & West Point
23 Fts. Montgomery & Clinton
24 Stony Point Battlefield
25 Springsteel Farm
26 Senate House
27 Clermont
28 Minisink Battlefield
29 Brandt's Camp
30 New Windsor Cantonment & Knox's HQ
31 Hasbrouck House
32 Fishkill Sites
33 Arnold's Cove
34 Hubbardton Battlefield

narrow strip meandered a few dirt roads. Threaded through the forest were lakes and rivers or streams, the only means of moving with comparative ease and speed from forest settlement to settlement, from the settlements to the seacoast ports, and from region to region. The two major waterways, the Hudson River–Mohawk River–Oneida Lake–Lake Ontario system and the Saint Lawrence–Richelieu–Champlain–George–Hudson system meet where Cohoes, New York, now stands, just above the city of Troy. These were the "roads" most frequently used by marauding Indian bands when they raided rich settlements along the Hudson and Mohawk valleys and in southern New England, and these were the "military highways" used by both the British and the French during their long struggle for control of the continent. Upon the control of these roads rested the fate of the infant republic.

The Montreal–New York waterway goes along the Saint Lawrence River to the Richelieu River, Lake Champlain, and Lake George and to a point a few miles north of where the Hudson River, flowing eastward from its source, Lake Tear of the Clouds, curves south and heads for the sea less than three hundred miles away. An alternative route carried one to the southern tip of Lake Champlain, then south along Wood Creek and across a narrow stretch of land to the Hudson. Except for the portages at the extremities of Lakes George and Champlain and a portage around the rapids in the Richelieu River, it was one continuous stretch of water along which moved rafts, scows, barges, sloops, gundalows, bateaux, canoes, and whatever else floated and could carry men, guns, and supplies. It was not, however, simply a matter of drifting with the current. All the waterways in this north-south system flow north except for the Hudson, so that in traveling from north to south one had to move against the current until the Hudson was reached. Conversely, traveling north from the Hudson was a lot simpler.

It will be even simpler for you in this era of turnpikes and thruways, from whichever direction you approach Fort Ticonderoga. From the north or south, take the Adirondack Northway (Interstate 87) to Exit 28 (Schroon Lake and Brant Lake), then State Highway 73 east to the village of Ticonderoga. From the west and southeast, take Interstate 90 to Exit 24 to the Northway north and follow it to Exit 28 as above. From due east or northeast, take U.S. Route 7 through Vermont to either Vermont 17 (and the bridge across Lake Champlain at Chimney Point and then 9N south), or to Route 74, or Route 73 and the ferry that crosses the lake directly north of the fort.

If you do not reach Ticonderoga well before dark and so wish to rest overnight before assaulting the fort, you will find comparatively few motels in and around Ticonderoga village, despite the crowd of visitors that come to the fort every summer. Hague, on Lake George, ten miles to the south along 9N, is a delightful spot on what I think is one of the most beautiful lakes in the world, but it has even fewer accommodations than Ticonderoga. It might be wise to stop an hour or so from the fort at some place where accommodations are more plentiful. In Bolton Landing, about fifteen miles south of Hague along 9N, the motels line both sides of the road. Burlington, Vermont, fifty miles north of Ticonderoga on the east side of Champlain, has a goodly number of hotels and motels.

Signs in Ticonderoga direct you out of town to the fort, as well as to Mounts Hope and Defiance which we will visit later. On the way through Ticonderoga, you will pass or cross over a waterfall or two and see the stream that goes through the village. This is Ticonderoga Creek which empties the waters of Lake George into Champlain, and this land you are driving through is all part of the portage area which travelers moving between the two lakes had to cross. After two miles you will come to the stone gateway to the promontory on which Fort Ticonderoga stands. A mile-long approach road leads through a lovely wooded area to the fort entrance. The road is lined with monuments and memorials to the men and military units—French, British, and American—that have served in and around the fort. At one point you may want to stop to inspect a reconstructed section of log wall that marks the site of the defenses Montcalm built when he defended the fort from the British in 1758. Near the parking field are picnic tables and barbecue sites under the trees, a lunch room, comfort stations, souvenirs, and the ticket booth.

The fort is open to the public every day from mid-May to mid-October between 8 A.M. and 6 P.M. In July and August visiting hours are extended to 7 P.M. Adult admission is $1.50; children aged ten to fourteen years pay $1.00; children under ten are admitted free. School classes accompanied by their teachers may be admitted free upon written application to the Fort Ticonderoga Association, Ticonderoga, New York. Bathing suits and portable radios are not permitted; dogs on leash and cameras are.

The admission fees support a nonprofit educational organization formed by members of the Pell family, which has owned and maintained the fort and surrounding ground since William Ferris Pell bought it in 1840. At that time it was nothing but a shell of its former self. Burgoyne had captured it in 1777, but abandoned it a few months later. It was never again garrisoned, though the site was kept under constant surveillance by both Continentals and redcoats to ensure that neither made the attempt. After the Treaty of Paris, its military value fell to rock bottom, and it was forgotten by everyone except the local inhabitants, who, like the citizens of Rome following the fall of the empire, quarried the local ruin for their own purposes. They pried loose stones from the walls of the fort and other structures and incorporated them into their farms and buildings until there was little left but the foundations. In the **Fort Ticonderoga Museum** are a number of paintings from the nineteenth century showing the fort in various stages of dismemberment. In 1908 Stephen Pell, great-grandson of William Ferris Pell, began rebuilding the walls on the old foundations. Although the fort has been almost completely restored, the work is still in progress at this writing, with an interior blockhouse tower and another barracks building almost completed.

Fort Ticonderoga was originally built by the French as an outpost for Fort St. Frederic at Crown Point farther down the lake (remember, down-lake is north). It was called Carillon because the noise of the creek water falling over the rocks as it tumbled out of Lake George and into Champlain sounded to the builders of the fort like chimes. I listened very hard from several likely positions on the ramparts but was unable to hear so much as a tinkle. Originally the fort consisted of squared-off timbers laid horizontally and backed by embankments, which were able to withstand the artillery of the times and could be easily repaired. Since, however, the wood eventually rotted and presented a fire hazard when dry, the French gradually substituted stone for wood and finally produced a completely stone fort. During the French and Indian War, Carillon was attacked on July 8, 1758, by the British, who tried to frontally assault the log wall that the commander, the Marquis de Montcalm, had built across the promontory. The attackers lost almost 3,000 men out of 15,000 against the loss of 300 defenders out of 3,500. The British left but returned under General Jeffrey Amherst one year later, by which time the French garrison had been drastically reduced. After a four-day siege, Amherst invested the fort, but not before the French had evacuated their troops and blown up their powder. Amherst repaired the damage and renamed the fort Ticonderoga. For the next sixteen years it was occupied by the British.

When open warfare broke out between King George III and his American colonists and the Americans began to put together an army, more than one wise rebel head realized that no army could last long without artillery and remembered that "Fort Ti" was well supplied with guns.

The immediate need was for cannon to strengthen the American siege lines around Boston. Two schemes were hatched simultaneously. Early in May, 1775, Benedict Arnold, a successful Connecticut merchant and smuggler and a recently elected captain of militia, sold the idea of capturing Fort Ticonderoga to the Massachusetts Committee of Safety. The committee commissioned Arnold as a colonel and authorized him to recruit a company of four hundred men for the purpose. At the same time the Connecticut assembly presented a similar plan to Ethan Allen and suggested that he and his Green Mountain Boys follow through. Arnold got wind of the Connecticut plan and, leaving his recruiting officers to form his company for him, rode to Castleton, Vermont, where Allen's men were gathering for the attack.

Arnold showed his written commission and attempted to take over command of the expedition, but the men refused to follow anyone but their own leader. Arnold then rode to Hand's Cove on the eastern shore of Lake Champlain, about two miles across from the fort, where Allen was making preparations for the assault, and got him to agree to share the command.

Since this is the first time Benedict Arnold appeared on the American stage, let us take a close look at the man who was to switch roles in the coming drama from hero to archvillain. Mark M. Boatner, in his *Encyclopedia of the American Revolution,* gives this description: "Five feet nine inches tall, thick set . . . icy grey eyes set off by black hair and a swarthy complexion [perhaps from long months at sea; he owned his own ships and had traded in the West Indies] . . . tremendously energetic and restless . . . unusually strong and possessing great stamina." Boatner also cites a drawing of Arnold done from life by a French artist, which shows Arnold with a beaky nose, a heavy jutting jaw, and a sloping brow.

The assault party of two to three hundred men assembled at Hand's Cove on the east shore of Lake Champlain near the present town of Shoreham, Vermont. Allen had sent a detachment to Skenesboro (Whitehall, New York), farther south on the lake, to capture boats for the crossing from Philip Skenes, the town's founder. Skenes, a Tory, was planning with the British to form a separate state or province in the Champlain area that would encompass parts of New York and New Hampshire, which then included the New Hampshire Grants (now Vermont). This made him a special target for Ethan Allen who had different plans for his native New Hampshire Grants.

When the detachment failed to return by just before dawn on Wednesday, May 10, Allen decided to move without them. He ordered eighty-three of his men into a couple of scows, the only boats available, and, with Arnold sticking to his side like glue, rowed across the lake through a succession of wind and rain squalls that threatened to upset the clumsy craft but covered their approach from the fort's defenders. By the time they landed, it was too light to send the boats back for more men, so Allen decided to press the attack with the men at hand, less than one-third of his total strength. They proved more than adequate for the job.

The fort was manned at the time by a detachment of forty-three men, some of whom had wives and children living with them, about twenty altogether. They were commanded by Captain William Delaplace and Lieutenant Jocelyn Feltham. Delaplace had reported suspicious Patriot activity around the fort earlier in the year, and General Thomas Gage, British commander in chief in America, had warned him to prepare for a possible surprise attack. Nevertheless, the south wall of the fort was in a state of disrepair, and it was from this direction that Allen had decided to attack at a point known as the Grenadier's Redoubt. Following a road or trail through the thick woods that covered the ground to the south of the fort, the attackers got up to the wall without being detected by the sentries. They found the south gate closed, but in the gate was a wicket wide enough to admit two men at a time which had, for some reason, been left open. Through this the rebels filtered until they were discovered by a sentry, who aimed his gun and pulled the trigger. The gun misfired and the sentry ran for the interior of the fort, yelling the alarm at the top of his lungs. A second sentry moved to the attack with his bayonet. Allen hit him over the head with the flat of his sword and stretched him out. The attackers charged into the fort whooping and yelling.

Entering the parade ground, now called the Place des Armes, they formed up back to back facing the barracks where the garrison was still asleep. Delaplace and Feltham were in their quarters on the second floor of the barracks, still snug abed.

The lieutenant, who later described the event in a written account, remembers that he was awakened by shouts of "No quarter! No quarter!" from the attacking force. He ran to Delaplace's room, pants in hand, and tried to rouse that gentleman to his senses.

By that time Allen and Arnold, with drawn swords, were coming up the wooden outside stairs that led to the top floor, demanding the fort's surrender; that is to say, Allen was bellowing, "Come on out, you damn old rat!" or words to that effect, while, as Feltham recalls, Arnold seconded him "in a genteel manner." The two startled Britons tried to stall, hoping their men would soon sally forth to the rescue, but by then the Green Mountain Boys had swarmed into the barracks and awakened the redcoats in their own inimitable fashion. Allen swore that if one of the defenders fired so much as a single shot, the entire garrison and the women and children would pay with their lives. Delaplace swallowed his chagrin and surrendered.

For the record, Allen's great dramatic and oft-quoted line "In the name of the Great Jehovah and the Continental Congress" never echoed from the walls of Ticonderoga. It was not given form or breath until Allen "recalled" the phrase in his own published account of the affair, which did not appear until 1779.

The Patriots captured seventy-eight guns in good condition, six mortars, three howitzers, thousands of cannonballs, thirty thousand flints, and other supplies at Ticonderoga and Crown Point, which they seized the next day. The British were marched away to prison in Hartford, Connecticut. During the days immediately following, Arnold tried for a glory all his own by leading his Connecticut volunteers, who had finally caught up with him, in a raid on St. Johns (Saint-Jean) near the head of the Richelieu River which destroyed some ships and captured supplies and prisoners. Allen tried to do him one better with his own St. Johns expedition to capture and hold the position, but he failed in the face of superior British forces.

Colonel Henry Knox arrived at Ticonderoga in December with a plan for what he later called the "noble train of artillery." He loaded fifty or sixty guns and mortars on forty-two sledges pulled by eighty yoke of oxen and started them south. By January 7, 1776, he had reached the southern end of Lake George, a distance of more than thirty miles, over hills and through forest. He still had three hundred miles to go, and go he did through Saratoga, Albany, Kinderhook, and Claverack, over the snow-covered Berkshires to Framingham (twenty miles from Cambridge, Massachusetts), which he reached by January 25. Three of the mortars weighed a ton each; total tonnage was about 119,900 pounds, and just to make the whole business a sporting proposition, the convoy carried an additional 2,300 pounds of lead and a supply of flints. The guns were eventually installed on Dorchester Heights, overlooking Boston, and were a strong factor in the British decision to evacuate the city.

On my first visit to Fort Ti in 1934, one simply paid admission and walked about exploring and looking completely on one's own. On my last visit a piper wearing the tartan of the Black Watch regiment, which lost many men before the blazing guns of Montcalm's forces, was stationed in the entranceway, where he piped to attract a group of visitors for a tour. During the spring and summer months the fort is manned by a company of these guides, usually college students dressed in colonial military costumes. During July and August they load and fire muskets and go through a cannon drill that ends with their firing a four-and-a-half-inch mortar at a target across the lake.

The fort is four-sided and faces south on its long axis. Each of its four corners is built out to form an arrowhead-shaped bastion. Additionally, in front of the west and north sides are freestanding triangular bastions called demilunes, which are connected to the fort proper by wooden bridges that could be raised if the bastions were captured by enemy forces. The demilunes were designed to protect the flat curtain walls on the west and north sides of the fort. These sides face land approaches where heavy artillery might have been placed to knock holes through them, for flat walls were particularly vulnerable to this kind of attack. The demilunes, with their apexes pointed outward, presented angled walls off which cannonballs and shells would have been deflected to the side. Notice that the walls of each corner bastion are also built at angles that would deflect cannonballs. A covered way on the west side guards the entrance.

To enter, walk up an incline that brings you to the brow of the promontory with the south outer wall on your right and the inner walls of the fort towering over you on your left. Mounted on the wall of the fort to the left as you walk up (actually the outer wall of the covered way) are a line of plaques citing the main details of the fort's history. A little way farther you are on a level stretch of ground inside the south outer wall with the arched entrance to the parade ground on your left and a row of cannon aimed through gunports at the lake on your right. Upon a platform built into an angle of the wall, a flagpole sports a snapping flag, busily flaunting itself at the clouds in the brisk wind that usually blows down-lake.

At this point you are looking south upstream along Lake Champlain. On your right is Mount Defiance, beyond which, but invisible from here, is Lake George. Mount Defiance, by the way, was called "Rattlesnake Mount" by the French, who, we assume, had good reason for doing so. The Americans neglected to fortify it even though it overlooks the fort, because they believed it was inaccessible. Burgoyne thought otherwise on his later campaign south and proved it to his great advantage and to the Americans' discomfort. Once his guns were in position overlooking the fort, they seemed to have no recourse but to evacuate the premises.

The rapids through which George empties into Champlain are a little southwest of the fort, not visible to you. To the left across the lake is Vermont. Mount Independence looms over the Vermont shore, and if you look closely (there are coin-operated telescopes spotted along the wall should you neglect to bring your binoculars), you will see the ruins of earthworks in a clearing near the top, all that remains of a large star-shaped stockade and line of redoubts and trenches the Americans built there in 1776. At the foot of the mount, a neck of land sticks out toward the New York shore with a quarter mile of water in between. A bridge of boats spanned that gap, while just to the north a log boom with iron chains attached was intended to halt British ships.

Off on the horizon to the east are the Green Mountains of Vermont. To the west and north stretch the hills and peaks of the Adirondacks. It is a truly beautiful view with the waters of the lake below you, the wooded hills towering above the fort, and the green farmlands of Vermont and New York filling in the near and middle distances. You will find this view even more impressive when you reach the top of the bastions behind you.

As you look at the lake and the land around the fort, keep in mind that the cleared fields were probably still part of the forest in the eighteenth century, a forest of huge trees and thick, tangled underbrush. The mountains remain as they were, and the nearby hills may have looked very much as they do today. Discount the smog that sometimes lies over the lake from the power-plant chimneys a few miles down-lake. And remember that directly in front of the south wall, between the wall and the lake shore, was a cluster of houses, the ruins of some of which you can see at the water's edge. They are all that is left of the civilian quarters that crowded the slope. There is a small door in the south wall, by the way, through which you can follow a narrow dirt path which probably led down to a landing where supplies were unloaded and then carried back up into the fort. The village was destroyed by the French in 1759, when they evacuated the fort.

The guns along this rampart are French and Spanish, but none of them was in the fort during its years of active service. In fact, only two guns of all those now in the fort actually saw service at Ticonderoga. One fell from a sledge in Knox's Noble Train of Artillery during the journey south, went through the ice of the Mohawk River, and was recovered in recent times. The other was dug up under the north wall of the fort after its presence was made known to Mrs. Samuel Pell in a dream, according to the guides. They will point them out to you on request if they neglect to mention them during the tour.

This south outer wall was built by the British after 1759. During the French tenancy a storehouse shaped somewhat like a square demilune with a cannon on its roof was situated just a little south and east of the arch leading into the interior. As you pass through the arch, you will note on your right a plaque bearing the names of some of the illustrious personages who have gone before you. The list includes Benjamin Franklin, Washington, Generals Burgoyne and Amherst, Ethan Allen, Benedict Arnold, and Lafayette.

Coming out of the archway you will find yourself in a rectangular open area called the **Place des Armes**, the central parade ground. Opposite you on the other side of the parade ground is the rear of the north curtain wall. To your right is the partially restored East Barracks. To the left is the reconstructed West Barracks, where the British garrison was caught in bed that early May morning. The wooden steps now going up to the second floor replace the original steps which Allen and Arnold mounted to demand the Fort's surrender.

The rest of the fort is fascinating to explore. Underneath some of the bastions are dungeons, storehouses, and other quarters, many of them open to the public. Ramps lead from the Place des Armes to the ramparts, with the most impressive view of the surrounding area, and wooden bridges, as I mentioned before, lead out to the demilunes. The museum is in the South Barracks, the building through which the archway leads, and it contains an excellent collection of period guns and other weapons, articles of clothing, and many utensils of eighteenth-century military and civilian life, many of them found in and around the fort. Among the exhibits in the showcases are an excellent demonstration of knapping, the process by which gun flints were shaped; an exhibit showing what the military man of the day could expect in the way of medical attention (part of this exhibit are musket balls with the toothmarks of the men who chewed on them during surgery or punishment); a hollow silver bullet that once held a message from the British General Clinton to Burgoyne telling him of the capture of the Hudson River forts (the British soldier who carried the message tried, when discovered, to swallow the bullet and was hanged as a spy); a rum horn made by Paul Revere; and a number of intriguing old maps. There are dioramas illustrating the highlights of the fort's history and several rooms set up as examples of the original quarters, including a soldier's canteen, the officer of the day's quarters, a blacksmith shop, and so on.

You can easily spend the better part of a day at Fort Ticonderoga and count it well spent. Before you leave, however, as you go back out toward the admission gate, turn to your right at the foot of the west demilune and enter the covered way. You will know it by the low stone wall that parallels the wall of the demilune with a wide ditch, the "covered way," in between. It continues around the apex of the demilune and along the other short wall of the triangle. This was always a feature of the best-designed fortresses of that time. It was intended as a position from which garrison members could make a close-in defense of the fort should attackers get near enough to be below the angle of deflection of the guns on the ramparts. The defenders stood against the stone wall and fired or threw hand grenades over the top at the attackers, who had first to negotiate another stone wall beyond and then to climb up a rise of ground. The men in the covered way were supported by their comrades-in-arms stationed above them on the demilune, but their main purpose was to keep the attackers from raising scaling ladders against the walls. You can, if you like, walk around most of the fort's perimeter at the foot of its walls for a good look at the construction. You can tell by the difference in the color of the mortar between the stones where the old foundations end and the reconstructed walls begin.

CROWN POINT

To reach Crown Point, parallel the route Ethan Allen's men took the day after the capture of Fort Ticonderoga. These men were under the command of Seth Warner, who later took part in the actions at Hubbardton and Bennington. Warner had been sent back to ferry over more men from Hand's Cove the night Ethan Allen crossed Lake Champlain. Two days later, on Friday, May 12, Warner led a force down-lake and captured Crown Point. Follow 9N and 22 (they are one road) to the village of Crown Point. Four miles north of the village you reach a turnoff marked by a large sign pointing the way to the Fort Crown Point reservation and campsites and the bridge to Vermont. Total distance from Ticonderoga is approximately eleven miles.

The Crown Point reservation is a well-developed public recreation area, as well as a historic landmark. It is a public campsite, and a very pretty one at that, right on the shore of Lake Champlain. There are picnic facilities, a public playground, comfort stations, refreshments, drinking water, and a museum that contains artifacts and exhibits connected with the site. The road from 9N also leads onto the Champlain Bridge, which goes across the lake to Chimney Point, Vermont. It is a beautiful area, with the broad fields and rolling hills of the Champlain shores stretching all about, mountains ringing the horizons, and the lovely lake in the foreground with the majestic, graceful curve of the bridge rising above it. If I were a camper I would go out of my way to get a Crown Point site.

☆

The story of Crown Point began with the appearance on these shores of Samuel de Champlain, the French explorer and founder of the city of Quebec, who in 1609 discovered the lake that bears his name. Champlain was accompanied on his voyage by a war party of Hurons who came to grips with a band of Iroquois, their hereditary enemies, close to this site. Champlain intervened on the part of the Hurons, frightening the Iroquois with his muskets, thus incurring their enmity for everything and everyone French, a bias that cost the French heavily in lives and in tactical advantage during their long struggle with the British.

The first fort here was Fort St. Frederic, built by the French in 1731. It was the target of at least two determined British efforts to capture the headwaters of the lake in 1755 and 1756. Amherst finally succeeded after his capture of Ticonderoga in 1759, but again, as at Fort Ti, the French managed to evacuate their forces and blow up the fort. Amherst then built a fort a few hundred yards away, called Crown Point or Fort Amherst. The interior buildings were destroyed in 1773 by a fire that was never satisfactorily explained although a court of inquiry was held. The ramparts, however, remained intact. The British planned to rebuild the fort but somehow never got around to it. Seth Warner captured the post in 1775, adding to the supply of cannon already captured at Ticonderoga, and supplementing the number of English prisoners held by the Americans by nine redcoats and ten women and children. It was at Crown Point and Ticonderoga that General Schuyler mustered his men and ships during the summer of 1775 and launched the American invasion of Canada. The site was reoccupied by the British on October 14, 1776, after the Montgomery-Arnold invasion of Canada had been repulsed, and held by them until November 3 of the same year. Burgoyne occupied it next in June, 1777, at the beginning of his offensive, but it was again abandoned by the British after Burgoyne's defeat at Saratoga the following October.

This is a very impressive ruin and one that will invite you to climb about and explore. An exhibit in the museum will fill you in on the history of the fort through pictures and diagrams. The Crown Point Foundation has instituted a self-guided walking tour on the site complete with a map, provided at the museum, marked with numbered sites and with detailed explanations. From one end of a parking area nearby a dirt road leads to the fort. The entrance is through an opening in the huge overgrown embankments surrounding the fort on all sides. You enter onto the parade ground, now overgrown with grass. To the left are the half-ruined remains of two long, two-story stone structures with gaping windows and doors, undoubtedly troop quarters. You can walk into the rooms through the doorways and see the remains of the fireplaces that once kept the occupants warm against the heavy snows and sweeping winds of the northern winters. On the opposite side of the parade ground are two freestanding crumbling brick chimneys that mark the site of two other smaller buildings. Scrambling up the embankment, you will find a narrow footpath at the top along which you can traverse the entire perimeter of the fort, looking out over the waters of the lake on the lakeside. At intervals you may notice what look like indentations in the ramparts. These mark the places where the Americans dug down in the earthen defenses to uncover guns that the British had buried. Many of the Crown Point guns became part of Knox's Noble Train of Artillery after they were brought up-lake to Ticonderoga. To the left of the barracks is an old well, now surrounded by a fence, and above that, on a platform on the embankment, a flagpole marks the spot where the Union Jack and the early American flags once flew.

There is the same general air about Fort Crown Point that one feels in the far more ancient ruins of Rome and Pompeii, occasioned by the still-standing walls with nothing within but rubble overgrown with weeds, and the heaps of tumbled stone marking sites where structures once stood that can only be guessed at now. You will notice, however, fresh mortar here and there, indicating some effort has been made to keep the walls from deteriorating any further. You get a better idea here than at Fort Ti about the dimensions of these frontier fortifications. There are fewer buildings to obstruct the view, and from almost any position on top of the ramparts, you can look across the space the fort occupied and get a good idea of the distance between outer walls. You can easily determine, by the course of the footpath on top of the embankment, that the fort was roughly star-shaped. Looking out over the surrounding terrain from the top of the ramparts one would never know that when the fort was an active British post, a number of houses and shops, quite a little village in fact, were built up here, over the years. The settlement provided living quarters for many officers and their families and it offered some of the amenities of life ordinarily missing at a military post in a wilderness area. Though the remains of the settlement are hidden from all but practiced eyes, archaeologists working on the site have identified the locations of an apothecary shop, a tavern, and other buildings.

After inspecting Fort Crown Point, you can walk the short distance to the ruins of **Fort St. Frederic,** close to the bridge. Most of the remaining fort is protected by a fence. All that was left after the French evacuation were the low remains of the walls and some of the buildings, heaps of rubble, and the earthen ramparts. This is a relic of the French and Indian War and played no part in the events of the American Revolution. There are, however, other Revolutionary War sites nearby. According to archaeologists working for New York State Historic Trust and Preservation, when the American invasion force in Canada retreated back to Crown Point, Benedict Arnold built a blockhouse there. Probably he was preparing for some kind of stand against the British Army under Generals Carleton and Burgoyne, whose forces were being marshaled on the Richelieu River for an invasion of New York. Evidence of this blockhouse has been found in letters sent by Arnold from Crown Point. When the Americans retreated up-lake to Ticonderoga, the British reoccupied Crown Point and Carleton ordered another blockhouse built. State archaeologists have located the sites of both structures but at this writing, they are keeping them concealed to prevent amateur archaeologists from spoiling the sites before sufficient funds are raised to allow a proper survey and dig. Visitors to Crown Point during the Bicentennial may find that the sites have been opened to them, with the new archaeological digs completed for their inspection, thus rounding out the story of Crown Point. Northward now the road leads, to the Canadian theater of operations.

II.

INVADING THE "FOURTEENTH COLONY"

ILE-AUX-NOIX

From Crown Point travel north on 9N to Elizabethport, where 9N turns west, and follow it to the Interstate 87 interchange. Take 87 north to Canada where it becomes Canadian Highway 15. After passing through Canadian inspection at the border, continue on 15 to the exit for 52 east. On 52 eastbound follow the signs for Lacolle about three miles away. At Lacolle continue on 52 for another three miles to Cantic on the Richelieu River. Turn left (north) onto 9B for a five-mile drive to St. Paul de-l'Ile-aux-Noix where you should look for the signs directing you to Fort Lennox National Historic Park. They will indicate a right turn onto a road that runs through a residential area and finally dead-ends at a ferry landing. There is parking near the ferry, and a combined ticket office/lunch counter where you can buy ferry tickets for $0.50.

The ferry goes to Ile-aux-Noix (Nut Island), so called because of the walnut trees that once grew there. The boat is an open affair with a bench around the sides and a scow-like bow. The ferry runs subject to demand, and the trip takes about ten minutes against the current. On the island a path from the ferry dock leads up to the fort and the grounds around it, which have been made into a very pleasant park.

Before you proceed any farther, have a seat on one of the benches overlooking the ferry landing and take stock of the situation, yours and the historic. As far as you are concerned, notice the nearby public phone booth. If you should visit the island during the off-season or on a day when few other visitors accompany you, the ferry will not hang around

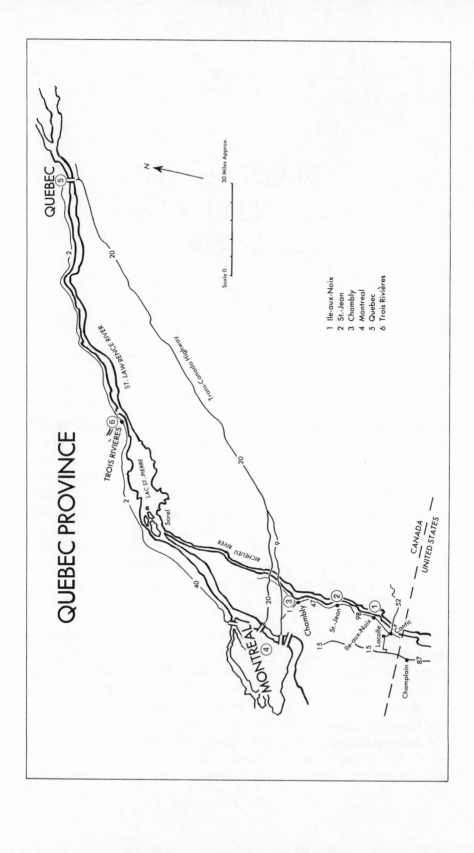

QUEBEC PROVINCE

QUEBEC ⑤

TROIS RIVIÈRES ⑥

MONTREAL ④

ST. LAWRENCE RIVER

LAC ST. PIERRE

Sorel

RICHELIEU RIVER

Trans-Canada Highway

Chambly

St.-Jean

Ile-aux-Noix

Lacolle

Contie

Champlain

CANADA
UNITED STATES

1 Ile-aux-Noix
2 St.-Jean
3 Chambly
4 Montreal
5 Quebec
6 Trois Rivières

Scale 0   30 Miles Approx.

N

waiting for you but will return to its home dock. When you are ready to return to your car, call the ferry ticket counter: the number is printed on the ticket. Then sit down to rest your weary feet, while you contemplate the pleasant prospect before you and watch the little water bug of a ferry speeding upstream in your direction in answer to your summons.

As far as history is concerned, turn your attention to Canada, just as the thoughts of many people in the colonies turned there during the early days of the Revolution. It was a perfectly natural thing to do, for it was in Canada, just over the northern horizon, that the British were making preparations to invade. When General Sir William Howe and his troops evacuated Boston in March, 1776, they sailed north to Halifax, where the British planned to move next against New York.

Canada was, however, more than a staging area for invasions; it was a constant source of American fear and annoyance for reasons incorporated in the Quebec Act, one of those pieces of parliamentary legislation known as the Intolerable Acts by which the British Parliament did all it could to arouse the feelings of the colonists against the crown. The Quebec Act had been enacted in 1774 to establish a permanent system of administration in Canada. It granted religious freedom to French Canadians and permitted them to continue many of the legal and political institutions they had maintained under French rule. From a New Englander's point of view this, in itself, was cause for alarm, for it meant that French Catholicism would predominate. It brought visions to New England minds of hordes of Indians, converted to the Cross and papistry by Canadian priests, descending on New England towns and farms as the instruments of a new inquisition, North American style.

The Quebec Act went even further. It gave Canada the legal right to claim all the land north of the Ohio River, east of the Mississippi, south of the Great Lakes, and west of the Appalachian mountain ranges, a vast piece of real estate which interested many New England residents, particularly in Connecticut, Pennsylvania, and Virginia.

To many Americans, it seemed only natural to assume that the Canadians would be just as fed up with British rule as they were, and that all the British colonies in North America would unite in a common effort against the British crown. The "fourteenth colony" was how these Americans referred to Canada, and it was as a fourteenth colony that they expected Canada to respond.

Unfortunately, the rebels first approached their Canadian neighbors in a manner hardly calculated to arouse confidence in their motives. First came Benedict Arnold's raid on St. Johns, followed by Ethan Allen's attempt to second the motion. Then came an armed invasion aimed at conquering and holding all of Canada by force. That the Second Continental Congress referred to Canadians as the "oppressed inhabitants of Canada" and, in authorizing the invasion, expressed the sincere hope that this act would not be "disagreeable to the Canadians" made very little impression on the poor "oppressed." Most Canadians today refer to the Quebec Act as their Magna Carta. In 1774 the act was accepted by most of their ancestors, especially by the *habitants*, the French Canadian peasants, who were particularly pleased by the religious provisions. Some Canadians were sympathetic to the rebel cause, but most remained neutral, as indifferent to British efforts to enlist them in the service of the crown as they were to efforts to get them to join the rebellion. Two companies of Canadian volunteers were formed to serve with the Continental Army, but there were willing hearts aplenty when the call went out for men to help repulse the American attacks on Montreal and Quebec.

The invasion had been suggested to Washington by Benedict Arnold soon after his St. Johns adventure. Washington had taken a great liking to Arnold and thought the idea worth a try. It seemed like a good chance to deal a blow at British invasion preparations before they were launched and to gain the support of the Canadians, or so he believed. Congress thought so too, and the plans went forward immediately.

It was to be a two-pronged attack, with two armies entering Canada at different points and then combining to capture Quebec, the Canadian capital and the colony's largest and strongest city. General Philip Schuyler, in charge of the entire operation, was to take the Montreal–New York waterway route to the Saint Lawrence, capturing Montreal along the way after taking the string of forts that guarded the Richelieu. Colonel Benedict Arnold was to move up the Kennebec River through Maine to the Dead River, then go by portage into Lake Megantic, which would take him into the Chaudière River and then into the Saint Lawrence just west of Quebec. Opposing them was the governor general of Canada, General Guy Carleton, who was much respected and beloved by the French Canadians but who had few regular troops at his disposal with which to resist the attack he knew was coming. The virtue of the American strategy was its audaciousness, but it had to be carried out at once before the British could gather enough reinforcements to withstand the assault and move their fleet into position around Quebec. The plan, however, was hastily and therefore inadequately prepared, and in that lay its eventual failure. For instance, Arnold depended on maps that gave him a completely erroneous idea of the route he was to travel. It was actually twice as long as the maps showed and beset with more portages, rapids, swamps, and other obstacles than his best intelligence was able to ascertain. Add to this the fact that he made the attempt during the late northern fall and you will understand why his march is rated alongside Xenophon's march to the sea and similar military epics. We will follow him through the wilderness when we turn our attention to the Revolutionary War sites of New England.

Schuyler's second-in-command, the Irish-born General Richard Montgomery, a veteran of sixteen years of service in the British army, headed north along Lake Champlain with 1,200 troops on August 28, 1775. He was not supposed to move quite that soon, but Schuyler had gone to Albany to attend a conference with certain Indian tribes aimed at keeping them neutral and while he was gone Montgomery learned that two gunboats being built at St. Johns were nearing completion. Their entrance into active service might have given the British control of Champlain, which the rebels felt they could not allow at that time. Without waiting to hear from his commanding officer, Montgomery decided to move north at once. In addition to his men, he had a few pieces of artillery, one sloop, one schooner, and a variety of smaller vessels including bateaux, rowing galleys, canoes, and whatnots. Schuyler returned to Crown Point after the army had gone and found a boat waiting to take him after it. Following in haste, he caught up with Montgomery on Monday, September 4, and the invaders spent their first night on Canadian soil, camped on Ile-aux-Noix.

There are no specific ruins or buildings to see on Ile-aux-Noix or even any remains to remind us of the American presence except the island itself. Fort Lennox, which occupies the southern tip of the island, was built during the War of 1812. However, Ile-aux-Noix became the American invaders' main base of supplies during their march up the Richelieu to Montreal. After the defeat at Quebec, they returned here to spend most of the spring and summer of 1776. In June a smallpox epidemic carried off from fifteen to twenty of them a day. The sick were cared for and buried on a smaller island a little farther down-river, which was appropriately dubbed "Hospital Island." The cemetery presently on the island contains the bodies of members of the Royal Canadian Army.

Ile-aux-Noix is an excellent example of a fortified position that appears to be effective because of its position athwart a major artery of supply—at least, that is how the French considered it when they first built a fort here in 1759 as a backup position should Carillon and Crown Point fall to the British. Actually, it was rendered ineffective quite easily by any force that decided to bypass it through the heavy forests that covered both banks of the river and a large part of the surrounding country. As a result, it was necessary for the island's garrison to maintain constant patrol activity along both banks and for some distance away from the river.

Fort Lennox is interesting in itself and is in excellent condition, with a wet moat that becomes operational during the summer months. There are comfort stations in one of the fort buildings, an information booth in a separate building, and picnic tables under pleasant groves of trees at the river's edge, but no refreshments, so drinks and sandwiches must be brought with you. It is a great place for a lunch break if you have driven up from the States in the morning or down from Montreal, which you might decide to make your headquarters as you explore the sites connected with the American campaign in the northern area. There is also a small but very well-kept museum in the fort, chronicling the history of the site.

When you return to your car at the ferry landing on the mainland, before you drive away notice the historical marker under the Fort Lennox sign mentioning the American presence in 1775–76. You may find yourself taken aback at the de-emphasis on the importance of this as an American Revolutionary War site. Later on, when you find other historical markers commemorating actions that took place during the invasion, you will read accounts not exactly complimentary to the invaders. In fact, according to most of these markers the British Canadian forces were the good guys and Montgomery and Arnold's men were the bad guys: a matter of national perspective.

FORT SAINT-JEAN

Fifteen miles farther north on 9B (223) is Saint-Jean, referred to in accounts of the Revolution as either St. Johns or Fort Saint-Jean. This is the site of the fort that Arnold raided shortly after the capture of Ticonderoga and Ethan Allen tried to capture and hold. Most American sources refer to the establishment of a fort at Saint-Jean as no earlier than 1758. Jacques Castonguay, the chaplain at the Collège Militaire Royal de Saint-Jean, proves quite conclusively, however, in an impressively researched account called *The Unknown Fort,* that there had been a fort on the site since the French campaign against the Iroquois in 1666.

As you enter Saint-Jean, continue past the Information Booth (they were uninstructed about the fort when I visited) until you see on the right the buildings, grounds, gates, and guard booth of the Collège Militaire. If traffic allows, park the car for a moment at the side of the road, or drive slowly by. Just inside and to the left and right of the gates and bordering the road are grass-covered *mounds* of dirt. As far as I can determine at this time, they are all that is left of Fort Saint-Jean, aside from some artifacts that have been uncovered about the site. The rest of the fort lies buried under the buildings of the school. Yet there was a fort here for more than two hundred and fifty years, until as late as World War II; in 1775 it was the scene of a siege that proved to be crucial to the entire American campaign in Canada.

In the face of the threat of invasion, General Carleton had not wasted any time rounding up as many civilians as he could persuade to join the Canadian militia. Fort Saint-Jean was one of a string of forts making up the outer defenses of Montreal. Carleton sent as many men as he could spare from Montreal and Quebec to these forts, and he increased the garrison at Saint-Jean to a total of 500 regulars and 225 volunteers. The latter included some sailors recruited from the sloops and frigates that patrolled the river, some Canadian militia, and a number of Scottish emigrants to Canada who had joined up in the Royal Highland Emigrants.

Schuyler had received some reinforcements since arriving at Ile-aux-Noix and had about 1,700 men in his command. On September 6 he made his first move. Advancing his main body downstream toward Saint-Jean, he sent a patrol ahead to scout out the way. The army landed about a mile and a half south of the fort in a low, swampy area, but when the patrol was ambushed and lost about sixteen men, Schuyler became convinced that Saint-Jean was too strongly held and retreated to Ile-aux-Noix. On September 8 he issued a proclamation assuring the Canadian populace that he and his men were there to fight only the British and appealing to them to come forth and join the rebels. He got even less response than General Carleton did.

On September 10 Schuyler tried again. This time he sent 500 men downriver by night to bypass the fort and come down on it from the north. In the dark, this force collided with a detachment under Montgomery that had been sent forward to give them covering fire. Convinced they were being ambushed, the 500 stampeded back to their boats. They were rallied and sent forward to the attack again, but British artillery and a round or two of small-arms fire brought them to a halt and the whole thing was called off.

Schuyler became too ill to continue his command and had to be sent back to Albany, leaving Montgomery in charge. Montgomery reassumed the offensive and went into siege positions around Saint-Jean on September 17. Castonguay's book quotes the diaries of several British Canadian officers and soldiers who withstood the fifty-odd days of siege that followed. The garrison, under the command of Major Charles Preston, stood up to the ordeal bravely, enduring artillery fire, cold, hunger, and the lack of sufficient clothing.

During October an American force bypassed Saint-Jean again, this time going farther downstream to capture Fort Chambly, which gave them possession of a large storehouse of supplies, including food, gunpowder, and cannonballs, all of which made it possible to continue the siege of Fort Saint-Jean. On November 1 and 2 Montgomery tried to convince the garrison that there was no longer any hope of relief from the British Canadian forces that had attempted to break through to their rescue. As proof, he offered the word of a Montreal hairdresser, a M. Depane, who had fallen into American hands and been brought to Montgomery with this piece of news. According to one entry in a Fort Saint-Jean diary, a Lieutenant André of the Seventh Regiment was sent to confer with this prisoner to establish his veracity. On November 2 the terms of capitulation were drawn up and the next day the survivors of the siege marched out to become prisoners of war. Among them was that same lieutenant—John André—who was sent on parole to Pennsylvania, until he was formally exchanged and returned to duty in 1776 as a captain A.D.C. (aide de camp) to General Grey, then with the British occupation forces in Philadelphia. Here André met a certain young lady who eventually led him to his relationship with Benedict Arnold. Even then it was a small world.

Though the siege of Fort Saint-Jean was successful, it cost the Americans dearly in the long run. Major Preston had managed to hold up their advance on Quebec for two months—two months that gave General Carleton more time to organize his defenses, and kept Montgomery from reaching Quebec with his guns in time to join the gunless Arnold when he first appeared before the city. Had the siege not lasted that long, the outcome of the invasion of Canada and the future course of the war might have been changed, though whether the rebels could have held on to Canada in the face of an inevitable British counterattack is a matter for debate.

FORT CHAMBLY

To reach this point along Montgomery's route to Quebec, take Highway 47 north out of Saint-Jean along the Richelieu. This is a two-lane highway that winds and twists as it follows the river and will keep you well within the stated speed limits. This is all to the good, for it will permit you to enjoy a very pleasant drive through this peaceful, riparian landscape. At Chambly signs lead you to the fort, an unmistakable stone structure that resembles the remains of a medieval castle. It is certainly most unusual and was very different in its day from all other forts.

Parking is available just across the road, near a small, well-kept park. The site is located on the river edge of the town, which began as a French settlement in New France more than three hundred years ago. The fort is open to the public year-round from 9 A.M. to 6 P.M. Admission is free.

There has been a fort on this site since about 1665, when Captain Jacques de Chambly, in command of four companies of the Carignan-Salières Regiment, was sent up the "rivière des Iroquoise" to build one of several forts intended to protect the Saint Lawrence Valley settlements from Iroquois attack. The forts that have stood here have been destroyed at one time or another by fire or enemy action during the struggles between the French and Indians and the French and British that have swirled up and down the Richelieu. The present fort is, for the most part, a reconstructed shell of its former self. Built completely of stone, its four-sided shape is unusual because of the square towers, each like a medieval castle keep, that stand at the corners. It was a comparatively small fortification, but it occupied a most strategic position, where the Richelieu curves and widens at the foot of a stretch of brawling rapids. Anything moving up or down the river was bound to come under the guns of the fort just where the rapids end, a very narrow stretch of water indeed.

There is a small *museum* just off the main entrance that contains nothing related to the American attack and occupation. Opposite the museum, across the entry way, a small *theater* shows a charming fifteen-minute, three-projector slide film telling the story of the fort entirely without words—just sound effects and music. I strongly recommend that you see the film before you tour the fort. The children will love it. I stayed to see it twice.

The inner courtyard or parade ground is lined with the ruins of former buildings and quarters and with beds of flowers grouped around a central plot of grass. The stone towers at the corners are also in ruins. You can enter one, at ground level, to inspect what was a powder magazine. Signs at appropriate places indicate what was where: the hospital . . . officers' quarters . . . the chapel . . . the barracks. The museum and theater are housed in a long, reconstructed one-story building that stretches the interior length of the northern or entrance wall. Directly opposite, across the old parade ground, are comfort stations built into the remains of other structures.

On the river side, the wall has not been reconstructed but left open to the river, with just a low wall with an iron fence surmounting it to keep overeager sightseers from toppling over onto the rocky incline and paved apron below at the water's edge. From this vantage point, one can look north downstream across a wide bay where the river widens, fringed with marinas and the town of Chambly itself crowding down to the bank. Directly opposite you can see two islands side by side that force anyone coming downstream to seek passage toward the fort. Upstream, one looks south up the rapids toward Saint-Jean, the direction from which the Americans made their appearance on October 18.

The night before, 135 Americans under the command of Major John Brown had ambushed a supply column about two miles south of Chambly. The garrison sallied forth the next day to confront Brown's men, but he had been reinforced by 500 additional troops and the British were driven back to the fort. While the ambush was in progress, two American bateaux carrying nine-pound cannon slipped past Saint-Jean and Chambly and took up positions north of Chambly. The bateaux also carried 300 Canadian volunteers friendly to the American cause and 50 Americans.

Carleton had recognized the strategic importance of Chambly but did not see fit to garrison it with more than 88 men. Perhaps he felt that as long as Saint-Jean held out, Chambly would not fall. What he did not foresee was that the fall of Chambly would hasten the surrender of Saint-Jean. This is exactly what happened. The nine-pounders put a few shot through the walls of the fort, which were not protected by earthen embankments, and the men capitulated. The Americans captured 30 women and 51 children, all the members of the garrison, and, as we have already seen, a storehouse of much-needed supplies that enabled them to maintain the siege of Saint-Jean. The British regimental colors seized at Chambly were the first such trophies to be captured by the rebels and are now on display in the West Point Military Academy Museum.

During the remaining months of the American invasion and occupation Fort Chambly was used as a prison for Canadians who were actively opposed to the invaders. In 1777 it was one of the mustering places for Burgoyne's men as he prepared to move up the Richelieu into Lake Champlain to invade the thirteen colonies.

A short distance from the fort, and reached by following the road around the bend of the river downstream, is a small *cemetery* in which a monument commemorates the fort's defenders. Another granite stone has been erected nearby by the Saranac, New York, Chapter of the Daughters of the American Revolution (D.A.R.) to the memory of General John Thomas, who took over command of the American expeditionary force outside the walls of Quebec after they had been repulsed. Thomas got the remaining men back to Sorel, but he contracted smallpox, was taken to Chambly, and died here on June 2, 1776. This monument also commemorates the Americans under his command who died and were buried with him. There are no other monuments or any headstones in this little plot of ground, for they have long since fallen over and been taken away. Tall, ancient-looking trees shade the grass under which Thomas, his men, and their enemies sleep together. If you walk over to the river side of the cemetery, you can look a little way upstream at the fort for a new perspective.

The area around the fort has changed considerably, though it was settled at the time of the invasion. According to old prints hanging in the museum, the riverside was a beehive of activity. Chambly was a trading and shipping center and many of the town's commercial activities were carried on here under the protective guns of the fort. The builder of the original fort, Jacques de Chambly, was granted a seigneury (a landed estate) on the surrounding land. In 1673 he was appointed governor of Acadia, but before he left he and many of the men who were with him when he first came up the Richelieu established a settlement here, the first permanent European settlement on this river. The men stayed behind and it eventually became the modern town that bears their benefactor's name.

MONTREAL

Montreal fell to the invading Americans on November 13, eleven days after the fall of Saint-Jean. There had been a premature attempt by Ethan Allen and John Brown to capture the city on September 25 using a number of Canadian volunteers whom Allen had managed to recruit up and down the banks of the Richelieu. However, the plan of attack drawn up by the two commanders went awry and the affair ended with Allen's capture by Carleton's men.

The modern city has overgrown whatever vestiges remain of that attack or the subsequent short campaign by Montgomery that brought about the city's fall. At the time there were a number of forts and city walls, but they no longer exist. Several plaques in the downtown areas of Montreal along the Saint Lawrence River mark the sites of forts, but there is nothing to show that any of them was connected with the invasion. Contacting the Canadian authorities concerned with historic sites brought no results. They could not offer so much as a clue as to the exact whereabouts of sites in or immediately around the city that were worth investigating. You are certainly free to poke around Montreal on your own, following up whatever clues you feel are relevant, but I am afraid it will only prove to be a waste of time. These sites have suffered the same fate that befell most Revolutionary War sites in New York City: urbanization has swallowed them up. The course of history now swings northeast along the Saint Lawrence River. We have come to the northern terminus of the great Montreal–New York waterway system. Now we turn toward the citadel city on the cliffs overlooking the river where Montgomery and his men met their fate.

QUEBEC

By taking the Trans-Canada Highway west for 160 of its 5,000 miles, you can cover the distance from Montreal to Quebec in a few hours. The Trans-Canada is a mostly four-lane, modern highway, which is to say it is a monotonous drive with gradual turns, gradual hills, and a steady sixty-mile-an-hour speed limit. There are service stations, restaurants, and motels at intervals off the interchange exits. The highway runs parallel to the north bend of the Saint Lawrence River, down which Montgomery sailed to his rendezvous with Arnold at Quebec.

When you get to the Quebec exit, number 193 on the province map, you will enter the city over the Pierre Laporte Bridge. The outskirts are well supplied with motels and gas stations; in other words they are much like the outskirts of most North American cities.

An alternate and more interesting route, if you have the time, is Highway 2, reached by taking Highway 40 out of Montreal. Hugging the north bank of the Saint Lawrence, Highway 2 takes you through the little French Canadian towns and cities that line the river. It also gives you a chance to see the Saint Lawrence Valley and the great locks of the Saint Lawrence Seaway. I followed this route some years ago on my first trip through Canada by car and found it fascinating. Quebec Province is French Canadian to the core, and though English is spoken on the highway, you will frequently come to places whre French alone is used, either because the inhabitants speak English poorly or because, as militant Québecois, they insist you meet them on their own grounds.

☆

QUEBEC

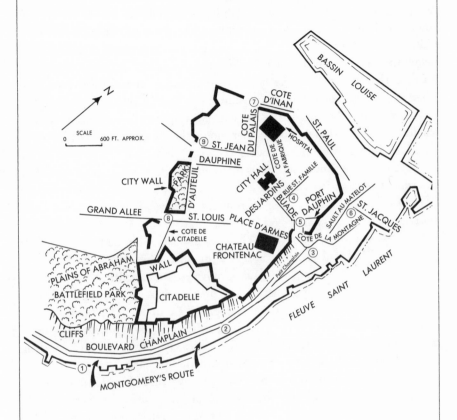

1 Wolf's Cove (Arnold Landed Here)

2 Block House (approx.)

3 Breakneck Steps

4 Notre Dame Seminary (Amer. Prisoners)

5 Prescott Gate Site

6 Barricade Site

7 St. Nicholas Gate Site

8 Montgomery's First Burial

9 American Feint

Quebec is a wonderful city from anyone's point of view and, I suspect, a good place to live. It is the only walled city left on the North American continent, a city of great charm and character, a European city in the midst of the general American culture that pervades even Canada. The modern suburbs west of the old city walls are neat, clean and attractive. The industrial suburbs to the north are as smoky and drab as any English Midlands factory or mining town. The oldest parts of the city strung out below the cliffs that line the river below the Citadel and the Château Frontenac are slummy and picturesque. I found that as I walked the streets of old Quebec it was easy to imagine I had stepped into an old print or painting of a seventeenth- or eighteenth-century town. At night the ancient atmosphere is enhanced by the shadows and half-lights that gather along the twisting streets and alleys that lead into private inner courts.

At the same time Quebec has many of the characteristics of a modern metropolis: attractive shops, excellent restaurants, good hotels, bustling crowds, and, of course, lots of tourists. Quebec is not an excessively tourist-oriented city, however, and the natives do not seem to exploit their visitors unduly. To these chrome- and steel-blinded eyes, Quebec presents a delightful prospect and is a joy and delight to visit.

So much for paeans of praise; now to practicalities. If you can, stay inside the old city, where most of the sites are located, either at a hotel or in some place that rents rooms to tourists. The Grande-Allée close to the Saint-Louis Gate is lined with boarding houses and small hotels with Victorian facades, but I cannot say how good any of them is, not having stayed there or known anyone who has.

There are also motels along the highways that thread the outskirts. If you come off the Quebec Bridge on your way into the city you will come to a traffic circle at the head of the Boulevard Wilfrid-Laurier. Around that traffic circle are located a number of good motels. Many other good motels are located on the other side of the bridge, along the roads leading to it. Of course in the very heart of the old town itself is the world-famous Château Frontenac—expensive but very, very good and wonderfully located on the cliffs overlooking the river and the lower town.

For reasons which I will explain, you should enter the city along the Boulevard Wilfrid-Laurier, which runs into the Grande-Allée, which in turn enters the old city through the Saint-Louis Gate. Traffic conditions in old Quebec are difficult and can be chaotic. Almost every street, avenue, and alley is one-way, usually not in your favor. My advice is to park your car as quickly as possible and walk, not a difficult prospect to face, for the old city does not cover an immense area and the distances from point to point are not very great. You should be able to cover all the sites within one or two days. Quebec is a city made for walking, despite the literal ups and downs you will meet along the way.

There are several places to park in the old town, including a park-and-lock on Saint-Stanislas, a garage on Avenue Saint-Louis a block or two above the Château Frontenac to your right as you near the hotel, and a number of free parking areas below the Frontenac and the Place du Fort. I found that the best place to park for the one- or two-day visitor is in a lot in a parklike area just inside the city wall on D'Auteuil. Parking in Quebec is fairly cheap, but this lot charges only $0.25 an hour with a maximum charge of $2.00. It is not easy to get to, however, unless you know how. When you come in through the Saint-Louis Gate you will be on Avenue Saint-Louis. The first intersection you will come to is D'Auteuil, but D'Auteuil is one-way, the wrong way for you. Continue on Saint-Louis to the intersection with Sainte-Ursule and turn left. Go left again on Sainte-Anne, which takes you back to D'Auteuil. The entrance to the parking lot is directly opposite you on the other side of D'Auteuil.

At one end of this lot is the gathering place for the horse-drawn calèches that take you meandering through the old city. The drivers come here to water their horses, eat lunch, and take on or discharge passengers. Just beyond is a one-story brick building, the government tourist office, which is staffed with knowledgeable types who have helpful information at their fingertips. The office is well supplied with excellent maps of Quebec, which are yours for the taking. Lest we forget, there are also rest rooms available there.

Before you tuck your car away, however, consider this. You should begin your tour of the siege of Quebec at Wolfe's Cove, which is west of the old city below the Plains of Abraham at the foot of the cliffs. You can get there by car, but the street you will then want to follow back up the cliffs, the Petit Champlain, is one-way against you. Taking a taxi or calèche to the cove cuts the Gordian knot, but a calèche is not cheap, and I cannot vouch for the cabs. You can walk, but it is a long hike. I suggest that you follow the route I will now lay out by car to the plaque beneath the Citadel; then return to the city, park, and continue the rest of the tour from the top or bottom of the Petit Champlain.

To begin at the beginning. As you came toward the old part of the city along the Grande-Allée, you passed the **Plains of Abraham** on which the French forces of the Marquis de Montcalm and the British under James Wolfe battled for possession of the city in 1759 and on which Arnold camped in 1775. The battleground is now a park, the Parc des Champs de Bataille, with cannons and markers denoting the positions of the units during the 1759 battle. I did not find a single marker, and I think I scoured the area quite thoroughly, for the positions of the American raiders.

Entering the park, follow the road through the beautifully landscaped grounds until you come to a stop sign. Just beyond is a roundabout and a parking area overlooking the Saint Lawrence where you can pull up to enjoy the view. Mark the spot upstream near the Quebec Bridge where the Chaudière River enters the Saint Lawrence at Point Lévis, the spot where Arnold and his men finally arrived after their epic trek from Maine.

A road leading to the right from the stop sign takes you down to the river embankment. Along the way watch for a marker that indicates **Wolfe's Cove,** directly below, where Wolfe disembarked with his men. It was to this same cove that Benedict Arnold brought his men after a two-mile row across the Saint Lawrence on Monday night, November 13, 1775. Arnold had started up the Kennebec with 1,100 men. Instead of 180 miles, he had had to travel 350 through a trackless wilderness. It took him not twenty days, as he had expected, but forty-five. He arrived at the Saint Lawrence with 675 men left from his original force; 300 had turned back midway in the march, and the rest had been evacuated or had wandered off or died of exposure and disease.

Having been apprised of Arnold's approach, Lieutenant Governor Cramahé, who was nervously awaiting Carleton's arrival from Montreal, had ordered the south bank of the Saint Lawrence swept clean of small boats. Arnold arrived at Point Lévis November 9, and rounded up enough canoes and other craft to effect a crossing after his men had been fed and rested sufficiently to proceed. Some local Abenaki Indians who enlisted under him found about forty vessels which would have to maneuver around two British warships, the sloop *Hunter* and the frigate *Lizard,* which were swinging on their anchor cables in midstream while their small boats constantly patrolled both banks of the river looking for signs of the Americans.

The row across the river to Wolfe's Cove was accomplished in the dead of night; Arnold's men had to pass in absolute silence between the two men-of-war. After three round trips 500 men had been ferried over. A patrol boat stuck its nose into Wolfe's Cove to investigate a bonfire

Arnold had thoughtfully built on the bank and had to be fired on. Without waiting for any more reinforcements, Arnold led the men at hand up the same path Wolfe's men had used to reach the Plains of Abraham. Some days before, Allan Maclean and his Royal Highland Emigrants had joined the city's defenders and were waiting on the walls for Arnold to make his move. Without guns to batter down the walls and with only 500 ragged men armed with 400 serviceable muskets—100 were too dangerous to fire—Arnold nevertheless sent three messages to the walls demanding the city's surrender. Each time the answer was a volley of musket fire deliberately aimed at the parley flag. Arnold decided that wisdom was the better part of valor and that he would wait for Montgomery, while blockading the city on the land side. The Canadian winter was closing in, and food and fuel were in short supply within the city whose French Canadian inhabitants were still not enthusiastically supporting the British cause. Ice now blocked the Saint Lawrence and Carleton could not expect reinforcements of any great size or support from the British fleet until the next spring.

Arnold kept up the siege for about six days; then, fearful a sortie from the city would reveal his weaknesses, he pulled back under cover of darkness to Pointe-aux-Trembles twenty miles upstream. Meanwhile the defenders of Quebec were joined by General Carleton who had escaped from Montreal.

When you leave the Plains of Abraham and continue down to the river, past the marker for Wolfe's Cove, you will eventually come out on the embankment that now runs around the foot of the cliffs below the city. Most of this land is industrial fill, for accounts of both the British and the American landings speak of cliffs that fall almost abruptly into the river with only narrow shingles of rock at their foot to give invaders a foothold. You will come out at a stop light on a wide boulevard, the Boulevard Champlain, opposite a group of oil-storage tanks. Turn left and follow it back toward the city, driving through Wolfe's Cove on the way. After two miles you will reach rows of houses along the cliff side of the road; then the **Citadel** will appear on the cliffs above. Slow down at this point so as not to miss the marker bolted to the cliff directly beneath the Citadel:

"Here stood the undaunted fifty safeguarding Canada, defeating Montgomery at the Près-de-Ville barricade on the last day of 1775, Guy Carleton commanding at Quebec."

This is where the trail starts that will lead you through the events of the night of December 31, 1775, and the following morning, as the old year died and the new year, the year of American independence, saw the light of its first day.

General Montgomery arrived at Pointe-aux-Trembles and met Arnold December 2 with about three hundred men, some artillery, and some much-needed food and clothing, including a large number of red British army coats captured at Montreal which Arnold's freezing men quickly put on despite the hated color. The bitter winds of the rapidly approaching Canadian winter had made them color-blind. With their forces now combined and Montgomery in charge of the entire operation under General Schuyler (Schuyler was in Albany keeping an eye on operations and trying to keep the supplies and reinforcements moving into Canada), the American expeditionary force returned to the Plains of Abraham and besieged Quebec.

Montgomery had lost all the Connecticut men under his command after the fall of Montreal: when their term of enlistment had expired, they could not be persuaded to see the rest of the campaign through. His position before Quebec was far from secure. His guns were not heavy enough to batter down the city's walls. He could probably hold his siege lines through the winter, despite the bitter cold, but come spring the ice-locked Saint Lawrence would be open, and the British navy would undoubtedly appear with a formidable army on board. The enlistment term of his Massachusetts men was up at the end of December. Montgomery had no choice but to try to take the city at once or the invasion would come to nothing.

Montgomery himself was in a personally dangerous position. Native Americans fighting against the British crown were considered rebels; if captured, they were imprisoned. Montgomery, however, and other native Englishmen like him who had cast their lot with the new republic were considered traitors. If captured, they faced a voyage in irons to England, a trial in a British court, and death at rope's end.

Montgomery sent an old woman into Quebec with a letter to Carleton demanding the city's surrender. Carleton is supposed to have ordered a drummer boy to take the letter from her with a pair of fire tongs and burn it in the fireplace without opening it. Carleton would not treat with either the traitor Montgomery or the rebel Arnold. Montgomery had, in fact, served with the British army in Canada during the French and Indian War and lived in Quebec for a time. He had soldiered with some of the very men who now stared down their gun barrels at him, and some of the inhabitants of the town he had besieged remembered him with affection. He has been described as tall and graceful, with a bright, intelligent face and an engaging personality. In parliamentary debate Edmund Burke spoke of Montgomery as "the hero who in one campaign had conquered two-thirds of Canada" while the British army had allowed itself to be shut up in Boston. Lord North, in reply, admitted that Montgomery was "brave . . . able . . . humane . . . generous . . . ," but that he was "only a brave, able, humane and generous rebel." His former compatriots were not about to excuse his present actions, even though he had sold his commission in the army, settled down on his own farm in King's Bridge, New York, with an American-born wife, and served in the first provincial congress in New York.

Montgomery waited for a snowstorm to cover the assault. Carleton, inside the walls, guessed that Montgomery would attack the lower town below the cliffs and disposed his defense accordingly. The snow started to fall on December 31. That night three rockets arched upward from the American lines and the defenders of Quebec sprang to their posts. As the American and British guns dueled with each other and detachments feinted toward the gates of the city, Arnold moved off with his men to attack the lower town from the northern side, while Montgomery, with 300 New Yorkers, climbed through the snow down the cliff-side to Wolfe's Cove. For two miles he and his men, carrying scaling ladders, scrambled over cakes of ice piled up against the base of the cliffs by the river current. Finally they reached a point about fifty yards from where you are now standing, below the cliffs of Point Diamond. Montgomery had to carry the two palisades and the blockhouse the defenders had prepared at this point and then rendezvous with Arnold and his men at the foot of Sault-au-Matelot, a street on the other side of Cape Diamond which leads into the upper town.

Montgomery had his men cut through the two wooden palisades. Beyond in the blockhouse, a single naval cannon pointed its ugly snout through an upper-story window in their direction. From above they could hear alarm bells ringing, and guns, muskets, and shells exploding. Inside the blockhouse a party of Canadian militia heard the sound of Montgomery's men cutting through the palisades. Some of them panicked and ran out the back door, but the rest stuck to their posts. One touched a match to the cannon just as Montgomery, followed by several officers and men, stepped through the hole in the second palisade and started for the blockhouse. There was a flash and a roar and the blockhouse defenders followed up with a volley of musket fire. Montgomery was killed at once, along with Captains John MacPherson and Jacob Cheeseman and several enlisted men. Aaron Burr, who had come up the Kennebec with Arnold only to transfer to Montgomery's command, was with Montgomery at the time but miraculously escaped injury. Dismayed by this turn of events, the senior officer remaining, Colonel Donald Campbell, ordered the rest of the men to retreat and led them to the rear.

Neither the blockhouse nor the wooden palisades exist any longer, but if you stand below the marker at the foot of the Citadel and—keeping a wary eye out for traffic—pace fifty yards in the direction you drove there from, you can mark the approximate spot at the foot of the cliff where Montgomery's attempt to storm the city came to an abrupt end.

The following morning the snow-covered bodies of the Americans were removed. Montgomery's rank was apparent, and he was identified by one of the Americans captured on the other side of town and by his old landlady. According to descriptions of what then occurred, Montgomery's body was carried around the cliff and up into the city. If you walk around the cliff from the plaque you will spot on your left a narrow one-way street called Petit Champlain; it is lined with old stone and frame houses and leads up the face of the cliff. Since there is no other street in the vicinity that fits the description, let us assume this is the route taken and follow the street up. It was probably once a path or trail that led from the Citadel to the riverbank below, hence the blockhouse to guard this entry into the city.

Petit Champlain leads to the foot of Breakneck Stairs, a flight of wooden steps scaling the last few feet of cliffside. They lead to Côte de la Montagne, the street where Montgomery and Arnold were supposed to rendezvous before driving on into the upper town. To the right, at the foot of the ramparts, is a plot of ground set off by a fence. A large, wooden cross marks the site of Quebec's first cemetery where some of the first residents and certain of their Indian friends are buried. Continue up the hill, around Montmorency Park with its statue to Archbishop de Montmorency Laval, to Du Fort and across Place du Fort to the front of the Château Frontenac. Turn to the right; you are now on **Avenue Saint-Louis,** which goes in the direction of the Saint-Louis Gate.

The accounts I have read state that Montgomery's body was taken up Saint-Louis to a house at 39A. Many of the private residences in old Quebec were in courtyards set back off the street and reached through archways in the side walls; many of those still standing are so situated. Number 39A Saint-Louis, however, is no longer in existence. You will find 41, but where 39A stood in its small courtyard is now a new office building.

A day or two later the body was taken to its burial spot. Continue along Saint-Louis to the gate. To your left a street called Côte de la Citadelle runs along the wall to the main visitor's entrance to the Citadel above. Turn left and as you walk up Côte de la Citadelle you will see on your right some army buildings grouped around a central courtyard which is reached through a gate. Just outside the gate to the right is a large **boulder** in the middle of a small plot of ground with a short flight of flagstone steps leading up to it. On the boulder is a bronze plaque which reads:

"In this place was buried on the fourth of January, 1776, along with his two aides de camp, MacPherson and Cheeseman, and certain of his soldiers, Richard Montgomery, the American general who was killed in the attack on Quebec on the thirty-first of December, 1775. In 1818 his remains were exhumed and removed to the precincts of St. Paul's Church, New York [City] where he is presently buried." Another plaque on a nearby wall marks where thirteen American soldiers who died in the assault are buried. A stone was placed over their grave by an unidentified group of American children.

Leaving the graves and that phase of the American attack behind you, retrace your steps along Côte de la Citadelle; continue across Saint-Louis and up D'Auteuil, passing the government information office and the parking lot. You are now walking parallel to the city wall. A short distance past the parking lot you will come to another gate at a street called Dauphine where stone towers flank the gate. A stairway leads to the top of the wall. From this vantage point you can look west over the streets beyond.

At the time of the American invasion, this area stretching west was countryside dotted with farms, cleared fields, and what were then suburban settlements. When Montgomery brought the army to the walls of Quebec after joining Arnold at Pointe-aux-Trembles, they closed in around this part of the city and down to the Saint Charles River which comes around Quebec to the north to empty into the Saint Lawrence. So close were the American positions to the walls that the besiegers could come near enough to touch the walls and the shut gates and still be out of range of the defenders above, who could get at them only by leaning far out over the ramparts, thus exposing themselves to American snipers. Continue to follow the wall until you reach the next street, Saint-Jean, where there is another and larger gate. It was here that some of the besiegers feinted toward the gate in an attempt to draw the attention of the defenders from Arnold's men.

Arnold's part of the plan was to skirt the northern wall down to the foot of a street called Sault-au-Matelot (sailor's leap) which still exists. It was known to be well defended. Arnold's mission was to carry these defenses and, advancing up Sault-au-Matelot, enter the lower town and link up with Montgomery on the Côte de la Montagne for the final push into the upper town.

Arnold got his men off on schedule. Reaching the wall, they began to skirt it—keeping about fifty feet beyond it, moving around the northernmost bastion, and then beginning the descent toward the river. Behind them, American artillery positioned as close to the walls as possible was firing at the city, church bells were ringing incessantly all over town, and the sky through the swirling snow reflected the muzzle flashes of the cannon, the glare of exploding shells, and the lesser flashes of muskets.

The area outside the wall at this point is now an industrial district; inside the wall there is no longer a street paralleling it to follow. You will have to turn right on Saint-Jean and follow this attractive shopping street to the next main intersection, where you will turn left onto Côte du Palais which, as its name implies, once ran alongside a palace. The palace no longer exists. Its place has been taken by the Hôtel-Dieu Hospital, which will be on your right as you proceed down the incline to the site of **Palace Gate.** At a point a short distance beyond the hospital, look for a plaque on the wall of a building to your left, marking the site of Palace, or St. Nicholas, Gate which was demolished in 1874.

It was just beyond this gate that the men on the wall spotted Arnold and his men, by the light of fire baskets hung over the wall, and opened fire. Sliding and slipping on the snow, the Americans forged ahead while their enemies above threw primitive hand grenades and rolled bombshells (shells that exploded like bombs) down the slope at them. Several men were hit, but the others went on as the defenders above ran along the wall firing at them, until they finally reached their first objective at the foot of the hill.

Now turn right onto Côte Dinan and follow the hill down until you reach the dock area in the lower city. Turn right on a street called Saint-Paul which will eventually bring you to the northern end of **Sault-au-Matelot.**

It was here the Americans came up against the first barricade. They charged forward in the face of enemy fire and Arnold went down with a ricochet through his leg and heel. Unable to walk without great difficulty, Arnold turned over his command to Daniel Morgan, the leader of the Virginia Rifles who had been in the vanguard during the long walk to Canada. Hobbling back to the rear, Arnold was again forced to run the gauntlet of enemy fire from above. He was hospitalized in a convent outside Quebec where he recuperated.

Walk one block up Sault-au-Matelot from Saint-Paul to an intersection with Saint-Jacques. On the wall of the post office building is a *plaque* which salutes the defenders of the city who repulsed and defeated Morgan's attack at this point. Morgan led the way up over the first barricade, which may have stood a little distance down toward Saint-Paul. Eyewitness accounts say he was the first up the ladder only to be knocked backward by the blast of musket fire that greeted his appearance. Picking himself up unhurt, he led the attack again, fell over the wall onto a gun carriage, and, after being joined by several others, captured the position, taking fifty prisoners whose presence he could ill afford, for they called for guards he could not spare. He then led a charge three hundred yards up Sault-au-Matelot to the next barrier. Instead of taking it as he could have (its defenders were in a panic and some confusion), Morgan allowed his subordinates to counsel caution. Most of the men in the command had not yet caught up with them and there were prisoners to guard, so Morgan was persuaded to wait.

It was a fatal error. By the time he had all his men with him, it was dawn and the defenders had rebuilt their forces. Morgan's attempts to take the barricade were repulsed. The garrison infiltrated the buildings around the Americans and drove them to cover in doorways and alleys. Dearborn's company, hurrying to the attackers' relief, was surprised and rendered ineffective outside Palace Gate by a shock force of two hundred of the city's defenders. This flying column then cut off Morgan's retreat, bottling him up inside Sault-au-Matelot. Some of his men got away across two miles of ice on the Saint Lawrence, but by 9 A.M. January 1, 1776, the rest had been forced to surrender. Morgan himself defied the surrounding guns and bayonets and refused to hand his sword over to anyone but a priest who was present in the crowd of onlookers that had gathered. A few other Americans tried to hide in alleys and streets of the old town, but a street-to-street search throughout New Year's Day flushed them out, and the attempt to capture the Canadian capital came to an inglorious end. Though the remaining Americans under Arnold, who was relieved by General Wooster April 2, maintained their positions west of the city until May, the coming of spring and the approach of the British fleet, added to an attack led by General Carleton, caused them to fall back along the Saint Lawrence to Sorel and eventually to Ile-aux-Noix.

There is little on Sault-au-Matelot, except the plaque, to remind you of the desperate action almost two hundred years ago. None of the buildings along the street date back to that period, but the street itself remains just as narrow as it was then. If you follow it away from the river to its upper end, you will come to the Côte de la Montagne where the two attacking forces were to have met. Turn right and follow Montagne, the route the Americans might have taken had they been victorious to that point. Montagne would have led them to Prescott Gate, no longer in existence, the last barrier before the upper town.

There is a steep climb ahead of you to Port Dauphin. Turn left on Dauphin and walk into Buade. On the right-hand side where Buade meets Ste. Famille, you will arrive at the Basilique Notre Dame. To the left of the Basilica is an iron gate which opens into the courtyard of the **Quebec Seminary**, where the captured American officers were imprisoned and where they planned and tried to carry out an escape that failed. The room in which the prisoners were kept was not open for viewing when I was there.

A visit to the Citadel, Quebec's famous fort situated on the highest point on the cliffs overlooking the river and the city, is worthwhile and the changing of the guard is a ceremony worth seeing. The present Citadel was not built until 1812. Only two of the buildings existed in 1775: the powder magazine, which is now the museum, and another building to which the American prisoners were transferred in irons after the escape attempt. It is situated behind the governor general's summer residence and is not open to the public. There is nothing in the museum associated with the siege or the attack.

One more point of interest should wind up your Quebec campaign. On the Place du Fort, opposite the Frontenac, is the **Musée du Fort**, where, standing before a diorama of Quebec and the surrounding area constructed to scale with tiny figures of soldiers in proper positions, one watches and listens as a son-et-lumière (sound and light) performance with recorded narration, music, smoke, and sound effects backed up by rear-screen projections, tells the history of the city. The last ten minutes are devoted to Montgomery's campaign. The museum is open from 9 A.M. to 11 P.M. in the summer and from 10 A.M. to 5 P.M. in the winter. Children under six are admitted free.

TROIS RIVIÈRES

One more Canadian site remains for you to visit, this one associated with the final American attempt to take Quebec. Retracing your route along the Trans-Canada Highway or along Route 2, you will come to Trois Rivières about midway between Montreal and Quebec. Route 2 goes through it. To reach it from the Trans-Canada, take Route 13 north to a bridge which takes you over the Saint Lawrence into the town.

By early June, 1776, the survivors of the Quebec expedition had returned to Sorel at the mouth of the Richelieu where they were joined by Brigadier Generals William Thompson and John Sullivan who had, respectively, 2,000 and 4,000 men under their command. Under orders from the Congress to try yet again to capture Quebec, Thompson moved his men down the Saint Lawrence on bateaux to first take Trois Rivières. Faulty intelligence had convinced Thompson and Sullivan that the town was held by only 800 men. Actually there were 6,000 redcoats under the command of General Simon Fraser, part of the force Burgoyne was beginning to assemble for an invasion of the colonies.

Thompson moved his men downriver on bateaux until they were about three miles from Trois Rivières. From there he moved forward on land. Among his commanders were Arthur St. Clair and Anthony Wayne, who had not yet earned his famous sobriquet, "Mad Anthony." Their French Canadian guide misled them, and they had to go through a swamp; as soon as they were out of that and back on the right road, they came under fire from several British ships and had to turn back into the swamp. Eventually they came to a clearing near the town where Wayne led a charge that sent part of the town's defenders running for their lives. A short distance farther, however, they encountered a greatly superior force dug in along a line of entrenchments and supported by the guns of ships on the river. Thompson tried one attack and was thrown back. Finding his command had fallen into disarray, he retreated. The men left to guard the bateaux were forced to escape with their craft to avoid capture, and the remainder made their escape through the swamps along the river. They were under almost constant attack from Indians and Canadian militia, not to mention the mosquitoes, reported to have been of monstrous size. Of the original two thousand, 1,100 managed to return to Sorel.

This final gasp of the American expeditionary force in Canada is marked on La Jeune Street in Trois Rivières by a *cairn* bearing a plaque marking the site where the British were dug in to await the enemy.

With Carleton threatening to move against them in force at any moment, the dispirited Americans evacuated Montreal, Chambly, and Saint-Jean and dropped back to Ile-aux-Noix where they were under attack from disease, as we have already learned, and finally returned to Crown Point. The invasion of Canada was over.

Now it is also time for you to leave the "fourteenth colony." Recross the border and head south on Interstate 87 to Exit 37 and Route 3 east to Plattsburgh and the Battle of Valcour Island.

III.

MOVING
SOUTH WITH BURGOYNE

No sooner were the invading Americans driven from the walls of Quebec and forced to retreat south, than the British began to gather men, ships, and supplies for the invasion of their rebellious American colonies. Their objective was threefold: to cut off New England, the "head" of the Revolution, from the other colonies by seizing the Hudson Valley and thus preventing the movement of men and supplies along the interior; to occupy New York from the sea; and to invade the Carolinas which were supposed to be hotbeds of Tory sentiment, thus giving them a strong foothold in the South.

Meanwhile, back at Crown Point, the rebel commanders decided it was impossible for them to hold Champlain without a fleet. Leaving a single regiment at Crown Point, they left for Forts Ticonderoga and George, with most of the army concentrated at Fort Ti, while Arnold, by virtue of his experience under civilian sail, began building a fleet to contest the inevitable British move onto the lake.

Arnold built his fleet at Skenesboro (now Whitehall, New York) at the southern end of Champlain and outfitted them at Ticonderoga and Crown Point. The British built and assembled their fleet at Fort St. Johns before sailing the ships up the Richelieu into Champlain. Some of the larger British ships on the Saint Lawrence had to be disassembled, hauled around the rapids above St. Johns in sections, and then reassembled. The two fleets converged at a battle off Valcour Island.

VALCOUR ISLAND

Exit from Interstate 87 at Plattsburgh and reassemble yourself at any one of the motels in the area, which are not always easy to get into. Nearby Plattsburgh Air Force Base attracts many visitors, including servicemen's families.

Valcour Island is about six miles south of Plattsburgh, about nine hundred yards off the west shore of the lake. You can find it easily by driving south on Route 9 until the island comes in sight off to your left. It is very much like it was at the time of the battle, with its sides coming down steeply to the water and its heavy growth of trees. Some open areas appear, but the island is uninhabited. A smaller island immediately to the south once held a blockhouse built by the French during their war with the Iroquois.

Opposite the southern end of the island, you will spot a marker set up by the D.A.R., commemorating the battle which occurred in the stretch of water between the shore you are standing on and the island, for about a half mile down-lake toward Plattsburgh, which did not exist at the time.

Both the British and the Americans had to build ships specially designed to maneuver in the comparatively shallow water of the lake. One British officer involved in the planning suggested using ships with a centerboard, an idea too avant-garde to be understood or adopted at the time. Most of the boats used were small craft propelled by small sails on short, stumpy masts, and by oars. Arnold formed his fleet around three sailing ships left over from the days of '75: the schooner *Liberty*, which had been captured at Skenesboro by the men Ethan Allen sent there for ships; the sloop *Enterprise*, which Arnold had captured in his raid on St. Johns after Ticonderoga; and the schooner *Royal Savage*, which had fallen into Montgomery's hands at the fall of Fort St. Johns. In addition he built another schooner called the *Revenge*; the cutter *Lee*; four galleys, the *Washington, Congress, Trumbull* and *Gates*, which used sails and oars and were about seventy-two feet long, twenty feet wide and six feet deep; and eight flatbottomed gundalows, which were open boats about fifty-three feet long, fifteen feet wide and almost four feet deep in the center. All of these boats were armed with heavy guns ranging from eighteen-pounders to two-pounders, and smaller swivel guns. They carried from forty-five to eighty men each; taken altogether, they were the first American naval fleet assembled.

Building these ships was a monumental feat in itself, for Arnold had nothing to work with but the trees in the forests. Local sawmills were pressed into service to produce the necessary planks, and most of the construction took place in a makeshift boatyard in Skenesboro, with inexperienced hands from the army drafted as boatwrights. Gradually skilled craftsmen began to come in from the colonies, lured by inflated wages. Arnold took personal charge of the shipbuilding and drove the men so well and so hard that the fleet was ready for action long before the British fleet was in any condition to take to the water.

The British fleet consisted of the three-masted sloop *Inflexible;* two schooners, the *Maria* and the *Carleton;* a large gundalow, the *Loyal Convert;* about twenty gunboats, each of which mounted one gun; four long boats which were armed with field cannon; twenty-four bateaux which carried provisions; and a 422-ton sailing scow, the *Thunderer,* which carried three hundred men and mounted howitzers, as well as twenty-four pound and six-pound guns. The *Thunderer* was ninety-two feet long and more than thirty-three feet wide, and would have been a formidable foe for Arnold's boats to tackle, had she ever taken part in the battle. Fortunately for the Americans, Arnold had disposed his fleet in such a way as to make this impossible.

Arnold placed his boats behind Valcour Island (between the island and the west shore), strung out in a line with their broadside guns facing south. Carleton came sailing south with all his ships, looking for the Americans, who, he had learned, were in the vicinity. On October 11 he came around Cumberland Head north of Valcour Island and bypassed Arnold without realizing it. By the time he saw his mistake, he had to come around and sail into the wind, which was blowing at a brisk rate from the north.

Arnold's line of battle was designed to give him the maximum advantage against a superior enemy force, but he made the initial mistake of sending some of the vessels, including the *Royal Savage,* out toward the British fleet. When he saw how many enemy ships he had to contend with, he ordered them back into the line. Most of the American crewmen were amateur sailors at best, and in the confusion and the tricky business of sailing into the wind in shoal waters, the *Royal Savage* ran aground on the southwest tip of Valcour Island, directly opposite the marker on Route 9. One of the British schooners, the *Carleton,* came abreast of the grounded ship and blasted her; but the same wind that had got the *Royal Savage* into trouble did as much for the *Carleton.* The *Carleton's* skipper anchored on a spring cable and prepared to blast the *Royal Savage* with further broadsides, supported by most of the British gunboats which lined up with the *Carleton* across the channel. A general engagement followed in which the *Carleton* was riddled and its commander severely wounded. The schooner finally had to be towed out of the action by several smaller boats.

The men on the *Royal Savage* continued to man her guns until a landing party of Indians and redcoats from another British ship drove them off, and the *Royal Savage* was burned. The fight raged on until the *Inflexible* managed to come up into the wind close enough to bring her guns into effective range. After five broadsides from the *Inflexible,* most of Arnold's guns were put out of action.

By that time it was getting dark. The engagement was broken off and the British held their positions, believing they had Arnold bottled up. They were prepared to destroy the American fleet completely the next day. Arnold, however, was not about to sit waiting calmly for annihilation. Under cover of a fog and with a good northeast wind at his back, he sailed his fleet in single file between the British line and the shore and escaped out into the lake. This means that the American fleet passed so close to shore at the point where you are standing, that had you been there, you could have heard the creak of muffled oars and the hushed voices of the men as the ships passed, one after the other. They left behind them the burned-out hulk of the *Royal Savage* and the *Philadelphia,* a gundalow which had sunk after nightfall.

Unfortunately, Arnold lost the wind. Despite his men's best efforts at the oars, they were only eight miles from the British ships by daybreak. Two gundalows too badly damaged to be repaired were scuttled; another foundered on a rock, and the rest fled south before the pursuing British fleet. By then the wind had turned and blew from the south, and both fleets had to row into it. When the wind turned again October 13, the British closed the gap and began to rake the Americans with broadsides. One galley, the *Washington,* was forced to surrender and the cutter *Lee* ran aground; but the *Congress,* Arnold's flagship, and four gundalows continued to resist, moving south as fast as they could. Recognizing Arnold on board the *Congress,* the British ships concentrated their attention on him. Arnold outwitted them again by turning into the wind and rowing (which the British could not do) across the lake to the Vermont shore, where he beached the remains of his fleet in Buttonmould Bay. Leaving the ships burning with their flags still flying, he and two hundred men marched ten miles to Crown Point, which the *Trumbull,* the *Enterprise, Revenge,* and *Liberty* had reached before him. With the British only hours away, Arnold burned the fort at Crown Point and withdrew to Fort Ticonderoga.

The Americans lost eleven of the fifteen vessels present at the battle and more than a hundred men killed, wounded, and captured. British losses were light, but the Americans had won something of great value: time. Because they had fought Carleton to a standstill, they made that cautious commander think twice before attempting to go any farther south. Ahead lay Fort Ticonderoga, which would have to be captured, and then a long trek down the waterway to Albany, neither of which could be accomplished before winter set in. More important than the battle was the presence of the American fleet, which made Carleton halt his advance at Fort St. Johns to build his own fleet—a delay some historians feel saved the American Revolution. And thus we are faced with a paradox of history, for the Champlain fleet was built by Benedict Arnold, who, through his boundless energy and personal drive, saved the very cause he attempted to betray four years later.

Archaeological operations, mostly amateur, have recovered several relics, including boats, from the waters off Valcour Island. Many of these have fallen into private hands and are scattered about the landscape. One of the most enthusiastic and persistent explorers of the site has been Frank Pabst, who runs a scuba diving store and the Valcour Island Campsite, three and a half miles south of Plattsburgh. Pabst has conducted underwater exploration with his diving group; has brought up many relics of the battle, including guns, shot, bayonets and utensils; and has located several of the boats that were sunk, including, he claims, the *Congress* and the others Arnold burned in Buttonmould Bay, a site covered in Book VII of this volume. Pabst will be happy to take you scuba-diving history buffs down to the wrecks, so long as they remain where they are. A museum with relics he found from the Arnold-Carleton encounter and the Battle of Champlain of 1814 has been planned by the Clinton County Historical Society for completion by 1976.

One other point of interest in the area is the **Kent-DeLord House** at 17 Cumberland Avenue in Plattsburgh. Cumberland Avenue borders the lake north of the town center. Several relics of the Battle of Valcour Island, including bar shot, anchors, chain shot, sounding weights, and some sections of what may have been the bulwarks of one of the boats, are on display in a shed behind the house. Inside the house, built in 1797, is the table at which Washington and the French commander Rochambeau sat while they held their last conference in the Webb home in Wethersfield, Connecticut, before they moved south to Yorktown. There is no explanation of how it came to Plattsburgh, but there it is, a valuable relic indeed of the Revolution and of Washington. The Kent-DeLord House is open year-round, except for a week at Christmas, from 10 A.M. until 4 P.M. The admission price of $1.00 for adults, $0.50 for children includes a guided tour through the house.

MOUNT HOPE AND MOUNT DEFIANCE

Returning south to the village of Ticonderoga, pick up the signs you noticed during your first visit indicating the route to Mount Hope, for the time has come to round out the story of Fort Ticonderoga and begin the story of General John Burgoyne's invasion of the colonies.

First let us catch up with the events of the Revolution between the Battle of Valcour Island and the day Burgoyne's invading forces appeared at the foot of Mount Hope in early summer, 1777. In 1776 Thomas Jefferson had written a document which the Continental Congress published as the young nation's Declaration of Independence. Then disaster followed on disaster. The British showed up in force in New York Harbor with their fleet and army under the command of the brothers Howe, Admiral Lord Richard Howe and General Sir William Howe. Carelessness and bad leadership lost Washington the Battle of Long Island. This was followed by the loss of the city of New York, a defeat at White Plains, and the Continental Army's retreat across the Hudson into New Jersey. With utter defeat staring the rebels in the face—the British had already declared that any who pledged their allegiance to the crown within sixty days would be pardoned, and hundreds took advantage of the amnesty—Washington crossed the Delaware on Christmas Eve and took a large force of Hessians by surprise in Trenton. Not giving his weary men time to rest properly, he followed up with a daringly successful attack on Princeton. With the Revolution given new life, Washington went into winter quarters in Morristown.

French assistance in the form of money and guns was beginning to reach the new government and its army, but the British were showing an increasing interest in the Hudson Valley. It was evident they would soon make a decisive move, probably from the north. That move was Burgoyne's. Burgoyne had gone in person to London to sell his plan of operations to King George. He was to come down from the north in the spring, along the Champlain-Hudson route to Albany, where he would be joined by a smaller force of regulars plus Indian and Canadian allies

who would come east from Fort Ontario through the Mohawk Valley.
At the same time General Howe would come up from New York City
and meet them above the Hudson Highlands. As in 1776, the idea was to
cut New England off from the other colonies.

General John Burgoyne was dubbed "Gentleman Johnny" because,
in an era when the press gang was the favorite method of recruiting
men into the armed forces where they were treated as though they were
insensible cattle, he opposed excessive corporal punishment and advocated
that officers treat the men under their command like human beings. A
successful politician, a fairly successful playwright, and the husband of
a famous heiress, he was much praised for his gallantry but was thought
by many of his contemporaries to be superficial.

He left St. Johns for the south in late June, 1777, preceded by a
flotilla of nine ships, which included the *Inflexible,* some of the American
vessels captured from Arnold's fleet, and about 10,500 British and German troops and a number of Indians and Canadians. One thousand members of his force were noncombatants and camp followers, including 500
soldiers' wives with offspring who were authorized to draw rations and
several women of higher rank with children, including the Baroness von
Riedesel, wife of Baron von Riedesel who was in command of the Hessians
and Brunswickers.

Burgoyne moved down the lake to Bouquet Ferry, approximately
forty miles north of Ticonderoga, where on June 23 he issued a proclamation summoning all Loyalists in the region he was about to invade to
come to his assistance and threatening to turn loose his Indian allies on
any who opposed him. His advance units under the command of General Simon Fraser had taken abandoned Crown Point, only ten miles
from Ticonderoga, on June 16.

The strategy that revolved around Fort Ticonderoga and its neighboring forts had not changed since it had fallen to Ethan Allen. The control of the portage area between Champlain and Lake George was as
important as ever, and in this control Mounts Hope, Defiance, and Independence all played a vital role. Mount Hope overlooks the creek connecting the two lakes.

General Fraser came down from Crown Point overland in command
of Burgoyne's advance corps and arrived at Mount Hope on July 2. The
rest of the army had deployed at Crown Point by that time. On July 2,
Fraser's units moved against Mount Hope. The tiny garrison set fire to
the log breastworks and retreated behind a prepared line at Fort Ticonderoga, the old French line of defense Montcalm had held successfully

nineteen years before, almost to the day. The British attacked and were thrown back, but the fall of Mount Hope meant that all communication between Fort Ti and the road south was cut off. Mount Hope was recaptured by the rebels two months later, after the Battle of Bennington, by Colonel John Brown, who was part of a raiding party sent out to harass Burgoyne's long supply line and to recapture Fort Ticonderoga, if possible. The raids took every British post around it, but failed to take Fort Ti itself. When the Americans withdrew, the British reoccupied these positions only to lose them again after Burgoyne's defeat at Saratoga. As the tides of war washed back and forth over the area, Mount Hope was recaptured by the British once more in 1780 and then changed hands for the last time when the Americans took it back in 1781 and held it until the end of the war.

Both Mount Hope and Mount Defiance are owned and run by a private, local organization headed by its founder, James M. Lonergan of Ticonderoga.

The Mount Hope site has been reconstructed on a hill near the fort that was first fortified by the Americans. The remains of the earthern breastworks have been enclosed in a wooden stockade and dressed up with a number of cannon Lonergan found at different sites and brought here. A reconstructed blockhouse has a small and not very well-arranged *museum,* which, nevertheless, displays some interesting old weapons and utensils, all found by Lonergan. Outside the blockhouse, in a shed, are the remains of a boat found under the waters of Champlain that might have been part of Arnold's fleet at the Battle of Valcour Island. The collection is a worthwhile sidelight, showing what an amateur archaeologist and historian might uncover if fortunate enough to live in or near so productive a site. There is no admission, but a collection box in the inevitable souvenir shop invites contributions.

The signs for Mount Defiance will take you from the village of Ticonderoga's Main Street to a toll booth at its foot. My admission cost me $3.00 for myself, wife, son, and car. The macadam road up is steep and narrow. Signs advise you to negotiate it in low gear, but I did not find this necessary, nor did I find it a difficult road to drive. As you go up, you will catch glimpses of Lake Champlain through the trees, giving promise of greater scenic delights ahead. The macadam road eventually gives way to a dirt road which leads a short distance to a parking area with several picnic tables set about on the rocks. Beyond that a paved pathway leads to the summit, which is crowned with a summit house, a large structure with picture windows all around and a sightdeck on the roof. Inside is a souvenir shop and a refreshment counter. The summit house features a taped account of the history of Mount Defiance played over a public-address system. A wooden fence encircles the site, with an occasional period cannon dressing up the scene.

This is the position the Americans neglected to fortify under the mistaken assumption that it was inaccessible. The fortifications on Mount Independence were not sufficient cover for Fort Ti, for they could be outflanked and the bridge, log boom, and iron chain easily captured. John Trumbull, who worked on the Fort Ticonderoga fortifications after its capture by the Americans, climbed 856 feet to the top of Mount Defiance to show that it was not inaccessible, but General Arthur St. Clair, in command at the fort, felt he did not have enough men to cover both positions and vetoed the idea.

When Burgoyne arrived, he sent his chief engineer, Lieutenant William Twiss, up Mount Defiance to see what he could see. Twiss saw what you now see, Fort Ticonderoga almost directly below. He reported to Burgoyne that the fort was within effective artillery range. This was something of an exaggeration, but it was good enough for Burgoyne, who sent for his commander of artillery, General William Phillips.

Phillips surveyed the position and is said to have remarked, "Where a goat can go, a man can go, and where a man can go, he can drag a gun."

And go they did, those British artillerists, cutting a road of sorts up the steep, rocky sides of Mount Defiance and dragging their guns behind them. Twiss had carried out his reconnaissance July 4. By noon of July 6, four twelve-pounders were in position ready to open fire on Fort Ticonderoga. The Americans, however, were not exactly taken by surprise, for they had seen the British preparations, guessed what was afoot, and immediately begun planning to deal with the new wrinkle.

The surprising part about this whole venture is the way both sides overestimated the threat posed by the guns on Mount Defiance. Big guns in those days had a total range of about a mile and a half, but an effective range of only three-quarters of a mile. The distance from the top of Mount Defiance to Fort Ticonderoga is a mile and a half as the crow flies. The Mount Defiance guns did effectively threaten the bridge at the foot of Mount Independence and any boats the Americans might have brought up to evacuate the garrison or to bring supplies. Whether or not the British could actually have hit the fort we shall never know. The Americans did not wait for them to try. Under cover of an artillery exchange, they pulled out of the fort on the night of July 5. Even though they were never fired, the guns of Mount Defiance had hit a target of a sort: American morale.

Nothing on Mount Defiance remains of the original British position, except for the hilltop. The views from this spot are magnificent, and the usual coin-operated telescopes will help you to enjoy them. To the west you look down on the village of Ticonderoga. Below you, just to the left of the village, you can see Ticonderoga Creek, the Lake George outlet. North the view is of Lake Champlain with the bridge at Crown Point, eighteen miles away, clearly visible. Almost directly below you is the promontory on which Fort Ticonderoga stands. From this vantage point, you can look down into the interior of Fort Ticonderoga and better understand why the occupants felt threatened that hot July day in 1777. To the west is Lake George, extending thirty-six miles to the south. Lake George, incidentally, is 210 feet higher than Lake Champlain, and its waters fall forty-five feet farther than the waters of Niagara Falls. Looking east you can see where Lake Champlain disappears south and the Adirondacks meet the Green Mountains of Vermont. It was up this southern part of the lake that Arnold's fleet passed in the summer of 1776 to be armed and supplied for the battle at Valcour Island.

As you stand on Mount Defiance, however, you are looking down on more than scenery. Below you stands the fort that for twenty-two years was a focal point of the opposing ambitions of the two leading European powers of the eighteenth century to control this vast, new continent and of the British and American forces early in the rebellion. Yet, in the course of three days, a small company of men and four pieces of artillery had changed all that. They had drawn the teeth of the dragon, disarmed the great, stone fortress down below, and rendered it impotent. Never again would Fort Ticonderoga play the role of linchpin, holding the great waterway system together.

BURGOYNE'S LINE OF MARCH

To follow Burgoyne on his march south, take Route 22 east and south out of Ticonderoga village for thirty-seven miles to **Whitehall,** New York. This was Skenesboro where Arnold built his Champlain fleet. The American withdrawal from Ticonderoga was well planned, but badly bungled by those entrusted with carrying it out. Nevertheless, it did accomplish its objective, which was to keep the main force intact and out of reach of Burgoyne who could easily have destroyed it.

St. Clair sent most of his supplies up Lake Champlain by boat, guarded by Colonel Pierce Long and four hundred New Hampshire men. Burgoyne burst through the boom at the foot of Mount Independence and sailed in pursuit, catching up with Long at Skenesboro while he was unloading. Most of the supplies fell into British hands, but Long's detachment managed to fight its way clear and continued retreating south. Burgoyne stayed in Skenesboro from July 9 to July 25 before moving on.

A small *museum* in Whitehall contains a scale model of Philip Skene's estate, showing the shipyard at the southernmost tip of Lake Champlain where Arnold's boats were built. Outside the museum a long, low shed, open on all sides, covers the remains of a vessel that took part in the Battle of Plattsburgh in 1814.

The site of the *shipyard* is marked, but difficult to find. It is off the lower end of Main Street, a short distance above the Whitehall Lock of the Hudson-Champlain Canal, lost amid a jumble of oil-storage tanks and industrial buildings. Follow Main Street to a lumberyard (it's the only one in town), then park and poke around to your right. Before the canal was built, the end of the lake formed a fishhook. The Skenesboro harbor was located inside the curve, protected by a bar which formed the shank of the hook.

Burgoyne was intent on getting to Albany where he expected to meet Lieutenant Colonel Barry St. Leger who was, supposedly, laying waste to the Mohawk Valley on his way east from Fort Ontario. He sent his guns and equipment by boat down Lake George, while he and his men cut their way south through the forest.

Route 22 south from Whitehall will take you along Burgoyne's line of march ten miles to the town of **Fort Ann,** near where Colonel Long turned and gave the pursuing British a good drubbing, and on to **Fort Edward** where General Philip Schuyler, in charge of operations against Burgoyne, had made his headquarters. St. Clair joined him there on July 12 and they decided to fall back farther south, burning and destroying everything en route that might be of help to the British and felling trees to block the trails. When U.S. Route 4 joins 22 below Whitehall, follow the signs for 4 as you look for markers on the sites of breastworks and other defenses the Americans set up against Burgoyne's progress. There are several in the vicinity of Schuylerville, including one near a gas station where Route 29 swings off to the west.

The drive down Routes 22 and 4 goes through the Hudson-Champlain Canal country, a rich and pleasant landscape with the canal off to your right, shaded by large overhanging trees, punctuated by occasional locks which are always interesting to watch in operation. Broad fields intersected by shaded lanes and roads stretch off in both directions, and you will welcome the chance the markers afford you to stop to sample the sun and air.

Coming south out of Fort Ann look for a marker on your right on a *memorial stone* surrounded by an iron fence. This marks the spot where Jane McCrea was buried, the heroine of a minor episode in the Burgoyne invasion that became a propaganda victory for the Americans. She was the twenty-three-year-old daughter of a Presbyterian minister and was affianced to David Jones, a Tory serving with Burgoyne. She had gone to Fort Edward, hoping to meet her fiancé when he arrived with the army, and was living with General Fraser's cousin, a Mrs. McNeil. On July 27 some of Burgoyne's Indians reached Fort Edward which, by that time, had been abandoned by the rebels. They seized the two women and took them back toward Fort Ann where Burgoyne's force had halted. They showed up in camp with Mrs. McNeil, who had been divested of her clothing, and Jane McCrea's scalp, which was identified by the unhappy Lieutenant Jones. No one to this day knows exactly what happened to the unfortunate young lady. The Wyandot Panther, one of the braves involved, was accused of the crime, but since Burgoyne could not afford to offend his Indian allies, he went unpunished. This occurred at a time when Indian depredations among the farms and settlements of eastern New York and western Vermont were arousing the settlers to action against Burgoyne, who was trying hard to rally Loyalist sentiment behind him as he advanced. He could also ill afford what next occurred in the western part of the state where St. Leger was preparing to move against Fort Stanwix and General Herkimer.

At this point, you are faced with several choices. You can follow the next events in sequential order, which means first traveling west to the Fort Stanwix site in Rome and the nearby Oriskany battlefield, then backtracking east and south to Hoosick Falls to cover the Battle of Bennington and returning north to Saratoga for the big battle of the campaign. Or you can proceed from Schuylerville to the Saratoga battlefield just a few miles to the south, then go to Rome and Bennington, or to Bennington and Rome, whichever fits in best with your plans. Either way, you face a round trip of almost two hundred and fifty miles to and from Rome and about a one-hundred-mile round trip to the Bennington battlefield. Of course, if you are a true-blue history buff, you will go all the way west to Oswego to visit the fort on Lake Ontario where St. Leger joined forces with Joseph Brant before setting out to ravage the Mohawk Valley and lay siege to Fort Stanwix.

Saratoga Springs is an excellent place to stay before you begin either trek. None of the old hotels with their wonderful verandas are still open; in fact only two are left, the Adelphi and the Rip Van Dam, and they are both ghosts of their former splendid selves. The town is still a spa and a popular resort, however, and offers a summer theater and music program at the Saratoga Arts Center and a number of motels to choose from.

FORT ONTARIO

To reach Fort Ontario, return to the Adirondack Northway via Route 29 to Route 9, then south on 9 to the first Interstate 87 interchange. Take 87 south to the interchange with Interstate 90, then 90 west to Exit 38, a distance of 138 miles. Coming off the interstate, take Route 57 north for another thirty miles to the city of Oswego where Fort Ontario sits on the shores of magnificent Lake Ontario.

Signs in Oswego will show you to the fort, an imposing structure set in a parklike area, with good parking facilities close to the entrance. The first version of this fort, a log palisade, was built in 1755 by the English who lost it to Montcalm in 1756. The second version, which stood from 1759 to 1814, was a square-timbered affair with stone and earth fill between the logs to form the ramparts. The present fort, built during the Civil War era, is earth with a masonry facing which was installed in 1863.

Fort Ontario is usually neglected by historians who deal with the Revolutionary War, possibly because it was not the scene of any large-scale military operations. However, it was of major importance to the people who lived along the Mohawk River as it was the originating point of frequent British attempts to raid and seize the valley. Its very presence at the head of the waterway system connecting the western part of New York with the major settlements to the east, was a constant menace to the welfare and well-being of adherents and sympathizers to the rebel cause.

In 1775 Guy Johnson, who had been chased out of Guy Hall, his home near Amsterdam, New York, by his rebel neighbors, held a conference here with the chiefs of the Iroquois tribes in an effort to enlist their aid in the Loyalist cause. He managed to sign up most of the tribes and then went to Canada to relay the happy news to Governor General Carle-

ton, to whom he next offered his services. He eventually returned to Fort
Ontario as the administrative officer in charge of St. Leger's expedition.

By the time revolutionary hostilities began, there was no longer a
regular garrison on duty at the fort, but that situation was soon corrected.
Lieutenant Colonel Barry St. Leger, an officer in the regular British army
who came by his French name through Huguenot ancestry, organized an
expedition in Montreal, then came up the Saint Lawrence and down
around the eastern shore of Lake Ontario to join forces with Joseph Brant
and his Indians here in 1777. St. Leger was to return to Fort Ontario
somewhat sooner than he had expected, retreating after his discomfiture,
which we will witness, at Fort Stanwix and Oriskany. As he continued
to fall back to Canada, he decided not to leave the fort's garrison in what
was then an exposed position and took them with him, abandoning the
fort. And in fact, the following summer of 1778, troops were sent from
Fort Stanwix under a Lieutenant McClellan to destroy the post. They
found it inhabited only by the members of a trader's family, who were
living in one of the fort's inner buildings. The wife, a fourteen-year-old
boy and several other children—the head of the family was off on a trading trip—were put aside, while all the log buildings inside the fort were
burned. Although McClellan's men did an excellent job on the inside,
they left the outside of the fort intact.

The Iroquois became apprehensive. Having cast their lot with the
British, they now found themselves open to retaliatory attack from the
colonists with no British military support at hand. At their insistence,
talks aimed at regarrisoning the fort began, but a proposed second conference during 1779 never materialized. During the years 1781–82, the
fort became a handy overnight stop for raiding parties heading into and
out of the interior of the state, thus maintaining the fort's wasp-nest
reputation among the Mohawk Valley settlers. Then in 1782 Canadian
Governor General Frederick Haldimand ordered the post regarrisoned,
which necessitated reconstructing the burned buildings. An answer was
attempted by Marinus Willett, a former member of the New York City
chapter of the Sons of Liberty who had been instrumental in arousing
rebel sentiment in that city. Willett had served in the Montgomery invasion of Canada and had been second-in-command at Fort Stanwix during
St. Leger's siege. In February, 1783, Willett led a force out of Fort Herkimer (Nicholas Herkimer's stockaded home) to Fort Ontario, via Fort
Stanwix. Marching most of the way on snowshoes, he attempted to
take Ontario by surprise. Wallace Workman, curator of Fort Ontario
and supervisor of the historic sites in New York from east of Oriskany
west, believes this operation was one of the last ordered by General

Washington. It was another attempt to prevent the British from launching a surprise attack through the Mohawk Valley. Unfortunately, Willett's men lost their way in the night and found themselves on the lake shore some distance west of the fort. By the time they retraced their steps, they had lost the element of surprise and gave up and went home.

Despite the Treaty of Paris and the end of the Revolutionary War, the British remained in command of the post until 1796. During the War of 1812 it was again an active post and was captured and destroyed by the British in 1814. It was regarrisoned and put on a state of alert during the Civil War for fear of British intervention. It was a military hospital camp during World War I and a training center for military police and anti-aircraft units during World War II. It was finally given up by the army in 1946.

At the time of my visit to the fort in 1970, the only aboveground evidence of the Revolutionary War period was part of the foundation of a building that was still being excavated and was not open to the public. By the time of the bicentennial, this and other remains will be on display, probably in a new Visitor's Center. I saw some of the work in progress in the fort's workshops, where skilled artisans and artists were preparing scale models, dioramas, and paintings, many of them dealing with the Revolutionary War period.

The present fort has little but the site itself at the mouth of the Oswego River to demonstrate its role during the Revolution. It is an extensive and complete fortification, which invites visitors to enter the reconstructed barracks and officers' quarters and to walk the ramparts. During the summer months a twelve-man garrison of college students, dressed in uniforms of the Civil War, carry out a thirty-minute infantry drill which ends with the loading and firing of a cannon. The drill is conducted in highly realistic fashion by sergeants who ball out enlisted men for not dressing ranks properly, for wearing sloppy uniforms, and for handling their rifles ineptly. Picnic tables are available in the park surrounding the fort.

Directly opposite the entrance to the fort, across the parade ground, is a rampart overlooking the lake and the mouth of the Oswego River, now the scene of modern industrial and shipping activities. Two of the first forts guarding the river mouth, including the 1755 original, stood on the hill on the opposite side until Montcalm destroyed them. During the Revolutionary War there were a number of buildings along the lake shore in this vicinity, but none are standing today. Along the lake shore due east of the fort is the post *cemetery,* which was moved to its present location from a previous site. It contains the graves of a Lieutenant Basil Dunbar of the Royal American Regiment, who was killed in a duel within the fort, and George Fikes of the King's Royal Regiment of New York, both of whom served at the fort with their units during the French and Indian and Revolutionary wars. Curator Workman has been told that both these gentlemen have been seen at various times over the years walking the ramparts. If the park and fort are ever open during the night hours, you may be fortunate enough to run into them yourself.

Fort Ontario is open to visitors year-round except for New Year's Day, Easter, Thanksgiving, and Christmas. Visiting hours are weekdays, 9 A.M. to 5 P.M.; Sundays, 1 P.M. to 5 P.M.

Oswego is an interesting old Great Lakes port at the mouth of the Oswego River. A series of locks takes ships through the center of town. An atomic power plant of the Niagara-Mohawk Power Corporation just to the north of the town, has a Visitor's Center which features a large, scale model of a "working" atomic power plant and a small exhibit room with fossils, local fish, and other wonders and delights. The town itself has a modern shopping area in the downtown section and a number of good motels and hotels. It's a good place to stay overnight after the long drive from the other side of the state.

FORT STANWIX

Lieutenant Colonel Barry St. Leger left the fort at Oswego July 26, 1777, with about 2,000 men, half of them Indians under Joseph Brant, the Mohawk war chief. His force also included 340 British regulars and a number of Tory volunteer units. Wise to the ways of the forest, the expedition traveled through the wilderness with some light pieces of artillery at about ten miles a day toward Fort Stanwix, along the traditional water route.

You can follow, or at least parallel, **St. Leger's route** on your way to Fort Stanwix by taking Route 57 south from Oswego. Route 57 follows the Oswego River to Three Rivers where the Oswego meets the Oneida River. You will have some difficulty going on along the Oneida River to its head in Oneida Lake, and I suggest you pick up an Oswego County map if you plan to try. After meandering around, pick up Route 31 at the eastern end of the lake and parallel the Mohawk River to Rome.

As far as I can determine, the exact route St. Leger followed has never been marked, though there is some talk of a Boy Scout effort to do so in time for the bicentennial. If you are not that much of a stickler for authenticity, leave 57 below Three Rivers where it meets Route 31, and follow 31 at a very unauthentic distance south of St. Leger's route into Rome and the site of Fort Stanwix.

If you are still in Schuylerville or Saratoga Springs and decide to join St. Leger at the end of his trek, I suggest you take Route 29 west to U.S. 9 south to the first Interstate 87 entrance. Continue south on 87 to Exit 24; then transfer onto Interstate 90 west for ninety-six miles. (Radar patrols are frequent.)

Leave 90 at Exit 32 and take Route 233 north to Rome, where the site of Fort Stanwix is located. Originally, the British built five forts in the area in 1755 to control the portage between Wood Creek and the Mohawk River, both now well within the city limits. The portage was called De-O-wain-sta by the Oneida Indians, meaning "the place where canoes are carried from one stream to another," and was known by the British as the Great Carrying Place, an important link along this major east-west water highway.

The forts also formed a bulwark of defense for the settlers in the Mohawk Valley against French and Indian raids, until the British were forced to burn them all in the face of a superior French force. It was then decided to replace the four smallest forts with one large fortress which would dominate the entire portage area. The original Fort Stanwix was then built in 1758, but was neglected and abandoned after the British took Canada. In 1768 it was the scene of a conference between the members of the Iroquois Confederation and Sir William Johnson (commissioner of Indian affairs for the British) which established the boundary line between Indian and settler territories. It played no further part in history until it was reoccupied and rehabilitated in June, 1776, by American revolutionary forces. For a while it was called Fort Schuyler in honor of General Schuyler, a leading and powerful figure in this part of the state. At that time it may have been garrisoned by as many as 800 men, the last 200 of whom managed to get into the fort just as St. Leger appeared with his men on August 3 and surrounded it.

The American garrison was under the command of Colonel Peter Gansevoort, and it had the honor of flying the Stars and Stripes for the first time in battle on August 3, the first day of the siege. Three days later General Herkimer and a relief column were ambushed at Oriskany a few miles away. Relief was delayed as a result, but the Indians lost so many during the battle that they lost heart. They were further dismayed by a raid the fort's defenders (led by Colonel Marinus Willett) carried out during the battle, which destroyed much of their encampment and left them with nothing to wear but what they had on at the time.

St. Leger tried to get Gansevoort to surrender, threatening the defenders and the settlers along the Mohawk with massacre if he didn't, but Gansevoort stubbornly refused. Not having heavy enough artillery to level the walls, the British started digging trenches toward two of the bastions, intending to advance under cover right up to the walls. By August 21 Gansevoort was preparing to fight his way out, when news reached him of a relief column coming to the rescue under the command of Benedict Arnold, who had been assigned to Schuyler's command after his return from Canada. Arnold actually had far fewer men than he needed to lift the siege, but St. Leger had no way of knowing that. Fearing he was about to be caught between the fort and the relief column, he decamped and headed back to Oswego. His flight is said to have been aided by a half-wit named Hon Yost Schuyler who wandered into the British camp, under Arnold's coaching, with a wild story concerning 3,000 Continentals headed in their direction. Arnold arrived on the twenty-fourth, and so ended the last important action to take place around Fort Stanwix.

When Fort Stanwix was taken over by the Americans in 1776, it consisted of a glacis (a cleared area of land that sloped up toward the fort, exposing attackers to the defenders' fire), a breastwork, a ditch, and a stockade fence in front of the walls. The walls were further defended by a line of sharp sticks, their points protruding outward. At each corner was a triangular bastion. There was also a covered way similar to the one at Fort Ticonderoga, a sally port (a small door through the outer wall), and a bridge leading to the gate. Inside were at least five structures used for supplies and the housing of the garrison.

After the walls were leveled in 1827, the high ground the fort stood on was eventually built over with private homes while the ubiquitous bulldozer took care of most of the area in the surrounding neighborhood. Today the site lies in the heart of downtown Rome, bounded by Dominick, Spring, Liberty, and James streets. Archaeological excavations to uncover traces of the fort began in 1965 and were completed in 1973 with the remains and evidence of about one third of the fort's structures exposed, enough to permit a complete reconstruction. The land where the fort stood has been included in a seventy-five-acre urban renewal plan featuring a fifteen-and-a-half-acre park. There, Fort Stanwix will be reconstructed at a cost of almost $9,000,000. The project is going forward under the aegis of the National Park Service, and they hope to have it completed by August, 1977, in time for the bicentennial of the British siege.

At present, a small, low building in the midst of the reconstruction site houses a museum displaying some of the artifacts uncovered on the site, maps, and detailed plans of the original fort and the restoration. Half-hourly tours, for which there is no charge, take visitors around the site, including the digs. If large numbers of people apply, the tours may be more frequent. Tours are conducted Monday through Friday during the winter and fall and on weekends as well between Memorial and Labor days. You can also walk or drive down to the banks of the Mohawk River and Wood Creek to look for the sites of the older forts, the British and Indian encampment, and the spot where the British gun batteries straddled what is now Ford Avenue. I poked around along the banks of the river, the far side of which is still mostly wooded, and found a few private homes, a tugboat landing, a few industrial sites, and a pathway that leads along the river bank and makes exploration easy, but nothing of any significance.

The siege and the successful resistance of the fort were more important to the inhabitants of the Mohawk Valley than to the total war effort, though local historians eagerly cite the defense of Stanwix and the Battle of Oriskany as a "turning point" in the war, fresh evidence of American spirit and fighting ability at a time when something was needed to revive flagging morale. In truth Oriskany was at best a draw, as we shall see, and that conclusion necessitates our leaning over backward a little. Similar claims, however, have been made by other local partisans for, respectively, the battles of Bennington, Princeton, Harlem Heights, Stony Point, Cowpens, Trenton, Saratoga, and even Hubbardton—in short for many major engagements fought during the Revolution and not a few small ones. Saratoga, Trenton, and Yorktown were decisive battles, but the proud description "turning point" could with some justification be applied to all the rest as well. Morale boosts were important to American armies under the command of men who were not, for the most part, professional soldiers with previous military experience under combat conditions. The armies were usually composed of militiamen, "warriors for the working day," who were forever threatening to go home as soon as their terms of enlistment were up and sometimes did. They were usually poorly equipped, poorly trained, rarely paid, ill-housed, ill-clothed, and ill-fed. Behind them was a home front riddled with Toryism and sectionalism—Schuyler was accused of abandoning New England to the enemy because he sent a relief force to Stanwix to save New York—while many New York and Philadelphia merchants toadied up shamelessly to the British when British forces occupied their cities. The country was governed by a Congress which did not have the reins of government firmly in hand and was still grappling with forming a national government of some sort in the middle of a war it was trying to wage with few clear sources of finance.

What then was the importance of Stanwix? From Burgoyne's point of view it was politically important, because its capture meant control of the Mohawk Valley and the western territories of New York State, where the settlers were split wide open over the issue of allegiance to the crown. It also meant maintaining a hold on the Iroquois, because if Stanwix didn't fall and the Americans maintained control of the region, the tribes were sure to waver in their allegiance. Who could blame these original Americans, who were doomed to watch their native land become the spoils of whichever of these two intruding opponents won the final outcome!

Fort Stanwix may be a difficult site to adjust to after Ticonderoga where the surrounding countryside and the fort itself bear a strong resemblance to the scene two hundred years ago. Unless you visit the site after the proposed reconstruction is completed, you will have to exercise your imagination to the fullest to counter the changes urbanization has wrought in an area that was once forest and swamp. No such problem will hinder your reconstruction of events when you visit the site of the Battle of Oriskany, however, where the major topographical features of the terrain remain unchanged.

ORISKANY

Oriskany is about five miles east of Rome. Take Mill Street out of town across a steel-girder bridge over the Mohawk River. At the intersection on the other side of the bridge, turn left and proceed to the next light. Around a traffic circle you will find Route 69 and signs directing you toward the battlefield. Route 69 goes along high ground through a short stretch of the Mohawk Valley to the entrance, which is marked on the left side of the road by a gate set between two stone posts. A sign hanging over the gate identifies the site as the **Oriskany battlefield,** and a tall monument inside the grounds, which is visible from the road, confirms it.

Follow the road through the gate to a small paved parking field. From there a gravel path leads down an incline to the Visitor's Center, which contains a central exhibit room and rest rooms. The exhibit room has several dioramas which are worth studying before touring the battlefield. One diorama showing the ambush gives a very good idea of the terrain at the time, the type of growth present, and the weather conditions. Others show Herkimer directing the battle from the foot of a beech tree, his subsequent death in his home, and Molly Brant, Joseph Brant's sister, relaying the news of the approach of Herkimer's men to St. Leger.

On the highest point of ground stands the granite-limestone *monument*, towering eighty-four feet above the field of battle. Standing at the monument with your back to Route 69, you are looking north by east across the valley of the Mohawk. The ground in front of you falls away into gently rolling fields and woodlands to the river. Beyond on the hilly horizon north of the river, a dish antenna marks Griffiss Air Force Base. Just below is a flat area, where you can sit on a comfortable bench and gaze off across the valley while you consider the circumstances of the battle.

Nicholas Herkimer, a general of militia and one of the leading rebel lights in Tryon County, had managed to raise about 800 militiamen from the area as soon as he heard of St. Leger's approach to Fort Stanwix. On August 4 he started off from Fort Dayton, situated in what was then called German Flats and is now the town of Herkimer, following a rough military supply road from Dayton to Stanwix. On the night of August 5, he camped about ten miles from Stanwix and sent messengers ahead to tell Gansevoort of his coming, suggesting that the fort's defenders create a diversion to cover his approach. Gansevoort was to fire a signal cannon to let him know when the action was taking place.

The next morning, on Wednesday, August 6, the wily old general wanted to sit tight until he heard the signal gun, but he weakened and gave way when his subordinate officers urged him to hurry to the fort's relief. Unknown to them, Molly Brant, who was Joseph Brant's sister and Sir William Johnson's mistress and mother of several of his children, had learned of the relief column and had sent a message to St. Leger. Brant and about 400 Indians and some Loyalist auxiliaries now lay in wait for Herkimer on both sides of the road at the point where it dipped down into a ravine and crossed a creek and marshy area.

The Indians lay low until Herkimer and many of his men were

well into the ravine before opening fire. At the first volley Herkimer and most of his officers went down, Herkimer with a bullet in one leg. Some of the militia ran, but most rallied and fought back. Herkimer had himself carried up the west slope of the ravine, and, with his back to a large beech tree, he lit his pipe and directed his men. The men formed a perimeter and managed to keep the line intact for about three-quarters of an hour. Then a storm broke, wet everyone's priming pan, and put a temporary end to the battle. The same storm delayed the start of Gansevoort's diversionary attack on the enemy camp. Herkimer took advantage of the lull to reorganize his men. The Indians had been having a field day, waiting for a militiaman to fire, then rushing in to tomahawk him before he could reload. Herkimer organized the men in pairs. While one reloaded, the other held his fire, waiting for the onrushing brave.

When the storm let up, some of the militia broke out of the ambush and formed a new line of defense on higher ground. About this time reinforcements came to Brant's aid from the siege lines around the fort. Turning their coats inside out, they tried to fool the Tryon County men into thinking they were friends; but one of the militiamen recognized a Tory neighbor, and a fierce hand-to-hand fight raged around the new perimeter. By this time the Indians had become discouraged over their losses, which have never been accurately determined, and quit. After six hours of fighting, the battle was over. Though they had sustained the brunt of an ambush and managed to get away intact, the battle was a defeat for the Americans since they did not succeed in relieving Fort Stanwix. Their determined stand, however, lowered the morale of St. Leger's Indians, who had been promised much loot and little fighting; their disillusionment eventually helped the British commander make up his mind to quit Fort Stanwix and retire in the direction whence he had come. The militia lost more than 160 killed and 50 wounded; several men were taken prisoner and the rest returned to Dayton. Herkimer died ten days later at his home after his leg had been amputated.

Standing at the battle monument, which marks the point where the Americans rallied after breaking out of the ambush, turn to your right and look down a gentle, grassy slope to a line of trees below you. Some distance down the slope you will see a granite marker. It is at the approximate site of the beech tree under which Herkimer sat during the battle.

The area at the time of the battle was heavily wooded and covered with first growth trees, hardwoods on the high ground, hemlocks and other soft woods in the ravine. The military supply road Herkimer was following was about 165 feet north of Route 69 and ran roughly parallel to it. If you stand about thirty feet to the left of the marker on the beech tree site, facing the ravine with Route 69 on your right, you will see two markers at the approximate site where the road crossed the ravine and then continued past where you are now standing to the granite monument behind you, and so on to the west.

Walk down the slope into the ravine, following a narrow, dirt footpath if you like. At the foot you will come to wet, marshy ground and the brook, now called Battle or Bloody Brook. The ground here is continually wet, as it was when Herkimer's men splashed across, and I advise you to wear overshoes to cross it, as I did. The growth is now quite young, but two hundred years ago the trees were huge, towering high overhead, and on every side were thick trunks, tangled underbrush, and fallen logs, making visibility difficult. If Herkimer had sent out flanking parties, he might have avoided what followed. Two wooden footbridges now cross the stream to the east slope of the ravine.

At the top of the eastern slope you will find three granite monuments at the end of a short spur of road, which leads in from Route 69 about a hundred yards east of the park entrance. They bear commemorative plaques dedicated to the militia of Tryon County who died in the battle and now lie in unmarked graves. Some of the dead were carried away by the survivors; others, according to one account, were found by Benedict Arnold and his men, who came by on their way to the relief of Stanwix and buried them in a common grave, which was never marked. Another account tells of the first settlers on the site finding the scattered remains on the battlefield and burying them in a common grave before clearing the land.

Returning to the granite monument overlooking the valley, read the plaques mounted on it, two of which are rosters of the men of the Tryon militia. Almost every family in the valley lost someone at Oriskany, and the effects of the battle on the valley's manpower were felt for many years after. This was one of the bloodiest engagements of the war, in terms of the ratio of casualties suffered to the number of men involved.

The Oriskany battlefield may be further enhanced by archaeological research, which is planned along the site of the old road, to be completed by the bicentennial of the battle in 1977. Now the site is a lovely park, overlooking a beautiful view across a section of the Mohawk Valley that was unsettled at the time of the battle. There are picnic tables set about, making it a good spot for the family to rest, enjoy lunch and the surroundings, and for the children to run about and stretch their legs before visiting General Herkimer's home to round out the story of Oriskany.

At this point you are faced with another choice, again depending on your schedule. For the shortest route, return toward Rome along Route 69 to Route 233, and take 233 south to Interstate 90 for a fast twenty-three-mile trip east to Exit 30; go off onto Route 5 to Little Falls. At Little Falls take Route 167 south to the intersection with Route 5S. Turn left onto 5S; a short distance farther you will see the sign for the **Herkimer Home**, indicating a left turn off the road. As an alternative route, if you have time, take Route 69 east to Utica, then Route 5 out of Utica east to Little Falls for an hour or so of driving through the scenic Mohawk River valley.

When Nicholas Herkimer settled on his 500 acres in 1754, he was living in a wilderness in the midst of the Iroquois Confederation. Two miles east was Indian Castle, the main village of the Mohawk tribe. Herkimer farmed the land, traded with the Indians, and served in the militia.

The house is a two-story, colonial red-brick building which you enter through the back door. The front of the house faces the river, and if you cross the grounds down the slope you will discover part of the walls of the old Erie Canal. The main canal along this stretch is now covered by plowed farmland.

The interior of the house has been partially restored to correct some Victorian atrocities a post-Civil War owner had committed, such as covering up the old fireplaces and partitioning some of the rooms into smaller rooms. The first room to the left as you enter is said by some historians to be the one in which Herkimer died; others dispute it. The dimensions of the room and the fireplace will recall the diorama you saw earlier at Oriskany.

The house is furnished with period furniture, but only a few of these items were actually there during Herkimer's occupancy. On an upper landing is a glass exhibit case which contains a German Bible printed in 1730. This was Herkimer's Bible, and it is opened to Psalm 38, which he read just before he died. Underneath the Bible is the sword he carried at Oriskany, and to one side is a piece of the beech tree under which he sat. Over this exhibit case hangs a photostat of the original deed to the house; elsewhere on the landing are the pistols the general carried at the battle. Most of the windows contain the original panes of glass, which were restored.

The lawns surrounding the house are beautifully kept and tree-shaded. To the left as you face the house is a low, stone archway leading into the *powder magazine* built into the side of some sloping ground. You may enter it to find a large, empty chamber in which the Herkimers kept their munitions, an obviously essential household item during their lifetime. The kitchen, which is open to visitors, is beneath the house directly under the dining room.

Off to one side, behind the house on a rise of ground, is a family *burial plot* containing the graves of many members of the Herkimer family, including the general and his brother. A tall, granite shaft similar to the one at Oriskany dominates the little cemetery. The General's final resting place is marked by a tombstone flanked by small American flags. According to the other tombstones, several of Herkimer's relatives were Revolutionary War veterans.

CHERRY VALLEY AND THE SCHOHARIE FORTS

Before you leave this part of the state to continue the Burgoyne story on the Bennington battlefield, you can choose to go south, as a matter of convenience, to cover the Cherry Valley Massacre and the forts along the Schoharie River. If you do, return to Route 5S, turn right and proceed to Canajoharie. At Canajoharie take Route 10 south to Route 20, then Route 20 west to the exit for Route 166 south, which will take you into Cherry Valley. While traveling along 20, watch for an overlook where you can pull off the road for a wonderful view of the Mohawk Valley with the Adirondack Mountains to the north. A historical marker describes in general detail the flow of events that moved across the scene before you.

The Cherry Valley Massacre is one of the best-known incidents of the war that was waged along the frontier during the Revolution. The settlement was established in 1740 and grew over the years, until by 1778 it represented a threat to Iroquois territory and towns, particularly the town of Unadilla, which was a staging area for attacks on the Mohawk Valley. Unadilla was destroyed in October, 1778, by Patriot forces, and, in retaliation, an attack on Cherry Valley was organized by Joseph Brant, the English-educated Iroquois chief, and Walter Butler, the New York Tory leader.

Most of the people of the valley were adherents to the rebel cause and had raised a company of rangers to serve with the Continental Army. This left the settlement exposed to attack until the state legislature supplied it with a company of rangers and the home of Colonel Samuel Campbell, one of the community's leading citizens, was fortified. Following the Battle of Oriskany, the situation in Cherry Valley became tense and uncertain. Small bands of Indians lurked on the outskirts, and farmers worked their fields under armed guard. In July, 1778, Colonel Ichabod Alden appeared to take command, ordered there by General Lafayette. He was accompanied by a regiment of Massachusetts men who were unfamiliar with Indian warfare. A new fort named after Alden was built, but otherwise the new commander proved to be badly suited for the job.

By early November, reports started coming to Alden warning of an approaching Indian attack, but he refused to believe them. It seemed too late in the season: snow had already fallen, and seasonal conditions throughout the area, which was still a wilderness beyond the settled regions, seemed too severe for campaigning, even by Indians. Nevertheless, a force of 700 Indians and Loyalist rangers had already completed a march of 150 miles down the Chemung River to the Susquehanna, north to Otsego Lake (where the present town of Cooperstown is located), and on to the vicinity of Cherry Valley. The Loyalists under Butler had marched from Fort Niagara, which was south of Lake Ontario and north of Lake Erie.

On the morning of November 11, a foggy, rainy Wednesday, the attackers moved toward the village. Many members of the 250-man garrison, including the officers, were either in their billets in private homes along the valley or visiting there. The first warning came from a horseman who pounded into the village, shouting that he had been fired on by Indians. Close behind him came the Senecas and Tories, heading first for the homes where the officers were staying. Alden, his officers, and a small headquarters company were at the home of Robert Wells, a short distance from the fort. Most were either killed or captured. Alden ran for the fort and was tomahawked before he could get there. The attackers fanned out through the village and settlement of forty homes, which covered about six miles in an imperfect semicircle. Before the day was over, thirty-odd civilians of the 300 residents had been killed, thirteen of them in the Wells house alone. Most of the garrison managed to get to the fort; those inhabitants who escaped the tomahawk and scalping knife either hid in the woods and hills or were taken alive. By the time the raiders left, the only buildings still standing were the fort, the church, and one or two homes. Everything else had been destroyed, including barns, outbuildings, crops, food supplies, and livestock. Seventy-one prisoners were taken away by Brant and Butler as they began the long march back to Fort Niagara. The next day most of the prisoners were released, except two women and seven children, who were kept as hostages against the release of the relatives of Tory officers being held prisoner in Albany.

Understandably, very little of the original settlement is left. Though the survivors returned and built anew, the settlement was destroyed again in a second, similar attack in 1780. Whatever was left standing after the first attack was leveled in the second, including the fort and the church. You can trace some of the incidents of the massacre through markers, however, by beginning with a visit to the **Cherry Valley Museum,** located on the town's main street in a house built in 1832. It is open daily from 9 A.M. to 6 P.M., May 30–September 30. Adult admission is $0.75; children are admitted free. A sign in front will help you find it.

Most of the material on exhibit is connected with the nineteenth century; but in the room to your right as you enter, you will find exhibits devoted to the Revolutionary War period, including a table-top topographical model of the valley and the settlement at the time of the massacre. Those sites connected with the events of November 11 are numbered, making it easy to follow the story from place to place. Other items in that room are relics of the massacre and of the Indian culture that developed in the valley long before the settlers appeared. There are some interesting pictures of the old settlement, including one of the Campbell house with the stockade around it and two blockhouses on the front lawn. How accurate the depiction is I cannot say, though the skulking figure in one corner, supposed to be that of Joseph Brant spying on the house, is an imaginative touch that makes it somewhat suspect.

To see the actual sites, proceed from the museum along Route 166, which follows an old Indian trail that ran between the Susquehanna and Mohawk valleys. In a block or two you will reach the town's center with its Civil War monument. At the traffic light, make a left onto Alden Street. A short distance down Alden Street you will see the Presbyterian Church on the left and beyond it, past several buildings, the *cemetery.* The entrance to the cemetery is flanked by two mortars on cement pedestals marking the site of Fort Alden. Inside and almost immediately to the right, an inscription on a marble slab identifies this as the site of the old church, the fort, and the stockade, which embraced about two acres and extended across the road. The ground on the other side of the road, which was once within the stockade, now contains a garage and filling station and a white, clapboard farmhouse.

To your right in the cemetery is a marble catafalque on a pedestal, atop a mound where the victims of the 1778 massacre were buried. The memorial was erected on the centennial of the massacre in 1878. Around the pedestal are inscribed the names of those killed, including Alden and fourteen members of the garrison. The graves of a number of Revolutionary War soldiers and veterans, some killed in other actions in the Mohawk Valley, are scattered throughout.

Continuing along Alden Street beyond the cemetery, look for a white marker surrounded by white posts on the right side of the road. It marks the spot where Alden was killed. A short distance past the **Alden memorial,** a dirt road goes winding up a hill to your right. Turn onto this road for a short distance until you come to the first driveway. At the end of the driveway is an old, white house with three chimneys. This is the **Willow Hill Farm**, on the site of the Wells house. It was from this spot that Alden tried to get to the fort; thirteen members of the Wells family were also killed here.

Retrace your steps into town to the light at the intersection of Main and Alden streets. Turn left onto Genesee Street and look for the Central School on the left. A marker on the grounds of the school identifies the spot from which the Sixth Massachusetts marched, on June 18, 1779, to join the force General James Clinton was assembling on Otsego Lake to march to Tioga, where he was to join General Sullivan for the Sullivan Expedition against the Iroquois. Sullivan's campaign was prompted by the Cherry Valley Massacre. The *map* inscribed on the plaque should intrigue you, for it shows the frontier area from Tioga (now Athens) in Pennsylvania to Minisink in southwestern New York and the Cherry Valley and Mohawk Valley areas, marking those sites connected with the campaigns and battles of the border war. This is the first of many bronze markers you will come across in the western part of New York, which mark the route of the Sullivan Expedition. You will find more when you follow Sullivan's route from Tioga to the valley of the Genesee in Volume II.

Some distance past the school, on the left side of the road, is a tall, white *marker* with a cross and circle at the top, surrounded by a chain fence. This is the site of the home of the Reverend Samuel Dunlop. Though the minister's life was spared through the intervention of an Indian chief named Little Aaron, Mrs. Dunlop was killed before his eyes. Dunlop was among those taken prisoner and released the next day. He moved to New Jersey with a daughter and survived his wife by only a year, a victim to the trauma he experienced that day.

From the Dunlop site, turn back into town and return to the traffic light. Turn left onto Montgomery Street and follow it out of town to the intersection with Old Fort Plain Road. Just beyond, up a rise of ground to the right, is a large, yellow and white house surrounded by spacious grounds. This is **Auchinbreck**. It stands on the site of the James Campbell house. Two pyramids of ten-inch shells in front of the house once marked the location of the stockade, which was built around the house in 1778, but they were not in evidence when we visited.

Turn right onto Old Fort Plain Road and follow it to its end at an intersection. Turn left and proceed through an underpass beneath railroad tracks to a dirt road which winds off to the left immediately after. Take that road until you come to a tall granite *pillar* on the right in front of a large boulder. According to local tradition, it was here Lieutenant Matthew Wormuth died in September, 1778. Wormuth, who was the scion of a local well-to-do family, had ridden to Cherry Valley to tell the inhabitants a Colonel Klock was on his way with a detachment of men. At the end of the day he was on his way home with a man named Peter Sitz, who was carrying dispatches, when they were challenged by a party of Indians hidden behind the rock. Setting spurs to their horses, they tried to escape but were shot down. Wormuth was only wounded, but as he lay on the ground he was killed and scalped. Tradition has it that the man who did the scalping was Joseph Brant who, as soon as he finished, recognized Wormuth as a close friend. According to Brant's account, he did not recognize the young man in his uniform. Wormuth was also buried in the Cherry Valley cemetery where you probably noticed his memorial.

Return to the village and retracing your route along 116, take Route 20 east to cover the Schoharie Valley campaign of Sir John Johnson in October, 1780. But before that, as you continue past the turnoff for Canajoharie, you will come into the town of Sharon Springs and then reach a sign noting "Sharon Center." A short distance beyond you will see a historical *marker* on the right side of the road with an arrow pointing to the right. On this site, early on the morning of Tuesday, July 10, 1781, 150 militia under the command of Colonel Marinus Willett, whose exploits you last heard about at Fort Stanwix, defeated a force of Tories and Indians at least three times larger in another incident in the border warfare. Willett had been at Fort Plank, which was located in what is now Canajoharie. He and his 400 men had been given the impossible job of protecting 5,000 settlers scattered over an area of 2,000 square miles. On July 9, smoke was seen rising from Currytown, which had been attacked by a Tory-Indian force under John Doxtader. A patrol brought Willett word that the enemy had made camp in a place which later came to be called Sharon Springs Swamp. He decided to attack.

Pull off onto the shoulder of the road and climb up the bank in the direction the arrow points. Now look north to the other side of Route 20 and notice the low ground that falls away quite sharply; this was probably the cedar swamp where the raiders were camped. By the morning of the tenth, however, they had moved out onto the high ground on your side of the road.

Though greatly outnumbered, Willett used guile to make up the difference. He formed his men into a crescent under cover of a dense growth of trees and underbrush. A small patrol then advanced from the center of the crescent, fired at the Tories and Indians, and retreated with the enemy after them. As soon as their pursuers were inside the crescent, Willett's concealed force opened fire, hitting the enemy from three sides. At the same time a small reserve force struck at one flank. Caught completely by surprise, Doxtader and his men put up a fight, but when Willett's men charged with the bayonet, they broke and ran. Fifty of the enemy were left dead on the field, and their camp with all the loot they had taken at Currytown fell into the hands of the Patriots. Willett lost five killed and nine wounded.

You can walk in from the road for about 200 feet until you come to a farm fence. Beyond is an orchard and higher ground, perhaps the high ground on which Doxtader and his men were camped when Willett made contact. Though there is nothing to indicate the direction from which Willett approached, we do know that Doxtader moved his men from low, swampy ground to high. Following the way the land rises from the north side of 20 toward the south, we may assume that Doxtader camped on the hill beyond the orchard, that Willett approached him from the vicinity of the area in which you are now standing, formed his crescent here, and lured him down off the hill and into the trap. In other words, the fighting may have taken place on the field you just crossed to the fence. This is all supposition, though it has a certain amount of known circumstances to back it up.

Continue east on Route 20 for about twenty-five miles to the Schoharie sites, until a road sign identifies Schoharie Creek to your right. At the juncture with Route 30, turn right on 30 and go south to where

30 joins Route 7 for a short distance. Turn right and then, shortly after, go away from 7 as 30 continues south to the left. Schoharie is now five miles away. Signs for the Old Stone Fort will begin to appear. After the first of these, another sign with letters burned into wood will appear on the left at an intersection. Turn left and look for an old marker for the **George Mann Tory Tavern** which was known in revolutionary days as the Brick House at the Forks in the Road. It's a colonial, brick building on a rise of ground, with a more recent white porch tacked on its front and a cupola on top.

Now look for a sign with a cannon painted on it, an arrow pointing left, and the words "800 feet." Follow the arrow and proceed toward Schoharie. A cemetery shows up on the left and some contemporary homes on the right. At the edge of the cemetery, a big, fieldstone, colonial building appears on the left with a sign in front announcing the **Old Stone Fort Museum.** Admission is $0.50 for adults, $0.25 for students. It is open daily from May 30 through Labor Day from 10 A.M. to 5 P.M., Sundays, noon to 5 P.M. In April and May and September through November, it is open daily except on Mondays, and on Sundays from 1 to 5 P.M.

This is a fascinating site and well worth an hour or two of your time, depending on your browsing capacity. It was built in 1772 as a church, the third of three built on or near the spot out of local stone by the Reformed Protestant High Dutch Church Society. Members of the congregation who helped erect the building had their names chiseled into the stone, but when the Revolution began and some of them made known their Loyalist sympathies, the Whigs chiseled the offenders' names right off. Originally the church sported a tower surmounted by a belfry, spire, and a metal weathercock made in Holland. The belfry and spire came down in 1830, but the old weathercock is on display inside.

As the Schoharie Valley became increasingly affected by the growing border warfare between the Patriot settlers and the Indians, the church was enclosed by a log stockade and made into a strong point called the Lower Fort. The other forts called the Middle and Upper Forts were built farther south along the creek.

According to Jephthah Simms's *History of Schoharie County,* the Lower Fort consisted of "an enclosure by strong pickets of about half an acre of ground embracing a stone church with blockhouses in the southwest and northeast corners mounting small cannon. Along the west side of the enclosure small huts were erected of rough boards for the summer residence of the inhabitants in that part of the valley with a board roof sloping from near the top of the pickets toward the center of the yard . . . Near the northeast corner or in that part of the enclosure toward the burying ground was a temporary tavern kept by Snyder a former innkeeper of that vicinity."

The "pickets" refer to a stockade. The half-acre would have enclosed part of the cemetery. Snyder's tavern refers to the Brick House at the Forks in the Road.

In September, 1780, Sir John Johnson left his base in Oswego and moved east with a mixed force of about 1,500 Tories, British soldiers, and Indians. Burning a number of farms along the Schoharie Valley on the way, he besieged the Lower Fort on Monday, October 16. The garrison consisted of about 200 men under the command of Major Melanchthon Woolsey and included, to Woolsey's eventual regret, Timothy Murphy, a well-known frontier marksman you will meet on the Saratoga battlefield where he became a legend. That action preceded the siege of the Lower Fort, and Murphy was by then probably the most famous marksman in the American army. In the Lower Fort he was a member of a company of sharpshooters stationed in the church tower.

Johnson opened his attack on October 17, but the fire from the fort was so accurate, the attackers were repulsed. Johnson then brought a swivel gun to bear and fired two balls through the roof. (You can see the hole made by one of them around the back of the church.) This so impressed Woolsey that he decided to surrender and sent a flag toward the British, only to have it fired upon by one of the sharpshooters in the tower. Twice more Woolsey sent out the flag, and twice more it was fired on. The culprit was, of course, Timothy Murphy. When the outraged Woolsey attempted to have him arrested, he found himself facing a mutiny in the ranks and even among some of his officers. Woolsey again ordered the white flag raised. This time Murphy swore to kill the man who carried out the order. While all this was going on, Johnson decided the stone building was too strong for his cannon to dent and gave up the siege. Evidently Murphy escaped the penalty for mutineers, for in 1781 he was at the siege of Yorktown as a member of the Pennsylvania Line under Wayne. He was married twice, produced a total of nine sons and four daughters, and lived to become a prosperous farmer and a local political power before dying in 1818 at the age of 67.

Today the interior of the fort is filled with a jumbled but fascinating collection of nineteenth-century memorabilia on the ground floor, including an ancient fire wagon, labeled "the oldest fire engine in the United

States," and a huge number of Indian artifacts on the second floor. The old weather vane is also on display. In a showcase near the visitor's register are several views of the church, including one showing the stockade around it and the spire on top. On the wall directly opposite the main entrance are two small stained-glass windows and a pillar marking the site of the old Dutch raised pulpit. The Reverend Johannes Schuyler, who served the church during the Revolution, is buried below the floor where the pulpit stood. Notice on the staircase landing, as you go up, a number of views of the Middle Fort, which is the site you will visit next. Notice also the framed copy of a map, discovered in the British Museum by someone in the American navy and copied in 1886. It was probably drawn by a British engineer and shows the forts along the Schoharie Creek. In a showcase on the second floor look for reconstructed views and descriptions of the Upper Fort in 1779, drawn by a local resident, W. E. Roscoe, who lived in Carlisle and visited the site in 1887 after studying all available accounts and maps. Roscoe also drew a map of the Schoharie Valley showing Johnson's invasion route and marking the significant sites along the way.

Outside to the right of the main entrance in the cemetery is a tall *pillar* over the grave of David Williams, one of the three men responsible for the capture of Major John André. Williams had moved to Schoharie County in 1805. Take the path that leads through the cemetery and follow it to where the ground falls away rather abruptly to Fox Creek on one side and Schoharie Creek to the left, emphasizing the obvious: the fort commanded the confluence of the two.

As you examine the old stone building, look to the right of the front entrance for the names of congregation members cut into the stone and the obvious places where names were obliterated. If you have trouble finding them, look directly under the memorial tablet to David Ellison. Around the back of the building, a sign indicates the hole made by Sir John's cannon shot in the wooden cornice just below the roof, as the arrow indicates.

If you walk down the road that leads past the Old Stone Fort and around a bend, you will find a white, frame home on the right, just before a bridge, with a marker identifying it as the *parsonage* of the Reverend Schuyler who is buried under the floor of the church.

At the time I visited, a new museum was being built on the side of the road opposite the Old Stone Fort. Chances are that by the time you visit the new museum will be open, displaying the exhibits in a much more effective fashion.

☆

From the Old Stone Fort continue south along Route 30, following the Schoharie for five miles to Middleburg. Shortly after the sign for Middleburg on the right is a marker on the site of the home of Captain George Rechtmyer who was in command of the Middle Fort in 1780. A short distance farther, you will find the marker for the approximate site of the fort on the left side of the road. I found the actual site by inquiring (in a hit-and-miss, but lucky fashion) of local inhabitants. A bit past the marker, you see on the right a sign for the Dutch Reformed Church; take the street leading to the east called Middle Fort Road. Middle Fort Road turns to parallel Route 30 and then curves again to meet it a little north of where you turned off. This is all to the good, however, for you are now only a quarter of a mile from the site of the fort. Look to the right and notice a ridgeline on the horizon beyond wide farmlands. Two private roads lead off Middle Fort Road to the right to the two farms that occupy the area between Middle Fort Road and the hills. Back there in the midst of what is now a cornfield, close to a stream that still flows across the fields, is where a stone house once stood enclosed by a stockade, in similar fashion to the Lower Fort. This was the **Middle Fort.** The site is on private property now, but the pastor of the Reformed Church back where you turned off Route 30 told me he knew the site and knew that plowing had turned up pieces of stone wall and brick. In fact, some of the fort's foundations have been taken out and placed in the foundation of the buildings near the church. According to one picture of the Middle Fort at the Old Stone Fort Museum, an effort was made to restore it in 1887. The kitchen remained, but the other buildings had disappeared by 1825.

According to Jephthah Simms's *Schoharie County and the Border Wars of New York*, if you had been standing in this area in 1780 and looking east, you would have seen the Middle Fort, or Fort Defiance as it was also called, "enclosing an area of ground larger than that picketed at the Lower Fort with blockhouses at the northeast and southwest where cannon were mounted. The principal entrance was on the south side. [As you face the site, south is to your right.] On each side of the gate were arranged the soldiers' barracks. Pickets as at the fort below were about a foot through and rose some ten feet from the ground with loopholes with which to fire on invaders. A brass nine-pound cannon was mounted on the southwest blockhouse and an identical one was mounted on the diagonal corner each of which, as the blockhouses projected, commanded two sides of the enclosure while along the eastern and western sides were arranged huts for citizens similar to those at the Lower Fort."

☆

As you continue into the town of Middleburg on your way to the **Upper Fort,** you come to a stop light where Route 30 south goes off to the right over a bridge that crosses Schoharie Creek. The sign for the right turn may fool you since it is also for 145 north, but cross the bridge and then make an almost immediate left turn which takes you south again on 30.

Beyond Middleburg keep a sharp eye out for the sign for Watson's Corners on your left, and then a marker for the site of Timothy Murphy's home. The marker for the Upper Fort will appear on the left side of the road not quite a quarter of a mile beyond the Murphy marker. According to the marker the fort stood five hundred feet off the road. The arrow points into the middle of a cornfield where the home of John Feake had been converted into a fortified position consisting of a large stockade enclosing four blockhouses, various dwelling houses, and earthworks. Just to the right is the home of the farmer who now owns the property. Look back in the direction from which you came and notice how the hills on the horizon fit the hills in Roscoe's sketch of the Upper Fort.

Simms wrote that at the Upper Fort as at the other two, a fair plot of ground was enclosed: "One side of this enclosure was picketed in while on its other side the breastwork was thrown over timbers and earth some eight or ten feet high and sufficiently thick to admit of drawing a wagon within its top with short pickets set in the outside timbers of the breastwork. A ditch surrounded the part thus constructed. Military barracks and small log huts were erected within the enclosure to accommodate the soldiers and the citizens. Blockhouses and sentry boxes were built in the northwest and southeast corners each mounting a small cannon and the guard inside. From its construction, this fort was probably better made in the name of fort than either of the others though some have stated that a moat partially surrounded the Middle Fort."

When Roscoe visited this site in 1887, he was guided by a grandson of Timothy Murphy who told him that pottery shards and brickwork had been uncovered in the fields during plowing. According to Roscoe, the Upper Fort was built chiefly of wood and so was the first of the three forts to decay and disappear. By 1800 very little was left. Roscoe determined the outlines of the fort area, which amounted to two and a half acres. His reconstruction shows three blockhouses whereas Simms talks of only two; otherwise his sketch corresponds closely with Simms's description. Note that the marker lists four blockhouses.

By the time you reach this point, you have covered Johnson's two-day Schoharie Valley raid, which we have to admit was successful. This valley had been one of the granary areas that fed Washington's army, turning out about 80,000 bushels per harvest. By the time Johnson's men left the Lower Fort on the seventeenth, the valley was in flames, and the homes of its Patriot citizens and their farmlands lay in ruins.

Standing here at the site of the Upper Fort, you have a beautiful, practically unobstructed view north up the Schoharie extending to the hills on the horizon. Looking at the fort site, remember that what is now open land was part of a farm in 1780 and probably very much as it is today in appearance.

BENNINGTON BATTLEFIELD

To get on to Bennington, after these diversions into the river valleys of central New York, return north along Route 30 to its juncture with Route 7, then take 7 east to Troy and beyond. If you decide to go directly to Bennington from Herkimer, return to Interstate 90 and take it to Exit 25, where you pick up Route 7 east through Troy, on the east bank of the Hudson River. About twenty-five miles east of Troy, Route 7 intersects Route 22. Take 22 north to the town of Hoosick Falls. You are now in Grandma Moses country; the pleasant, rolling farmlands around you may bring her canvases to mind. Continue north on 22 to a junction with Route 67. Turn right (east) on 67 for a few miles, until you reach the entrance to Bennington Battlefield State Park on your left. Though this battle bears the name of a Vermont town, the battlefield is in New York, just over the state line.

Through the park is a winding, rising, paved road that leads to a parking area near picnic tables set under the trees and a park headquarters which contains rest rooms. The road continues to a higher parking lot; a paved pathway from there leads to the highest point in the area, where a topographical *relief model* of the terrain, cast in bronze, is laid on a stone base. This is one of the best on-site devices I have yet seen to explain a battle. By referring to the relief model, you can pinpoint the important sites. Actually the total area encompassed by the scope of the battle, including bivouac areas and lines of advances and retreats, was about seven miles square and cannot be seen to its fullest extent from this point.

By the time Burgoyne reached Fort Edward on his march south on July 29, he was running short of supplies. He also needed horses for his Brunswick dragoons who had been marching along on foot, their primary function as cavalry completely lost to him. Baron von Riedesel suggested that an expedition, more properly a raiding party, be sent east into the

Connecticut River valley to gather supplies and horses. Burgoyne agreed, but extended its scope by ordering the expedition to continue south in support of the main body of the army, which was to advance to Albany to meet St. Leger. Burgoyne was sure that Seth Warner and his Green Mountain Boys, who had been organized into a regiment as a reward for their capture of Ticonderoga, were now at Bennington, and he wanted to protect his left flank. Ethan Allen was a paroled prisoner in New York City. (In return for not being confined, he had given his word of honor not to try to escape.) Warner had led St. Clair's rear guard during the retreat from Ticonderoga and was, in fact, at Manchester, twenty miles north of Bennington.

On August 11, 1777, the expedition moved out of Fort Miller, four miles north of a small creek, the Batten Kill, to a point just opposite Saratoga where the creek empties into the Hudson. It consisted of 800 men, 374 of them Germans, including a full military band and a large number of batmen (orderlies) for the officers; 300 Tories, Indians, and Canadians; and a small force of British army marksmen. With them they dragged a couple of three-pound cannon. Their orders were to sweep down the Connecticut Valley from Rockingham through Brattleboro and then march west to Albany. Their mission was to gather supplies, secure horses for the Brunswick dragoons, and enlist the support or at least the sympathy of the inhabitants along the way for the British cause and Burgoyne's mission, despite the fact that their commander, Lieutenant Colonel Friedrich Baum, spoke no English at all. Burgoyne sent Philip Skene along to assist the colonel with linguistical problems.

At the last minute Burgoyne changed Baum's orders. He had just received an intelligence report of a large rebel supply base at Bennington guarded by only a few hundred militia. Baum's orders now were to advance to Bennington and raid it.

In the meantime Vermont and New Hampshire were pooling their resources to meet the threatened attack and turned to John Stark to organize the effort. Stark had served with the Continental Army in charge of New Hampshire detachments at Bunker Hill, Trenton, and Princeton, but, despite his distinguished service, had been passed over for promotion by the Continental Congress. Chagrined, he had returned home to sit out the war like a New England Achilles. Now offered the command of the Vermont-New Hampshire defense effort, he agreed to accept only if it was kept independent of the Congress and the rest of the Continental Army.

His terms were met and he was commissioned on July 17. Within a week he had enlisted 1,500 militiamen and officers and by the thirtieth he was on his way to Manchester. The men carried their own private arms and were dressed in civilian clothing. At Manchester he was greeted by General Benjamin Lincoln, who had been sent by General Philip Schuyler to command the New England forces. Lincoln, who had led the unsuccessful American raid to try to recapture Ticonderoga while Burgoyne was coming south, met resistance from Stark when he attempted to incorporate Stark's command into his own. When Stark told Lincoln he was going to attack Burgoyne's left flank on his own, Lincoln decided he would try to get Schuyler to support the move, rather than risk the loss of this militia force through a direct confrontation with its hard-headed commander.

At Manchester Stark made contact with Seth Warner's Green Mountain Boys and then moved his force to Bennington, a move Burgoyne never detected. As Baum came south, his Indians destroyed homes and property on all sides, arousing the populace against and not for Burgoyne. The word of his advance came down to Stark who sent a small force eighteen miles to Cambridge (New York) on August 13 to check the advance. This detachment fired one volley at the enemy and then headed back to Bennington. Hearing that British regulars were coming along behind the Indians, Stark moved out on the fourteenth to meet them, sending word at the same time to Warner to march his men to Bennington at once.

Now aware there were many more men at Bennington than just a few hundred, Baum advanced more cautiously, reporting his reasons to Burgoyne. Orient yourself again by the relief map in front of you. You are facing south; north is behind you. To your right is the west from which Baum advanced along a road toward Bennington to the east on your left; you can mark the location of Bennington itself by the Bennington Battle Monument, clearly visible over the trees. To the northwest, Burgoyne was already moving toward Saratoga.

A second one-volley engagement took place at Sancoick's Mill to your right, along a stream you cannot see, when an advance party sent out by Stark made contact with the advancing British, fired once, and then retired. Baum then advanced to a bridge across the Walloomsac River at a point on your left front along the line of trees at the foot of the slope that marks the river. Stark was waiting for him on the opposite bank, but when the British made no move to cross and it started to rain heavily, Stark pulled back about a mile toward Bennington and camped for the rest of that day and night. In the meantime Baum requested reinforcements from Burgoyne, though, according to his messages, he did not really expect any serious opposition. He then divided his men into a number of small units and scattered them over a mile-square area, which embraces most of the area before you along the river.

Somewhat to your left, on a rise of ground now hidden by trees, the Indians took up a position on a small plateau. Just below them Baum's dragoons built a breastwork of earth and logs called the Dragoon Redoubt. On the other side of the river, close to the bridge, Baum's Tory contingent built another breastwork called the Tory Redoubt. Baum needed the bridge to continue his march toward Bennington, and he meant to hold it securely. Off to one side, on a high bank overlooking the crossing, he posted a number of German soldiers and British marksmen and one of his two guns. The Tory Redoubt was manned by about 150 men; the Dragoon Redoubt, the British main position, by about 200. Three smaller positions were established to support both the larger breastworks. Other units were located at various points along the riverbank toward the mill to guard the rear.

Burgoyne sent Baum reinforcements on the morning of August 15, about 650 Germans and a couple of six-pound guns under the command of Lieutenant Colonel Heinrich von Breymann. They had only twenty-five miles to march, but since Breymann insisted on stopping to dress ranks in true European fashion every twenty minutes or so, and since his men wore heavy, uncomfortable uniforms and carried immense, clumsy swords, their rate of advance was about half a mile an hour. When he camped for the first night in the field, he had covered all of eight miles.

Stark had been joined the night of August 15 by Warner, in advance of his men, and on August 16 he attacked. The plan of action he and Warner had devised was a classic double envelopment or pincer movement. One arm of the pincers, composed of 200 New Hampshire men, marched through the wooded hills to your left and hit the Dragoon Redoubt at about three in the afternoon. The other arm, 300 Vermonters and some Bennington militia, came around the other way and hit Baum's rear guard. A third column of 200 men came straight down the road and tried to envelop the Tory Redoubt, while an additional 100 attacked Baum's front.

Having committed the serious error of dividing his force into a number of small, vulnerable units, Baum continued to make mistakes. From his position on the Dragoon Redoubt, he saw the first pincer movement as it left Stark's camp and went off into the hills, but since he had such a low opinion of his opponents, he believed he was watching a retreat. When the same men started to infiltrate his position, he thought they were Tories coming to find safety behind his lines. The deception was further enhanced by the Americans who carried their rifles butt-up over their shoulders, Tory fashion. It was a trick that had served them well at the Battle of Hubbardton (on July 7), and it worked again at Bennington.

As the attacks opened, Baum's position was quickly engulfed from all sides. The Tory Redoubt did its best to resist, but while its defenders were reloading after their first volley, the rebels advanced so quickly and the developing noise of battle rattled them so effectively that they panicked and fled. The Indians gave up at once and left the field, never to be seen in those parts again. Most of the other small positions collapsed, but Baum stood fast in the Dragoon Redoubt for about two hours.

As the firing began, Stark left camp with the main force of about 1,300 men, marching up the Bennington Road in the direction of the fighting. He reportedly told his men, "We'll beat them before night, or Molly Stark will be a widow."

By then the survivors of the Tory Redoubt and the other positions had fled to the Dragoon Redoubt and British ammunition was running low. A wagon holding their reserve supply of ammunition caught fire and blew up, and the militia came charging up the slope for the death blow. The German dragoons pulled out their swords and started to cut their way out, but when Baum fell, mortally wounded in the stomach, they threw down their weapons and surrendered.

The time was 5 P.M. A half hour earlier, Breymann had reached Sancoick's Mill where he was met by refugees fleeing the battlefield. Small bands of militia were forming all around to harass him, but the stolid, methodical German soldiers plodded on. They might have turned the tide, for Stark's men were enjoying themselves in and around the Dragoon Redoubt, chasing the fleeing Germans and British, looting and drinking up Baum's supply of rum. They were really not prepared to meet this new threat, which was suddenly announced by the distant sound of musket fire.

What saved them and the day was the approach of Seth Warner's Green Mountain Boys who had marched to Bennington, stopped to load up with ammunition, and then been held up by rain which made them stop to dry out their muskets. They met Breymann's men near the present village of Walloomsac (New York), but had to fall back to better ground. The Germans attacked, using their two small cannon to good advantage, and a hot fire fight developed. Breymann tried to encircle one flank, but the Americans pulled an encircling movement of their own around the German encirclers, and the lines stabilized.

As darkness approached, Breymann's ammunition began to run out and he ordered his men to retreat. The militiamen immediately came swarming close around them, causing many of the exhausted Germans to drop their weapons and surrender. Following European custom, Breymann had his drummers beat for a parley, but to the New Englanders it was just a lot of noise and they went on firing. Breymann, though wounded, managed to get his men away virtually intact in the developing gloom of night. Stark arrived on the scene and called back his militiamen before they could lose themselves in the dark and start shooting at each other.

Stark later remarked that if the day had lasted an hour longer, he would have captured Breymann's command. Burgoyne said in retrospect that if Breymann had marched at the rate of two miles an hour for any twelve hours out of the thirty-two it took him to get to the battle, the outcome would have been very different. Both were probably correct. It certainly would have been different if Breymann and Baum had been able to present a united front to Stark's attack. According to some sources, the Americans lost thirty men killed and forty wounded, though forty killed and wounded may be more accurate; the raiding party lost 207 dead and 700 taken prisoners, including 32 officers. The Tory prisoners were bound and paraded through Bennington to suffer the contempt and scorn of the local inhabitants. The loot included hundreds of muskets and swords, four brass cannon, and four ammunition wagons. As a result Burgoyne did not get his, by now, desperately needed supplies or horses; the local populace was up in arms against him; and he had lost a number of good fighting men and officers he could ill afford to lose, about 10 percent of his total strength. All this had been accomplished by a militia superior in numbers, but untrained, poorly organized, and poorly equipped, facing 1,500 well-trained, well-equipped, well-organized regular soldiers.

Most of the area you now see is private property owned by local farmers, except for the 208-acre state park. A good part of the battlefield was private land at the time of the battle. In fact, according to a local historian, Mr. Cottrell, the population of this area was probably larger than it is today. He bases this on his own study of local records going back to an Indian attack in 1756. The value of the property lost and damaged in that raid amounted to 40,000 pounds, a sum which translated into modern currency would amount to several times that in dollars.

Most people during the colonial era put their money into land and homes; though building costs were much cheaper and much of the labor was not hired but home grown, the amount of property damage in 1750 indicates a much larger population along the Walloomsac River valley than at the present time.

You can walk down the slope before you toward the river and poke around along its banks, but nothing remains, or has been uncovered, to indicate definitely where the two redoubts were located. Take the park road back to the entrance and, turning to your left, follow the signs to the caretaker's house. This will lead you down a narrow road off to your right to the Walloomsac River at the site of the crossing Baum held on the first day of the battle. The caretaker's house, built about the time of the Civil War, occupies part of the British encampment site. Standing with your back to the house, you can see a white sign near the top of a high embankment that overlooks a railroad spur to your left. By walking down the spur, you eventually reach a spot from which you can read the words; it marks the position where some "German grenadiers" were stationed during the battle "with a cannon." Crossing the bridge, you will find a crossroads immediately to your left and another road to your right leading through a barnyard. Following the road to your right, you come after a few minutes' walk or drive to the top of a rise of ground from which, to your right, you can see the battle overlook, with its relief map, far above you and the broad fields in between along the river. According to maps of the area at the time of the battle, the road you are now on joined the Bennington Road Baum was following on the other side of the bridge. Thus, the old Bennington Road ran on the other side of the river, hugging the stream as it went along. Baum marched from the direction in which you are now headed, and Stark's men first encountered him close to the bridge you just crossed.

If you turn to the left after crossing the bridge and take Cottrell Road at the tiny crossroads, you will pass two cemeteries, one on your left and a larger one on the right opposite a large, brick farmhouse. Cannonballs that may have been fired from about two thousand feet away, perhaps from the grenadier position on the embankment over the railroad tracks, were found on the cornfield near the cemetery.

Cottrell Road takes you out to a state highway. A little farther is a marker near the site of a house to which Baum was carried and in which he died. According to the marker, he was buried a short distance west of the house on the bank of the Walloomsac River in an unmarked grave. A dirt road leads off to the right past this site. Follow this road for about a half mile. At the edge of a cornfield on the left side of the road close to a white, frame farmhouse is a marker identifying the site of Stark's encampment the night before the battle.

An interesting sidelight turned up in an account Cottrell ran across during his research on the battle. Colonel Baum, according to this account, was carrying about three thousand British pounds in gold to purchase the mounts for Burgoyne's dismounted cavalry. One of the militia officers relieved the dead colonel of this sum and used it to build a very substantial home in the vicinity.

But turn away now from the spoils of war to the west to follow Burgoyne's dwindling fortunes to Saratoga, the final scene of his military career and a genuine turning point for the better in the fortunes of the revolutionary cause.

SARATOGA

From Bennington battlefield, take Route 67 west to the intersection with Route 40. Continuing west, take the county road on the opposite side of the intersection across the Hudson through the town of Stillwater to U.S. 4 north out of Stillwater. You are now on the road Burgoyne meant to follow had he won the Battle of Saratoga. At that time, this was the main route leading from the north to Albany. About four miles from Stillwater, you will travel along the eastern edge of the battlefield with the Hudson River clearly visible on your right and Bemis Heights towering above you on your left. There is an entrance to the battlefield park on the left side of the road that will take you to the Visitor's Center where you should begin your tour.

If, on the other hand, you decided to do Saratoga before visiting Stanwix and Bennington, head south on Route 4 from Schuylerville and proceed as above, or head south out of Saratoga Springs on Route 9. Turn off several miles south of town onto Route 9P. A sign at the turn-off indicates that **Saratoga National Historic Park** lies to the east. Take 9P to Route 423 where another sign directs you left onto 423 for a five-mile drive to Route 32. A short distance along 32 brings you to a right-hand turn into the park.

Once in the park, drive a short distance from the entrance to the paved parking area in front of the Visitor's Center, a long, low, modern building set on a hill and reached by flights of paved steps and landscaped terraces. There are drinking fountains here, a fresh-water faucet for canteens and water jugs, picnic tables, rest rooms and, inside the Visitor's Center, vending machines. Because of the litter problem, that is the extent of the refreshment facilities available, even during the summer months when the battlefield sees most of its visitors. If you plan to eat lunch, bring all the fixings with you.

The Visitor's Center is open year-round, weather permitting, from 9 A.M. to 7 P.M. during the summer, and from 8 A.M. to 5 P.M. the rest of the year. The John Neilson House and the Freeman cabin are open only during the summer. The park roads are open from April 1 to November 30, weather permitting. There is no charge for admission.

In the Visitor's Center is a large exhibit room and, to one side, a smaller museum area. The *museum* exhibits artifacts dug up on the site and a series of dioramas illustrating incidents of the battle. Each diorama has a taped narration complete with sound effects. One of these may be a historical gaffe, according to William Meuse, park superintendent, because it shows Daniel Morgan at Freeman's Farm rallying his men with his turkey-bone whistle, a sound effect reproduced on the tape in a most realistic fashion. Recent research, however, has questioned whether Morgan and his Virginia riflemen were actually at the battle, where most historians have always believed them to have been, or at the Morristown encampment in New Jersey. This also throws a shadow over one of the most famous stories told about the battle, the saga of Timothy Murphy, as we shall see. Since most published accounts of the battle describe Morgan's men taking a prominent part in the action, I shall assume he was actually here until it's definitely proved otherwise.

A small *auditorium* off the museum shows a very good twelve-minute slide film with sound, which gives a capsule account of the battle and the events leading up to it. Plans for the bicentennial may include a more ambitious film to replace this, but that was only in the talking stage when I visited.

The main room has floor-to-ceiling windows along its west wall which allow an unobstructed, panoramic view of the battlefield. Directly in front of these windows is a large, table-top *scale model* of the view, showing the battlefield in minute detail, as it appeared during the days of battle, the disposition of both armies, the sites where the major actions took place, and all the salient topographical features, including Mill Creek, the Great Ravine, the cleared farmlands, the hilltops, Bemis Heights, the Hudson River, etc. You will undoubtedly spend a long time looking at the view, then examining the scale model, then checking it against the view, for this is an invaluable aid to familiarizing yourself with the terrain before you go out to see it close up.

Notice how much more woodland there was two hundred years ago and how many fewer cleared areas. There were several farms in the area, but today there is only one, which lies outside the park boundaries. The battlefield itself, however, is all contained within the park boundaries. An effort will be made by the bicentennial of the battle to reforest those areas that were forested and to clear whatever ground was clear in September, 1777, when Burgoyne's army first marched upon the field. The main topographical features to keep in mind are several hilltops and two ravines which cut through the battlefield from west to east. Along one runs a stream known as Mill Creek, which has a number of tributary branches. Mill Creek empties into the Hudson River just north of the northernmost American gun position overlooking the river. The other ravine is known as the Great Ravine. The hilltops are where the two armies made their camps, and they are marked by old farmland and buildings.

This is the moment, with the battlefield spread out before you, to review the immediate circumstances that led Burgoyne to the spot and what happened after he arrived. General Howe, lacking definite instructions from London to support Burgoyne, had sailed south from New York in an attempt to capture Philadelphia. Desperately short of supplies and apparently no longer able to expect a thrust up the Hudson from Howe to meet him, Burgoyne decided to gamble on getting through to Albany anyhow.

On September 13 he sent his men across a bridge of boats stretched between the banks of the Hudson River at Saratoga, now Schuylerville, thus cutting himself off from further contact with his home base in Canada. Since, however, he had to cross the river at some point to get to Albany, he felt that crossing at Saratoga was more advantageous. By this time he had only a handful of Indians left, the rest having been discouraged by what had happened at Bennington. As a result, his intelligence was sadly lacking. He knew that the rebels, under General Horatio Gates, who had replaced General Philip Schuyler in command of northern operations, were holding Bemis Heights, a series of bluffs overlooking the Albany Road where a curve in the river squeezed it into a narrow strip of land between the river and the high ground. From this position, as you will see, the Americans had a clear field of fire covering the river and the road. If he was to continue his advance, those guns would have to be taken.

Gates's army numbered about 7,000 men. Their positions had been fortified by Thaddeus Kosciuszko, the Polish volunteer who was to plan and build the defenses at West Point the following year. Uncertain of exactly how and where the main force of Americans was disposed because of the heavy forests between the two armies, Burgoyne moved south cautiously on Friday, September 19, in three columns. One column of 1,100 men, under Riedesel's command, moved down the Albany Road with the bateaux filled with his remaining supplies close behind. Burgoyne himself led a column of 1,100 men down the center axis of the advance about a mile or so in from the river. Brigadier General Simon Fraser, with 2,200 men, swung wide to the west and then moved south parallel to the other two columns. The three columns kept abreast of each other by firing guns to signal the start of the advance.

THE FIRST BATTLE OF SARATOGA (FREEMAN'S FARM)

The first Battle of Saratoga occurred on the first day of the advance and is also known as the Battle of Freeman's Farm, since it took place in the woods and cleared area around a log cabin, once part of a local farm. The reconstructed building can be seen from the Visitor's Center.

The Americans were camped inside a fortified position on the Neilson Farm, which belonged to a member of the Albany County militia, who sent his family south to safety as Burgoyne drew near. The barn had been fortified and made into the apex of the position with log and earth embankments thrown up on both sides facing generally north. Gates, a cautious type, was content to let Burgoyne come to him. But when American patrols along the east bank of the Hudson signaled Riedesel's advance down the Albany Road, Gates sent Morgan and his men to reconnoiter.

At Freeman's Farm, Morgan ran into a small advance party out ahead of Burgoyne's column and cut most of them down with one volley. Chasing after the survivors, the Virginians ran smack into a British regiment drawn up in battle formation in a clearing and were driven back by a return volley. Morgan rallied his men in the woods, using his famous turkey-bone whistle, while Benedict Arnold, who had been ordered to support Morgan if necessary, brought up additional troops. The skirmish grew rapidly into a major engagement as both Burgoyne and Arnold committed more men, and the battle swayed back and forth across the clearing near the farm and through the woods. The British would advance with bayonets fixed, only to have the American riflemen decimate their ranks as they fired from the shelter of the woods. As they retreated the Americans would hurry after them, only to be driven back as they came up against the re-formed British lines. The advantage of this kind of fighting lay with the Americans, who took cover behind the trees and underbrush and blazed away at the exposed British regiments trying to maintain typically European battle formations on typically American terrain. As a result, Burgoyne's center took severe punishment and his casualties were heavy.

About two in the afternoon, hearing the sound of guns off to his right, Riedesel sent Burgoyne four cannon, just in case he needed them, and need them he did. At 5 P.M. Burgoyne requested that Riedesel come to his assistance. Riedesel complied, pushing west toward Freeman's Farm with about half his men, hurrying along as fast as his stout legs could carry him, which was pretty fast, for he was an energetic and capable man. Arriving on the scene with most of his men strung out behind him, he found the American right flank exposed before him. Ordering his band (which he had brought along just in case he wanted some music) to play loudly and his men to make enough noise to sound like twice their number, he charged without hesitation. Heartened by Riedesel's appearance, Burgoyne attacked the Americans' line and, as darkness fell, forced them back into the forest, leaving him in possession of the field.

Technically Burgoyne had won the first round—he held the field of battle—but at a terrible price. Out of the 1,000 men he had committed to the fight—Fraser did not arrive until it was over—about 600 were killed, wounded, and captured. It was not the kind of victory he could afford. In fact, had the circumstances been somewhat altered, his campaign might have ended right then and there.

Arnold, who had been in command at Freeman's Farm, had ridden back to the camp on Bemis Heights to bring up additional reinforcements. When he arrived, Gates sent the reinforcements himself and ordered Arnold to remain in camp. Gates, a New Englander, had replaced Schuyler, a New Yorker, at the behest of the New England congressional delegation, who believed he could be counted on to give a higher priority to New England defense. Arnold had originally been attached to Schuyler's command by Washington and had stayed on as Schuyler's man after Gates took over, a fact which did not exactly endear Arnold to Gates. They were also two temperamentally different people, almost diametrically opposed in their approach to the conduct of the war. Arnold was bold, audacious, sometimes brash, and perhaps recklessly overconfident in his drive for personal success and recognition. Gates, the son of a duke's housekeeper, had been an officer in the British army before he resigned his commission and settled in the colonies with Washington's personal assistance. He gained Washington's favor as a military commander early in the war. He has been described as small, with a red face and thick spectacles. He had a way of peering when not wearing his glasses that made him look like a sly, little old granny, which earned him the nickname "Grandmother Gates." Like the Swedish playwright Strindberg, his mother's servant status is supposed to have influenced his entire life, making him critical of the British social-caste system and anxious to improve his own social status. Some conjecture has arisen among historians as to what would have happened had Gates allowed Arnold to return to the field. The Americans were still superior in numbers to their opponents even with Riedesel's men added to Burgoyne's. Some historians think Arnold might have rallied them and overwhelmed Burgoyne's men, who had sustained heavy losses and were exhausted.

Had Gates not been so cautious, he might also have taken advantage of the split in Riedesel's command. Fully realizing the risk, the doughty German had brought a full 500 of his men to Burgoyne's assistance, leaving only 600 to hold the road and guard the supply boats. Gates had easily twice that number of troops still in camp. Had he made the move and captured Burgoyne's remaining supplies, he would have left the British commander with no alternative but to surrender.

If, on the other hand, Burgoyne had attacked again the following day, Saturday, the twentieth, he might have caught Gates off balance, for the fight at Freeman's Farm had left the Americans in a disorganized, confused state. Although the British were in bad shape, they were regulars and might have rallied sufficiently to give Burgoyne the victory he needed so badly. Instead he gave his troops a day to rest, intending to try again on the twenty-first. That day, however, he received a letter from Clinton, written on September 12, saying he was about to sweep north up the Hudson. Thinking Clinton was now going to do what he insisted Howe should have done, Burgoyne decided to sit tight until he received further word from the south. As it happened, Clinton pushed off on October 3 to clear the Hudson Highlands of American fortifications. He captured and destroyed Forts Clinton and Montgomery, destroyed Fort Constitution opposite a point of land known then as the west point, raided and burned Kingston (then called Esopus) a little farther north, and then, fearful of overextending his lines, withdrew to New York City. Nevertheless, he wrote Burgoyne on October 8 from captured Fort Montgomery that there were now no further obstacles between himself and Gates, and that he hoped he had helped Burgoyne's efforts in some small way. Some small way indeed! The day before Clinton wrote that letter, Burgoyne made his final move and lost.

THE WAITING GAME

For three weeks Burgoyne maintained his position facing the American lines; at least as nearly as he could tell, they faced the American lines. His main fortifications were built in the Freeman's Farm area and included two redoubts, the Balcarres and Breymann redoubts. A third, larger redoubt, called the Great Redoubt, was built on high ground overlooking the river northeast of the farm where he based his supplies. Below it he built a bridge of boats across the river. During those three weeks, he continued to lose men through desertion until he was down to a muster of only 7,000 living on short rations consisting of salt pork and weevily flour. The Americans sat tight in their camp around the Neilson Farm, happy to let their numbers swell; additional militia and Continentals came in until there were 11,000 men on hand, all well fed and happy to be there.

Gates's extreme caution during the battle of September 19 had been occasioned by his army's lack of ammunition, particularly of paper cartridges. In those days each soldier carried the makings of his own ammunition—lead, powder, and paper. When the ammo he had been issued ran out, he melted down the lead and poured it into molds in the shape of musket balls. When they had cooled, he broke them out of the molds and filed off the rough edges. Then he poured his powder into pieces of paper which he rolled into cartridges that were inserted down the barrel of his musket before he put in his musket ball. The cartridge was ignited by the powder he poured into his priming pan.

Gates's army was to have been supplied by an arsenal at Stillwater, but the arsenal never came through. Instead his soldiers and their camp followers had to make their own cartridges. Only he and his chief of ordnance, Ebenezer Stevens, knew that the army had only three rounds of ammunition per man on hand after the first day's fighting, hardly enough for any extensive engagement. But during the three-week waiting period, General Schuyler kept the supplies rolling up from Albany despite his feud with Gates, thus correcting the situation.

The contrast between the two camps was marked not only by the number of fighting men and the amount of supplies, but also by the difference in morale. The British were apprehensive and very much aware of the gravity of their situation, but victory was in the air in the American camp. The Americans sent out daily patrols to harass Burgoyne who was never able to determine exactly what was going on in the American camp or, for that matter, exactly where it was. Every patrol he sent out was set upon by the ever-present militiamen lurking behind the trees and in the underbrush.

As you look out over the battlefield from the Visitor's Center it may be difficult to understand why this was so. When Burgoyne first moved out of Saratoga he was attempting to locate the American camp. Now here he was only a few miles away and still unsure of its location, still uncertain whether he could clear Bemis Heights. The picture becomes clearer, however, when you remember that most of the area was heavily wooded, a part of the great American wilderness forest, and in it Burgoyne was blind, for he had lost his eyes—his Indians.

THE SECOND BATTLE OF SARATOGA (BEMIS HEIGHTS)

On Tuesday, October 7, Burgoyne committed 600 Canadians and Tories and 1,500 regulars to what was supposed to be an armed reconnaissance to probe the American left where those obstructing gun batteries were located. Again advancing in three columns, with Fraser once more off to the right, the British moved slowly out of their entrenchments. After an advance of less than a mile, the main force formed into line at the edge of a wheatfield where the officers tried to see where the Americans were through their spy glasses, while a party of foragers mowed the wheat to feed the horses. When their presence was reported to Gates by his scouts, he ordered Morgan to move his command against Burgoyne's west or right flank and General Enoch Poor to bring his men against Burgoyne's east or left flank. Both British flanks over-extended the field and were covered by woods, which gave the attacking rebels the kind of cover they knew how to use.

Morgan was supposed to open the attack, but Poor got into position first, and the action began at about 2:30 P.M. The British on the left flank were on a rise of ground and had to fire downhill at the Americans, usually aiming too high.

Finally their commander, Major John Dyke Acland, ordered his men to "Fix bayonets and charge the damned rebels." The damned rebels met the charge with a murderous volley that mowed Acland's grenadiers down like tenpins and charged up the hill, completely overwhelming the survivors. Acland himself went down with lead in both legs. One of the rebels saved him from instant dispatch at the hands of a compatriot, and he was carried off the field to Poor's quarters at the Neilson Farm, a prisoner.

In the meantime, Morgan attacked the British right, commanded by Major Earl Alexander Balcarres, crumbling it up as he advanced. The

Germans in the center under Riedesel were now left exposed on both flanks, but stood their ground as the Americans massed for a frontal attack.

All this time Arnold, who had not been given another command following the battle at Freeman's Farm, was back in camp fuming and fussing. (He had threatened to leave for Albany some days before but had been persuaded to stay by the Schuyler faction.) He was now furious because Gates was sitting complacently in his tent and not moving his main force out to engage the enemy. (One account has it that Gates spent this time arguing with Sir Francis Clerke about the American Revolution. Clerke had been gravely wounded and captured while trying to convey Burgoyne's order to Balcarres to withdraw, and had been brought to the American commander's tent.) As the sounds of battle became louder in the distance, the rest of Gates's men began a spontaneous movement toward the fighting. Leaping on his horse, Arnold galloped off to join the fight. Gates sent an officer after him to order him back, but it was too late. Arnold had hurled himself into the thick of the fight, assuming command and leading an assault against the British center, which had now withdrawn into the Balcarres Redoubt along with the remnants of the flanking regiments. In the meantime Fraser hurried in to support Burgoyne's center, only to be shot down by an American marksman.

Tradition has it that the feat was accomplished by Timothy Murphy, one of Daniel Morgan's men, at the behest of Arnold who reportedly said: "That man on the grey horse is a host to himself and must be disposed of." The same Timothy Murphy was also given credit for wounding Sir Francis Clerke. There is some basis in fact for the story if Morgan's men were actually at the battle, for it was common practice to assign the best marksmen to snipe at enemy officers.

Unable to carry Balcarres Redoubt, Arnold then galloped to the other end of the field, riding through the fire of both armies as he rode between the lines. At the left end of the American line, he took command of several newly arrived units, led them in an attack that cleared the area between the Balcarres and Breymann redoubts of some smaller fortified positions, then raced back across the field to lead four other regiments in an assault on the rear of Breymann Redoubt. As he entered the redoubt, he was hit by a musket ball in the same leg—the left leg—that had been wounded at the Sault-au-Matelot barricade in Quebec. As the rebels poured into the redoubt, Breymann sabered down four of his own men who were attempting to lay down their arms and was then killed by a fifth before he could do any further damage.

Some of the German units attempted a counterattack to retake the redoubt, but were driven back; as darkness began to fall, Burgoyne slowly withdrew to a line just north of the Great Ravine.

So ended the second part of the Battle of Saratoga. The rebels lost about 150 men; the British lost four times as many and ten cannon. Their losses included some of their best officers, among them Simon Fraser. Altogether they had lost 1,200 men and a good part of their artillery at Saratoga. There was now nothing left but a retreat to Canada.

Before you move out to inspect the battlefield firsthand, take a minute to consider the role Arnold played during the fighting. There are two schools of thought regarding his conduct. In the days that followed Arnold became known as the "mad man of Saratoga," a nickname signifying not criticism but praise, for he was widely credited with having won the battle for Gates. Historians are split even today, however, over the necessity and importance of what he did at Saratoga. Those opposed say that most of the losses the Americans suffered at the second battle were caused by Arnold's impetuous and needless assaults against Balcarres Redoubt. They argue that Burgoyne's position had already deteriorated and that further casualties were not necessary. The pro-Arnold faction argues that Burgoyne's main force was still intact, that he could have retired behind his fortifications and waited to try again another day. They say that Arnold, like Burgoyne, believed Clinton was on his way north, and, thus, the Americans were in danger of being caught between two British armies. The antis say that the Breymann Redoubt had already fallen and that Arnold attacked after other American units were already entering the position from the front. The pros insist it was Arnold's instant understanding of the overall situation and his brilliant organization of the attack force that carried the redoubt, thus making Burgoyne's position impossible and forcing him to retreat. Interestingly enough, some of Arnold's staunchest defenders are British and include Burgoyne, who attributed his defeat to Arnold's leadership. It has been said that if he had been killed instead of wounded at Saratoga, "American posterity would have known fewer names brighter than that of Benedict Arnold."

TOURING SARATOGA BATTLEFIELD

Put aside a whole day for Saratoga. The area within the park encompasses four square miles and the battle sites are scattered throughout. A nine-mile paved road winds through nine sites, with parking areas at each site and paved paths leading to the various markers, memorials, and buildings. There is ample opportunity to walk about, as there are few fences or closed-off areas; the open fields (which were then heavily wooded), tangled ravines, and sloping hills are very inviting if you like to poke around off the beaten path. Each site features illustrative maps and diagrams, and some are equipped with audio tapes.

The driveway begins at one end of the parking lot below the Visitor's Center and is clearly marked by a sign that reads "Begin Historic Tour." The speed limit is thirty miles an hour; the road is wide enough for one car; and traffic is usually one-way, following a circular route that brings you back to the Visitor's Center parking lot. You can pick up a pamphlet at the Center which maps the drive and gives a brief description of each stop along the way.

The first stop is **Freeman's Farm** overlook, where you stand on the side of a hill looking east over the scene of the first day's fighting. On the horizon in front of you is a line of hills on the eastern bank of the Hudson, which cannot be seen because of the trees and bluffs in between. To the left is a reconstruction of the cabin that marked the first meeting between Morgan's Rifles and Burgoyne's scouting detachment. To the right you are looking toward Bemis Heights where the American gun positions that brought about the battle were located. The ground between Bemis Heights and the farm is the area Arnold and Poor crossed with their men when they came to reinforce Morgan. The battle developed to the east of the farm building; the lightly wooded ground east and north-east of the farm reconstruction marks the forest through which Morgan played his deadly game of tag with the British. The stockade you see in the middle distance directly in front of you is part of the Balcarres Redoubt which did not exist at the time of this first encounter. The granite marker clearly visible in the field before you was erected by the D.A.R. and merely commemorates the battle; it does not indicate a specific site.

Nothing much is known about the Freeman family, except that the men of the family were obligated to serve in the Albany County militia. One interesting item turned up recently was a bill presented by Freeman to the British for services rendered as a scout.

As you proceed to the next site, notice to your right a short, pointed *column* off the road, midway up a rise of ground. This monument is dedicated to Morgan and reads in part: "Here Morgan, reluctant to destroy so noble a foe, was forced by patriotic necessity to defeat and slay the gentle and gallant Fraser." The tablet was erected by Morgan's great-granddaughter, Virginia Neville Taylor. It would be a shame for the touching, Homeric sentiments here expressed by Morgan's fond descendant, if it is indeed ever proved that Morgan never took part in the battle.

Stop two is the **Neilson Farm** which you will see from the distance as you drive up. This was the apex of the American main line of defense, and was known as Fort Neilson. The white clapboard building is the original **Neilson farmhouse,** the only original building left on the battlefield. A recording inside the house states that General Enoch Poor and possibly Benedict Arnold were quartered here. According to contemporary accounts, Major Acland was brought here suffering from his leg wounds, and his wife, Lady Harriet, came to nurse him after being allowed through the lines of both armies. Lady Harriet, the daughter of the Earl of Ilchester, had been painted twice by Sir Joshua Reynolds. To get to her husband she had to travel down the Hudson in the midst of a storm. One account has it that the American sentry who challenged the boat was so startled to hear a woman's voice answer him from out of the wind and rain, that he kept her waiting for some time before allowing her to land. The story is probably apocryphal, and British at that; other accounts insist that she was kept waiting for only a short time before being escorted to her husband's side.

Behind the Neilson house are two other buildings, including a reconstructed *blockhouse* which was not there at the time of the battle and will be moved for the bicentennial. The very apex of the line was the Neilson barn which was reinforced and fortified, a type of early pillbox, if you will. There were heavy batteries of guns on either side, and it was protected by a breastwork of logs and trees that had been chopped down in front to give a clear field of fire. Some fallen trees were let lay as obstacles. A marker close to the house explains that you are standing on Bemis Heights and details, on a map, the locations of the American encampment and line. It was from this site that Morgan's Rifles and the other companies commanded by Poor and Arnold advanced to the north to engage the British at Freeman's Farm. The road you followed between the two sites cut across their path, at least in part.

A cannon behind the blockhouse is inscribed "Strasbourg, 1761." None of the guns on the battlefield, except for one or two that I will mention specifically, was used in the battle. Superintendent Meuse believes that the Americans used four-pound guns of Swedish manufacture; they had been originally sold to the French army, then taken out of service when the French switched to another type of gun, and sold to the American rebels as part of the trickle of aid the French sent to the colonies prior to the Battle of Saratoga. There is a gun, however, near the blockhouse on a carriage which is described by a marker as having been surrendered by Burgoyne as part of the terms of the Convention of Saratoga following the battle.

Standing near the Neilson House facing north, toward where the British camp was, you are standing in the midst of what was the American camp. Behind you are markers for the site of the hospital tents. To the right, out of sight, is the Hudson River and the site of the gun positions that overlooked it.

A number of granite monuments about this site are dedicated to individuals and units that took part in the battle. The most significant landmark is a line of wooden, blue and white *posts* set into the ground marking the line of the American fortifications laid out by Poor and Arnold. A nearby granite memorial is dedicated to Kosciuszko who built the fortifications, while beyond it is a memorial to Timothy Murphy. Though most of Gates's army consisted of militiamen from the surrounding counties, many of those killed in the battle are believed to have been buried in a common grave somewhere in this area. Extensive excavations, however, failed to turn up any evidence. Others were carried back to their homes to be buried in the parish churchyards of Albany and Saratoga counties, where the tombstones still standing and legible attest to the sacrifice they made on this field. You may run across them as you travel the county roads and byways of this part of New York State.

Before leaving the site, I suggest you take a last, good look at the view of the Adirondacks to the north and west, the Green Mountains of Vermont to the east, the Berkshires in Massachusetts to the southeast and the Catskills to the south, all in all a most impressive sight.

As you continue, the road goes around the foot of the hill and becomes a two-lane road just where a sign says you are now driving in the direction of the American river fortifications, Stop Three. Note that the line of blue and white posts outlining the American fortifications crosses the road from the left and continues on for some distance to the right, indicating the extent of this part of the American position.

The road leads into a curved cul-de-sac with parking spaces around the perimeter. You are now at the right anchor of the American line on **Bemis Heights.** Paved paths leading away from the parking area to the positions of the various batteries are mapped out on a nearby plaque. One path is marked "To the Audio Unit Point." Following this path you come to a hill overlooking a modern farm below you at the foot of a long, grassy slope. Beyond it through a fringe of trees you will catch glimpses of the Hudson River and the high ground beyond on the east bank. Here you see firsthand how the road below is caught in a narrow corridor between the river and the high ground on which you are now standing. Two hundred years ago, the river was in plain sight.

At the push of a button, the audio tape explains the position. The gun batteries extended for three-quarters of a mile or so to your right and left. Burgoyne was trying to outflank these guns and so had to move to the west. Behind you is a ravine which marks the right end of the American line. A line of white posts indicates the position. Three plaques illustrate the kind of fortifications that were built here, give a Patriot's-eye view of Burgoyne's invasion routes, and provide a relief map of the gun positions.

If you take the path back from the audio point, but then turn off to the right, you come out on the brow of the hill overlooking the farm. Here you see a bend in the river to your right. A plaque explains how the Americans forced the British into rough, wooded land where they could not use their artillery or accustomed infantry formations. Several photographs next to the plaque show how close these bluffs come to the river, giving the guns a clear field of fire over the river and up the narrow valley. There is also a picture of what the bluff looks like when viewed from below, a view you can see for yourself by taking Route 4 after you have finished the tour and stopping near the farm. It was a formidable barrier indeed.

Returning to the parking area, take the path to the left, and walk north along the top of the bluffs. A parallel path to your right, below the brow of the hill, marks the line of entrenchments the American soldiers dug so they would not be silhouetted against the sky while firing down the slope. I walked down this slope until I hit a wet, marshy area, then turned and climbed back up to see just what Burgoyne's men would have faced had they come down the river road, met the fire of the American guns and muskets from above, and then tried to take the position. It would have been Bunker Hill multiplied several times over, for here the rebels had cannon as well as flintlocks.

At the foot of the hill you will notice a wall of fitted stones, a wet area which was filled with water when I was there, and beyond that another wall. Beyond that wall is the farmyard and, obviously, private property. This was probably part of the Erie Canal, a branch of which extended north from Troy (where the main canal turned south to Albany) to the southern end of Champlain.

Following the northbound path on the top of the hill, you eventually dead-end in a round, paved cul-de-sac at the site of the **north redan,** a two-sided fieldwork of logs and earth facing the enemy and open to the rear. This was probably the position of the first guns that would have opened on Burgoyne had he come down the road. In 1777 the road turned here and followed a route across the field below you diagonally toward the river, which is marked by a line of trees.

Return to the audio point and this time take a dirt path to the south. A hundred yards or so along this path you will come to the site of the *south redan* with an illustrative plaque which also refers to a gun position immediately south. As you face the plaque, you are looking south across a ravine. The gun position mentioned was on the top of the hill on the other side of this ravine. The plaque also explains that Bemis Heights is named for Bemis Tavern, which was situated at the foot of these bluffs on the road below.

Yielding to curiosity and an urge to explore, I led an expedition of two—my son, Richard, and me—across the ravine, tasting a little of what Burgoyne's men faced as they pushed their way through the forest. If you are similarly tempted, be advised beforehand that you will have to find your own way across the ravine through thick undergrowth, down and up steep slopes, and across a stream at the bottom. On the top of the hill on the other side was an overgrown plowed field from which we had a very good view of the river looking south. At the eastern end of the field, we found what seemed to be the remains of an embankment, but we subsequently learned that bulldozers used in a sand-quarrying operation along Bemis Heights at the beginning of the century effectively leveled and buried whatever earthen works might have remained. In other words, unless you want the exercise, it is not worth your while to cross the ravine.

Regaining the delightfully cool and comfortable front seat of your car, leave Bemis Heights and continue to the next stop, the site of **Asa Chatfield's Farm**, an American observation post. Facing north by a little east, you look down a slope past a row of young trees, beyond which is another wooded slope where the American pickets were stationed. Beyond that is the **Middle Ravine.** The rising slope of that ravine, the northern slope, is where the opposing British pickets were stationed. The open areas around this site were probably wooded areas, according to the relief map on the site. The specific site of the Chatfield farmhouse is not marked.

As you proceed toward the next stop, you will come to a paved apron on the right side of the road which marks the Middle Ravine. A path leading from the road takes you to a granite marker at the spot where Major Acland was wounded on October 7. According to that marker, this, then, was where Enoch Poor's men overran the British left flank. Leading off to your right from the marker is a cleared path through the high grass, which allows you to look down into the ravine itself, where so much of the fighting took place during the second Battle of Saratoga. The ravine is still wooded, though perhaps not as heavily as it was then; it does give you a good idea of what the terrain must have been like. Incidentally, the path leading along the top of the ravine is not paved, but is made of a distinctly different kind of grass which is kept cut short. You will notice several of these grass pathways running across the battlefield. They are meant to mark the routes of whatever roads and trails existed at the time of the fighting.

Continuing along the tour road for a few hundred feet, you will find a granite marker on the left which marks the point where Poor opened his attack on the British left. At the next stop, an audio tape explains that the British line, with ten cannon, halted on the **Barber Wheatfield** directly in front of you. This was part of a local farm belonging to the Barber family. The British formed a battle line a thousand yards long, stretching across the field from where you are standing and into the field you can see on the other side of a row of trees. From this spot the American camp on Bemis Heights, near the left end of the American line, is about a mile to your left. Poor's attack hit the British line, Acland's command, at the spot on which you are standing. Morgan's attack came at the far end of the British line, beyond the other open field. From this position Burgoyne ordered his troops to fall back toward Balcarres Redoubt. If you face southeast toward the Hudson, you can see the Freeman Farm building off to your left, the direction the British retreated. Still facing southeast, you are looking along the British line of advance. Behind you and off to the right is a granite *monument* which marks the spot where Fraser fell. This would put Timothy Murphy, who was with Morgan's men, off on the British right flank to your right on the other side of the hill, where you came across the Morgan memorial erected by his great-granddaughter. If these two positions are correctly marked, with the hill between them, then Murphy must have been either up an extremely tall tree—and several accounts do say as much—or armed with a mortar.

On the whole, the appearance of this area is similar to what it was at the time of the battle, though if the British flanks were in wooded areas, then where you are now standing was either wooded or at the edge of a woods.

When I was there, the middle of the British line was marked by two guns, lying on the ground, which actually saw service during this battle and were surrendered when Burgoyne's men laid down their arms. By the time you arrive, these may be mounted on carriages, and, if you get there about the time of the bicentennial, they may not be the same guns. There are plans to substitute exact replicas for the originals, which are marked with engraved coats of arms and other devices too rare to lose through the friction of climbing dungarees and wandering, wondering hands.

The next stop along the tour is at **Balcarres Redoubt.** In this area a line of red and white posts marks the line of the British defenses. The path which leads to the redoubt goes first to a reconstructed log cabin representing the **Freeman cabin,** which stood on the site. As you walk up to the cabin, the posts marking the British line become strikingly evident around you. The cabin is furnished with a cornhusk bed, a period fireplace, and a life-size model of a British soldier. Most of the surrounding area is open, but we must assume much of it was then overgrown, since the cabin stood in a clearing in the woods.

After a short walk south from the cabin, you reach a plaque marking the site of the Balcarres Redoubt. The painted stakes in this area outline the redoubt's perimeter and extend around you in a circle. The redoubt was defended by 1,500 men and eight cannon. It was about 500 yards long and twelve to fourteen feet high. A short distance away a relief map describes the action around the redoubt. The assault Arnold led came over the wooded ridge directly in front of you, which is about a thousand yards away. A nearby granite marker memorializes Colonel Zebulon Bidwell of the Connecticut militia, who was killed during the first day's fighting on September 19. It was erected by the Bidwell family which goes all over the country putting up memorials to Bidwells on appropriate sites. In this case, they goofed. Zebulon is believed to have died in a swampy area below the redoubt. Nevertheless, the marker's date serves as a reminder that you are standing on the site of two battles that took place three weeks apart, but were fought over the same ground.

Walking along the path beyond the redoubt area, you next come to a marker for **Bloody Knoll.** The attackers lost more men between this point and the redoubt, now behind you, than at any other spot on the field. Ahead is a rise of ground leading to the top of a ridge and a log reconstruction of a British gun position which stood here at the time, an *outwork* intended to cover the approaches to the redoubt. According to the accompanying plaque, the reconstruction is a good example of this type of eighteenth-century fortification. Additional fortifications like this may be reconstructed on the site by the time the bicentennial of the battle rolls around.

The next stop is **Breymann Redoubt.** Again at this position red and white posts mark the line of the British fortifications. A footpath leads up a hill to the redoubt, but first you come to a carved *memorial* to Arnold's twice-wounded leg. It is a very realistic leg indeed, clad in a period boot, surmounted by an epaulette to indicate Arnold's rank, and resting on the end of a mortar. The memorial is surrounded by an iron picket fence and is, to the best of my knowledge, the only memorial in the world to anyone's leg.

A plaque on the site of the redoubt describes it in detail. Facing west, with the Arnold memorial to your right and the line of posts outlining the redoubt in front of you, you are facing the direction from which the main rebel attack came. Arnold and his men entered from behind you.

Leaving Breymann Redoubt, the road now takes you to the eighth stop, the site of **Burgoyne's headquarters** after the first battle. A somewhat misleading plaque tells you that Burgoyne set up his headquarters by the spring before you, seemingly indicating a wet area at your feet. A dirt path from the parking area, however, leads you across another trickle of water and into the field where Burgoyne's tent was pitched. This is where Burgoyne planned the Freeman Farm fortifications, where he sweated out the three-week waiting period, and where he eventually planned his last advance.

The road now leads to the last stop on the tour, the site of the **Great Redoubt.** A footpath leads to the brow of a hill, your closest point of the day to Route 4 and the river. This is the southernmost of four or five bluffs which extend from this spot toward the river. This bluff and the two to the north made up the fortified position known as the Great Redoubt. After the second battle, Burgoyne himself retreated to the bluff on your left. Directly below you, where the river is so close you think you can reach it with a stone, is where Burgoyne had a bridge of boats built. The British army hospital was below the bluffs and somewhat north, close to the river.

It was within this redoubt that Fraser was buried. All through the night of October 7 he had lain dying, tended by the Baroness von Riedesel, in a farmhouse which stood at the foot of the middle bluff. At his own request, he was buried within the redoubt on the evening of

October 8. According to some accounts, American gunners, possibly in position on the bluffs south of where you are standing, misunderstood the ceremony taking place and fired on the funeral, their balls coming close enough to throw dust into the face of the officiating chaplain. Legend has it that when they realized what was happening, they fired memorial salutes instead to their fallen foe.

From this point Burgoyne retreated north back to Saratoga. Ironically enough, from here he could see quite a distance downstream even as you can. Ahead of him stretched the road to Albany, but beyond the hills to the south, forever beyond his sight, lay the guns of Bemis Heights, the rock on which his ambitious plans foundered.

If you have spent most of the day touring Saratoga battlefield, by the time you visit the Great Redoubt the sun is low on the horizon behind you, and the fields and hills across the river are streaked with the long shadows of grazing cattle, a lovely, peaceful scene inducing a quiet feeling in mind and heart. Not so Burgoyne's mind and heart on the evening of October 8 as the body of one of his ablest commanders sank out of sight into the receiving earth. Whatever long shadows he saw that day could only have portended the dark, uncertain future that stretched immediately before him in the final scenes of Saratoga.

A short distance from the Great Redoubt along the road leading back to the Visitor's Center, a paved turnoff leads into another picnic area, which provides picnic tables, but no facilities for fires and no refreshments.

During the summer months guides and others dressed in colonial costume are stationed throughout the battlefield to explain the sites and answer questions. Their duties also include rolling paper cartridges as described earlier, an activity in which you are invited to join, and the loading and firing of guns and muskets.

OLD SARATOGA (SCHUYLERVILLE) AND THE CONVENTION OF SARATOGA

The story of Saratoga by no means ends with the battle of October 7. Like the Burgoyne invasion, it dragged on for several days more until finally, after several anticlimaxes, came the surrender ceremony.

To follow the story, take the turnoff to U.S. 4 a short distance before the parking area on the road back to the Visitor's Center. A small sign indicates the turnoff, so keep your eyes peeled. Turn north on U.S. 4 toward Schuylerville along the route Burgoyne followed as he left the battlefield. He stopped long enough to bury Fraser; then, leaving campfires burning in the Great Redoubt, folded his tents "like the Arabs, and as silently stole away."

Gates had sent a force of 1,300 Massachusetts militia to block this expected move. The militia crossed the Hudson and moved north along the eastern bank, then recrossed the river at old Saratoga (Schuylerville) and took up a position right across Burgoyne's route. But, since many of these men had to go back to the main camp at Bemis Heights to draw supplies, Burgoyne was able to slip by during the night of the eighth and the following day. It was raining heavily by then and his men marched slowly, trying to give the bateaux a chance to keep up. American patrols harassed them constantly, hanging on to their flank and rear, capturing most of the boats and many of the baggage wagons. Finally, they reached Saratoga and went into camp in a well-defended position.

Drive considerably below the speed limit on U.S. 4 to catch the historic markers during the few minutes it takes to get to Schuylerville. The first marker shows up on the right at the site of **Dovegat House,** Burgoyne's headquarters during the advance and retreat of the British army. The original house's site is now occupied by an old farmhouse with a cupola on top of the roof.

A mile or so farther north is a marker smack in the front yard of a converted mobile home, part of a row of recently built small homes. This marker is somewhat suspect. It states that this is the site of **Gates's head-quarters** prior to Burgoyne's surrender. I have been informed by reliable authorities, however, that some markers along this route have been taken from their original positions and relocated in certain front yards to give the inhabitants whatever benefits and advantages they might hope to accrue from residing on an "authentic" historic site. Perhaps validity will have been restored by the time you pass along this way.

A half mile farther, a marker to the right indicates where a series of *forts* important to the area were built; they may have commanded this stretch of river during the long period of conflict between the French and the British. This is now plowed farmland. I stopped there briefly, but could see nothing remotely like the remains of any fort. This marker, however, should alert you to the next one coming up, which is most pertinent to your search.

It occurs about a half mile farther on the left and marks the site of Burgoyne's surrender. Actually it marks the site of what is known as the **Field of Grounded Arms,** the place where the surrendering British stacked their arms. The exact site is probably on the opposite side of the road, between the road and the river. At that time this was all open fields, floodplains onto which the Hudson spilled whenever the melting snows and heavy rains of spring caused it to overextend its banks. Most of the Field of Grounded Arms is now privately owned, and the rest has been made into a bathing and recreation area for the residents of Schuylerville.

A short distance north of the Field of Grounded Arms, you come to the entrance to the **Philip Schuyler House** on the right side of the road. There is a small parking space off the road from which you can walk to the house across the spacious tree-shaded grounds.

This house, maintained by the National Park Service, sits in a twenty-five-acre park which is part of, though separate from, the Saratoga battle area. This was Schuyler's country home to which he intended to retire from the family mansion in Albany. The property had originally been acquired by his great-uncle as part of the Saratoga Patent of 1684, which took in all of what is now Saratoga County and more. The first house was burned during a French and Indian raid in 1745. History repeated itself on October 10, 1777, when Burgoyne reluctantly destroyed this one the day after occupying it, rather than allow it to be used for cover by the encircling rebel forces. As soon as the British surrendered, however, Schuyler put a number of soldier-masons and civilian carpenters to work (one account says he also used British prisoners), and, within seventeen days, with his own sawmill going full blast, he had rebuilt the house on the old foundations. Of course he had lost all his furnishings, but he simply sent to the Albany mansion for more. In the meantime, he had Burgoyne and his staff brought to Albany where he put them up at the mansion, thus heaping coals on the head of the British prisoner, who is said to have apologized more than once for having burned his host's lovely country home. Schuyler took it all very philosophically, telling Burgoyne that, had he been in his place, he would have done exactly the same thing.

The house is well worth going through. The furniture inside is all pre-1790, but none of it was in the original or the rebuilt house, though there are one or two pieces that did belong to the Schuylers. The negotiations for the surrender and the surrender itself took place on Schuyler land not far from the house.

Before going in, notice the plaques with relief maps showing the British and American lines at the time of the surrender and the position of the British on October 10 when they got back to Saratoga. Another plaque shows a picture of what the house looked like originally and gives the history of the estate. Among the items inside is a virginal made in Vermont by the country's earliest piano manufacturers; a lap desk for

use in the field during military campaigns; dining-room chairs with ex-
tra-wide seats, typical of the furniture of the Dutch who settled the upper Hudson valley; a Chippendale table in the dining room, which belonged to the general and his wife; two knockdown beds in an upstairs
room, which were carried by officers in the field; a child's drawer bed
that pulls out from under a larger bed; and a bowfront chest of drawers,
which also belonged to the Schuylers, in the master bedroom. The
kitchen, which is a cookhouse around to the back, features a taped com-
mentary in the character of an upstate servant, who explains that the
kitchen was built later than the rest of the house after two years of cooking in the basement. The herb garden behind the house marks the site of
what was once the kitchen garden.

Take a moment or so now to consider what happened in this area
following the battle farther south. On October 10, Gates finally decided
to follow up his victory by pursuing the British. Burgoyne had sent a
small detachment north to build a bridge at Fort Edward, over which
his army could retreat across the Hudson. Gates believed that this was
the main body of the British army and that only a rear guard had been
left at old Saratoga; he proceeded, accordingly, to move his men in the
direction of the town. Luckily for him, a deserter revealed the truth, and
Gates was able to pull back and avoid a blunder that might have reopened
the way for Burgoyne to move on Albany, had it resulted in an American
defeat.

Instead Gates went into siege positions surrounding the British on
the east, west, and south. Burgoyne held a council of war to consider the
possibilities and finally decided to listen to Riedesel, who advised him to
abandon the heavy equipment and slip away during the night to the
north. Unfortunately, he had waited a day too long. John Stark, with
1,100 militiamen from New Hampshire and a battery of guns, had overcome his anger by then and returned to the army. Slipping into position
to the north, he cut off Burgoyne's retreat. The British army was now
surrounded by 20,000 American militiamen and Continentals, all eager
for the kill. The Americans bombarded the town for six days and nights,
according to the memoirs of Madame Riedesel who spent the time with
her children in a cellar crowded with wounded soldiers. Burgoyne spent
the same period in General Schuyler's home drinking champagne with
his mistress, she also noted.

On Monday, October 13, Burgoyne requested a parley with Gates
and asked for surrender terms. Then followed one of the slickest maneu-
vers ever attempted by a commanding general who knows his number

is up, but refuses to accept the inevitable. Burgoyne insisted on calling the surrender a "convention," not a capitulation. Gates was no match for the wily Englishman, though he had originally insisted on unconditional surrender—a blunder on his part because no one knew at the time whether Clinton was coming to Burgoyne's assistance. Burgoyne suggested that his men be paroled after giving their word not to serve in North America for the remainder of the war and Gates agreed, not realizing he was freeing more than 5,000 trained British regulars for use against American allies in Europe. Gates then overplayed his hand by demanding the actual surrender take place quickly. This got Burgoyne's wind up and he stalled, asking for time to go over the details of the surrender agreement.

On October 15, Burgoyne was informed by messenger that Clinton had reached Esopus and was probably on his way to Albany. Burgoyne then wanted to call off the surrender, but his commanders told him he could not honorably withdraw from the agreement and threw doubt—wise men that they were—on the messenger's report. To stall for more time until he could clarify the situation, Burgoyne asked Gates to verify the strength of the American army. He had been told that a large force of militiamen had left Gates's command and suspected that the Americans no longer possessed their superiority in numbers. What had really happened was that several hundred of the militia had reached the end of their enlistment and were heading home. Gates now told Burgoyne to either surrender or fight. Burgoyne stalled a little longer, but finally gave in to his advisors and surrendered on Friday, October 17.

On that day Burgoyne rode out of camp in all his regalia and decorations to meet Gates the conqueror, a little, bespectacled man in very plain clothes. While they were at dinner the British soldiery laid down their arms on the Field of Grounded Arms. Gates did not allow any of his soldiers to witness the event; but as the British regulars marched away, they found the road lined with rebel militiamen, standing silently in ranks. An American band struck up "Yankee Doodle," and as the British troops marched past, Gates and Burgoyne came out to watch. At this point Burgoyne handed over his sword and Gates handed it back.

According to some accounts, as soon as the British soldiers had got clear of their American captors, they began to complain about their misfortunes. By this time they were surrounded by American camp followers and a crowd of local inhabitants who had suffered misfortunes of their own at the hands of British foragers and their Indian friends. When they heard the redcoats complaining, they talked about dusting their backs for them. There was also some talk about massacring the few Indians still with the British who were now prisoners. A motion was passed and seconded that Burgoyne be sent to Albany in tar and feathers. The militia intervened, however, and Gates detailed a special escort to protect the captive general as he was taken away.

The prisoners of war were now known as the Convention Army and numbered just a little less than 5,000. They were supposed to march to Boston, board ship, and return to England. Congress, however, was up in arms about the terms Gates had agreed to, and so was the British General Howe, who hated the thought of seeing so many fine regulars go to waste when he needed them so badly.

The prisoners got as far as Cambridge, Massachusetts. By that time Howe was trying to get them shipped to England via a British-held port, preferably New York. The Americans immediately saw this as a scheme by which Howe meant to reinforce his army. On its part, Congress was trying to find some way to get out of the surrender agreement without sacrificing national honor. First they said the British had not turned in as much equipment as they should have, only 600-odd cartridge boxes having been surrendered. Then Burgoyne wrote to Gates complaining about the treatment his troops had received and stated his opinion that the terms of the convention had been violated and therefore public faith was broken. Congress took this statement to mean that Burgoyne was disavowing the terms of the agreement and put off the embarkation until the convention was ratified by the crown.

In December the British ships that were to carry the men to England appeared off Boston harbor, but were refused entry. In the meantime General Clinton, who had replaced General Howe as the British commander in chief, received orders from the King to ratify the convention. Congress pretended to believe the orders were forged and demanded that a witness be produced who could swear he had seen the King sign the order. The whole sorry mess wound up with Burgoyne and two other officers returning to England while the rest of his men sat, or more properly, marched out the war as prisoners. They spent a year in Massachusetts and Vermont. Then in 1779 they were marched for twelve weeks on starvation rations through the snows of January and February to Charlottesville, Virginia, accompanied by the Baroness von Riedesel and her daughters, who refused to leave the baron's side. As they passed through Pennsylvania, most of the Hessian prisoners slipped away, giving a good many families with German names now living in Pennsylvania their start. The prisoners were moved around several times after that, especially as the war moved into southern theaters and the approach of

Cornwallis threatened to liberate them. By the end of the war, less than half were still in captivity, and most of those elected to go back to England.

The guns captured at Saratoga were shipped south and eventually wound up in storage at West Point, where some can be seen on display at Trophy Point, overlooking the river their commander had hoped to dominate. Recent research has revealed that Howe had indeed planned to bypass the convention. He intended to order the British repatriation ships to New York instead of Southampton and to exchange the troops on board for American prisoners.

The Battle of Saratoga and Burgoyne's surrender were, in every sense of the word, the turning point of the American Revolution; the results meant much more than the lifting of American morale after the loss of Philadelphia, more than the surrender of several thousand men. Up to that time, the French had cast a sympathetic eye on the American rebels, as they would have on any party who made trouble for their ancient British enemies, but had held back from becoming directly involved. After Saratoga, however, the French attitude changed. After all, an army of trained, disciplined British and German regulars, with all their guns and equipment, had been made to surrender to a makeshift army composed in part of American militiamen. The British posts north of Saratoga were hurriedly withdrawn into Canada. Of the original thirteen colonies, the British crown could claim to control effectively only the areas around New York City and Philadelphia and Rhode Island.

Within five months of Saratoga, the French government recognized the American republic and signed a formal and open alliance. Not only money and cannon could now be expected from France, but French fighting men and the French navy as well. France was moving toward war with England, as was Spain and even Holland, despite the Dutch-British alliance. The outcome would be an entente opposing British commercial and naval power that would siphon off into the Caribbean and elsewhere some of the military energy the British were expending on the North American mainland. In a sense, the American Revolution after Saratoga became the world's first world war, for before it was over most of Europe, including Austria, Prussia, and even Russia, was striving to upset the British commercial applecart.

IV.

UP THE HUDSON
WITH CLINTON
AND OTHERS

By Saratoga American and British strategy planners were concentrating on the final link in the chain of waterways connecting Canada and New York, the Hudson River, particularly the 160 or so miles of it between Albany and New York City. Ticonderoga and the other northern forts had been rendered harmless either through capture or through being by-passed. The Americans had tried a Canadian invasion and had failed. Then the British had tried to use the route for another round of the invasion game only to have Burgoyne come a cropper at Bemis Heights. And even before Saratoga, Clinton's attempt to break the rebel hold on that part of the river running through the Hudson Highlands was, as we shall see, only partially successful. When all was said and done, he did not have the muscle to retain control, much less march north to pry Burgoyne out of Gates's trap. The new French alliance promising to bring the French fleet into American waters would soon place a higher premium on New England ports.

The Hudson River was now more than just a single link in a greater system; it was a belt holding the colonies together. With the British fleet sailing virtually unopposed along the Atlantic coast, communications between New England, the Middle Atlantic states, and the South depended on the few roads connecting these widely separated regions. All of these roads had to cross the Hudson. Some historians believe today that even had the British gained control of the Hudson and cut off the New England "head" from the rest of the revolutionary body, the revolutionary army under Washington would still have been free to maneuver and fight, and the outcome of the war would not have been materially affected. No one at the time, however, had the advantage of hindsight. As far as the British and the Americans were concerned, the Hudson, with its ocean tides reaching upstream almost as far as Albany making the river navigable by large vessels, including the biggest war-ships, and with a predominantly Tory population living along its valley, was the prize plum of the war. It brought Burgoyne down from Canada, brought Clinton up from New York City, brought about a major effort on the part of the Continental Congress and its army to fortify its mountains, and brought Arnold and André to grief over West Point.

We shall explore the revolutionary sites along the Hudson with all of this in mind, first proceeding north along the west side from the New York–New Jersey line, then crossing over at the present town of Kingston and coming south along the east bank. In the process we will trace two chapters in the story of the Revolution, Clinton's expedition and the West Point treason plot. At the same time we will cover a number of sites associated with the Continental Army, particularly with the days of its final encampments. This will require some traveling back and forth, but the story is so absorbing, and the scenery so inviting, I am sure you will welcome the opportunity to become familiar with one of the most beautiful regions in the United States.

CLINTON RAIDS THE HIGHLANDS

North of New York City a chain of mountains spreads across the Hudson Valley from east to west. The southern limit of this region is at Bear Mountain, the northern limit at Kingston, with twenty miles of river in between, twisting and winding between the hills, finding a sinuous pathway through a veritable gorge. On either side of this gorge the highlands tower a thousand and more feet above the river, and on their cliff sides are numerous places where guns and forts can and did perch.

In May, 1775, shortly after Ethan Allen took Fort Ticonderoga, the Continental Congress attempted to secure the southern end of the waterway system by authorizing the building of three forts. The north-ernmost, Fort Constitution, was built on an island opposite that west point of land where the river goes into one of its convulsive turns through the highlands. The island was called Martelaar's Rock for a party of Dutch settlers who had been "martyred" there by a band of local Indians. The island has since been renamed Constitution Island, either in honor of the British constitution which many American patriots professed to support during the early days of the Revolution, or for Fort Constitution. About ten miles south was Fort Montgomery, probably named for the American commander who died at Quebec, built on the north bank of Popolopen Creek, which empties into the Hudson immediately north of where Bear Mountain on the west bank and Anthony's Nose on the east force the river into the first coil of an S curve. Since the Fort Montgomery site was dominated by higher ground on the south bank of the creek, a third fort, Fort Clinton, was constructed there to protect Fort Montgomery. A bridge across Popolopen Creek allowed contact between the two.

Between Bear Mountain and Anthony's Nose the rebels stretched an iron chain and a stout log boom to obstruct river traffic. Additional but smaller fortifications included Fort Independence, about three miles below Bear Mountain on the east bank, guarding the approaches to Peekskill Bay and the city of Peekskill at its eastern end. Three miles south as the crow flies, a small outpost called Fort Lafayette guarded the eastern landing of King's Ferry on Verplanck's Point, directly opposite Stony Point.

In addition, but not to be taken seriously, was a chevaux-de-frise, a line of iron-pointed stakes embedded in large, stone-filled cribs submerged along a stretch of flats between the west bank of the Hudson near New Windsor out to Polopel's Island just below Kingston. Any vessel driven upon it was supposed to have its bottom ripped open, a theory that was never proved since the British refused to cooperate. The chevaux-de-frise was further enhanced by a log boom and iron chain.

You may shake your head in disbelief and smile at the quaint ideas our ancestors had about the effectiveness of these forts and devices. Actually, the chevaux-de-frise aside, they really did know what they were doing. Where it runs through the highland gorge for twenty miles, the Hudson River presented a tricky problem in navigation for wooden, wind-driven vessels. The tide changes twice a day, now flowing upstream, now down. The gorge presses in on the river at certain places, making the current run stronger and swifter. At the same time the gorge is wide enough to allow winds of considerable force to blow north, then south through its steep, rocky corridors. Those vagrant winds and changing currents called for top-notch seamanship; a helmsman could never be sure but that just around the next bend he would find himself suddenly forced onto the rocky shore either to right or left. Those responsible for constructing the forts and placing the chains and booms had chosen sites that overlooked the river where navigation was the most difficult. The fortifying of the most important site, however, the west point and the heights around and above it, would have to wait until another year of war had earned the planners enough experience to realize their neglect.

Sir Henry Clinton was placed in a dilemma when Howe sailed away with most of the army based in New York. Left with about 7,000 regulars and Tories to defend the city, he came under increasing pressure from Burgoyne for support. Clinton was a British career-officer whose father, a British admiral, had been first the governor of Newfoundland and then of New York. Sir Henry, reared in New York Province, had returned to England during his youth to enter the army and had distinguished himself in active service on the Continent during the Seven Years' War.

A happy marriage ended tragically with his wife's death which brought on a temporary emotional and mental breakdown according to Professor William B. Willcox who has edited his very extensive memoirs. Clinton also seems to have had a strong emotional attachment to his adjutant general, Major John André, who was executed as a spy, and grieved intensely for him. He was forever getting into disputes with his superiors over matters of strategy, and though he was usually right and went out of his way to point this out to the gentlemen in question, he and his brilliant suggestions were constantly shunted aside, which may have been lucky for the American cause.

As Howe's second-in-command, Clinton was afraid to move to Burgoyne's support with so few men, though he could see quite plainly that the rebels would eventually move in force themselves either against him or Burgoyne. When Burgoyne began to press him harder for support during September, 1777, just before the Battle of Freeman's Farm, Clinton was already proposing to move against Forts Montgomery and Clinton, but was waiting for more men. Finally on September 24, the reinforcements he was expecting arrived from England, giving him an army of almost 7,000 regulars besides his 3,000 Tories. On Friday, October 3, he marched 3,000 regulars and Tory volunteers aboard the ships Howe had left him and sailed north up the Hudson.

The rebel forces along the Hudson Valley were not caught flat-footed by this move. They had been expecting Clinton to attack the Hudson forts for some time and General Washington had sent frequent warnings to the officers in the area to keep on the alert. The work on Forts Montgomery and Clinton had progressed slowly since construction had begun in the spring of 1776. By the time Clinton came north Fort Clinton was in the final stages, but Fort Montgomery was still open to the rear. The builders of Fort Constitution had run into early difficulties with the civilian engineer who had been hired to plan and supervise the work, as we shall see when we visit the island, and as a result, it too was not yet completed. The log boom and chain were in position from Anthony's Nose to the west bank. Available to the rebels was also a small flotilla of ships and boats, which included two small frigates, the *Congress* and the *Montgomery*, two oar-propelled galleys, and a sloop.

Major General Israel Putnam had been in command of the Hudson Highlands defenses since early 1777. Though Washington had kept an anxious eye over the highlands' defenses, he had been forced to pull troops out of the area to reinforce the fighting in New Jersey and Pennsylvania. As a result, by October, 1777, Putnam had about 1,000 Continental soldiers and 400 militiamen camped around Peekskill and only about 600 militia holding the forts on the west bank. The forts were coincidentally commanded by two brothers named Clinton, George and James. Both had been born and reared in New York, the sons of Charles Clinton, a British army officer. Both had seen service in the New York militia during the French and Indian War, and both were members of the provincial assembly. George had been a delegate to the Continental Congress before he was put in charge of building the Hudson River defenses, a post he filled conscientiously but anxiously, for he freely admitted he did not have the knowledge or experience to do the job without expert help.

In April, 1777, George Clinton had been elected governor and lieutenant governor of New York. He declined the honor of being his own lieutenant governor, but accepted the job of the state's first executive. He continued to fulfill his military duties, and when word came to him from Putnam that Clinton was on the move, he hurried down from a meeting of the state assembly at Esopus to take up his post as commander of Fort Montgomery. The British had already carried out one raid that year; on March 23 they had raided Peekskill, driving off the town's defenders and destroying large quantities of supplies. On July 1, Washington urged George Clinton to call out the militia, because he was sure Sir William Howe was about to advance against the highland forts. Then came Burgoyne's thrust from the north, obviously aimed at the Hudson Valley, and Howe's mysterious exit from New York City and disappearance at sea. Finally on October 3, Clinton was about to open the attack and you must hurry north to join him.

☆

From New York City, take the George Washington Bridge across the Hudson and then Route 9W north to Stony Point. From Saratoga, take 87 south to the Albany connection to the New York Thruway; take the thruway to the Nyacks exit (ignore the West Nyack exit) and proceed north on 9W as above. Two exits later on 84, take 9W south to Stony Point.

On October 4, Clinton landed some of his men at Tarrytown opposite Nyack, near where the Tappan Zee Bridge now spans the three-mile width of the river. He then proceeded up the river to Verplanck's Point, where he landed a larger number of troops the next day. By this time, beacon fires were burning atop the highland peaks, the signal guns were roaring out the alarm, and the militia companies on both banks were mustering and hurrying to their posts. George Clinton was coming down the Hudson by boat. General Israel Putnam, never much of a field commander despite his doughty service at Bunker Hill, Long Island, and Philadelphia, was sure Clinton was about to move against Peekskill. Clinton obliged him by capturing the small garrison at Verplanck's Point and leaving 400 men on shore, causing Putnam to withdraw into the hills east of Peekskill and call for reinforcements from Forts Clinton and Montgomery.

At Stony Point, follow the signs from 9W to the battlefield park and climb the path that takes you through the sites of the battle that occurred less than two years after Clinton's expedition. We will be going over this ground again when we cover the battle. Follow this path to the top of the hill overlooking the Hudson. Looking off at an angle to your left across the river, you can see the protruding bulge in the east bank that marks Verplanck's Point and the eastern terminus of King's Ferry. Then find the side path that takes you to the north side of Stony Point overlooking **Tomkins Cove.** Directly below is the spot where Clinton landed the main body of his troops at the western ferry landing on the morning of Monday, October 6, under cover of fog, leaving Putnam in the hills above Peekskill and George and James Clinton at Popolopen Creek wondering what he was up to. Four years later, on August 20 and 21, 1781, the Continental Army and their French allies would land here on their way to the victory at Yorktown.

Nothing remains of either ferry landing. The river edge at Verplanck's Point has been altered drastically by fill placed there by the railroad for a roadbed. An oil-storage area and private homes occupy most of the point at this writing. In Tomkins Cove there is only a rocky beach and no evidence on the bank to show the trail Clinton's men followed as they moved away from the river first west, then north to out-flank Forts Clinton and Montgomery.

As you continue north from Stony Point on 9W, you will find yourself winding and climbing around the eastern flank of Dunderberg Mountain. Clinton's army followed a trail over the top of a smaller peak immediately south of Dunderberg, called the Bockberg, and then through a pass called the Timp around Dunderberg on its western flank. Contemporary accounts describe the trail as a narrow road in very bad condition. Anthony Wayne led his men over part of it as he marched to attack Stony Point two years later and had no better opinion of the route. When you visit Stony Point again to follow the battle there, you will travel over some of the route, now paved and named.

Clinton sent on an advance force of 900 men under Lieutenant Colonel Mungo Campbell to carry out the first part of his well-planned strategy. Campbell led his men through the Timp below the summit of Dunderberg, a narrow path leading between rough, wooded slopes that could have been defended easily by a few men. In fact the pass had been surveyed by the Americans, who had decided it was impassable. It seemed to have been a common failing among the rebels to assume, as they did at Mount Defiance, what the enemy could or could not do.

North of Dunderberg the advance party reached an area still known as Doodletown, about two miles from Fort Clinton, where it split into two groups. One went west on a seven-mile march around Bear Mountain to take Fort Montgomery from the rear, while the other went east around the mountain to take up attack positions around Fort Clinton.

Despite the morning fog, Governor Clinton's scouts had detected the landing and reported it to him. Clinton immediately sent to Putnam for reinforcements. By that time Putnam had also learned of the landing on the west bank and was now convinced the attack was going to be directed, not against Peekskill, but against Fort Montgomery; he had already sent a note to Clinton promising reinforcements.

Clinton sent out a patrol of about thirty men to locate the enemy, whose exact movements were still hidden from him. The patrol ran into the British at Doodletown and a hot skirmish ensued; the patrol withdrew only with great difficulty to get the word back to Clinton. Then a scout brought word of Campbell's movement around Bear Mountain and part of the British strategy became apparent. Knowing only too well how weak in men he was, Clinton, nevertheless, decided to fight a series of delaying actions outside the forts in the hope of holding up the British advance until Putnam's reinforcements could arrive. One hundred militia and Continentals were sent out toward Doodletown and a large gun in Fort Montgomery was ordered to a position west of the fort to intercept Campbell.

The Bear Mountain area, including Doodletown and the remains of Fort Clinton, is now part of a large and very popular state park. Unfortunately Doodletown is in a section of the park closed to the public, a situation I hope will be changed by the time of the bicentennial of this action. If you follow 9W into **Bear Mountain Park,** however, you can visit most of the sites. Park your car in the very large parking lot near the Bear Mountain Inn and prepare to do some walking, much the best way to get around the area.

Walk from the parking lot (the parking fee in the summer is $1.00) back to the Inn. A short distance north of the Inn, a path leads to the southern edge of a large pond called **Hessian Lake.** Somewhere nearby, perhaps where the Inn now stands or where 9W runs, was a low, stone wall behind which the 100 sent out toward Doodletown took up a position to await the advancing British. One story says Hessian Lake was so named because the bodies of Hessian troops were thrown into it after the battle. The source is an account of a visit paid by Dr. Timothy Dwight, an American army chaplain who visited the sites of the forts in May, 1778, and reported that he saw the bodies of some of the defenders in a small pond near Fort Montgomery, not Fort Clinton. A fire fight developed here as the defenders behind the wall put up a stiff resistance before being gradually forced back into Fort Clinton.

In the meantime, that solo gun from Fort Montgomery under the command of Captain Ephraim Fenno, who was covered by about 120 men, was causing great confusion in the ranks of Campbell's command. Grapeshot and musket fire drove the attackers back time and again, until Campbell outflanked the gun, causing the gunners to spike the piece and retire to Fort Montgomery. A second gun was ordered out to cover the retreat and though it too had to be abandoned, it gave the men a chance to get back into the shelter of the fort with few losses. Unfortunately, Captain Fenno delayed his own retreat too long and was captured. The rest of the British force now hurried up to join the advance parties and invest both forts. With Sir Henry Clinton himself on the scene what might be called the Battle of the Clintons now began in earnest, with Sir Henry attacking and George and James defending.

Continuing from Hessian Lake, find the signs for the nature and history trails and enjoy a very pleasant walk through the woods on the east side of the mountain. It will lead you past the bear pits, animal cages, and the nature museum, and then on to the history trail, which goes to a second *museum* devoted to the area's history. This museum stands in the middle of what was a star-shaped redoubt located on the highest point inside **Fort Clinton.** If you face west toward the mountain, the ramparts would have been all around you, and you would have been at the southeastern corner of the fort. Behind you and to your right is the Bear Mountain Bridge. Directly to your right, out of sight and down at the north foot of the mountain is Popolopen Creek. On the other side of the creek, on the high ground, stood Fort Montgomery. Somewhere beyond the westernmost wall of Fort Clinton was a smaller redoubt known as the West Redoubt. The bird cages are located on what was then a line of redoubts. One of the barracks was located somewhere to your front at a distance between you and the western ramparts. Another larger L-shaped building was off to your left front, beyond the star redoubt, in the approximate center of the fort area.

I can think of no better observation post than the inside of Fort Clinton from which to watch the ensuing battle. By the time both forts were completely invested by the attackers, it was late afternoon and there weren't many daylight hours left. The British attacked continuously for three hours, advancing up to the walls again and again, only to be thrown back by the defenders, many of whom had only their muskets, no bayonets or smaller arms. The British guns kept up a steady bombardment and what American guns were left answered them back. In the meantime Putnam had not yet sent reinforcements, because he was still fearful of the troops Sir Henry had left at Verplanck's Point. Putnam thought there were about 1,500, but actually there were no more than three or four hundred, just enough to keep Putnam wondering. The three British warships and several troop transports anchored in Peekskill Bay did little to allay his fears. When he went down to the shore of the bay to investigate, however, and heard the noise of battle from across the river, he sent 500 men to reinforce the forts. The men intended to cross the river on one of two American frigates north of the log boom, but by the time they got there they were cut off from the forts and were forced to remain on board, helpless witnesses to what happened next.

By five in the afternoon, three British galleys and several smaller vessels had fought their way upstream against the tide to a position off the mouth of Popolopen Creek and opened fire on the forts and the flotilla on the other side of the chain. The forts and the boats replied, and the artillery exchange grew into a mutual bombardment.

About this time Campbell approached Fort Montgomery under a white flag and met with Lieutenant Colonel William S. Livingston, acting for Governor Clinton. Campbell suggested that the fort surrender within five minutes or face further bloodshed. Livingston assured Campbell that the defenders had no thought of surrendering, but that if the attackers surrendered, they could expect to be treated well.

A few minutes after this exchange, the British attacked in full force and Campbell was killed. This time, however, the attackers swept up to and over the exhausted defenders and the fighting continued inside Montgomery. In the meantime the attack was pressed hard against Fort Clinton, where the British were having a more difficult time. Fort Clinton, though smaller than Montgomery, was surrounded by rougher terrain and was more strongly built. Many of the officers on the British side went down before its walls, including Count Grabouski, a Polish nobleman who was Sir Henry's A.D.C. The outcome, however, was never in doubt, and within a few minutes after Montgomery fell, Clinton followed suit.

By this time night was falling quickly and the scene was rapidly becoming obscured. Taking advantage of the fading light, many of the defenders managed to hack their way out and get lost in the surrounding forest and ravines. A witness to the battle says that the garrison of Fort Clinton continued to fight in good order as it retreated across the parade ground, the open area directly in front of you, before firing one last volley and throwing down its arms.

Governor George Clinton escaped and got across the river in a boat. James Clinton, wounded in one leg by a bayonet, got away too and lived to father DeWitt Clinton, the builder of the Erie Canal. A number of other officers also got clear, but 263 Americans, including 26 commissioned officers, were captured. Accounts of British losses vary from 41 killed and 142 wounded, to 300 killed and wounded. Sir Henry himself narrowly escaped being killed by grapeshot. One source says the British carried Fort Montgomery with few losses and that most of the garrison got away. Most accounts agree, however, that American losses were high. Out of the more than 600 militiamen and Continental soldiers serving in both forts, 250 were killed, wounded, and reported missing.

By this time the American flotilla was trying to escape upstream and not making much headway against the tide, which was on the ebb. One of the frigates, the *Montgomery*, drifted down toward the log boom; it and two of the galleys were set afire to prevent the British taking possession. The flames lit up the sides of Anthony's Nose, the mouth of the creek, and Bear Mountain with a fearful light, while the gorge echoed and re-echoed to the sounds of explosions as the flames reached the cannon on board. One or two final explosions eventually extinguished the flames, and the gorge was again covered by the darkness.

The second frigate, the *Congress*, went aground near Fort Constitution and was also burned. The crews of both vessels and the troops aboard all escaped.

The history museum contains several showcases filled with relics of the battle and the fort, found on and around the site. There are also several well-done dioramas of the battle and one excellent reconstruction of the gun platform that ran along the rampart paralleling the river.

A short distance from the museum, close to the west tower of the Bear Mountain Bridge, you will find several links of the *iron chain* that once stretched across the river below. British workmen cut the chain loose on October 8. The day before, October 7, Fort Clinton had been renamed Fort Vaughan by the victorious Sir Henry in honor of Major General John Vaughan, who had participated in its capture. On the same day Fort Constitution was abandoned by its defenders when a flag of truce was sent upstream accompanied by a demand of surrender. The garrison responded by firing on the flag and left. By October 15, Sir Henry had decided it would take too many men to defend Fort Montgomery and ordered it destroyed.

Leaving Bear Mountain, drive a short distance north on 9W to a traffic circle, then continue on 9W north in the direction of West Point. Just beyond the traffic circle, the road passes over a viaduct that bridges **Popolopen Gorge.** You can park your car at the side of the road on either side of the viaduct (or walk there from the Inn in the park) for a look up the gorge. Though private homes show through the trees here and there, this is still a wild, rough place that well deserves its name, the Hell Hole. Up at the head of the gorge is Torne Hill, where Captain Fenno served his gun so well before the British moved past him and down the gorge toward the fort.

The site of **Fort Montgomery** lies somewhere north of the viaduct, and it covers an extensive piece of land—the original site measured about 1,300 by 800 feet—that actually extends both right and left of 9W. Archaeological work began here some years ago and was completed shortly before this writing, after twelve or thirteen structures had been located and the foundations and other remains of seven of them were exposed. With the permission of the archaeologist in charge, I toured the site, breaking through heavy summer underbrush to find piles of rubble, walls, the remains of a "necessary," the fort's northern redoubt, and a gun battery overlooking the Hudson, as well as the foundation walls of barracks' buildings and the fort's magazine. All that was left of the necessary, besides an accompanying pile of rock and brick, was a rectangular pit about eight feet deep lined with stone—an example of a colonial cesspool. The brick carefully heaped up at some sites suggests that certain structures inside the fort were sizeable.

The New York State Historic Trust and Preservation people intend to stabilize the ruins just as they are so that visitors to the site, following a self-guiding walking tour path, can see the remains as the archaeologists found them, including what is left of the Grand Battery on the river. Open-sided sheds will probably be built to protect the sites from the weather, and interpretative signs and illustrations will be posted everywhere to give the visitor a vivid picture of the fort and the life within it. At the time of my visit, all of this was projected for the future, hopefully in time for the bicentennial of the fort's capture. Until then I am honor bound not to reveal the location of the site in the interest of protecting it from vandalism and over-enthusiastic would-be archaeologists. Unguided attempts to find these remains would be most unwise. The remains are well guarded by thickets of brambles, thorny berry bushes and, at certain times of the year, copperheads. Everywhere there are unexpected piles of rock underfoot ready to twist an ankle, stretch a tendon, or break a bone. Here and there, usually concealed by underbrush, are old wells without covers and several deep pits or caves lined with mossy smooth, slippery rock formations that drop suddenly into deep pools of slime-covered water.

In the later years of the war, the Fort Montgomery site became a campground for American troops. General Anthony Wayne paused here to rest and catch up with his correspondence both before and after the capture of Stony Point. In August, 1779, Colonel Rufus Putnam built a small moon-shaped battery along the line of the old fort. Some of the remains on the site are of this redoubt. The garrison at West Point, after its establishment in 1778, used the site as an advanced observation post from which any British move in the direction of the West Point forts could be detected well in advance of an attack.

Before leaving these sites, I suggest you treat yourself to a bird's-eye view of this part of Sir Henry Clinton's campaign by driving or hiking to the top of **Bear Mountain.** The road to the top, called Perkin's Drive, begins at a traffic circle inside the park grounds immediately south of the parking lot and athletic field. Signs along the way indicate you are traveling west toward a junction with the Palisades Interstate Parkway and Route 6. When you reach a point about a third of the way up, however, where the road begins to descend to the western foot of the mountain, you will see another road leading off to the right, marked by a small booth and a gate which bars the road to automobile traffic during the winter. In the summer a parking fee of $0.25 gives you admission to the summit.

Markers along the summit road indicate various features below, and one such marker is at an overlook, a hundred feet or so from the summit, above Popolopen Gorge. The best view, however, is from a stone tower with an enclosed observation deck on the top. The view from the base of the tower is quite satisfactory, if you would rather not climb the winding flight of steps inside. A number of coin-operated telescopes with directions attached for locating various landmarks are also available.

The view is magnificent. Below you the Hudson River stretches to the north and south. Immediately to the south the nearest mountain is the Dunderberg, where you can make out the Timp through which Campbell led Clinton's advance party. Peekskill Bay is at its eastern foot. South of that, the bulge of land jutting out into the river is Stony Point; the waters just to its north, where a line of World War II Victory ships is moored (part of the famous Hudson River Mothball Fleet), is where Clinton landed his troops. On the opposite side of the river is Verplanck's Point, marked by a cluster of white oil-storage tanks. Below you to the north is Popolopen Gorge and the creek clearly marked by a railroad bridge stretched across its mouth. From this height the ruins of Fort Montgomery are not evident, but the site of the fort and its approaches are completely exposed to your view. Most of the gorge is clearly visible as is Torne Hill at the top. The iron chain and the boom were anchored on this side of the river at a point a short distance north of the mouth of the creek. Bear Mountain Bridge, linking the two sides of the river, ends at Anthony's Nose on the east side.

To the north the Hudson Highlands stretch to the horizon where a bend of the river hides West Point and Constitution Island which we will soon visit. Northward along the eastern bank, hidden among the hills, are several of the sites connected with the Arnold–André affair which we'll also see. The conical hill so prominent on that side of the river is Sugarloaf, whose slopes once sported rebel gun batteries.

You get a better view to the west from the top of the tower, a panorama of wooded, rolling hills which hide the remains of some of the foundries and mines that supplied the rebel armies in the area with armaments. The hills, which also hide a number of very lovely lakes, are part of Harriman State Park. The roads through this area are well paved and well marked and take you to excellent fishing and swimming facilities within a few minutes of Bear Mountain.

All around, the heartland of the Revolution is spread out before you like a relief map, the most precise, most realistic relief map possible. There is an excellent picnic area on the summit, with tables and benches, water fountains, a parking area around the southern brow of the hill, and individual parking spaces close to many of the picnic tables. Food and drinks for the troops, however, will have to be transported from the park area below.

There are other picnic areas in the vicinity of the Inn as well as a snack counter and a restaurant with an outdoor terrace overlooking Hessian Lake in the Inn itself. The Inn is open year-round and the great, rustic building has cavernous lounges with enormous fireplaces and comfortable log furniture. The recreational facilities include a public swimming pool, saddle horses, baseball and football fields, outdoor ice-skating rink, sledding slopes, and a ski run, where eastern seaboard jumping competitions are held every January. You may want to make Bear Mountain your headquarters while you follow the American Revolution up and down the Hudson Valley.

After the forts fell, Governor Clinton made his way to General Putnam's headquarters for a council of war. The next day Putnam's army withdrew up the valley to a position across the Albany Post Road a few miles south of the village of Fishkill.

On October 11 four British ships sailed north to breach the chevaux-de-frise at Kingston and reconnoitered as far as Poughkeepsie without meeting any resistance. Four days later on Wednesday, October 15, a fleet of thirty-odd ships, carrying about 1,600 troops under the command of Major General Vaughan, sailed north in what was described as an attempt to assist Burgoyne by creating a diversion. This was the move Burgoyne received advance word of, which very nearly made him withdraw from the surrender agreement.

On the evening of October 15, the fleet spent the night six miles below Kingston. You can reach Kingston in much less time by driving north from Fort Montgomery along 9W, over Storm King Mountain with its wonderful overlook, and on to Newburgh. At Newburgh you have a choice: you can continue along 9W to Kingston; or, take Interstate

84 west to the New York State Thruway, then the thruway for half an hour or so to the Kingston exit. The 9W route goes through all the towns in between and is a more interesting road to travel, but the thruway is faster.

On the morning of October 16, the British went ashore at Kingston, then called Esopus, attacked two American gun positions near the landing, and proceeded to burn the town because it was considered a hotbed of revolutionary sentiment. The British had good reason to feel about Esopus as they did, for it was the legislative captial of the newly declared sovereign state of New York. Governor George Clinton had hurried to Fort Montgomery just a few days before from Kingston, where he had been attending a session of the New York State Assembly in the Senate House, now a Kingston landmark.

Coming off the thruway at Exit 19, take Interstate 587 east a short distance to Albany Avenue; make a right onto Albany Avenue and take it to Clinton Avenue. The **Senate House** lies on the left side of Clinton Avenue where it meets North Front Street. Originally this was the home of Colonel Wessel Ten Broeck who built it in 1676 when Esopus was a pioneer settlement surrounded by a wooden stockade. The Senate House faces the crest of a hill along which the stockade ran. During the British raid of 1777, the Senate House was partially destroyed. The walls now standing are all that was left of the first building. The period furnishings are not original to the house. To the right as you enter, in the dining room, is a painting attributed to Benjamin West, *The Death of Count Pulaski,* memorializing a Polish volunteer who died in a cavalry charge at Savannah, Georgia. There is a small museum behind the house opposite a very pretty period garden. Admission to the Senate House is free. It is open weekdays from 9 A.M. to 5 P.M. and Sundays from 1 P.M. to 5 P.M.

To one side of the Senate House is a convenient municipal parking lot where you can leave your car if you want to spend an hour or so walking around this charming, old river-town, finding some of the other landmarks. For example, walk back up Clinton Avenue in the direction from which you came and turn right at the first intersection to Fair Street, then left onto Fair Street for several blocks to Maiden Lane. There on the left side of the intersection, a marker identifies the **Elmendorf Tavern** where the state committee of safety met in 1777. The tavern is at present the office and residence of a physician and was not open to the public at the time of my visit. A fine old fieldstone structure with the old shutters still in place, it is obviously well cared for. A number of maps and pamphlets available at the Senate House direct you to other interesting old houses in and around Kingston and will also help you

mark the perimeter of the seventeenth-century stockade that once protected the town from its unfriendly Indian neighbors.

After doing as much damage as possible in Esopus, Vaughan continued to dawdle along the Hudson for another day or two until word
came that Burgoyne had surrendered and gone into captivity. Then Sir
Henry received instructions from Sir William Howe to send 4,500 reinforcements to Philadelphia, which pretty well put a crimp into any idea
he might have had about proceeding north. On October 26 Fort Montgomery and the bridge across Popolopen Creek were burned by Clinton's
rear guard as his troops and ships slowly withdrew to New York City.
A day or two later, the last of the British ships dropped anchor in New
York Harbor and Clinton's Hudson campaign was over.

As a campaign it had been highly successful. The Hudson forts had
been captured; the river chain removed; the American river flotilla destroyed; sixty-seven pieces of American artillery captured, along with
large quantities of shot, ammunition, and powder. Great stores of supplies
had been destroyed; the countryside along the river had been left in a
shambles; and, out of three hundred homes in Esopus, only one was left
standing. In just twenty days, Clinton had laid waste all the rebels had
worked so hard to achieve in more than two years. His strategy had been
brilliantly planned and flawlessly carried out at the cost of only a handful
of casualties. And even though he had not helped Burgoyne out of his
predicament, his approach up the Hudson made Gates so nervous that he
was willing to accept a "convention" rather than the usual surrender.

Leave Kingston via the Kingston–Rhinecliff Bridge for the east side
of the Hudson on your way to the high-water mark of the Clinton cam-
paign. On the east side take Route 9G north, then turn east on County
Road 6 to the entrance to **Clermont Park,** which is maintained by the
Taconic State Park Commission and is located on the grounds of the
Robert R. Livingston estate.

This is one of the most beautiful sites along your route through
history, perhaps the most beautiful. The grounds extend just a few feet
above the Hudson River. The view across the river is of the low-lying
hills on the western bank with the Catskill Mountains spread out behind
them as a backdrop. There is a long parking lot and, just beyond a rise
of ground, a line of picnic tables overlooking the river, many of them
shaded by big, old trees. There are also comfort stations, drinking fountains, and charcoal burners.

The house is surrounded by spacious lawns bordered by flower beds, with a separate lawn set off by a hedge, which encloses some statuary. The house and the grounds are a 13,000-acre section, called Clermont, of a larger 160,000-acre estate, which had been assembled by the first Robert Livingston during the late 1600s when the region was predominately Dutch. His grandson, Robert R. Livingston, was a delegate to the Continental Congress in 1776 and a member of the committee appointed to draft the Declaration of Independence, which he did not sign, being absent from Philadelphia at the time of the signing.

Robert R. built a house called Belvedere on this site, where Governor George Clinton and his wife came to confer with him concerning the defense of the Hudson Highlands. Vaughan sailed his ships up to this point after burning Kingston and anchored in the waters immediately south of the house. His men came ashore and burned Belvedere, but Robert II's mother, who also made her home in Belvedere, began to rebuild as soon as Vaughan had left. The British were then just forty-six miles south of Albany. At several places on the grounds are the remains of the basements of ruined buildings, some of which may be restored by the time of the bicentennial. The house itself was gutted, but the outside walls were left standing, making Mrs. Livingston's job a little easier. During the reconstruction General and Mrs. Washington came to visit and were entertained in the basement, where furnished apartments and cooking facilities had been set up.

Clermont is open daily to the public from mid-April to mid-November from 9 A.M. to 5 P.M. Guided tours take groups of ten visitors at a time through the house. I found it time well spent. The furnishings will intrigue any lover of antiques, and the walls are hung with some exceedingly valuable paintings, including a Gilbert Stuart and a portrait of General Richard Montgomery, who was married to Janet Livingston, Robert R.'s daughter. Since Richard was absent at the time, the portrait was posed for by his sister wearing one of his uniforms. Robert R. Livingston, as United States minister to France, negotiated the Louisiana Purchase, which more than doubled the land area of the young nation. He also helped finance Robert Fulton's first steamboat, which was named, appropriately enough, the *Clermont* and which sailed up the river as far as Clermont on her maiden voyage.

I heartily recommend that when you do the Clinton campaign you plan to stop for an outdoor lunch or dinner at Clermont. It is the perfect spot to reach after a long day's walking and climbing and driving, with its tree-shaded lawns and gardens and river views so well designed to rest the eyes and relax the mind.

WEST POINT

Having taken your rest, retrace your route across the Kingston–Rhinecliff Bridge, return to the New York State Thruway and go south as far as Newburgh. Leaving the thruway at Exit 17, take Route 17K east to 9W, then continue south along 9W to the south side of Storm King Mountain. A few miles or so farther, take a left turn onto Route 218 which will take you into the town of Highland Falls and up to Thayer Gate, the south entrance to the West Point Military Reservation.

A mile or so farther north along 9W, a new entrance to the reservation has been built; it is marked by signs for 218, Highland Falls, and West Point. If you use this entrance, turn off 9W at that exit and continue straight ahead to a point below Fort Putnam and behind and above Michie Stadium. Several large parking fields were being paved there at the time of this writing.

Before you begin your Revolutionary War tour of West Point, you should go up to **Fort Putnam**, the highest available point overlooking the reservation, for a bird's-eye view of it, the river, Constitution Island, and the surrounding country, all of which constituted a vital strategic whole during the Revolution. If you are at Thayer Gate, follow 218 up to and through it. The military police at the booth will automatically wave you on, unless there is a traffic tie-up (which occurs when the West Point football team plays in the home stadium). The reservation is also a national monument and park, open to the public at all times of the year, even after dark. Detailed maps of the reservation are available for the asking at the M.P. booth.

Once inside the gate, follow Thayer Road, named for Sylvanus Thayer, the United States Military Academy's founding and guiding spirit. The Hotel Thayer is on your right—it accommodates anyone who cares to sign the register—and the post-detachment athletic field and parade ground are on your left. At the first intersection, which comes up shortly, turn left onto Mills Road and drive up the side of a hill until you come to Lusk Reservoir on your right and Michie Stadium on your left. A short distance north of the stadium and around a curve you will see on your left an unpaved road which leads up to Fort Putnam. It usually has a chain stretched across it to prevent cars from using it.

From then on you must go on foot. There is very little parking in that area. In fact, parking on the whole at the Point is difficult. One way of avoiding this is to take one of the tour buses that leave from Highland

Falls at stated times, but that ties you to the bus schedule, which you may find restricting. The road in front of the stadium widens into an extensive apron where you might park if the stadium is not in use. You may be forced to find parking down below in the large parking field across Thayer Road from the parade ground, or in the Fort Clinton area, or at any one of a number of oddly-placed spots about the post.

The parking field opposite the parade ground is large and accommodates several hundred cars, but there are a surprising number of civilians working on the post or at the academy, and their cars plus the cars belonging to military personnel, plus the cars belonging to the usual sightseers, often fill it to capacity. You may have better luck after lunch or late in the morning when some civilian workers and military personnel finish tours of duty and leave.

This can all mean quite a hike to Fort Put, but it is definitely the place to get to before you start hoofing it all over the Point. It is a stiff climb for part of the way (stay to the left); the last 200 feet or so are up an ungraded, stony path, but the location and the view are well worth it. Having attained—puffing—the fort, climb a little farther, up the stone steps to the eastern ramparts. At the highest possible point, lean against the rough, comforting stones, while you look at the Point spread out below you, the surrounding hills, the broad, majestic Hudson widening to the north with Polopel's Island in the distance, the fields and hills of Putnam County beyond, and in between the Point and the east bank—somewhat to your left—a long, wide, wooded piece of land that hardly looks like an island from where you're standing, but is actually Constitution Island.

With Sir Henry Clinton and his marauding troops safely tucked away in New York City, and a good part of them on their way to join Howe's army in Philadelphia, the rebels again began to think of ways to keep the river open and to protect the highlands. It was probably Washington who saw the answer to the problem. In December, 1777, less than two months after Clinton had knocked the highland defenses into a cocked hat, he wrote to General Putnam recommending that a strong position be built on the "west point of land" directly opposite Constitution Island, which was, itself, too vulnerable to attack from the river and from any hostile force that could place guns on the point. The point was also an ideal spot to block the river with a chain, for here the river makes two turns that are almost right angles. All vessels sailing in either direction had to lose way and come about in order to negotiate each turn. A British square-rigged warship, attempting the maneuver, would be brought directly under batteries placed on the heights, with sails slack and the ship not firmly under control, and then onto the chain.

At the time, Putnam's Continentals and militia and the Corps of Invalids (veterans who, because of wounds and other disabling factors, could perform only limited service) were encamped around the town of Fishkill just across the river. On Tuesday, January 20, 1778, a detachment of men from a Massachusetts brigade crossed the frozen river and climbed the rocky slopes on the west bank to a plateau covered with scrub pine. That area is now below you, and now encompasses the parade ground known as the Plain, several athletic fields, the academy's academic buildings, and officers' and professors' quarters. In 1778 it was privately-owned land, held under royal patent by a Captain Charles Congreve. Naturally, the royal patent was a worthless document as far as the men from Massachusetts were concerned, and they had no compunctions about cutting down some of the trees to make themselves shelters, before starting to build fortifications on the edge of the cliffs overlooking the river.

At first the work was under the direction of a Frenchman, Lieutenant Colonel Louis Dashax de la Radière, who by March gave up the job because of various difficulties. The work was then taken over by Thaddeus Kosciuszko who had fortified Bemis Heights for Gates and was now a full colonel at the direction of Congress. During the following twenty-eight months, Kosciuszko planned and supervised the construction of a number of forts, gun-emplacements, and garrison buildings, turning the once desolate plateau and surrounding hills into a formidable position, called by Washington the "key to America," which, in the opinion of some historians, neutralized Sir Henry Clinton's position in New York City.

The West Point defenses included Fort Arnold at the eastern edge (it was renamed Fort Clinton after Arnold's defection); Sherburne's Redoubt supporting Fort Clinton; Fort Putnam where you are now standing, which was named for Colonel Rufus Putnam who commanded the Massachusetts regiment that built it; three redoubts, named Webb, Wyllis, and Meigs for their commanders under Putnam and covering the southern approaches to the point; four additional redoubts on the hills behind you; and, along the shoreline overlooking the channel between the Point and Constitution Island and facing upriver from what is now Trophy Point, a number of gun batteries.

The Marquis de Chastellux, who came to America with Rochambeau and kept a diary of his travels, visited West Point in November, 1780, coming across the river from Fishkill via a dock located somewhere between Beacon and Garrison. His impression of West Point was that of a ring of forts perched on the heights forming an amphitheater, all protecting each other. In addition there were a number of fortifications and gun positions built on Constitution Island, which we shall tour when we have finished with West Point, as well as two redoubts, the Northern and Southern redoubts, located on the east side of the river at sites near the modern town of Garrison.

The ramparts of these forts were at first made of earth and logs, which proved to be a fire hazard, especially during the winter months when the Point was lashed by winds blowing along the river corridor between the hills. A Major Bauman, writing from the Point during that period, tells of fires, fanned by the wind, eating away at the outer fortifications. Eventually the wooden ramparts were replaced by stone, as you can see by the stone walls around you.

Winter duty at the Point during the Revolution was not welcomed by the Continental soldiers who had to serve here. Available housing consisted of log huts chinked against the wind, like the hutments at Valley Forge. Fuel was in plentiful supply in the surrounding woods, but had to be chopped with bare, freezing hands. Clothing was, as usual, in short supply, and so was the food. The men on garrison duty in these redoubts had their own name for the place—Purgatory Point.

From Fort Putnam you get an excellent perspective of West Point's strategic value, which was increased by the iron chain and log boom stretched across the river between the Point and Constitution Island. Most of Fort Putnam has been reconstructed out of the original stones, which were allowed to tumble from position and lie where they fell. The West Point archives and other sources have pictures of the ruins of Fort Putnam showing civilians and cadets lounging about or enjoying picnics with their female friends during the nineteenth century, for the ruined fort with its arched powder magazines was a romantic spot to visit. Even today, during the summer months, it is not unusual to find several cadets sprawled out on the grassy ramparts sunbathing. Children have a ball climbing all over the place.

Fort Putnam has undergone some changes since it was first built in 1778. The reconstruction was undertaken early in this century without sufficient research. Its present reconstructed appearance leaves much to be desired in historical accuracy.

Unlike Fort Clinton and the river redoubts, Putnam was probably not originally built of earth walls and logs, since it was thought of as a last-ditch position. It protected Fort Clinton below from land attack from the west and south. If the British had advanced upriver along the west bank, first coming north by ship and then landing at the site of Fort

Montgomery for an overland attack, they would have come along the ridgeline extending from north to south, which was protected by Redoubts Wyllis, Webb, and Meigs. It was understood among the American commanders that the British were entirely capable of launching such an attack. Had they been successful in taking Webb and Wyllis and the redoubts to the west, Putnam would have been under orders to hold out at any cost. If Putnam fell, the Plain below would have been lost and the rest of the garrison hemmed in against the river.

Fortunately, such an attack was never mounted and the Point never heard a shot fired in anger, but its forts were supposed to be in a constant state of preparation for such a possibility. Putnam's stone walls, or scarp as they are known in military parlance, were surmounted by a parapet made of fascines—wickerwork baskets filled with earth and bound together to form a continuous wall capable of absorbing the shock of shells and cannonballs. The garrison took shelter behind the fascines rather than the rock scarp, because earth was a much better defense against the solid projectiles of the time; rock was likely to shatter under the impact and fill the air with flying fragments as deadly as shrapnel.

The lists of ordnance for Fort Putnam called for sixteen guns, but there were only fourteeen pieces that could be used; two guns were unmounted and could not be fired. The fourteen pieces consisted of one fourpounder of iron, another of brass, four three-and-a-half-pounders of brass, one six-pounder of iron, one twelve-pounder of iron, five eighteenpounders of iron and one nine-pounder of iron. All these were mounted either on naval gun mounts made of wood or on field artillery mounts with wheels on either side. For the most part, their muzzles pointed west and south in the direction from which the British could be expected.

According to sources contemporary to the time, about 150 men manned Fort Putnam and were housed in either one or two barracks buildings. A diagram of the fort, drawn by Lieutenant Seth Eastman in about 1837, shows the remains of a building foundation wall somewhere inside the northern walls. The chambers hollowed out into the rock below the level of the walls, by the way, had curved arches, not the flat arches you see now.

You can make an almost complete circuit of the ramparts of Fort Putnam looking down all around you at the steep approaches, or across the ravines and ridges to the west and south. The walls are pierced by gun openings at regular intervals and one or two old cannon are placed in realistic positions. Most of the powder magazines and storerooms have iron bars placed across their entrances to prevent accidents.

Some of these rooms have fireplaces, suggesting they were either where the garrison kept warm or where they heated hot shot. One of the rooms can be entered; it's a large, empty cave of a place with a dirt floor. The entrance to this fort is through two curtain walls built several feet apart to form a passage covered from possible enemy fire. Once inside, you are on a lower level from which steps cut into the stone lead up to the ramparts.

Back at the eastern ramparts again, notice as you look out across the Plain at the cliffside overlooking the river a parking area bounded on the east and north by raised mounds of earth, which may look somewhat foreshortened in height from this elevation. These are the remains of Fort Clinton, the next site to visit.

The redoubts that covered the approaches to Fort Putnam were on the lower hills surrounding the hill you are on. Most of their sites are so covered by trees and underbrush that it is difficult to find remains, if there are any. An aerial photo I have seen did reveal the outlines of what is believed to have been Webb Redoubt, somewhere to the south and east of Putnam.

None of the garrison buildings built here during the Revolutionary War still exist. They were demolished, either by fire or by the wrecker's crowbar, as the academy grew and expanded after its founding in 1802. There are several paintings of the Point, however, showing it at various times during its first fifty years before all the original buildings disappeared. Some of these pictures are in the few published histories of the Point; a few are in the West Point Museum. The best of them may be found at either the New-York Historical Society Library in New York City, or adorning the walls of the Officers' Mess at West Point; they are by a modern artist, Walter S. Sturgill, who attempted, on the basis of his own extensive research, to reconstruct the Point in paintings as it appeared from the Revolutionary War years through the following century. Among the buildings Sturgill shows in one of his early views is a blockhouse which may have stood overlooking the river south of Fort Clinton.

As you look out over the Point now, it takes a conscious effort of the viewer's imagination to see it as it was when Continental soldiers mounted regular guard duty on the forts' walls and stood to the guns along the river, when General Washington made frequent visits and tours of inspection as he traveled back and forth between his headquarters in Newport or Fishkill and New Jersey and Pennsylvania. You would have to erase all the buildings you see now: the flagpole and victory statue at Trophy Point, the well-tended parade ground, the athletic fields with their tiers of benches, the parked cars, the numerous houses and estates showing through the trees on the eastern bank of the river, and the steam- and diesel-powered river traffic. Instead, picture a wide, bare area whose most prominent feature, a long, wooden barracks known appropriately enough as the Long Barracks, is located almost in the center of the Plain. There is a smaller wooden structure to the east of the Long Barracks and beyond it, overlooking the river, Fort Clinton. Directly below Fort Putnam stands a row of small, frame buildings in which the officers lived. You might not have been able to see them from here; the slope of ground below probably cut them off from view. Off to the left you might have seen a row of tents and log cabins which sheltered most of the enlisted personnel. Off to the edge of the plateau, Fort Clinton's log and earth walls are pierced by gunports between which the sentries pace back and forth, their muskets held upright between arms folded across chests, eighteenth-century fashion. To the right through a densely wooded area a single road leads to the south. Below you on the hilltops, the smaller redoubts are clearly visible with their guns jutting out toward the river. Below you and somewhat to the left, where the present superintendent's and commandant's houses now stand, one or two frame buildings with peaked roofs and brick chimneys are the on-post headquarters of the fort's commanders. Off to the right, north of Trophy Point where the ground drops off, is Yankeetown, so called because the enlisted men live there in log huts. Constitution Island is fringed on the river side by a number of small, stone and log forts and gun batteries. (One period drawing shows it from a river-level angle with what look like crenelated battlements against the sky.) Off to the right, across the river where a cluster of houses close to the water mark the river hamlet of Garrison Landing, is a landing and a path leading up from it that disappears among the trees. The path leads to two comfortable homes where West Point commandants live off-post. If you see in your mind's eye a small boat tied up at the landing with a couple of fellows in Continental blues lounging in or around it, you will know the commandant is taking his ease; that would be the barge that carries him across the river to and from the Point. Looking north up the river, you see the sails of the wide-beamed Hudson River sloops and the smaller sails of shallops flitting from bank to bank. Beyond the spires of the churches of ruined Esopus show past Polopel's Island.

Come back down from old Fort Put and continue along Mills Road in the direction you were traveling when you reached the stadium and the reservoir. Mills Road follows the slope down to an intersection with Washington Road. To your left Washington Road leads to the old cadet chapel and the cemetery, two sites you might want to visit. The walls of the chapel are decorated with black marble plaques bearing in gold letters the names of all the generals who commanded the Revolutionary Army. One plaque, however, bears only the words "Major General" and gives a birth date. The name and date of death are missing—Benedict Arnold, June, 1801. In the cemetery you will find the graves of soldiers and civilians whose names filled the history books you read in school.

Turn right onto Washington Road to Trophy Point, which you will know by the victory monument on its tall pillar. Then follow the signs around a traffic circle and onto Thayer Road, heading back toward the academic buildings with the parade ground on your right and the athletic fields on your left. About midway along the parade ground you will see a road leading off to your left to the large parking field. Turn onto this road and follow it past the parking field, along a narrower road until it turns to the left and enters another large parking area. To your right the ground seems to slope up into a long, low rise. That slope and rise are the remains of the ramparts of **Fort Clinton.** You can climb up onto them and walk along the top, looking down onto the river below, examining the old guns laid out in rows, and looking for those Burgoyne surrendered at Saratoga.

Fort Clinton, originally Fort Arnold, covered a fairly wide area, according to drawings of the time, particularly those of a French officer named Villefranche who replaced Kosciuszko. Kosciuszko could not get on with Benedict Arnold when he commanded the post and asked to be transferred to the staff of General Gates, Arnold's archenemy. Villefranche's map of the Point shows Fort Clinton with four triangular bastions reminiscent of the bastions of Forts Ticonderoga and Stanwix. The present ramparts have been graded and grassed. The old fort towered up above the cliff's edge, probably with a line of fascines forming a parapet along the stone scarp. A log palisade extended around the perimeter of the fort, presenting another obstacle to any attacking force. Inside the fort's perimeter a number of barracks buildings and bombproofs (shelters from exploding projectiles) protected its garrison. Below the cliff, on a flat piece of ground about halfway down to the river, a water battery added its fire power to the fort above.

Now turn your back to the river, face the parked cars below and the athletic field beyond, and look down into what was the interior of Fort Clinton. If you walk back to the south end of the rampart where it slopes down gradually, you will find a one-way road leading around its foot. A plaque set into the stone outerworks identifies the site. Walk along the perimeter of the old fort with its walls towering above you on the left and continue to follow the road until it brings you to **Trophy Point,** with its Civil War monument. You will pause here, whether you plan to or not, and stand for a moment looking upriver at one of the most photographed, most painted of all American views. For a few miles north the river flows through its highland. Constitution Island is now to your right front.

Before you leave Trophy Point, find the links of the great *iron chain* that extended from a cove close by to Constitution Island. The chain was forged at the Sterling Iron Works about twenty-five miles west of the Point. Each link was about twelve inches wide, eighteen inches long, and was made of bar iron about two inches square. The largest links weighed 130 pounds, the smallest from 98 to 109 pounds, and the entire chain, about 186 tons. It was attached by huge staples to pointed timbers that buoyed it up so it was just below the surface of the water. The ends were fixed to two large cribbage blocks, one on each side of the river, and every winter the entire contraption was windlassed back to the Point to prevent its breaking under the pressure of the huge cakes of ice that moved up and down the river with the tides. It was placed in position by Captain Thomas Machin, an artillery officer and a veteran of Bunker Hill and Fort Montgomery.

Follow a path to the right down from Trophy Point or the road to the left that goes down to the river in a gradual descent. At the river is a landing near an open area on the riverbank and a number of warehouses. Walk out onto the pier and look upstream, following with your eye the shoreline on the left. The highland falls off into a valley, called Washington Valley, with Storm King Mountain towering over it. You can see a number of buildings and roads, including a very large building near the water, the athletic fieldhouse. Somewhere in that area Washington used to pitch his tent; he preferred sleeping under canvas close to the river to sleeping in the bed that was always ready for him in the post-headquarters building. You can drive or walk to the valley in a few minutes from where you are now, but there is nothing there to mark the actual site of the tent. Directly across the river from this landing is Constitution Island, and if you look closely you can spot a stone redoubt at its northern end.

Turning to your left, walk past a boathouse to a curved, fieldstone arch bearing plaques on either side to the memory of two cadets. The footpath which led to the chain battery and the gun positions along the river begins here. The path is now incorporated in the famous Flirtation

Walk along which the cadets take their sweethearts when they are in a romantic mood. According to signs along this path and others, visitors are not permitted unless accompanied by a cadet. Unless some provision is made for tours or limited, controlled access, you may have to skip this part of the West Point story. If, however, you manage to come armed with some type of dispensation, or a cadet, the following sites are what you can expect to find. (There is another way to get to Kosciuszko's Garden at the end of the path, which I will describe at the site.) The walk along this river path is a pleasant, tree-shaded hike, with some gentle ups and downs and some not so gentle ones. The river is a few feet below you, the woody shores of Constitution Island are visible across the narrow channel, and since few of the sightseers who visit the Point come down here, the peace and quiet is broken only by an occasional train rushing by behind Constitution Island or the rasp of a motorboat.

Along the way you will pass inscriptions cut into the rocks commemorating battles of the Mexican War. One that is high up on a cliff and difficult to find commemorates the Battle of Yorktown. Then comes Gee's Point with its electronically-controlled lighthouse, and then, facing the river, a marble bench with a flight of stone steps leading up to it, called the Sheridan Memorial. The sites you particularly want to see are those marking the chain and water batteries. You come first to the *chain battery* a short distance past Kissing Rock, a large rock which protrudes over the path. It is identified by a plaque fastened to the rock wall on the right side. As you pass the plaque, the path curves to follow the curve of the cove in which the chain was fastened. At the midpoint of the chain battery is an earthern parapet; a wide, cleared area behind it marks the spot where a small unit armed with muskets covered the chain anchor. The words "chain battery" are cut into one of the stones. Passing the lighthouse and the Mexican War rock carvings, you will come to a rock inscription on higher ground which marks the site of a *water battery,* where guns were placed to cover the channel.

Toward the end of this twenty- or thirty-minute walk, the path climbs somewhat steeply, leading you along the foot of a cement retaining wall, then finally onto a small, flagstoned terrace with a spring bubbling up in a stone basin at one end, flower beds and ornamental bushes and trees all around, a sheer, rock wall to one side, and a flight of steps leading up to a higher terrace, where the spring gushes from a pipe into a stone basin inside a brick springhouse. Iron benches on the terraces invite you to sit a while to enjoy the peace and sunshine, just as Kosciuszko did two hundred years ago; for this is *Kosciuszko's Garden,* a private retreat he built for himself, where he loved to come to read and contemplate during the long months he spent building the fortifications. In his day there were no buildings beetling overhead or neatly paved terraces. Everywhere was the native rock, and the steps were set into the natural slope of the ground. According to photographs, as recently as 1950 the rock garden did not exist, and the whole area presented a much more natural appearance, with fern and wild, flowering plants overrunning it. It was much more the secluded spot Kosciuszko knew and much more a part of the surrounding terrain. Now, however, on the river side an ugly steel catwalk, only partially hidden by a row of hemlock, leads to tennis courts directly below at the water's edge, while overhead the very contemporary bowed window of the Officers' Club intrudes against the sky. Under the circumstances, perhaps the best possible answer was this more formal, carefully tended arrangement.

If you cannot get to the garden along the river path, turn right from the West Point Museum and walk along the road on top of the palisades above the river. On your right you will pass the Officers' Club and Cullum Hall. As you face Cullum Hall, notice a cement sidewalk along the right side of the building. Walk along it and down three flights of steps onto a paved terrace, a parking area. Turn left and keep to the right side of the parking area as you walk behind Cullum Hall, so that you do not miss the narrow, steep steps leading down from the terrace. They lead to more steps that take you to Kosciuszko's Garden.

Eating and refreshment facilities at the Point are limited for the general public. Only officers and their guests are allowed to eat in the Officers' Club, but the Hotel Thayer's dining room is open daily. I have also seen a mobile hot dog stand take up a position near Trophy Point and successfully hold it. The village of Highland Falls, just outside Thayer Gate, has restaurants and lunch counters. There is a refreshment stand with rest rooms in a long, low building at the south end of the post-detachment athletic field, just at the intersection of Mills and Thayer roads where you turned left to go to Fort Putnam. There is also a snack bar in the building at the far or north end of this athletic field. This is a long way off, however, if you find yourself at lunchtime at Trophy Point at the opposite end of the reservation, and you don't care to lose your parking spot. By and large, a visit to West Point calls for a picnic. There are no picnic facilities as such, but there are shaded, grassy areas everywhere, some close to the river, and a great lack of signs saying "No picnicking." I have seen parties of visitors dining alfresco along Fort Clinton's ramparts and at Trophy Point.

There are several public comfort stations on the reservation. One is below and north of Trophy Point to the right as you face the river. A path north of the flagpole off Washington Road leads down to it. Another is located on the right side of Thayer Road about a half mile north of the Thayer Hotel. You can find a third comfort station north of Lusk Reservoir on Mills Road. It is in a small building on the right-hand side, and it comes up a short distance after the road has taken a sharp curve to get around the north end of the reservoir.

CONSTITUTION ISLAND

The most convenient way to get to Constitution Island is from West Point. At the time of this writing, the island was reserved for the use of the cadet corps as a picnic and recreation area. The Constitution Island Association, a private organization, conducts tours of the Warner House, the only building on the island. Boats leave from the West Point dock on Wednesday afternoons only. The association requires that you write to it care of the West Point post office (Constitution Island Association, West Point, New York, will do) to make reservations; thirty or more visitors are accommodated at a time. Though the tour centers around the Warner House, you can probably get to see the fortified positions near the house. The first year these tours were conducted was 1970, however, and some more frequent schedule may have been worked out by 1976.

There is also a land route to the island from the east bank of the river. This requires you to cross the river over the Bear Mountain Bridge; then make a left onto Route 9D and follow it north for about ten miles to the village of Cold Spring. Turn left onto Main Street and follow it past the railroad station and over a bridge to the west side of the New York Central tracks. A street to your left called Market Street parallels the tracks. Drive south along Market Street as far as you can; then park and continue to follow the road alongside the tracks. After a while you will be walking along a causeway that crosses a tidal marsh and eventually comes to Constitution Island. The distance between Cold Spring and the island is about a mile.

Strictly speaking, this is not a public thoroughfare. Your presence on the island, if detected, will certainly be questioned. Constitution Island is off-limits to the general public except for the Warner House tour. The provisions of the agreement under which the island was turned over by its owners to the federal government for use by the cadets of

West Point seem to make the restriction necessary. Some way may be found, at least for the bicentennial, to relax these rules, perhaps to permit controlled guided tours.

This is one Revolutionary War site that is comparatively untouched and unspoiled. No reconstruction work has been done on any of its fortifications. The dirt ramparts and the stone walls are as the Continental soldiers left them, allowing for the gradual attrition of time and weather. This was the first highland site on which fortifications were attempted in 1775. The work was under the supervision of a congressional commission that hired Bernard Romans, an engineer, to survey the island, design the fortifications, and supervise their construction. Romans submitted his report in September, 1775, dated from "Martelaar's Rock or Martyr's Reach." In this report, interestingly enough, Romans suggested stationing a small battery on the west point opposite.

Romans's plans called for a series of batteries, blockhouses, and barracks, and work was started that same month. A great deal of money went into the project, but somehow the commissioners lost confidence both in Romans and in the site, and he and they argued over the relative values of the island and other proposed sites, some of which the commissioners believed to be superior. Romans himself suggested that the river passage at Anthony's Nose and "Pooploop's [sic] Kill" be fortified, but he went on building, or trying to build, on the island. Finally in December, 1775, a three-man investigating committee recommended to Congress that the work on Fort Constitution be abandoned and the major effort made at the Fort Montgomery site. Romans took his case to both the New York Provincial Congress and the Continental Congress, but finally in January, 1776, Congress ordered work on "Martler's [sic] Rock" brought to a halt. The timber set aside for some of the barracks was sent to the other fort sites, and Fort Constitution was garrisoned in its uncompleted state. It was entirely abandoned to the British, as you know, who removed the guns and destroyed as much as they could. The island was regarrisoned when West Point was refortified, and its defenses rebuilt and extended under Kosciuszko's supervision.

A small farm at the south end of the island, belonging to a man named Bunn, had been abandoned before it was first fortified. In the early part of the nineteenth century, the island was bought by the Warner family, and the two Warner sisters, Susan and Anna B., maintained the present house and the farm until they sold it in 1915 to the federal government to become part of the West Point reservation.

☆

If the rules are relaxed for the bicentennial, begin your tour at the landing dock on the island, the site where the east end of the West Point chain was anchored, in the cove to the left of the dock. Walk up from the dock toward the Warner House, but before you get there, at a flower garden that lines the path take a turnoff to the right leading to the first of the island's seven redoubts. The island is wooded and shady, a very pleasant prospect in warm weather if there is a breeze on the river. On a muggy summer day, however, the heat under the trees can be oppressive.

About the only work being done on the island when I was there was the clearing of paths making the redoubts easily accessible. Small army-green signs point the way. All in all, the redoubts mounted about forty-one guns, all of them on the river side of the island. You can visit every redoubt if you like; but since most are exactly alike, I concentrated on those that are unique and particularly well preserved. The path to the first redoubt, called the **Cliffside Redoubt,** mounts a gradual slope that ends at earth ramparts and stone walls. This redoubt was about thirty feet long and fifteen feet wide, and is typical of most of these sites.

The path then leads to the **Gravel Hill Redoubt,** so named because the ground on that site is very gravelly. This must have been a very extensive work, some fifty or sixty feet long. It is presently marked by two long mounds, the remains of the breastworks, with a depression between suggesting an entrenchment. Its long axis faces the river and it makes a right angle with the side of the hill on which the Cliffside Redoubt is located. Romans's original plan was to extend the Gravel Hill Redoubt up the hill until the two redoubts became one long position.

Retrace your steps to the Warner House and walk around to the rear where you will see a *stone wall,* part of the house that stands out among all the clapboard and shingling. This wall is believed to have been part of a barracks which housed some of the 400 Continental troops who were stationed here from 1778 on. According to one account, the island's first settler, Farmer Bunn, returned to the island after the war was over and claimed the federal government owed him the buildings as payment for the changes made on his property. Secretary of War Knox, so the story goes, agreed to pay him one-fifth of what he was claiming. And so this one wall was left standing.

Coming back to the front of the house, take the dirt road leading off to the right or north. It passes an open field on the right bordered by a stone wall. Picnic tables in the field testify not that you can picnic here, but that West Point cadets can and do during off-duty hours. At the far end of the field, you will notice at one side a pile of tumbled stones marking the site of one of the Continental Army buildings, possibly a storehouse. This pile of tumbled stones is only one of many you will see all over the island. They probably all mark sites where Revolutionary War buildings stood; some are the remains of soldiers' hutments. Though the island is well wooded, the number of these stone piles suggests that timber may not have been as plentiful then as it is now, causing the soldiers to use the stones which abound on the island to build walls, saving whatever wood they had for roofing.

Redoubt Six is your next stop, overlooking the river and marked by a Revolutionary War cannon which was placed there in 1925 to commemorate the 170th anniversary of the island's first fortification. The redoubt itself, also called Romans's Redoubt, is below the gun on the right. The breastwork in this position consists of earth piled up over rock. A rocky slope leads from the gun down into the redoubt's interior, which has one stone wall in very good condition fronting on the river. Behind this wall is a depression believed to be the collapsed remains of a bombproof—a stone or earthern shelter against exploding projectiles in use then, including mortar shells, which were fired from mortars with their own fuses burning, and hand grenades.

Leaving Romans's Redoubt, follow the path back to the road. At that point you will see a tangled mass of rocks, trees, vines, and shrubs off the path believed to mark the site of another barracks building. If you poke around in the rubble you may find pieces of colonial brick.

The path now goes up a steep, rocky slope for a vigorous five- or ten-minute climb to **Redoubt Seven** at the northern tip of the island. This is the most sophisticated and most complete Revolutionary War structure on the island. The walls of this small fort, which it was, are easily eight to ten feet high, almost two feet thick, made completely of fitted stone with a curtain wall to protect the entrance. There was a window in the river wall directly opposite the entrance, but the Civilian Conservation Corps walled it up for some reason in the 1930s. Perhaps you will notice after you have been in it for a while that this redoubt is oddly shaped. Some of the angles where the walls meet are not right angles but obtuse, suggesting that the builders started out to erect something very different —perhaps simply three-sided breastworks—then changed their minds and made it an enclosed, four-wall structure.

Take the path back from Redoubt Seven to the foot of the hill, but instead of continuing, go off into the woods until you find a low, three-sided stone structure with a good-sized pine tree growing in the opening. This is what remains of one of the enlisted men's *hutments*. A little farther on, you will find the stone remains of yet another hutment whose resourceful builders took advantage of a large boulder which they used as the back of their fireplace. Rocks were piled on top of each other to form the walls, and there they are, still in place, just as they were piled two hundred years ago.

There are at least fifteen to eighteen of these sites around the island that have been found and identified. They are usually off the paths under trees, hidden by undergrowth; some marked only by tumbled piles of stone; some, like the two I have described, retaining the shape of the walls.

"TREASON OF THE BLACKEST DYE . . ."

These were the words that headed General Washington's orderly book on the morning of September 24, 1780: "Treason of the Blackest Dye was yesterday discovered. . . . Gen'l Arnold who commanded at West Point lost to every sentiment of Honour of Private and Publick Obligation, was about to Deliver the important post into the hands of the enemy. . . ."

So Washington expressed his horror and shock over Benedict Arnold's treasonous plot and his despair as well, for if Arnold, the most popular hero besides himself that the Revolution had produced, in whom Washington had placed his confidence, could be bought to sell out a cause he had fought and bled for, then who could be trusted!

Washington's reaction reflected the nation's. Understanding the strategic importance of the post at that time, you can grasp the enormity of the crime within that context and realize what a profound effect it had not only on Washington, but on every highly placed military and civilian official and on the general public. The Patriots' cause had reached its lowest ebb, despite Saratoga and the French alliance. In December, 1778, Savannah had fallen to the British and a royal government had been reestablished in Georgia. In May, 1780, General Clinton had captured Charleston and forced the surrender of General Lincoln and 2,500 men, the only army the Americans had in the South. A counterattack led by Gates had ended in disaster at Camden, South Carolina, in August, 1780. The disclosure of Arnold's treachery coming after all that had the impact of a well-placed, well-timed bomb.

Arnold had always been an ambitious man. In civilian life as a merchant, he had indulged in privateering, a fancy name for smuggling and sometimes outright piracy. As a soldier he boldly and often rashly gambled for high stakes without reserves to fall back on. He was as brave as a lion, never hesitating to risk his own life—or his followers' lives, as some historians are quick to point out.

Arnold should have risen high, but his sense of loyalty and honor and his devotion to the American cause were no match for his vaulting ambition and chronic need for money. The Continental Congress did little to bolster his moral fiber: they passed him over when promotions were being handed out to men who were not as deserving, or so Arnold thought, and perhaps with good cause. Add to this his own personal misfortunes—he had lost his wife, had been left with three young sons to care for, had an indigent, maiden sister to support and a twice-wounded leg that kept him away from the fighting and a chance for further glory —and perhaps you can grasp his frame of mind when Washington appointed him military governor of Philadelphia once the British had evacuated the city in June, 1778. However, since Congress had paid him public honor in February of that same year for his part in the Saratoga campaign and had promoted him to major general, placing him highest in rank over Gates, Schuyler, Lincoln, and several other general officers, the man seems to have been motivated more by his need for money than by anything else.

As soon as he was in command in Philadelphia he set about satisfying that need, which was not abated in the least when he moved into a handsome house owned by John Penn (William Penn's grandson), formerly General Howe's quarters, took up a style of living far beyond his resources, and began playing the privateer with army supplies. Patriotic elements finally lodged charges against him in Congress. He was courtmartialed, but let off with a reprimand which Washington himself delivered in the mildest possible terms; yet Arnold was very angry because he had not been completely exonerated.

At the time, the city's populace was divided into Patriots, Loyalists, and those who professed to be neutral. Arnold, who was 37, was attracted to eighteen-year-old Peggy Shippen, one of Philadelphia's prettiest and liveliest social lights. Peggy, the daughter of a neutral, Edward Shippen, fell in love with Arnold at first sight and set her cap for him. The attraction was mutual and they were married in April, 1779. A month later, Arnold decided to sell his services to the British.

He began by contacting a Tory living in Philadelphia who put him in touch with Sir Henry Clinton, who passed the matter on to John André whom we last saw marching out of Fort St. Johns into captivity. André was now a major and Sir Henry's acting adjutant general. Using the name John Anderson, André began a correspondence with Arnold who passed along several tidbits of information, including the news that the French commander Rochambeau was approaching America with an army and the French fleet.

Over a long period of time, Arnold and Sir Henry Clinton, who had succeeded Howe as commander in chief, discussed, through André, ways in which Arnold might be useful to the crown. Peggy was in on the whole thing from the beginning. In fact, she and André had been good friends during the British occupation of Philadelphia. He had drawn her portrait. Pretending to discuss millinery, André corresponded with Arnold through Peggy, talking in his letters about the latest fashions from Paris, but actually keeping the discussion going between his chief and the traitor.

Finally Arnold saw his opportunity in newly fortified West Point, which needed a commander. He began to pressure Washington to give him the command while offering its surrender to Sir Henry for 20,000 pounds, a sum equal to thirty times as much in modern pounds or $1,440,000, according to the present rate of exchange. Sir Henry agreed to this, provided Arnold could work out a satisfactory plan and actually deliver. Furthermore, he assured Arnold that if anything went wrong, he would not be left holding the bag.

Washington was seriously considering Arnold's request for the West Point post, but he had a change of heart and on August 1, 1780, thinking this fire-breathing war-horse would surely prefer a more active assignment, decided to give him command of the light infantry. Peggy Arnold first heard this news at a dinner party and went into hysterics, creating a scene which was witnessed by Aaron Burr, an old friend, who was supposedly bemused by her behavior.

Arnold hastened to tell Washington that his old leg wound prevented his accepting so active a role and renewed his request for the West Point post. Washington reconsidered and on August 3 gave him the command, not only of West Point but also of Verplanck's Point, Stony Point (which had been captured by the British and then retaken by Anthony Wayne), and other posts and positions from Fishkill to North Castle.

This was exactly what Arnold wanted, and he began to put his plan into operation. Taking advantage of a commander's privilege, he moved Peggy and their first child (they eventually had four sons) to the home of Beverley Robinson, a Tory serving with the British in New York City. His home in Garrison, New York, was in the hands of the rebels and was very convenient, since it was just across the river from West Point.

Despite Washington's instructions, Arnold allowed the Point's fortifications to fall into a general state of disrepair. He also made contact with several people in the area who would work with him, including Joshua Hett Smith who lived near King's Ferry.

The scheme he finally came up with required that Sir Henry's representative, Major André, meet with him to arrange for the actual surrender. The lines between the two opposing armies in New York State had always been tenuous in Westchester County, a no-man's-land where partisans of both sides plundered and looted at will. There was a great deal of trafficking back and forth and exchanges of letters and messages between civilians on both sides, so no one would be unduly suspicious of a request from Colonel Beverley Robinson to meet with the commander of West Point to discuss his home. André, under the pseudonym Anderson, would come along. At some time during the conference, he and Arnold would go off to one side and get down to the real business of the meeting. Contact between the two parties would be made from H.M.S. *Vulture,* which was usually on picket duty off Spuyten Duyvil at the north end of Manhattan Island.

ANDRÉ'S LANDING

Early in the week of September 17, the *Vulture* sailed upriver, supposedly on a reconnaissance mission, and took up a position south of King's Ferry. It is now time for you to be in on the rendezvous, so drive south from West Point along 9W for about thirty or forty minutes. You will pass Bear Mountain, then Stony Point, then West Haverstraw and Haverstraw. Look off to your left as you pass Haverstraw and notice the wide bay. During the Revolution the town was a known base of rebel supplies. In 1776 a British fleet dropped anchor in this bay and attempted to land a raiding party, but it was driven off by the local militia. Beyond Haverstraw, just beyond the traffic light, watch the left-hand side of the road for an overlook marked by a dirt area wide enough for ten or fifteen cars. During the summer there is usually a mobile hot dog stand stationed there doing a good business. Pull into the parking area and, facing traffic, walk south for about a thousand feet to two **boulders** with plaques and a mount for a missing Revolutionary War cannon placed between them.

On the night of Thursday, September 21, the *Vulture* was anchored in midstream a little south of where you are now. Toward midnight, Joshua Smith was rowed out to the ship by Samuel and John Calhoon (or Colquhoun), two brothers who were tenants of his, and returned with André, who was known to Smith as John Anderson. Smith car-

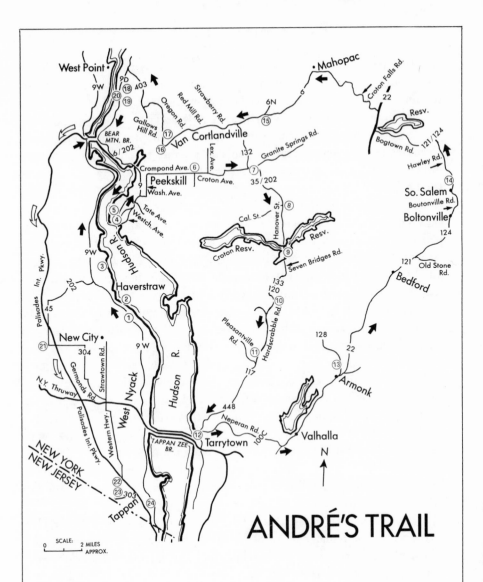

ANDRÉ'S TRAIL

1 André's Landing (Overlook)

2 André's Landing

3 Treason House Site

4 Verplanck's Pt./Post Hancock Hse.

5 Fort Lafayette

6 Andreas Miller Hse. Site

7 André Meets Patrol

8 Underhill House

9 Pine Bridge—Smith Turns Back

10 Yellow House—André Asks Directions

11 André's Spring

12 André's Capture Site

13 Jameson's H.Q.

14 Jacob Gilbert House Site André Writes to Washington

15 Sybil Ruddington Marker

16 St. Peter's Churchyard

17 Continental Village

18 Sugar Loaf

19 Robinson's House Site

20 Arnold's Lane

21 Coe's Tavern Site

22 Bogart Farm

23 Continental Army Camp Site

24 Mablie's Tavern De Windt—André's Execution

ried two papers signed by Arnold. One was a pass that allowed him to go through American patrols and also contained instructions for André to come ashore for the meeting. The other granted Smith and "Anderson" permission to pass the guards at King's Ferry.

André came ashore with Smith and met Arnold in the woods at the river's edge on a spot, according to one plaque, toward which the gun is pointed. The other plaque says the site of the meeting lies between the boulder and the river.

You can reach the landing site, or at least what local tradition has preserved as the site, by backtracking a short distance north along 9W. As you again pass the traffic light, look to your right for a road going off down the hill. Take that road; you will immediately cross the railroad tracks and continue down the slope of the palisades. Within a short distance, you will come to an intersection with a road that comes in from the right at an acute angle. Turn right onto that road and follow it beyond a traprock mill and silos which take up both sides of the road and the riverbank. The road goes under two covered conveyor belts and past a white clapboard cottage on the right, the traprock company's field office. A short distance farther, you will reach a row of small, one-family homes on both sides of the road, just before the paved road goes to dirt. Two old, cement gateposts minus gates mark what was at one time a park area. If the road is not too muddy or icy, drive on; otherwise park and walk in 270 paces to a small parking space which has been dug out of the hillside to the right. A sign facing you prohibits vehicles from proceeding any farther.

Pick your way down the hill to the river, noting as you get close to the water the remains of an old road marked by stone retaining walls. When you are on the rocky shoreline, look for a granite **boulder** about four feet long, three feet high, and two feet across. At high tide it will be partially submerged, but at low tide it will be completely dry except for its base which was partially cemented down at some time. There is an inscription on the river side of the boulder which you can read only if you can scramble out on the small rocks around it or if you can climb up on the boulder itself and look down at the other side: "André the Spy landed here, September 21, 1780."

On the night of the meeting, the *Vulture* was anchored a short distance downriver. André scrambled ashore in this cove; met Arnold, who was waiting under the trees; and the two men talked until dawn. Since it was then too light for André to return to the ship, they proceeded north three miles to Smith's home, probably following the *old road,* part of which you found on the bank just above the shoreline. It is possible the old road has now become part of the paved road you took to this spot. At the time, there was a brickworks, about where the trap-rock plant is now, whose products were shipped south from docks along this stretch of riverbank. It was a busy area in the daytime, probably with quite a bit of foot and wagon traffic along the road just above.

You can catch up with the two conspirators by driving back up the slope to 9W. Turn right onto the highway and travel north past Haverstraw and West Haverstraw for about three miles. Look for the New York State Rehabilitation Hospital on the left at the top of a rise of ground overlooking the river. A historical marker on the left side of the road identifies the site of **Treason House,** Joshua Smith's home. The house, which stood where the present hospital is now, was destroyed by fire toward the end of the last century.

André was supposed to return to the *Vulture* the following night, but Colonel James Livingston, in command of American troops on the opposite side of the river, became incensed at the *Vulture*'s presence and opened fire with two cannon, forcing the vessel to retreat downstream. This left André stranded. He was under orders from Clinton not to go behind enemy lines, not to put on a disguise of any kind, and not to carry any papers with him. By this time, however, he had a number of documents Arnold had handed him which gave full details of the strength of the garrison and the disposition of the defenses at West Point. When he was told it was impossible to get back to the *Vulture,* he was faced with the necessity of returning to his own lines overland through rebel-held territory.

FOLLOWING IN ANDRÉ'S FOOTSTEPS

From this point on, André's path led steadily downhill. You can follow his progress to disaster from the site of Smith's house to the site of his execution. But it will take a long day at least, winding in and out of the hills of Westchester County.

Many of these sites I discovered myself, but for several, I am indebted to local historians Mrs. Josephine Watts of Suffern, New York, and John Focht of Garrison, New York, who published a very good pamphlet on the trail. Focht, who did most of the research, worked with members of the Westchester and Tappan Historical societies and used a map drawn up by William Abbatt for his *Crisis of the American Revolution,* which was published in 1899 and is still one of the best accounts of the Arnold-André affair. Some parts of the trail are obscure and the history buff attempting to follow it can find himself bogged down in a maze of nameless, narrow, winding roads, some of them dirt and slippery in wet or cold weather, in remote backcountry areas of Westchester where houses, gas stations, and other amenities are few and far between.

There is evidence to show that Arnold intended all along for André to return to the British lines overland, but since, as Carl Van Doren points out in *The Secret History of the American Revolution,* it was not in Arnold's interest to place André in danger, Arnold probably thought he was doing the wise thing. He wrote André a pass to get him through the American lines as "John Anderson," left him with Smith who was to guide him back, and went by barge upstream to his headquarters. Late Friday afternoon, September 22, Smith and André crossed the river via King's Ferry, which is no longer in operation.

You will have to catch up with them circuitously. Continue north along 9W to the Bear Mountain Traffic Circle; bearing right at the circle, cross the river on the Bear Mountain Bridge. At the east end of the bridge, turn right and take Routes 6–202 up around Anthony's Nose.

As you come down the south flank of the mountain, you will pass on your left an entrance to Camp Smith, a New York State National Guard training camp, then come to a traffic circle where Route 9 south joins 6–202. Continue south on 9–6–202. When Routes 6 and 202 go off, continue along 9 until you see the sign for New York 9A–Welcher Avenue–Buchanan and look for Tate Avenue at a traffic light. Turn right onto Tate Avenue for a half-mile drive to King's Ferry Road. Turn right onto King's Ferry Road. In a short distance, it will bring you to a causeway with the Hudson to your left beyond a row of mobile homes and what looks like a large pond to the right. Stop to read the historical marker at the right, and notice a white, clapboard house on a rock foundation, also to the right. This is **Verplanck's Point**, the eastern terminus of King's Ferry from Stony Point. The ferry landing was located about where the mobile homes are now, directly opposite the house. A section of the old landing was in existence until quite recently. The pond, two hundred years ago a swamp, was created by the causeway built by an ice company.

The house is the **Post–Hancock House**, though its colonial character has been disguised by a porch and the clapboarding, which either replaced or covered the original exterior. The house is privately owned and cannot be visited, but the present occupants assured me nothing of the original interior remains. According to the marker, the seventeenth- and eighteenth-century occupants operated the ferry; Colonel Livingston had his headquarters in it; and on this spot, in 1782, Washington presented medals to the three men who captured André.

Smith and André landed here and André continued on alone for a short distance while Smith stopped to talk with that same Colonel Livingston who was the cause of André's predicament. These military outposts were situated to intercept travelers passing through this disputed area, and Livingston questioned Smith closely. Smith told him he was accompanying a gentleman who was on his way to meet General Arnold, accepted letters from Livingston for Arnold and General Clinton (one of the American Clintons), and caught up with André who, understandably, was in a hurry to get to White Plains.

Before you catch up to them, take a few minutes to locate another site close by with which André was connected on a previous occasion. Drive over the causeway into Verplanck until you come to Broadway. Turn left and go three blocks to Third Street. Turn right onto Third, then left onto Lafayette Drive. The drive winds around and takes you up onto high ground through a residential area containing small, one-family homes. Though there is no marker, this is approximately where **Fort Lafayette** stood; for it seems only natural that a fort would have occupied the highest ground in the vicinity to dominate the ferry and the road leading to it. You can find your way down to the river just below, if you like, to see the approximate site where Sir Henry Clinton's men came ashore before taking Stony Point. It was here in 1779, fourteen months before André and Smith passed by, that Captain John André came ashore and persuaded the garrison of Fort Lafayette to surrender.

Return to Third Street and take it back to Broadway; turn right to Sixth Street, then left to Westchester Avenue. Turn left onto Westchester Avenue, and drive to the intersection of Westchester and Tate avenues and 9A. Turn left onto 9A and proceed north into Peekskill. When 9A meets Route 9, continue ahead across Route 9 onto Welcher Avenue, a short street that will take you to Washington Street, the first intersection after Route 9. Turn left onto Washington Street and proceed to South Street, driving through south Peekskill. Turn right onto South Street, which ends at a major shopping street at a traffic light. Turn right and then immediately left, following the signs indicating Routes 6, 202, and 35. When you reach South Broad Street, another major intersection with a traffic light, turn right again; look at once for signs for 202 and 35, indicating a left turn. Make that turn left and go up a hill with private homes and a rocky wooded slope to your right and

Peekskill below to your left. You are on **Crompond Road** and back on the road André and Smith followed.

Watch for a sign on the right for Bear Mountain Parkway (Route 6). Two traffic lights beyond that is an intersection with Croton Avenue, and a short distance beyond, another with Lexington Avenue. Somewhere between the two intersections ran a brook and alongside that brook, in what was the town of Crompond, stood the Andreas Miller House where André and Smith spent Friday night after meeting an American patrol a little farther on.

Drive on to the site of that encounter, passing under the Taconic State Parkway and Mohansic State Park to the right. Shortly after Route 132 comes in from the left, Routes 35–202 take a sharp curving right to head south. The road going on ahead at the point of the curve is Granite Springs Road. At about this spot, Smith and André ran into a patrol commanded by militia Captain Samuel Webb, who knew André by sight but failed to recognize him, perhaps because it was about nine in the evening and dark. Webb questioned them and advised them to proceed no farther until daybreak for fear of running into Loyalist patrols. André would have welcomed such a meeting, but not daring to say so, he turned back with Smith to the Andreas Miller House where, according to Smith, they had to share the same bed.

The next morning, Saturday, September 23, André and Smith were up and on the road before sunrise. Follow them by continuing south along 35 and 202 into the town of Yorktown Heights. When you come to a flashing red light at an intersection with Route 118, bear left. Passing the Yorktown Heights Engine Company No. 1 on your left, you will find yourself on Hanover Street, which will take you up a hill and into a semirural area. At the bottom of a hill, you will come to the intersection of Hanover and California streets. Turn right onto California Street and park in front of the corner house to your right. A clapboard, colonial house with a peaked roof and an obviously new wing, this is the **Underhill House** at which Smith and André stopped for breakfast that morning. A plaque celebrating the occasion has been placed on the Hanover Street side of the house near the front. The house is privately owned.

Having eaten, André and his companion continued south. Follow them by continuing along Hanover Street to an intersection with Route 118. Turn left onto 118 and take it a short distance to a traffic circle, where you will pick up Route 100 south. In no time at all, you will come to **Pine Bridge,** a steel girder bridge which crosses what is now the Croton Reservoir. When André and Smith came this way, it was only the Croton River. A historical marker on the right side of the road identifies it as a military crossing. It was here Smith's nervousness over the possibility of running into Loyalist patrols, he later said, got the better of him and he turned back, leaving André to continue his journey alone over roads unfamiliar to him.

Ahead of André lay only fifteen miles to his own lines; when he arrived, the plan to capture West Point would become operational. Those fifteen miles, however, lay through a no-man's-land in which the Cow Boys, who were Loyalist, and the Skinners, who were rebels, conducted a guerrilla war whose main losers were the local inhabitants. The Skinners, for instance, were permitted to investigate anyone who crossed their path and could keep anything of value they found.

André crossed the river at a spot which is now underwater a hundred yards or so upstream to your left. Drive over the bridge, continue south along 100, and watch for Seven Bridges Road, onto which you make a left turn. At the intersection with Route 133, turn right onto 133 and take it to Route 120, where you make a left turn. Take the next right, which is Hardscrabble Road, and after the turn notice the large, yellow, clapboard *house* to your left at the intersection where André stopped to ask directions.

Continue along Hardscrabble Road, looking for 80 Hardscrabble Road, which is a good distance farther south. When you reach 100 Hardscrabble Road, look for a yellow, clapboard house on the right called Medlar Hill. Diagonally opposite it, on the left side of the road, you will find a *springhouse* with a peaked, shingle roof, stone retaining walls on either side, and what looks like a large, wooden well lid in front of it. A stream of water issues from the foot of the hill and flows past the springhouse. A plaque set into a granite boulder tells you that André stopped here to water his horse.

According to Van Doren, André learned from a boy at this point that the Skinners were active on the White Plains Road and he decided to travel on the Tarrytown Road to the west. According to sources referred to by Watts and Focht, André did not hear about the Skinners until he reached the Sloats Hammond House, which stood about where Hawthorne traffic interchange is now. Since it is no longer standing, proceed directly to Tarrytown as André probably did. Continue south along Hardscrabble Road to Pleasantville Road. Turn left onto Pleasantville Road and take it to Route 117. Turn right onto 117, and take it west to Route 448. Turning left onto 448, take it to Route 9; turn left onto 9 and drive south into Tarrytown.

TARRYTOWN—THE CAPTURE

Actually when André turned south, he traveled along the old Albany Post Road, some of which I suspect now exists as Route 448 and parts of Route 9, so you are at least approximating his route.

As you go through bustling Tarrytown, you will come to a park area on the right with paved paths, benches, shrubbery, and two small bridges that cross a meandering brook. Immediately off the road, at the main entrance to the park, is a *statue* of a man in Continental Army dress leaning on a musket. Erected in 1853, this monument marks the site of André's capture. There are several side streets going off the left side of the road, and I suggest you find parking there and walk back to the park.

According to several accounts, André came from the north along the Albany Post Road at about ten or eleven o'clock Saturday morning and crossed a little brook then called Clark's Kill, now known as André Brook. Here he was stopped by three members of the Skinner gang, part of a larger force on the lookout for cattle stolen the day before by the Cow Boys. The three—John Paulding, Isaac van Wart, and David Williams—had been in hiding 150 feet south of the brook, where they had a clear view of the road. A split-rail fence ran along the road and Isaac van Wart was behind it as a lookout, while the other two probably reclined at their ease on the grass. Isaac saw André come into sight as he breasted a small hill just the other side of the brook. By the time the unsuspecting André arrived at the bridge, he found three flint-locks pointed at him over the fence.

According to André's information, there should have been no American patrols this far south, and when he was challenged and saw that Paulding was wearing a red Hessian coat, he said, "Gentlemen, I hope you belong to our party?"

"Which party?" he was asked, and replied, "The lower party," meaning the British, in lower Westchester.

One of the militiamen then said something that led André to believe they were friendly, upon which he is reported to have said: "I am a British officer out of the country on particular business, and I hope you will not detain me a minute." To prove he was indeed an officer and gentleman, he showed them a gold watch he had received at the court of Saxe Coburg during a visit to the Continent some years before.

Showing a gold watch to men who had a license to loot was like bringing a starving man to a banquet table and waving a chicken leg under his nose. André was made to dismount and was then taken into the bushes near the brook and stripped. Off came his boots as well, and there were the papers inside his stockings. He was then told to dress and David Williams, according to his testimony, asked what he would give them if they let him go. André offered any sum of money they requested or anything else, but by then the three were beginning to suspect they had come across someone quite extraordinary and were not about to let him out of their clutches. Now fully aware he had fallen in with the wrong party, André showed them Arnold's pass, which might have gotten him through if he had produced it at once, but it was too late for that. The three militiamen decided to take him to an American headquarters at what was then North Castle and is now Armonk.

Since they stopped with their prisoner at a nearby tavern for light refreshments, you have time to take a look around the site before going on with the patrol. Despite its position in the midst of a suburban city, the site retains some of its original character, particularly the **brook** which comes trickling out from under Route 9 and goes under two stone bridges inside the park. Route 9 follows to some extent the old Albany Post Road, which may have come over a bridge just in front of the monument. Take a good look at the statue on top of the monument. It is said to be a portrait of John Paulding wearing his Hessian coat. Curiously enough, the statue was the gift of a wealthy citizen of North Tarrytown whose name was John Anderson, the fictitious name André was using.

Continue south along Route 9 into the heart of Tarrytown to a busy intersection with a traffic light. To the left, the intersecting street is Neperan Road. Turn left onto Neperan Road, and drive up over the hills above Tarrytown. You may want to stop at the **Historical Society of the Tarrytowns** at 1 Grove Street at the corner of Grove Street and Neperan Road. There, in a room called the Captors' Room, are a number of relics and memorabilia connected with André, the three militiamen, and the capture. One wall is covered with a number of paintings portraying the event. Some are obviously wild stretches of the imagination, but one or two may be substantially correct in their details.

You are now faced with a choice. If you have the time and the inclination, you can follow, approximately, the roads André traveled with his captors. Or, you can go directly from Tarrytown to the

Robinson House where the plot was completely exposed. If you choose to go with André, follow the directions in the next paragraph. If not, return to Route 9 and take it north to Routes 6 and 202 which take you up and around Anthony's Nose. On the west side of the mountain, the road dips down to the entrance to the Bear Mountain Bridge. Continue ahead past the bridge onto Route 9D north. About four miles beyond the bridge, notice a conical hill on your left about a quarter of a mile from the road. A historical marker on your right identifies it as Sugarloaf, where the Continental Army maintained a gun battery. A few hundred feet farther is a contemporary, two-story, white farmhouse facing north. Immediately beyond it, a second marker on the right denotes the site of Robinson House where you should catch up on the uncovering of the Arnold-André plot.

To follow the prisoner's route, continue along Neperan Road. You will pass through a reservoir park area and go under the overpasses for the Saw Mill River Parkway and the New York Central Railroad before entering a landscaped industrial area. Look for a historical *marker* on the left side of the road not far from a contemporary factory or office building. The marker commemorates the site of the house in which John Paulding was born.

Drive on until you come to Route 100C, which makes a right-angle turn. Signs for 100C indicate the road directly ahead and the one to your left. Turn left onto 100C (east) and follow it to a traffic light where it runs into Route 100. Continue directly ahead onto Route 100, passing Westchester County Community College on your left, until you come to a road juncture with signs for Valhalla. Turn left and go into Valhalla to a stop sign where the Valhalla firehouse faces you from the other side of the intersection. Turn right onto Valhalla's main street with the Taconic State Parkway immediately to the right. Eventually you will enter a parklike area intersected by roads connecting with major Westchester parkways. You will also note to your left the face of a dam which forms Kensico Reservoir. Shortly after the dam, the parklike area will be replaced by a business-residential area. When you come to the first traffic light, Route 22 comes in at an acute angle from your left and continues on ahead of you. Make a sharp left turn and take Route 22 north.

JAMESON'S HEADQUARTERS

Route 22 is a four-lane highway, skirting the Kensico Reservoir to your left. At 5.2 miles, you will see the first signs for Armonk. A mile farther is a juncture with Route 128 at a traffic light. Turn left and drive through the village of Armonk, just off 22. As you come out of the town, look for the "End 40 Mile Speed" sign and clock 0.5 mile to a road coming in from the right. Turn right along a piece of road about fifteen feet long to High Street. Turn left onto High Street; in less than a hundred yards, look for Greenway Road going off to the right. You can park on High Street or pull off onto Greenway Road and park where it curves to the left.

To the right is a swimming club pool and cabana. To the left is a grassy, shaded plot of ground on which some sort of digging was going on when I visited. Directly opposite the Greenway Road intersection, about fifty feet off High Street down in a grassy hollow, is a tall, granite *slab* with small plantings around it, surrounded on three sides by stone walls. About twenty or thirty feet behind it, at the top of another slope, runs Route 128. Walk down into the hollow to confront the stone, and you are standing on the site of a building in which Colonel John Jameson of the Continental Army had his headquarters. I have not been able to ascertain whether the stone walls are the remains of the building's foundations or merely retaining walls.

On this site a curious twist of fate occurred which might still have saved André, but for a timely intervention. Before André came up-river, Arnold had passed along instructions to all commanders in the area that someone called "John Anderson" might be coming from New York City and that he should be sent to his headquarters. André's appearance puzzled Jameson. Here was the John Anderson in question, but coming from the wrong direction. Furthermore, he had certain documents that seemed to be dangerous to the American cause should they fall into the wrong hands. Jameson decided to play it safe. He sent "Anderson" under escort to Arnold and the papers by courier to General Washington, who was on his way west from Connecticut where he had been conferring with Rochambeau, the commander of the French forces in America.

Prisoner and papers were sent on their respective ways. André and escort went off along what is now Route 128 north toward Peekskill via the bridge over the Croton River. Shortly after, Major Benjamin Tallmadge, who was engaged in secret service work for Washington, came to North Castle, heard about the affair, and persuaded Jameson to have André brought back.

When Tallmadge confronted André, he became highly suspicious. The more he observed André, according to his own account of the affair, the more Tallmadge became convinced that "Mr. Anderson" was not who he said he was, but he could not convince Jameson to do anything more than to continue to hold André.

A series of unbelievable coincidences and missed opportunities then occurred. Early the next morning, Sunday, September 24, André was transferred to another post at Lower Salem, now called South Salem, near Connecticut. Jameson wrote a report of the incident and sent it to Arnold at his headquarters, the Robinson House in Garrison, opposite West Point. The courier with the papers had not been able to find Washington in Danbury and brought them back. When André learned the papers had been sent to Washington, he realized the jig was up and wrote Washington a letter in which he revealed his true identity. This was sent with the incriminating evidence by another messenger to Arnold's headquarters, where Washington was expected. On that same day, Joshua Hett Smith had dinner at Robinson House, where he probably told Arnold that "Anderson" was safely through the American lines.

THE PRISONER'S ROUTE

For the next installment of this tale of hugger mugger on the Hudson, return along Route 128 to Route 22; turn left, and drive north toward South Salem through a semirural area. In 7.2 miles, you will reach the village of Bedford. Shortly after you leave Bedford, turn right onto Route 121 which comes in from the right. In 1.6 miles, 121 is joined by 137 north and 137 south goes off to the right. Turn right onto 137 south in the direction of Pound Ridge. In 1.9 miles, turn left onto Old Stone Road. Almost immediately, you will come to a fork in the road with a triangle of ground separating the two roads that meet.

Though there will probably be a dearth of street signs, bear right to stay on Old Stone Road. This is backcountry Westchester, a rural area with fields and woods on both sides and only occasional homes where you might stop for directions. In many respects, the countryside is probably very like what André was escorted through. Since the woods are so obviously young, however, no older than sixty or seventy years, and since there are many stone walls running through them, I suspect there were more open fields under cultivation two hundred years ago.

In 0.9 mile, the paved road runs out and you are on a narrow dirt road for 0.2 mile. In 0.5 mile you reach a juncture with Route 124. Turn left onto 124 for 1.7 miles to Boutonville Road, which comes in suddenly at the foot of a hill, just around a curve. The sign for Boutonville Road is narrow and wooden in the shape of a pointing hand, painted white and not very conspicuous. If you pass it by, you will see a dirt road shortly after to your right leading to a park entrance. You can turn around there and retrace your steps to the turnoff.

You are back again on a narrow, winding road which goes to dirt in 0.3 mile, then back to pavement after another mile. When you reach Route 35, continue on Boutonville Road. In a mile and a half a stop sign will bring you to a halt at Spring Street. Turn left onto Spring Street. Spring Street takes you into **South Salem** with its tall, white-spired Presbyterian Church built in 1752 to the right. South Salem is a tiny, picturesque hamlet in which Spring Street rapidly becomes Main Street. (Spring Street goes off to the left.) Continue along Main Street 0.7 mile, to a point just before the intersection with Bouton Road. To your left, set into a stone wall is a *plaque*. Up behind it on a rise of ground, a stretch of lawn leads to a modern, one-family home.

The plaque marks the site of the home of Jacob Gilbert which stood behind the wall. It was to this place that André was brought and in the house that originally stood here that he wrote his letter of confession to Washington. In this letter, he told Washington that he was Major John André, adjutant general of the British army, that he had come into the American lines to meet someone who was to "give me intelligence," and in the process had been forced into "the vile condition of an enemy in disguise within your posts." On the next day, Monday, September 25, André was sent on to Robinson House in the company of Benjamin Tallmadge, who was to be his companion almost constantly until the day of his execution.

To follow André's progress to Robinson House, continue along Main Street to Oscaleta Road, which comes in from the left. Turn onto Oscaleta Road and in 0.65 mile you will arrive at an intersection where Benedict Road comes in from the left and seemingly continues off to the right. Actually, the road going to the right is Hawley Road, though there may be no road sign to identify it. Turn right onto Hawley Road. In 0.6 mile, Hawley Road curves sharply to the right and in another half mile forks. Bear right and continue another 1.1 miles to an intersection with Route 121 at a stop sign. Turn left onto 121, which quickly becomes 121 and 124.

In approximately 1.1 miles you will come to Bogtown Road, a narrow, two-lane road to the right. Take it 1.2 miles, past Titicus Reservoir on the right, to a stop sign; turn left into the village of Purdys. The street you are on will take you down a slope to a stop sign at Route 116. Make a right, then left for Route 22 north toward Croton Falls. You are now on Route 22S going to Route 22; bear left on 22 north, called Sun

Valley Road. In 9.7 miles you will come to a road and a sign pointing the way to Lake Mahopac. Turn left onto what is actually Croton Falls Road which will eventually take you across a causeway between two bodies of water.

At a sign for Lake Mahopac indicating a left turn, bear left; in four miles you will come to a traffic light at an intersection with Route 6. Turn left onto Route 6 and in about 0.5 mile, as you come into the town of Mahopac, Route 6 meets 6N, which goes to the right. At the intersection is a traffic light and a historical *marker* for Sybil Ruddington, the "Paul Revere of Westchester County," who rode a locally famous number of miles to rouse the militia during the British raid on Danbury (Book X).

Continue along 6N in a westerly direction until it rejoins Route 6 at a traffic light. Turn right and continue west along 6 under the overpass for the Taconic Parkway, keeping your eyes open for Strawberry Road which goes off to the right at a traffic light. Follow Strawberry Road to an intersection with a stop sign. Here the road signs may be confusing. The road coming in from the left is Lexington Road; the road going to the right is Red Mill Road. Turn right onto Red Mill Road and follow it to another intersection with a traffic light. No matter what the road signs say, cross the intersection and take the road which continues straight ahead, Oregon Road. In about two miles, you will come into Van Cortlandtville where you will pass two modern cemeteries before coming to old **St. Peter's churchyard** on the left side of the road. John Paulding is buried in that cemetery, his grave marked by a monument. Also buried here, according to the plaque on the main entrance gatepost, is Seth Pomeroy, "the first commander of the American army as senior brigadier general in 1775." The inscription is somewhat misleading. Congress made Pomeroy a brigadier general after the Battle of Bunker Hill in which he served as a volunteer, despite his sixty-nine years. He declined the honor, preferring to remain with his state's militia, but was technically the senior brigadier before Washington assumed command.

Continue on to Gallows Hill Road and turn right. In 1.7 miles, Gallows Hill Road forks. An inscribed granite boulder at the fork marks the site of **Continental Village**, a major supply depot which was burned by the British on October 9, 1777, during Clinton's attack on the Hudson Valley forts.

Continue beyond the monument on the dirt road that goes up the hill ahead (Gallows Hill Road goes to the right). In a half mile you will see a road to the left. Take it 5.2 miles to a steep incline where a sign warns you to blow your horn; on the other side of the incline is a road coming in from the left. Continue on another 0.2 mile, as the road becomes paved, to Route 9.

If the roads are not icy or otherwise impassable, and if you want to stay strictly to André's route, turn right and head north toward Garrison. In about a quarter of a mile, you will come to the Garrison Garage. To the left, a dirt road climbs a hill. Follow it through a lovely wooded area, up and down the hill, until it comes to Route 9D. Otherwise, turn left onto Route 9 and take it a short distance to Route 403 which goes off at an acute angle to the right. Turn right onto 403 and take it to Route 9D.

No matter which way you have come to Route 9D, turn left onto 9D and head south for the Robinson House site. Once you are on 9D, notice the prominent hill to your left front. Seen from the other side of the river farther south, that hill is a perfect sugarloaf, which gives it its name. This side of **Sugarloaf** was the site of a gun battery, part of the American defense system on the east bank of the river. Next, note the Highlands Country Club golf course on the right. Shortly after it, about 0.7 mile since turning onto 9D, you will see a marker on the right near the entrance to a dirt road. Ignore it for the moment, and look for another marker on the left which marks the site of **Robinson House.**

ROBINSON HOUSE—THE PLOT REVEALED

You should pause to examine the site and consider the events that transpired here. There are a few places along the road where you can pull over far enough to get out of the traffic. You can also park down that dirt road, Arnold's Lane, near the other marker and walk back to the site. The road on the side near the Robinson House marker is bordered by a line of trees and a stone wall. On the other side of the wall is a broad pasture, then a red barn at the end of a wide, dirt road. Facing north, just beyond two large stone pillars that flank the entrance, is a white, frame farmhouse. Facing this house, on the other side of the driveway, is a grassy area with a few shade trees. The Robinson House stood approximately on that spot. A little farther on in the farmyard is a covered well.

A few miles north of here on 9D, in the town of Cold Spring, the Putnam County Historical Society sponsors a *museum,* about one hundred feet off the road at 63 Chestnut Street, which is crammed full of all kinds of relics and memorabilia from Putnam County during the Revolutionary War. In their files are two photographs of Robinson House taken just before it burned in 1892. The pictures show a white, frame, colonial farmhouse with two wings added, several dormer windows on the upper story, a veranda running around two sides, and a circular driveway in front. According to a period watercolor, the house's long axis ran east and west, which indicates that the front faced south. The position of Arnold's Lane about fifty feet north of the house on the opposite side of 9D suggests that, since the lane connected the house with the river landing and Arnold dashed down it without being seen by those in the house, it must have led to the back door on the north side.

One of the tenants in the house now on the property told me that amateur archaeologists have gone down into an underground chamber somewhere near the well and emerged with old hats and other items. I took a peek down the well, but saw nothing but a lot of water. I did find another well behind the barn which had rungs leading down, but since that too was flooded I did not investigate any further. The property is now owned by a local resident who has closed off the barnyard and the Robinson House area with a fence.

On Sunday, September 24, Washington changed his mind. Instead of coming on to Robinson House that evening, he decided to spend the night in Fishkill. Joshua Hett Smith, who had stopped at Robinson House to see Arnold after leaving André at the Croton River, had gotten into a sharp argument at dinner with Arnold's aides, Lieutenant Colonel Richard Varick and Major David Franks. Smith's brother, William, was a notorious Tory, which made Joshua somewhat suspect in the eyes of the local Patriots. Varick and Franks suspected, however, that Smith and Arnold were involved in some commercial scheme, similar to those that had got their commander into hot water in Philadelphia. After the meal, Smith continued on his way to Fishkill while Arnold sharply reprimanded Franks for insulting his guest. When Smith got to Fishkill, he dined at the same house where Washington was staying, but they had no contact. At the time, Smith was unknown to Washington.

By breakfast time, Monday morning, September 25, neither of Jameson's two messengers had arrived at Robinson House. About 9 A.M., Alexander Hamilton and another of Washington's aides arrived to say the commander in chief had stopped to inspect some fortifications en route and would be late for breakfast. The meal proceeded with Arnold and his aides now joined by Hamilton and the other officer. Peggy was not feeling well and was upstairs in bed with the baby. During the meal, the messenger bearing Jameson's report on André's apprehension arrived and delivered it to Arnold, who read it, quietly told the messenger not to mention the report to any one, excused himself, and went upstairs to see Peggy. He told her they were all in the soup, said good-bye, and came back downstairs. Major Franks told him Washington was approaching the house. Arnold said to inform the general he had to get to West Point at once, dashed out of the house around the back way, got on a horse, and galloped down to the Robinson House landing on the river. There he got into his barge and had himself rowed downriver to the *Vulture*.

Washington reached the house about 10:30, accompanied by the Marquis de Lafayette and Henry Knox, among others. He was surprised at not finding the Arnolds at table, had his breakfast, and then crossed the river to the Point where he expected to meet Arnold. Arnold was not to be found. Instead, the commander in chief found the fortifications in a deplorable state.

In the meantime, back at the Robinson House, Peggy had gone into a fit of hysterics, accusing Colonel Varick of planning to have her child murdered. She went down on her knees and begged him to spare the child. The two aides and Arnold's physician got her, still raving, back into bed. By this time, both aides had spoken to Jameson's messenger and also discovered their commander had not gone across the river to West Point, but downstream; they still tended to give him the benefit of the doubt.

Washington returned to the house at four in the afternoon. By then, Jameson's second messenger had arrived. Washington was handed first the papers found on André, then Jameson's report to Arnold. After reading André's letter, he knew the worst. He immediately sent Hamilton racing south to try to intercept Arnold, who was by that time safely on board the *Vulture*. Sometime after Hamilton left, a messenger brought Washington a letter from Arnold, brought ashore under a flag of truce, explaining that "Love to my country actuates my present conduct" and pleading for good treatment for Peggy and her child because, he said, she knew nothing of what was going on. Peggy continued the mad act in front of Washington and Lafayette and Hamilton, who all knew her from the old Philadelphia days. They believed her madness and sent her back to her family in Philadelphia.

Leaving the house site, walk along the road to **Arnold's Lane,** so named on a signpost and otherwise identified by a marker pointing it out as the path along which Arnold fled. You can follow it down to the river, a pleasant distance of about a quarter of a mile. At the foot of the lane is a town dump, alongside the inevitable New York Central tracks, with the river beyond. The land on the other side of the tracks rises into a wooded, rocky knoll overlooking the river, an ideal spot for a picnic, if you don't mind the passing of an occasional train. Looking across the river and upstream, you can see the buildings of West Point and mark the present West Point Landing, which is approximately the site of the old landing. You can also understand how much luck was on Arnold's side, for he went down the river with the ebbing morning tide. If his rowers had been forced to struggle against a rising tide later in the day, Hamilton might have been able to intercept him at Verplanck's Point. The two men who rowed Arnold to the *Vulture*, both Continental soldiers, were imprisoned for their pains by the British; they were unwitting accomplices and refused to follow their commander into the British army.

According to the sketch Benson Lossing made of Robinson Landing for his Fieldbook, the landing was located on the south or downriver side of the knoll. I had been told that sandstone steps were to be found at the water's edge, but though my son Richard and I searched every inch of waterline on the south side of the knoll, not a step did we find there. We did, however, find two sandstone steps on the knoll itself which lead up onto an outcropping of rock facing west on the river. If these steps were part of the landing area two hundred years ago, then they have felt the pressure of a score of well-known feet, not only Arnold's but Washington's, Lafayette's, Beverley Robinson's, and Hamilton's, to mention only a few.

André was brought to Robinson House, probably on Monday, but never saw Washington. Joshua Smith was apprehended and the two prisoners were taken to West Point, then downriver by barge to Stony Point, and from there overland to Tappan.

If you want to explore 9D north for a few miles, you will find markers identifying the general sites on which particular detachments of Continental soldiers and militiamen camped during the Revolution. A short distance past Arnold's Lane, at a crossroads to the left, is **Mandeville House,** a colonial house once used by West Point commanders as an offpost home. West, on the turnoff to Mandeville House, is the hamlet of **Garrison Landing** with its old, deserted riverboat landing and a fine old two-story house which may have been an inn for ferry travelers.

To follow André, take 9D south to the Bear Mountain Bridge. As you pass the Robinson House site, note the marker on the left side of the road for Sugarloaf. Then keep your eyes open for another marker on the right, about two miles or so south, at the intersection of a road going down the hill to your right and the hamlet of Manitou on the riverbank. The marker says that the site of the eastern anchor of the Fort Montgomery *chain* is nearby. This marker must have been moved from another and more likely site, for when you get down to Manitou and look across the river, the Fort Montgomery site is too far to the south. From all accounts and according to the maps I have seen of the Popolopen forts and the chain, the chain stretched directly across the river to Anthony's Nose from Fort Montgomery.

Continue south, and in a short time you will see another marker to the right for Camp Smith, a National Guard camp. It appears just before the small plaza at the east end of the Bear Mountain Bridge. Where it stands is where the chain marker should be, for below you at the river line, at the foot of Anthony's Nose, is where the chain must have been anchored.

Again, if you do not want to follow the whole André route, but wish to get on to where he finally met his unfortunate fate, cross the Bear Mountain Bridge and take the Palisades Interstate Parkway to the Tappan exit, Exit 5, a twenty- or thirty-minute drive.

Coming off the parkway, proceed south on Route 303 to Tappan. At Oak Tree Road, which is marked by a traffic light and a small shopping center on one corner, turn right and drive the few blocks into Tappan (which was sometimes called Orangetown). You will pass the DeWint House on your left, which you will visit shortly. A short block past DeWint House is Main Street, the heart of Tappan. Everything in town you will want to see is within walking distance; indeed, Tappan is a town to walk through, for it has to a surprising extent retained some of its eighteenth-century flavor. On the opposite side of Main Street is **Mablie's Tavern,** now a restaurant called '76 House.

If you are following the more exact route, cross the river and get back onto Routes 9W and 202 heading south. In West Haverstraw, turn right onto Railroad Avenue, then left onto Central Highway, which is also Main Street. Then turn right on Route 202. Watch for the intersection with Route 45 which comes in at Mt. Ivy, a busy intersection marked by a traffic light. Turn left on 45 and then left at the next light onto New Hempstead Road. Shortly after the turn, notice the church near the intersection where Old Schoolhouse Road goes off to the left. Coe Tavern, which stood on the corner of New Hempstead and Old Schoolhouse Roads opposite the church is supposed to have played host to the prisoners and their escort for a short time, but the story has not been confirmed. There was a militia guard post at this point during the Revolution.

From here to Tappan, you wll be traveling on old roads well marked on late eighteenth-century maps of this area. New Hempstead Road takes you down a series of hills to Main Street in the village of New City. Turn right onto Main Street and proceed south, noticing the new courthouse to your right a block and a half after the turn. Clarkstown Courthouse is marked on the old maps and was probably the reason for the little settlement that eventually grew into the modern bustling village you are now driving through.

New City's Main Street dead-ends, but just before it does, look for the turnoff to the left onto new Route 304, a four-lane highway. Turn right onto 304 and take it to the next traffic light at Germonds Road; then turn left and go along Germonds Road for 0.3 mile, at which point Germonds Road goes to the right. Continue on Germonds Road, noticing in 0.3 mile an old Dutch farmhouse on your right in a little park adjacent to a more recent and very handsome white, clapboard farmhouse. In 0.6 mile farther along Germonds Road, you will see on a rise of ground to your left, an old cemetery with many graves dating to the eighteenth century.

When you get to a four-way stop with a flashing traffic light, turn right onto Strawtown Road, a road along which Henry Lee's Legion clattered frequently as they performed patrol duty in the region. In a quarter of a mile you will arrive at another intersection with a traffic light and will probably see to your right a signpost identifying this region as part of the West Nyack Historic Zone. The three-story building to your right is the Clarksville Inn; it dates to the early nineteenth century and still entertains the public as a restaurant. Turn left at the light onto West Nyack Road and drive through the hamlet of West Nyack. At Western Highway turn right, continuing to dog André's footsteps as he rode on with his armed escort to Tappan.

You have been traveling through a semirural-suburban area and now will parallel the Hackensack River for a while on the right. In 2.4 miles you will come to a traffic light in Blauvelt; in 2.7 miles you will pass St. Dominican College on the right, and in 3.4 miles you will be at the intersection of Orangeburg Road, marked by a traffic light. In 4.5 miles look for a historic marker on the right side of the road at the foot of a driveway that leads to a modern one-family home. It marks the site of the **Bogart farm** in which Lafayette lived briefly in 1780. A spring somewhere in the vicinity was used by the Continental Army when it was encamped on the ridge to the west, or behind the house. The marker suggests that the spring was situated on the opposite side of the road which is now occupied by a number of small houses of the type built by the army for enlisted personnel and their families. If the spring was located there, it has long since disappeared. In 0.1 mile farther, a second marker on the right, at the intersection of Washington Avenue, identifies the ridge to the west, or right, as the campsite of the Continental Army

in 1782 after its return from Yorktown when it was on its way to the
New Windsor encampment near Newburgh. I drove up to the top of the
ridge, most of which is now occupied by one-family homes on small plots
and a contemporary school, but saw nothing to indicate any of the features of the encampment.

Western Highway soon ends in Old Tappan Road, which runs at
right angles to it. You are now in Tappan, which was sometimes called
Orangetown. Turn left and proceed across railroad tracks and on down
to the traffic light at King's Highway, Tappan's main street. To your left
is an imposing, red brick church with a historic marker beside it. Ahead
a short block is the DeWint House. Turn right at this light and find
Mablie's Tavern, now a restaurant called '76 House.

TAPPAN—DETENTION, TRIAL, AND EXECUTION

Always a tavern of some sort, this is where André was kept during
his trial and immediately prior to his execution. It started its historical
career when a number of local people gathered in its public room to draw
up the Orangetown Resolutions on July 4, 1774. They began by protest-
ing their eagerness to remain loyal to the crown, went on to object to
certain acts of Parliament, and ended by calling for the cessation of all
imports and exports to and from Great Britain and the West Indies.

In revolutionary times, much of the clientele consisted of the officers
of the Continental Army. According to a sign over the bar presently in
use, it is the very bar on which a host of heroes leaned while they drank
their rum or gin. A photograph of the tavern in *Southeastern New York,
Volume II* (if you are a New Yorker, your local library may have it),
shows it in a deplorable condition sometime early in this century. The
entire front of the building had been either demolished or allowed to
disintegrate so badly that nothing was left of the porch and the entire
front wall. What you are looking at now is mostly an excellent restoration.

The interior is a picturesque dining room done in colonial style with
a variety of pictures and relics of the period decorating the walls, many
of them associated with the prisoner who was confined here. The room
in which he stayed is to one side, closed off from the dining room by a
Dutch door with the upper part open so that you may look in. It is a
small, narrow room; in André's time it contained a mirror that he used
to draw a self-portrait during the last hours of his life. In the DeWint
House is a small drawing of the tavern during André's imprisonment,
which shows the windows boarded up to prevent his escape.

The building is a low, stone, Dutch-style farmhouse with a high peaked roof and an overhang front and back. At some time during its long career, a small porch was added to the front. A state historical marker at the front identifies it. A paved parking lot to one side accommodates patrons of the restaurant only. The village has a number of homes dating back to revolutionary and colonial times, as well as a cemetery whose tombstones go back to the seventeenth century.

Leaving '76 House, turn left and walk back one short block to Old Tappan Road. On the opposite side, on King's Highway, is that church with the historical marker outside. This is the **Tappan Reformed Church** which stands, as the marker explains, on the site of the old Dutch church in which André's trial was held. A bronze plaque on the church elaborates further: "The Reformed Dutch Church of Tappan (the original church) organized in 1694 was used during the Revolution as a military hospital and prison, and the trials of both André and Joshua Hett Smith for treason were held here in 1780."

So few words to cover what was one of the most grotesque and pitiful episodes in American history. On September 29, a special board of inquiry, which included Generals Lafayette, Steuben, St. Clair, James Clinton, John Stark, Henry Knox, and others, examined André and all the evidence. Among the evidence were letters from Sir Henry Clinton insisting André had been sent on shore under a flag of truce as an emissary from Clinton and that on shore he had acted under Arnold's orders, and therefore could not be considered a spy. André, on the other hand, was the very soul of honor and admitted freely that he had not come ashore under a flag of truce.

The letters that passed between Clinton and Washington are a revelation of eighteenth-century ideas concerning honor and the qualities of a gentleman. Clinton swore up and down there was a flag of truce and André was acting as a British officer under his command. Washington answered by handling the matter in a forthright and dignified fashion. The sticking point was André himself, who would not go back on the social code under which he had been reared and educated, not even to save his own life. He also attempted to trade in on that code by claiming the kinship then prevalent among military officers, no matter which side they served. Every officer was perforce a gentleman, and a gentleman in the eighteenth century was very definitely superior to the ordinary run of men like Timothy Murphy, for example, who was criticized by certain of his compatriots of higher standing for shooting down Simon Fraser, a gentleman.

Though neither he nor Clinton could bring themselves to admit the truth, André had acted the part of and done the work of a spy, conspiring with a traitor who was attempting to sell his comrades-in-arms and his country literally down the river. So thought the board of inquiry and so thought Washington when he issued the general order for André's execution by hanging, the punishment usually reserved for spies. Considering this too shameful a death for a soldier who had been captured doing his honorable duty, André wrote to Washington asking him to change the penalty to death by shooting. The letter was carried from the tavern to Washington at the DeWint House. Washington never answered and in fact refused to see the prisoner, was not present at the board of inquiry at any time, and on the morning of the execution ordered the shutters of his office closed, so that he could not see the death procession as it left the tavern and headed for the rope.

The execution date was orginally set for October 1, but Washington received a communication from Sir Henry requesting a delay to give three emissaries time to explain the true facts. Washington postponed the event until the next day, though he must have been certain in his own mind that the three would have nothing new to offer. Some historians suspect that Washington's own officers were trying to delay the execution and arrange an exchange of André for Arnold. André had made a favorable impression on them. He was young, good-looking, talented in a dilettantish way (he was handy with brush and pen, having done a very creditable portrait of Peggy Shippen before her marriage, as we have noted, as well as one or two self-portraits, and had also written some light verse, including a poem entitled "The Cow Chace" which ridiculed Anthony Wayne's frantic attempts to capture a blockhouse at Bull's Ferry, New Jersey), and was plentifully supplied with the social graces considered desirable at the time. There are some who believe that Hamilton wrote to Clinton, suggesting the exchange and disguising his handwriting, though André himself would not hear of it. Hamilton is also supposed to have held André's execution against Washington, though the break between the two did not occur until some four months later.

Clinton's emissaries, headed by Major General James Robertson, had nothing to say that could possibly have changed Washington's mind. All the facts were in and all they had to add was a plea from Sir Henry that Washington release André as a personal favor to him, a request that seems incredible under the circumstances.

And so André was taken out of the tavern on the morning of October 2, 1780, a lovely Monday morning in the fall, and marched to his

death. It was a fine fall day with the leaves turning and the sun still
warm when I took that path myself, walking left from '76 House, as
I suggest you do. None of the buildings now on Main Street or in the
immediate vicinity were standing at that time, nor were any of the homes
I passed along the way; nor was there music as there was for André, who
marched along to the fifes and drums playing a piece called "The Blue
Bird." No one paid me any attention, but the people from Tappan and
the neighboring farms turned out to watch and weep over the death of
one so young and fair.

At the intersection, turn left onto Old Tappan Road. Along the way
you will pass old, frame houses and new cottages, cross railroad tracks,
walk sometimes in the road for the lack of a sidewalk, and climb up a
steepening incline. At what seems to be the top of the hill, a street to the
right called **André's Hill** leads higher still. Follow this street to a circular
area at the very top, with houses and their driveways on every side. The
houses are probably no more than twenty years old, and may be even
more recent. A photograph in the second volume of *Southeastern New
York* shows the same site without houses, with trees and some scant undergrowth in their place, and all around, an unobstructed view of the valley
below and the town off to the right. The core of the circle is a large stone
surrounded by an iron fence. The stone has quotes from Arthur Stanley,
Dean of Westminster, Washington, and Virgil.

When he saw the gibbet and the horse-drawn cart standing under
it, André drew back in horror; not having had any answer from Washington to his plea for a soldier's death, he left the tavern believing
Washington would allow him this. He climbed up onto the wagon without
any assistance; waved away the hangman who, not having a black hood,
had blackened his face with pitch; and adjusted the noose around his own
neck. All the while the band was playing a death march while the American officers with whom he had associated—Lafayette and Hamilton were
reported among the onlookers—were in tears.

When asked if he had anything to say, he said, "I have nothing more
to say gentleman, but this: that you will all bear me witness to the world
that I met my fate as becomes a soldier." Then he bowed to his friends
in the crowd, tied a white silk handkerchief over his eyes, and stood
waiting as the orders for his execution were read aloud. The drums rolled,
the wagon moved forward, and the affair was ended, at least for André.

Arnold had written again to Washington, resigning his commission
in the Continental Army, as if that were necessary. By the time André

died Arnold had accepted 6,315 pounds from Sir Henry and a commission in the British army as a brigadier general. When he heard of the death sentence he wrote again, threatening to kill every American prisoner who fell into his hands if it was carried out. He fought actively against his former countrymen and comrades-in-arms, led the savage raid on New London in 1781, and participated in the fighting in Virginia. He spent several years in Canada as a merchant in the West Indies trade and had an illegitimate child while there by a woman not identified to this day. Then Peggy and the children, his sister, Hannah, and his sons by his first marriage joined him. By 1791 Benedict, Peggy, and sons had settled in London. Hannah and the other boys remained in Canada. Peggy was given a yearly pension by the crown of 500 pounds, and 100 pounds was also given yearly to each of her children. Arnold died in June, 1801, at the age of sixty; the story that he called for his old Continental uniform on his deathbed is apocryphal. Peggy died in 1804, at forty-four. Her sons all served in the British army and a great-grandson was a British major general in World War I.

On August 15, 1821, a British man-of-war sailed up the Hudson to the Tappan Landing. There an emissary from the Duke of York disembarked, proceeded to the village, and then to André's burial place, where he supervised the exhumation of the body. Two cedar trees had been planted at the foot of the grave and a peach tree, placed by an unknown woman, was at the head. The cedar trees, which were about ten feet high by that time, were taken to England and made into snuff boxes. The peach tree presented the resurrectionists with some difficulty, for its roots had penetrated the coffin and entwined themselves around the corpse's skull. The body was placed in a metal sarcophagus, covered with royal purple, and taken to England where it was reburied in Westminster Abbey on November 20.

DE WINT HOUSE

A few minutes' walk will take you to the DeWint House on Oak Tree Road which meets King's Highway to the right as you leave '76 House. There are a number of houses in Connecticut, New York, New Jersey, Rhode Island, and Pennsylvania in which Washington stayed for varying lengths of time. Since he was the commander in chief of the American forces, any place he stayed automatically became his headquarters, and most of these landmarks claim the honor. Technically the claim is correct, but few of them actually saw the general in residence for any significant length of time. DeWint House is one of the few in which Washington's periods of residence (he was here several times) had some historical significance.

It is a small house (the smallness of some of these homes of wealth and importance is always a surprise to me) made of native sandstone and brick with a typically Dutch, high-peaked, steeply sloping roof which flattens out into overhangs at front and back and has brick chimneys at each end. It is set back from the surrounding streets in the midst of a twelve-acre grassed and shaded plot with a brook running through one end. A driveway from the street leads to a paved parking area. This is a registered national historic landmark and is maintained by the National Park Service. It is open daily from 10 A.M. to 4 P.M. and admission is free. There are two buildings in the little park, a carriage house built about 1800, which is now used as a museum, and the DeWint House.

Daniel DeClark built the house in 1700, then sold it to Johannes DeWint in 1746. Washington stayed here on four separate occasions between August, 1780, and November, 1783. It was during his second visit, from September 28 to October 7, 1780, that André was tried and hanged. The DeWint family, with the general's consent, provided the food the prisoner ate. Those same shutters that were shut on the day of execution are still there, beside the same windows.

After the British surrender at Yorktown and the signing of the peace treaty, Sir Guy Carleton traveled up the Hudson to meet with Washington at Tappan to arrange for the evacuation of the British army from New York City. Washington entertained the general and his staff at dinner in the DeWint House. The meal was supervised by Samuel Fraunces, the proprietor of Fraunces Tavern in New York City. On the next day Washington returned the visit, going out on the river to the British man-of-war that had brought Sir Guy to Tappan. This was the first occasion on which the British navy fired a salute to an American flag. The agreement governing the withdrawal was drawn up and signed in the house.

The last time Washington stayed here was through necessity, though undoubtedly he welcomed the opportunity. In November, 1783, the general and his party were on their way from Hackensack, New Jersey, to West Point when they were caught in a heavy snowstorm and were forced to seek shelter. The DeWints and one of the other old Dutch families in the neighborhood, the Blauvelts, entertained him until the storm was over and he could continue his journey.

In 1931 the property was bought by the Free Masons of New York State, who restored it and made it into a shrine in honor of Washington, the most illustrious American ever to belong to the order. The seller, Rogers D. Small, specified in the bill of sale that with the house also went "one black oblong wooden table, one pair of antique brass andirons, one built-in kitchen cabinet, one flint-lock gun of the revolutionary period," all in what is now the kitchen, and "one wooden hat rack having five or six pegs now in the kitchen closet, original pictorial tiles, about seventy-nine in number." All of these to the best of his knowledge and belief were in the house during Washington's visits.

The carriage house *museum* has a number of interesting relics which were found around the DeWint House or in the vicinity, including a spy glass carried by one of the members of Washington's staff, the original key to Mablie's Tavern, and what is purported to be Washington's death mask hanging on one wall in an enclosed glass-fronted box.

About 40 percent of the present furnishings were there originally. Of the two big rooms on the ground floor off the entrance, one is now the front parlor and features the fireplace with the seventy-nine pictorial tiles mentioned in the bill of sale. The kitchen was originally the main room, and most of the articles mentioned by Small are in this room. The round table in the parlor is reportedly the one on which Washington signed the order for André's execution and at which he and Carleton drew up the plans for the British evacuation.

The house and its grounds are worth a look around. During the restoration it was necessary to replace some of the original Dutch bricks, which were then used for the walk now in front. There is a southern magnolia tree behind the house which is unique for the size it has managed to attain, despite the northern winters. The pole well is not original, but was placed there to enhance the atmosphere. There are benches and a drinking fountain, but no picnicking facilities. There are no motels or other accommodations in or near Tappan, for it is off well-traveled roads; but it is within a half hour or so of a number of good motels along 9W and off the New York Thruway.

Leaving pathos and gibbets behind, return to Tappan's principal intersection and, with '76 House on your left, turn onto Old Tappan Road and head east for the scene of a massacre.

BAYLOR'S MASSACRE

Old Tappan Road leads through a pleasant, semirural area away from Tappan, which was called New Tappan in revolutionary times, over the New Jersey border to Old Tappan. After two or so miles the road curves sharply right and then goes over a bridge across the Hackensack River. Immediately beyond the bridge, Old Tappan Road comes to a stop sign at an intersection with River Vale Road. Turn right and look to your right for a wide drive divided by a grass mall, leading into a new subdevelopment. Turn onto the drive and notice the memorial park to the right with new plantings of young trees, gravel walks, and an old *millstone*. On the millstone is a bronze plaque telling the story of the massacre and the restoration of the site. The millstone marks the burial site of some of the victims.

The little park has been built on the site of an eighteenth-century tannery whose soaking vats were dug into the banks of the Hackensack River close by. The area to the south of Old Tappan Road was known as Haring Town, after the Haring Farm. River Vale Road was known as Overkill Road. The area between Old Tappan Road and the river was called Old Tappan, and the area on the north side of the river and Overkill Road was known as the Overkill neighborhood.

Along River Vale Road stood six buildings in 1778 in which about 120 men and officers of the Third Light Dragoons of the Continental Army were quartered on Sunday night, September 27, 1778. At the time the British were gathering supplies for an expeditionary force Clinton was sending to the West Indies. Cornwallis, with about 5,000 troops, had been sent from New York across the Hudson to forage and had taken up positions from what is now River Edge to Englewood, New Jersey. The Americans had responded by setting up an opposing line from Newark, New Jersey, to what was then Clarkstown in what is now Rockland County, New York. The Third Dragoons, part of this perimeter, were a lightly-armed reconnaissance and escort unit under the command of Colonel George Baylor, aged twenty-six, the scion of a socially-prominent Virginia family. Baylor had served briefly as an A.D.C. to Washington, who knew his family well. His second-in-command was Major Alexander Clough, who has been described by historians as an experienced officer.

Baylor had moved the dragoons to Haring Town to keep an eye on the British. He and Clough were billeted in the home of Cornelius Haring, a local Tory. A guard was posted on the bridge over the Hackensack, probably at the point where River Vale Road now crosses the river. Another command of about 400 militia was stationed at New Tappan. Cornwallis learned of the presence of these American troops and decided to attack them as a defense measure before they could attack his foraging parties. He sent Major General Charles "No-flint" Grey up Kinderkemack Road (which still exists) in command of four regiments, which included units of the British Light Infantry. Grey got his nickname from the Paoli Massacre in 1777 in Pennsylvania when he had ordered his men to remove the flints from their guns, so no accidental discharge would warn Anthony Wayne's men of their approach.

Grey's men came marching first up Kinderkemack Road, then along what is now Piermont Road, and finally north along River Vale Road. Flanking parties were detached to surround the homes and barns in which the dragoons were sleeping. They overpowered the guard at the bridge and, at 2 A.M. on the morning of the twenty-eighth, attacked. The dragoons, taken entirely by surprise, put up only a feeble defense. Sixty-seven of the enlisted men were killed, wounded, or made prisoners and thirty-seven escaped. Eleven were killed at once; four others died later. Thirteen were wounded and recovered. Eight of the thirty-nine taken prisoner were also wounded.

The killing was done with the bayonet. D. Bennett Mazur's account of the action (in a report on archaeological work done on the site) said the British pressed the attack shouting, "Kill him!" and "Skiver him!" as they mercilessly bayoneted the dragoons, who tried to hide or get away. Some of the dragoons were wounded many times; one or two were stabbed sixteen times or more; and others were clubbed to death after being bayoneted. Baylor and Clough were pushed into the chimney of the house in which they were billeted and there bayoneted. Baylor was taken prisoner (though wounded), but eventually released. He finally died of the effects of his wounds two years later. Clough reportedly died several days later, after being taken with many of the other wounded to the church in New Tappan (the same church in which André was tried) and then to Orangetown by members of the local militia; but certain archaeological evidence found on the site seems to prove otherwise, as we shall see. The account of the massacre spread through both armies. Congress ordered an investigation and the British Light Infantry were credited, even by their comrades, with being a barbarous outfit.

It is now believed that all of the dead dragoons may have been buried near the site, many in the tannery vats, which had been abandoned some years before. Archaeological excavations carried out in 1967 uncovered three vats in which four skeletons were found, easily identified as dragoons by the buttons and artifacts found with them. Among the relics found with one skeleton were the buttons and stock buckle of an officer. The only officer known to have been near death that night was Clough, and this find suggests he may have died immediately or shortly after and was buried with the others on the site. The burial spot was marked for years by the old millstone, which was used in the tannery to grind bark for the tannic acid used in curing hides. Sometime after the event, the great stone was moved onto the property of a local farmer and was then placed, with a plaque, on the grounds of a local school. It has now resumed its function as a grave marker in the memorial park. Somewhere under the park are the remains of the old vats and the reinterred remains of some of the dragoons who died just across the road. The remains of the other victims were either destroyed during the building and farming operations that disturbed the site, or buried in a yet-to-be-discovered grave.

Look around the park and stroll the banks of the Hackensack as far as you are able. There is a footpath along the riverbank on which Arie Blauvelt's tannery once stood. Blauvelt has been a well-known name in these parts and in Rockland County for over two hundred years. Before the white settlers came, this was a camping spot of the local Indians, who left many artifacts of their Stone Age culture.

Leaving the park, return to River Vale Road and turn right. Some distance farther on the left is a senior citizens' home. On that spot stood the Haring House in which Baylor and Clough were sleeping on the night of the massacre. Now turn around and return along River Vale Road. On your right is where the barns the enlisted men were billeted in were situated. The British came up the road you are traveling. The detachments that encircled the barns came over the ground to your right and over the grounds of the Edgewood Country Club, which you will come to just opposite the intersection with Old Tappan Road. Notice the new blue and white historical marker a short distance beyond that intersection on your right. A little way farther Piermont Road comes in from the right; the British marched along it as they approached Overkill Road.

The area bears a strong resemblance to what it was like then, despite the real estate development and other homes. The country club, the tree-shaded roads, the winding river, and a semirural aspect have saved for Old Tappan much of its older atmosphere and appearance.

Return to Tappan along Old Tappan Road and head north again for a final swing through the Hudson Valley to cover a battle, one of Washington's most important headquarters, and several Continental Army sites, including the last encampment. Begin by backtracking from Tappan. Take Oak Tree Road to Route 303. Take 303 to the Palisades Interstate Parkway, and follow the parkway north to the Stony Point–Route 210 exit. At the stop sign immediately off the exit ramp, turn left to the next stop sign; then turn right onto Route 210 and head east toward the village of Stony Point.

THE STORMING OF STONY POINT

Follow winding, twisting Route 210 through a rural area with a brook to your right and a wooded ridgeline to your left. There are turn-offs here and there that you don't want to take; make sure you remain on 210. About two miles from the parkway, you will spot an old, white sign hanging on the right side of the road. An arrow points to a road which intersects 210 from the left. The sign informs you that a mile in the direction indicated is the site of **Springsteel Farm**, where General Wayne and his men assembled before they attacked the British at Stony Point. Follow the arrow north for about a mile to the intersection with Frank Road. Frank Road follows what was the first road over the Ramapo Hills, a military supply road. It is also the road Wayne's men marched along on their way to the assault.

Frank Road takes you to an open, grassy plot of ground on your right, close to the entrance to Camp Bulowa, a local Boy Scout camp. Park in the grassy area and look to your left. On the opposite side of the road is a boulder bearing a plaque, surrounded by a low, white picket fence. The boulder marks the spot where the Springsteel farmhouse stood. In that farmhouse Wayne rested the night of the assault and reviewed his plans with his officers for the last time. The farmlands then in the immediate vicinity were the final assembly point for his men.

A brook close to the farmhouse provided the men with much welcome water, for they had just marched sixteen miles over narrow, rough roads from their marshaling area at Sandy Beach, north of Fort Montgomery. Close to the farmhouse site, in the direction of the present house, is a narrow waterway which is usually dry whenever I visit the spot. The late I. W. Sklarsky, a writer and resident of the village of Tomkins Cove, wrote a book on the battle, called *The Revolution's Boldest Venture,* in which he describes a brook issuing from under a huge boulder. I hunted high and low and investigated every boulder in sight, including a truly huge one just across the road at the edge of a low, marshy area, but I was not able to locate the brook. You may have better luck, but I suspect the brook has either dried up or shifted its banks.

As you stand with your back to the marker facing east in the direction of the river, notice a wooded hill toward your right front. This hill screened the attacking force from the British, one reason this site was selected for the jumping-off place.

☆

This is a good time to pause and flash back a year and more before the Arnold-André affair to the summer of 1779, when the Stony Point action occurred. Arnold, who was then military governor in Philadelphia, was already in contact with Sir Henry Clinton. The Hudson Valley had been quiet during the winter and early spring of '79. The Americans had remained in their encampments north of Westchester, while they busied themselves fortifying West Point on the opposite bank. Sir Henry brooded in New York City, his thoughts still tending northward up the great river and northeastward toward Connecticut, from whose shores American raiding parties preyed on British shipping on Long Island Sound. In London Lord George Germain, newly appointed head of the war office, had devised a strategy aimed at driving Washington inland. Clinton, however, was on the scene and knew better than Germain the supply problems that would have to be met if British forces were to chase the Continentals into the wilderness west of the Hudson. Clinton hoped to do what other British generals before him had tried in Pennsylvania and New Jersey: lure Washington into open battle, enticing him to pit his relatively inexperienced, haphazardly equipped soldiers against the superior training and equipment of the British redcoats. Sir Henry thought and schemed and finally bestirred himself.

On Monday, May 30, he personally led an expedition up the Hudson, consisting of 6,000 regulars, Hessian and British, embarked on more than 120 sailing ships and flatbottomed vessels. The next day, May 31, they seized Stony Point on the west bank and on June 1, Fort Lafayette on the opposite bank at Verplanck's Point. A small American detachment on Stony Point set fire to the blockhouse they had erected and vacated the premises. On Verplanck's Point, Captain John André approached Fort Lafayette after a short, token bombardment and persuaded the garrison of seventy-five North Carolinians and one officer to surrender.

The significance of the move was immediately and painfully apparent to General Washington. Stony Point and Verplanck's Point were, respectively, the western and eastern landings of King's Ferry, a vital link connecting east-west roads from the towns and seaports of New England to New Jersey, Pennsylvania, and the southern states. Historians differ as to whether Clinton was trying to revive the old strategy of severing New England from the rest of the colonies. There were other aspects to this situation, however, that posed a positive danger to the American cause. King's Ferry marked the closest point to New York City at which the rebels could operate safely. Now that it was in British hands, those limits of safety had been pushed considerably northward, perhaps as much as twelve miles north to newly-fortified West Point, Washington's "key to the Continent."

The capture of Stony Point, however, was mostly bait in a trap. Sir Henry followed up with a series of devastating raids into Connecticut. Fairfield and Norwalk were invested and burned; New Haven ransacked, the countryside laid waste, and the citizenry harried: all designed to lure Washington away from the safety of the highlands. These were intolerable acts the Americans could not afford to ignore, but their response was not quite what Sir Henry expected or desired. Washington took immediate counter steps. He concentrated his forces at strategic points along the Hudson Valley should the British attempt to attack West Point, moved his headquarters to New Windsor behind the lines, and began to plan the recapture of Stony Point. A number of reconnaissance missions scouted out the defenses the British were building there. An American army officer, Allen McLane, escorted a local widow, who was visiting her sons, into the fort under a flag of truce and came away with a report on its state of partial readiness. Washington himself reconnoitered the Point several times from the nearby hills and decided the situation required the special talents of Anthony Wayne.

This is not the first time we have seen Wayne in action, nor will it be the last. We recall him as one of the commanders leading the attempt to take Trois Rivières during the closing phases of the invasion of Canada. In our travels through the Pennsylvania sites, we shall meet him again on the Brandywine, at Germantown and Paoli, and in New Jersey on Monmouth battlefield. These were all engagements which had occurred before this stop in history.

The Battle of Stony Point was Wayne's very own. Though Washington had laid down the general plan of attack, it was Wayne's sole responsibility, from the planning of the actual assault to its conclusion. It was here he earned his sobriquet, "Mad Anthony," for his audacity and seeming recklessness.

A native son of Pennsylvania, he had been educated at his uncle's academy in Philadelphia, then had spent a year working as an agent and surveyor for a land company. The job took him twice to Nova Scotia on surveying trips, and many a road and town line in Pennsylvania today owe their existence to Wayne's facility with his transit. In 1774 he was elected to the Pennsylvania legislature and the state committee of safety. Though he was well read in military history, at the outbreak of hostilities he was as inexperienced in battle as were most other American commanders. He had a natural talent for command, however; his fellow Pennsylvanians seemed eager to follow him; and he seemed to relish the rigors of campaigning and the dangers of the battlefield. Though he was not always a successful commander, he invariably displayed great courage and daring. He had suffered one humiliating defeat, the nighttime massacre of his men at Paoli, a disaster which had taught him a lesson he was about to apply in the coming engagement.

Following the Battle of Monmouth, he had been replaced as commander of the Pennsylvania Line by Arthur St. Clair, that same St. Clair who, you will remember, surrendered Fort Ticonderoga to the British without firing a shot. Wayne, a brigadier general, was asked to take command of a brigade, a colonel's post. Feeling slighted and more than a little disillusioned, Wayne saw his men safely into winter quarters and then rode back to Pennsylvania on a leave of absence. Resuming his seat in the assembly, he persuaded the state to make retirement provisions for its veterans against the day they would be out of service. He took the precaution of writing to Washington, explaining that his absence from the army was only temporary and that he would appreciate it if his old commander would entrust to him the command of the new light infantry brigade then being organized. He waited patiently on his farm in Waynesborough, a family man once again, enjoying the company of his wife, young son and daughter until word came of Clinton's move to Stony Point, followed by a message from Washington asking him to return to active duty.

As a battle site, Stony Point has several unusual features. Very little archaeological digging or restoration has been done, though some landscaping was done when it was made into a state park. Despite its modern character as a public park, it is comparatively out of the way and unadvertised and therefore relatively unknown. The battle itself consisted of a single action within a small, well-defined area. Finally, many of the routes followed by the attacking force still exist or can be traced, allowing us to follow the movements of troops prior to the fighting over the same terrain.

You can easily fight the battle of Stony Point in one day; the distances involved add up to only twenty or so miles, some of which can be covered on foot if you so choose. I suggest you begin with the preceding sites and storm the position in the afternoon.

Wayne was in command of a brigade of the newly formed light infantry numbering about twelve hundred men. Light infantry was a European innovation that had become a regular part of standing armies of the time. British regiments usually included two companies known as light infantry or grenadiers, lightly equipped, lightly armed units which were used as advanced skirmishers and to guard the flank of the regiment against surprise attack. The Continental Army had had several units of light infantry before Stony Point under various commanders. Wayne's command was yet another attempt to establish and standardize this kind of a unit as a regular part of army organization.

One half of Wayne's command went into camp at **Sandy Beach,** a river's edge spot about five miles below West Point and two miles north of Fort Montgomery. I did my best to find the site one windy, cloudy Sunday. I began in the town of Fort Montgomery just the other side of the traffic circle beyond Bear Mountain Park at the northern end of the Palisades Parkway. First I drove to the historical marker on the right side of 9W marking the fort, then continued north, turning off 9W onto 218, the road that leads to Highland Falls and West Point, so as to keep close to the river. After passing two mobile-home parks I wandered into a small maze of development roads, one with the intriguing name Revolutionary Road, but could not get close enough to the riverbank to investigate. Finally I gave up there and continued north until I passed the sign for Highland Falls. Just beyond I entered the grounds of a large, private estate whose owner, intrigued by my search, allowed me to park my car and showed me how to get down to the shoreline. She also pointed out Sugarloaf almost directly across the river, the same Sugarloaf Mountain which is just south of the Beverley Robinson House site. This made it immediately clear I had come much too far north.

With the sky occasionally spitting rain, I took an enjoyable walk along the riverbank as far south as Fort Montgomery, a distance of about three miles, looking for any site that might warrant the name Sandy Beach. It was supposed to have been located on the farmland of a Benjamin Jacques, but though there are a number of farms and homes in the area, the most promising site I found was the mobile-home park area. This was about a mile below the point where I had begun my walk, placing it about the right distance above Fort Montgomery. Just before I came to this spot, I noted a brook brawling its way down the rock-torn slope on its way to the river; at the mobile park itself, there is good water which is being pumped and stored for the residents of the park. This and the fact that the shoreline flattens out there into a wide, grassy slope more gradual than the rocky shores that line this part of the Hudson, leads me to speculate that there is where Wayne's men might have camped.

Wayne's command consisted of four regiments, each divided into two battalions. The first regiment was under the command of Colonel Christian Febiger, a Danish volunteer who had been at Bunker Hill and

Quebec. Major Thomas Posey of Virginia, destined to become the second governor of Indiana, was in command of Febiger's second battalion. The first battalion was under Lieutenant Colonel Louis de Fleury, a French volunteer.

The second regiment of Pennsylvania and Maryland troops was commanded by Colonel Richard Butler. The third regiment (stationed on the other side of the river so as not to arouse the suspicions of the British, who would have noticed so many men living and training together in so conspicuous an area) was commanded by Colonel Return Jonathan Meigs, who had been captured at Quebec and then exchanged. The fourth was commanded by Colonel Rufus Putnam, but it was led into action at Stony Point by his second-in-command, Lieutenant Colonel William Hull.

These were all men noted for their bravery and competence, culled from crack battalions in Washington's immediate command. They were low on food and rum, a situation Wayne did his best to relieve. "Dandy Wayne," as his officers called him, was also very uniform-conscious and was distressed by his men's lack of them. He had designed for himself a uniform featuring light blue as the dominant color with sleeves on the shirt that protruded below the cuffs of his coat. Wayne was not able to do much about the uniforming of his men, but he did manage to see to their arming. Once the basic strategy of the attack was set, he had his noncommissioned officers carry spontoons—tall, spear-like weapons with pointed blades at the top and short crossbars just below the hafts. The men drilled daily with the bayonet, following Baron von Steuben's infantry manual. No one knew what they were training for, since the purpose of their mission had not yet been revealed to anyone except their commander.

Washington invited Wayne to join him on a reconnaissance on July 6 on the top of **Buckberg Mountain,** which lies a mile northwest of Stony Point. You can join the party by returning to 210 and continuing into the village of Stony Point. Where 210 ends at a juncture with 9W, turn left (north) onto 9W and drive for about a mile to the village of Tomkins Cove. Keep a sharp eye out for Buckberg Road on your left which leaves 9W at a climbing diagonal. A historical marker just off 9W will inform you that "In 1776–1783 this was an important military route over the Dunderberg to Doodletown, Fort Clinton, Montgomery, and West Point." Follow Buckberg Road past pleasant homes and gardens on both sides until you come to a historical marker on the right side of the road which reads: "Buckberg Mountain. Here Generals Washington and

Wayne surveyed the British fort on Stony Point and planned the victory of July 15–16 of 1779."

There is no place to park except on the shoulder of the road, but since traffic is light, that does not present any great problem. You are almost at the top of the mountain. The highest point is to your left across the road where the wooded slope goes up for a short distance, the site where the two men stood as they peered down at the Point. That is private property, however, and you will have to be content with trying to catch a glimpse of the view below from the tangled, brushy plot of ground next to the marker. You will notice, as I did, that it is quite difficult to see the river and Stony Point from this position because of the trees, though it may be somewhat better during the late fall and winter when the foliage is gone. The rest of the area on that side of the road is occupied by a white, frame house and its grounds. The occupants allowed me on the property, and by walking to the eastern edge of their lawn I was able to see a wonderful view of the river, the cove, Verplanck's Point directly across the river and Stony Point itself below. However you get to see this view, keep in mind that in 1779 none of the homes you passed on your way up or those in the immediate vicinity were in existence. Most of the people now living on Buckberg had to have top soil trucked in to cover bare, rock areas in order to grow lawns and shrubs. Therefore, we may safely assume that most of the area was too rocky to support more than low, scraggly growth and that Wayne and Washington had little trouble seeing the Point.

Washington had come to this site several times after the British captured the position to see for himself what kind of progress they were making with their fortifications. Though only the west and north slopes were visible, the Point had been cleared of trees and enough could be seen to formulate a plan of attack. What Washington had in mind was a surprise attack, covered either by night or by a storm if one should come along at the right moment and preferably by both. The attackers were not to give away their numbers or positions with small arms fire, but were to rely on bayonets.

"General," the impetuous Wayne said as they peered through their spy glasses at the British, "I'll storm Hell if you'll only plan it."

To which Washington replied, "Perhaps you had better try Stony Point first."

Even after two centuries, one can hear the tone of voice the words imply. Stony Point today is shaded by tall cedars and a variety of other arboreal plants, not to mention the shrubs and lawns planted by the New York State Parks Department and the wild flowers, grasses, and bushes that have sprung up over the years. What the reconnoiterers saw was a bare, stony peninsula with steep, rocky sides sloping sharply down into the river. Originally the peninsula had been an island, but Washington had started the first garrison to work on a causeway to the shore. The causeway was never completed and high tide still presented a water barrier to anyone approaching from the west, but to all intents and purposes, the island had been joined to the shore.

The British had cut down whatever trees the rocky soil supported and had cleared the woods and vegetation from the approaches to deny cover to any forces attempting to retake the site, utilizing the timber in the construction of their fortifications. On the highest part of the Point, 150 feet above the river, the Americans could see a fort almost completely enclosed with seven or eight batteries, some fifteen guns in all. The observers must also have noticed that a system of communications trenches was being dug connecting the gun positions.

Well in front of the fort was an abatis, a barrier of tree trunks sharpened to points which protruded forward in the direction of probable attack, extending across the width of the peninsula from water line to water line. Two hundred yards or so west of that was yet another abatis which also extended completely across the peninsula. Both abatises curved in at the ends to face anyone attempting to climb either slope from any angle. Between them several guns and fortified positions took advantage of natural strong points and chevaux-de-frise littered the open areas. West of the second abatis, advance, fortified positions covered all avenues of approach to the causeway. As you go over the ground you will see for yourself how much advantage the defenders had and why the attack strategy was dictated by the nature of the terrain. "Little Gibraltar" the British called the place, a most appropriate name.

The British garrison totaled 625 officers and men, under the command of Lieutenant Colonel Henry Johnson, including Highland Grenadiers and a number of Americans loyal to the crown. Against them Wayne was bringing 1,200 of his light infantry, a reserve of three hundred under General Muhlenburg and Henry Lee and his mounted troops for reconnaissance and security. For once numerical superiority lay with the rebels. The British by this time were aware an attack was being prepared. That they were not more cautious and on guard was their own fault. However, they could call on naval support in the event of a siege and the guns on the Point covered the surrounding area in every direction for at least half a mile. Incidentally, Lee was the famous "Light Horse Harry" Lee, one of the Continental Army's few cavalry commanders. He had already served with distinction during the Philadelphia campaign and was to cover himself with glory at Paulus Hook and during the southern campaigns. He was also destined to father the future commander of Confederate forces, Robert E. Lee. Lee's job was to patrol roads and trails in the Stony Point area, keeping tabs on suspected British agents, harassing British patrols and foraging parties, taking prisoners for information, and seeing to it that no word of the American preparations reached British ears via the local inhabitants.

A British deserter revealed that the shoreline close to the southern side of the Point was a sandy beach occasionally flooded by the tide and guarded by a small abatis. This morsel of information clarified the plan of attack in Washington's mind, and he passed it on to Wayne who subsequently made some adjustments to suit the terrain and other circumstances. An intensive period of training began at Sandy Beach, though no one except one or two officers besides Wayne knew about the attack. On July 14 the third and fourth regiments joined the other two and Wayne's Corps of Light Infantry was ready to move. On the fifteenth, a Thursday, the entire command fell in for regular morning inspection and were ordered to march out. Heading south they passed the ruins of Fort Montgomery, then swung west to pass around Torne Hill on the north side of Popolopen Gorge.

You can follow their route for a little way by picking up old Route 9W just north of the Bear Mountain traffic circle. As you come off the viaduct on 9W look for a road going off and down to your left with an ordinary signpost reading "old 9W." Follow this road around a series of sharp curves until, quite suddenly, you come upon a road to your left going up a steep incline. A marker on your left as you turn onto this road tells you that "July 15, 1779, the Light Infantry of the American Army under General Wayne marched over this road to storm Stony Point." Following in the footsteps of the light infantry you will pass a number of trailer camps and small private homes in a very rustic setting. To your left the ground falls away steeply into Popolopen Gorge. Beyond it you will see the north slope of Bear Mountain and along its flank the Palisades Parkway. At this point you are traveling across the south flank of Torne Hill whose bare, craggy top, immediately north of Bear Mountain, overlooks Popolopen Gorge. After marching four miles along this road, their passage screened from possible observers on the river by the mountains, the men were halted on the Clement farm in an area known as Queensboro where a village, long since gone, was built after the Revolution. Resuming their march they turned south to cross the western end of the Dunderberg, down to Springsteel Farm.

I clocked four miles along this road leading west from Fort Montgomery and after passing through lands which are probably part of the West Point reservation, found myself driving alongside a man-made lake with a spillway and concrete dam at the east end. It was therefore impossible to turn left as Wayne's men had done to march south, nor was there any trace of a road, as far as I could see, on the other side of the lake. It seemed as though the lake had covered that portion of the route.

Reviewing the situation while taking my ease at the Springsteel Farm site, I concluded that the road or trail the light infantry took from Queensboro is no longer in existence or not marked. However, from Springsteel Farm you can follow the routes the assault parties used to get to Stony Point for most of the way. Return to 9W, head south back to Stony Point and return to Springsteel Farm.

Wayne is said to have used elaborate security precautions during the hours immediately preceding the attack. All civilians who happened to be abroad that night were escorted to their homes; a screen of pickets surrounded the Point itself, and even the assembly area at the farm was sealed off to prevent faint hearts and traitors from going over to the enemy with news of what was afoot. One source says that Wayne had all the local farm dogs killed to prevent their raising any commotion as his men moved from the farm to the Point, but I have not been able to find confirmation of this anywhere else.

The men were formed into three columns. Two columns were to converge on the Point from the north and south simultaneously. The third column was to approach over the causeway and open fire upon the defenders to create a diversion. These men were the only ones allowed to carry loaded rifles. The men in the two flanking columns were under orders not to fire their guns under any circumstances. Any man who disobeyed this order was to be killed on the spot by his commanding officer. Each man wore a white piece of paper in his hat to distinguish him from the enemy. Surprise was the very essence of this operation, for the bayonet alone was to carry home the point of the American argument.

Each of the flanking columns was preceded by an officer and twenty men called "forlorn hopes." Their job was to take care of the sentinels and to cut a way through the abatises.

Behind them came 150 men who were to get through the fallen barriers and dash for the top, fighting their way into the British positions crying "The fort's our own!" as loud as they could.

The rest of the men were to follow up with the knockout punch.

Wayne was with the column attacking from the south. The central or diversionary column was under the command of Major Hardy Murfree for whom Murfreesport in Pennsylvania was named. The first man to enter the fort was to receive a promotion and a reward of $500; the second would be given $400; the third, $300; the fourth, $200; and the fifth, $100.

At 11:30 that night, the columns came to attention and moved out. There was only a mile and a half between them and their objective. Move out with them by returning along Frank Road in the direction from which you came. A hundred yards or so along you will come to a stop sign at an intersection. At this point the southern attack column continued straight ahead onto Crickettown Road, which is what Frank Road becomes. The northern column turned left and followed what is now called **Wayne Avenue.** You go along with them down Wayne Avenue toward the river. On your left between houses and trees, you can look across a valley to Buckberg Mountain where you reconnoitered the fort earlier in the day. Small private homes appear along both sides of the road as you come down into the village of Stony Point and to a junction with 9W. At that point you cannot go ahead any farther, for the road does not continue on the other side of 9W. The river is less than a mile away and we must assume that the northern column still had road ahead to take it down to the point of attack. In fact, just across 9W is where Murfree's column headed right to march to the causeway.

Turn around and return along Wayne Avenue to the Frank Road intersection; then make a left onto Crickettown Road. Now you are moving south with Wayne and the southern column. At Heights Road turn left and follow it down into the village of Stony Point. As the river comes into view below, Heights Road runs into Ten Eyck Road, which takes you to Liberty Drive, and so on to 9W. Here the road runs out, just as Wayne Avenue did. However, if you turn left onto 9W and proceed north for a short distance, you will come to a road which turns off sharply to the right. Whether this is actually the road along which Wayne continued his approach is a matter of conjecture, but it will take you to the river on the south side of Stony Point at about the right distance from it. A quarter of a mile from 9W you will come to a railroad overpass. Just beyond is a dirt road. You are now on the riverbank with marinas and boatyards all about. Turn left onto the dirt road and follow it as far as you can to a wide, grassy area restricted, according to hand-lettered signs here and there, to boat owners. I was not challenged, but there does not really seem to be any reason why I should have been.

Leave your car, walk toward the water, and look to your left. **Stony Point** is about a quarter of a mile away, jutting out into the water. Remember that if you had been standing here in July, 1779, during daylight hours, you would have seen the abatises and gun positions quite clearly. At midnight of July 15, when Wayne and his men reached this shore, they might have just been able to make out the Point, a dark mass against the starry sky with perhaps the glow from a fire showing from the fort 150 feet above them.

You can walk along the riverbank toward the Point for as far as possible, but whether you will be walking over the same ground the light infantry trod is debatable. The railroad put down a right-of-way and the extent to which they used fill and changed the shoreline is unknown. Pick your way between the piles of boat-building materials, over the sandy ground which is dotted with clumps of high, coarse grass. Cattails ahead show that the same marshy area Wayne's men confronted is still in existence. Finally you will come to the place where the riverbank curves west and a narrow arm of watery marsh separates you from the south flank of Stony Point.

Wayne had expected to find this ground dry, but the tide was in, and his men were forced to step into the water and wade the rest of the way. At that moment a British sentry on picket duty along the shore thought he heard something and fired. The attackers pushed on as the alarm spread and rolling drums called the Point's defenders to their posts. At almost the same moment, the northern column attacked and the battle was joined.

In the face of musket, rifle, and cannon fire from above, the forlorn hopes of the southern column gained the side of the Point and went to work with their axes on the first abatis. The advanced party swarmed through the breach and started to work its way up the steep, rocky slope. Wayne stepped through the abatis and started after them, only to be hit a glancing blow in the head. Down he went as his men swept on without him.

In true cliff-hanger fashion, leave Wayne's fate hanging in the balance and drive back the way you came. Before you reach 9W turn right onto Park Avenue, which runs parallel to 9W at a distance east, and follow it to the entrance of **Stony Point State Park**. You will know you are there by a sharp turn in the road to the right (the road ahead is marked private) that leads through a wooded area with a high rise of ground on your right.

If you do not choose to go through the painstaking effort of following the routes of attack, proceed directly to the battlefield by following 9W north through the village of Stony Point until you see a marker on the left side of the road reading "Stony Point battlefield" with an arrow pointing off to your right. The marker appears rather abruptly and it's not a very big one, so drive slowly and be prepared for it. Turn onto the road indicated and follow it toward the river. You will pass private homes as you drive down the sloping ground with only one additional marker, no more conspicuous than the one on 9W, to indicate you are on the right road.

Both routes take you to the entrance to the park, where you will pass over the causeway built by the Continentals. It has since been widened and its height probably raised somewhat. It is now thick with planted trees and undergrowth, a factor you should immediately discount, for the British cut down every bit of cover on the causeway and along its approaches. Note a historical marker on your left, but pass it by for the time being; you will return shortly. A stone archway inscribed "Stony Point State Park" marks your entrance onto state land. Directly beyond is a wooden bridge which goes over the railroad cut. Follow the road around the caretaker's house (it was abandoned the last time I was there because of a fire) down to an open, grassy area with parking spaces indicated by low, log barriers. Beyond the barriers are picnic tables, beyond them the river and the marshy shoreline along which Wayne's column approached. You are looking south toward the boatyards and marina where you were following the opening phase of the attack a short time ago.

Other picnic tables are scattered throughout the park, some on high ground overlooking the river. There are also rest rooms, water fountains, and a *museum* containing relics of the battle, maps, and other displays. Paved and gravel footpaths lead everywhere with signs and arrows pointing the way and markers at all pertinent sites. There are shade trees and grassy slopes everywhere with good views of the river from almost every height, all in all a delightful prospect for an afternoon spent in history and the outdoors.

Return on foot to the marker you passed as you entered the park and place yourself back in the action, this time with Murfree's men. From now on you will be better able to appreciate the Washington-Wayne plan of attack. The marker reads "Major Murfree with Massachusetts and North Carolina companies engaged British outposts here by firing to cover the two flank movements." This describes Murfree's role only in part. Murfree had his men commence firing as soon as he heard the commotion from above which told him the British had sprung to their posts to meet the threat of the two flanking columns. Straight ahead of you is where the British pickets were stationed when they challenged Murfree's advance. Walk back into the park over the ground Murfree's men covered as they drove the pickets back. The British responded just as Wayne thought they would. Colonel Johnson, freshly aroused from sleep, came charging down the hill with six companies of men convinced that the main attack was coming across the causeway. As the south column of attackers gained the slopes behind him, they cut him off from the central redoubt. When he realized his mistake he tried to get back, only to find himself caught between Wayne's men and Murfree's column. By that time the Americans were in the main redoubt and he was forced to surrender.

As you walk, notice the terrain which Murfree and his men faced, the rapidly and steeply rising ground ahead and to the left with a swampy ravine to the right, dangerous and difficult terrain for any attacking force to overcome, especially in the face of well-armed, well-equipped, well-dug-in forces. Now you can see for yourself how the nature of the terrain dictated flanking, surprise attacks—an audacious way of overcoming the lack of cover and the threat of the British artillery.

As you walk still farther into the park, you will find markers identifying the positions of the two abatises, the places where British guns were placed, the very spots where the attackers entered the British works, the central redoubt, and the place in the central redoubt where the final hand-to-hand melee took place.

The gun positions are usually marked by depressions in the ground and sometimes by period cannon, none of which were on the scene during the battle. One marker denotes the supply road the British used to get to the central redoubt. The central redoubt itself was perched atop a huge outcropping of rocks, the very top of the point which presents a formidable obstacle that must be flanked by anyone approaching from the downhill side. A cannon placed at the brink of this huge rock formation and pointed downhill faces the climber as he approaches and the effect is quite overpowering, even though you know the gun is not loaded and the barrels of a hundred Brown Besses are not aimed in your direction.

When you get to the marker on the site where Colonel Butler led the advanced party of the northern column into the British works, look off to your left into Tomkins Cove and the ground that column traversed to reach the Point. Beyond this marker the site of the main *redoubt* is marked by a large circle of fieldstones fitted roughly together and then, a little way farther up, a still larger circle which includes most of the top of the Point, about two hundred feet in circumference. From this position the British had an unsurpassed view of this section of the river and complete control of the ferry. The sites of both landings may be seen in Tomkins Cove and on Verplanck's Point, which is presently occupied by several colonies of oil-storage tanks. In Tomkins Cove may also be seen the remains of the Mothball Fleet, tankers and Liberty ships of World War II, veterans of the South Pacific and the Murmansk run, now retired upriver to swing on their cables. Downslope, were the trees not present, you might see what the British garrisons saw in that direction —all of the rest of the Point as far as the shoreline (which would have been visible in both directions for some distance), the high ground sloping up and inland, and on the skyline the Ramapo Hills which had hidden Wayne's line of approach. Immediately to the east of the redoubt, behind you, is the Coast Guard lighthouse, erected on the very spot once occupied by the blockhouse built by the first American garrison.

Sit down and take a moment or two to conclude the story of the storming of Stony Point. The two attack columns from north and south made their way up the slopes in the face of heavy British musket and cannon fire. The aim of anyone firing downhill, however, is notoriously bad, so the casualties were not crippling, though seventeen out of twenty of the northern column's forlorn hopes were either killed or wounded. Murfree had drawn Colonel Johnson and a considerable number of his garrison off to the foot of the Point. Colonel Butler and his advance party entered the British positions from the north. Wayne, with his forehead creased by grapeshot, lay on the south slope attended by two aides. Fearing he had been seriously wounded, he pleaded to be carried to the top so that he could die within the redoubt, secure in the knowledge of victory.

Lieutenant Colonel François Louis Teissèdre de Fleury, with Wayne's column, was the first to enter the British works shouting, "The fort's our own!" as per his orders.

Fleury, scion of a noble family, was yet another of those French volunteers who willingly risked life and limb in the cause of American liberty, a cause which diametrically opposed the concept of royalty and the doctrine of the divine right of kings. Fleury had served with distinction at Brandywine and Monmouth and for six weeks in Fort Mifflin when it was under siege. He was subsequently guillotined in Paris, a victim of the Terror, though he fought for the French republic when the European powers invaded her in their attempt to restore the monarchy.

Lieutenant George Knox, also with Wayne's column, was the second to enter the main redoubt, to be followed by a Sergeant Baker who was bleeding from four different wounds. Right after them were Sergeant Spencer and Sergeant Donlop who was also wounded. The British were now split into small, isolated pockets of resistance all over the site, each surrounded by shouting Americans advancing on them with bayonets at the ready. Revenge for Paoli, Baylor's Massacre, the Hancock Massacre, and half a dozen other bloody incidents must have been uppermost in many a rebel's mind that night, no less in those of the British soldiers who cried out for quarter. Under the rules of war pertaining at that time, night attackers were not obliged to give quarter, but with admirable restraint the Continentals overlooked the rules, curbed their instinct for vengeance, and called upon the redcoats to throw down their arms. All of them did so at once with the exception of a captain named Tew who refused. He was promptly bayoneted to death, thus earning for himself the dubious distinction of being the only British officer to die on Stony Point.

The attack had been launched a few minutes after midnight. Less than an hour later, it was all over and Stony Point was back in American hands. One British officer escaped by jumping into the river and swimming out to the British sloop *Vulture,* the very ship that was to carry André to his rendezvous with Arnold fourteen months later. On Verplanck's Point the British occupying Fort Lafayette heard the sound of fighting die away and wondered who had won. The cheers of the victors told them nothing, but the guns of Stony Point spoke volumes when the Americans turned them around and fired in their direction. The *Vulture* slipped her cables and dropped downstream out of range.

In the full flush of victory, few in the attacking force realized their general was not with them to celebrate until Wayne, bleeding but conscious and still in command of himself and the situation, was carried into the redoubt. He was not dying but only slightly wounded, fully able to enjoy the fruits of his careful planning and exactly-timed strategy.

The Americans lost 15 killed and 83 wounded. The British lost 20 killed, 74 wounded, 58 missing and 472 captured, which included the wounded. The value of the captured stores and supplies, which came to about $180,655, was divided among the victors on a share basis according to rank, the way whaling crews used to share in the profits of their voyages. The shares ranged from Wayne's $1,420.51 to a private's $78.92. The rewards promised to the first five men to enter the fort were eventually voted by Congress and paid. Fleury was awarded a congressional medal for his part in the action, one of only eight medals Congress handed out during the war. Wayne and Major John Stewart, one of the officers commanding the southern column, were also medal recipients.

Washington had planned to take Fort Lafayette as well. All that was needed to put that phase of the plan into operation was definite word from Wayne that Stony Point had fallen.

At 2 A.M. on the morning of July 16, Wayne wrote to Washington: "The fort and garrison with Colonel Johnson are ours. Our officers and men behaved like men who are determined to be free."

The note was dispatched immediately. Troops were standing by at West Point and Continental Village east of Peekskill ready to move on Verplanck's Point. Wayne's note went astray and there was a grand mix-up concerning marching orders and siege equipment. By the time the attack force was in position around Fort Lafayette, Clinton had received word of Stony Point and had sent reinforcements hurrying north, causing the Americans to abandon the attempt. Washington decided he did not have enough men available to defend Stony Point and ordered the British-built defenses razed and the guns removed. Wayne and his men withdrew on the eighteenth, but not before Washington himself had come to inspect the scene and congratulate the victors personally. Three American deserters who had been captured in the redoubt were hanged at the flagpole, a site marked by the present flagpole.

As many of the guns as possible were transferred to the galley *Lady Washington,* only to be lost in the river when the galley came under fire from an eighteen-pounder on Verplanck's Point and had to be beached and burned to escape capture. On the very next day, July 19, Clinton's men reoccupied Stony Point and subsequently rebuilt the works, this time completely enclosing the fort. The damage to the British cause, however, was irreversible. American morale had been given a tremendous boost. Wayne's exploit had forced Clinton to call a halt to the British activities in New England and to concentrate most of his command along the lower Hudson valley to keep an eye on Washington.

Wayne's Light Infantry went into camp at Fort Montgomery for several months until it was decided to take Stony Point again. With this in mind Wayne marched his men downriver, this time in full view of the British. Finding the defenses too strong, however, Wayne continued his line of march through Haverstraw and on into New Jersey where the brigade took up patrol duties. Clinton finally realized he would not be able to keep a grip on King's Ferry through the coming winter and ordered both Stony Point and Fort Lafayette abandoned. His attempts to capture and control the Hudson Highlands by force of arms and to trap Washington had come to naught. Another way would have to be found, perhaps through treachery. We know, however, what became of that scheme. In retrospect, Stony Point ended Clinton's Hudson strategy. It was the last important action fought in the northern states. After Stony Point most of the action was transferred to southern theaters of operation.

Sklarsky reports that in 1953, landscaping operations at Stony Point uncovered the skeletons of several British soldiers identifiable by the buttons of their uniforms. In response to a request from Great Britain, the United States government had the remains returned to their native land.

Today picnic tables dominate the ground. A depression in the ground is a clear indication of the redoubt walls and the area behind them. There are markers identifying the site as the central redoubt and one which states that the final combat was fought in this area between American bayonets and British muskets. About thirty feet south of the central redoubt another marker says Wayne was wounded near the spot by British grapeshot. "Near" in this case means a distance down the slope, of course. You will have to walk south from the marker to the edge of the slope to look down toward the real spot. A short distance down this slope and off to the right you will come across yet another marker for the main gate to the redoubt. Here again is a depression between the remains of an embankment. To the right of this marker, another identifies the spot where Fleury entered the ramparts. A path leads from this spot, which you can follow or charge along it with Fleury if you're so inclined, into the central redoubt position. Up at the very top, a depression with some tumbled rocks lying about probably marks yet another gun position. A flight of stone steps leads to the base of the lighthouse. The view is magnificent and a picnic table is available, a wonderful spot for lunch if the wind isn't too strong.

At this point you are closer than you will be from any other point in New York to the site of one of the many border battles between British-Indian allies and rebel settlers. This calls for a detour; since the region in which it is located was part of the frontier it is still off the beaten track, so to speak. There's nothing for it but to go out of your way if you want to be in on the Battle of Minisink.

BATTLE OF MINISINK

If you are going to Minisink from Stony Point, return to the Palisades Interstate Parkway; take it north for a short distance to U.S. 6

west, and then take 6 through the northernmost section of Bear Mountain–Harriman State Park until you reach Route 17. At that point, follow signs onto the new Route 17, which is called the Quickway. Since 6 west actually joins 17, you won't go wrong if you follow the signs for Route 6. If you are coming from either north or south of Stony Point, take the New York State Thruway to the Quickway exit and then the Quickway west about fifteen miles to Goshen.

The Goshen exit goes onto Route 207, which takes you into town almost immediately. Drive through the center of town, across railroad tracks and past a war memorial on the right; shortly after that you will come to a large, buff, brick building also on the right, the county office building. Next to it, encircled by an iron picket fence, is a *memorial column* to the men who fell in the Battle of Minisink. The monument stands in Goshen because most of the militiamen came from the Goshen region and marched from Goshen as they followed Joseph Brant's trail.

A raid on the village of Minisink had occurred on the night of July 19–20 (Monday-Tuesday), 1779, carried out by Joseph Brant, the Mohawk chief, at the head of a combined force of Indians and Tories. There is some speculation among historians as to where Minisink was located. Benson J. Lossing places it about ten miles northwest of Goshen, which would put it at a point midway between the present towns of Otisville and Howells (both are on Route 211) and about two miles northeast and northwest of Otisville and Howells respectively. Others claim that Port Jervis is the town in question; indeed, Port Jervis was called Minisink at the time. There were also three Indian villages in this area which used the name Minisink, including Minisink Ford on the Delaware River, where the battle following the raid occurred.

Also obscure is Brant's purpose. At the time the American General John Sullivan was preparing an expedition up the Wyoming Valley in Pennsylvania to the Iroquois heartland, and it is possible Brant was trying to either slow down his progress or create a diversion. On the other hand, since only three or four Minisink inhabitants were killed, and many cattle and supplies were taken, it is possible Brant's purpose was only the gathering of supplies.

The Minisink fort, a mill, and a number of houses and barns were burned. The inhabitants put up little resistance; some of them made it into Goshen where the word was spread that Brant was on the loose. The militia gathered and pushed off in pursuit on July 21 under the command of Lieutenant Colonel Benjamin Tusten, a local physician. The next day they were joined by Colonel John Hathorn and a small number of reinforcements. Hathorn assumed command and they continued after Brant, who was headed for the Delaware River which he meant to cross with his booty.

If you are a horse fan and particularly a devotee of trotting horses, you may want to visit the Trotters Hall of Fame, an excellent museum in Goshen only a block or two beyond the memorial. There is a well-known trotting track in town, just behind the museum, where races are held early in July. This is trotting country and for anyone interested in the improvement of the breed, Goshen is Jerusalem.

Return to the Quickway, Route 17; take it for less than a quarter of a mile (you will go on and then off again) to the exit for 17M. Follow 17M to Interstate 84 and take 84 west to Port Jervis. As you come off 84 at the Port Jervis exit, keep driving straight ahead; don't take Route 23 which goes down into New Jersey. You are at the point where New Jersey, New York, and Pennsylvania meet.

Take Route 97 north out of Port Jervis following the scenic Delaware River just off to your left. This is truly beautiful country with wooded hills to right and left forming a gorge through which the river, frequently showing white water, flows. Route 97 follows the river for miles, hugging it around every twist and turn. The result is a drive that reveals one lovely river view after another. The Delaware is a favorite with canoeists whom you may see frequently.

Route 97 will take you into Sullivan County and finally into Barryville. The speed limit drops as you come into town and almost immediately you will find a historical marker on the right at a filling station. It stands on the bank of a brook and tells you that Brant and his men camped here after the raid on July 21 and that the pursuing militia camped three miles up the brook.

Immediately after the marker, Route 55 comes in from the east or right. We followed it for the prescribed three miles with the brook almost constantly in sight, first on one side and then on the other side of the road. The three-mile mark is at a point just beyond a county highway department depot on the right. The brook is off the road on the left side. If the militia did indeed camp here, they were very close to Brant's force, which squares with all accounts. As they came upon the remains of Brant's fires the next day, they learned the force they were pursuing was larger than they had thought, and there was some debate about the advisability of continuing. It was finally decided to continue and on they went.

Return to Route 97 and clock 2.8 miles from the junction with 55 to a second marker. It says it marks the ravine up which Brant led forty of his men to ambush the militiamen, who were on a hill to the west; but there is no hill to the west, only the Delaware River. This suggests that the marker may have been moved to this more traveled road. The hill in question lies not to the west, your left, but to your right, or east and north and some distance farther. In 0.4 mile along 97, a third marker commemorates the battle "on this hill," to your right. More confusion. The hill on which the battle took place is actually farther. In 0.7 mile you come to a sign for Minisink Ford. Now you are really hot. In another 0.3 mile you will come to another marker on the left for the Battle of Minisink. You are also at a sign for a toll bridge, which is off to the left where Route 590 crosses the Delaware River. Immediately to the right is a sign for the **Minisink battlefield** which is now 3,000 feet up the hill. Before you visit the battlefield, take note of the toll bridge. It was built by John Augustus Roebling, who also built the Brooklyn Bridge, and is somehow reminiscent of that famous span. Perhaps it is the huge, round cables that hold up the roadbed, which was made of loose, wooden planks when we drove over it. Certainly it is a most unusual design for a bridge in such an out-of-the-way place.

Drive up the hill on County Road 168 past a few private homes and driveways, through a wooded area until you see a sign reading "Minisink Battlefield Historic Site. Public Invited." The road curves at that point, but a sign reading "monument" displays an arrow indicating the direction you should follow. Continue on up the hill along a park road. At the top of the hill is a picnic area with parking spaces, tables, fireplaces, rest rooms, and water. From there a walking trail takes you over this battlefield on which the pursuers became the entrapped and then the pursued.

Those among the Goshen militia who had argued against continuing the pursuit were here vindicated in a manner they foresaw but would rather have avoided. A detachment under Captain Bezaleel Tyler went ahead of the main body, while Hathorn planned to catch Brant as he was fording the river. Brant, who was well aware of his pursuers, had left a rear guard, which picked off Tyler but did not stop his men from coming on. With the two main forces out of sight of each other because of the hills and woods, Brant led his detachment up the ravine you passed along 97 and set up an ambush behind the militia. Most of his supplies and equipment were already across the river, and the militia, realizing they were too late, started back for Goshen.

Almost at once they found themselves ambushed. Brant tried to get them to surrender, but one of the militiamen took a shot that would have killed him if it had not hit his belt. General firing then broke out. During the fight part of the militia was cut off from the rest. The main body took up strong defensive positions on this hill and held out until almost nightfall. As their ammunition began to run out, Brant noticed that a militiaman covering one spot in the Patriots' defenses had been hit and his position was uncovered. The Indians attacked at that point, breached the militia defense line, and began to massacre as many as they could get their hands on. Tusten, who had sheltered the wounded under an overhanging rock, was killed along with seventeen of his patients. Others were killed as they tried to escape down the hill or across the river. Altogether about forty-five Americans were killed, those whose names are listed on the monument in Goshen. Hathorn got away with about twenty-nine others.

From the picnic area, two paths lead off in different directions, one to Indian Rock according to a sign. You should follow the other path. It will take you first to a large, graveled area with benches set around a *monument* which was erected in 1879 on the centennial of the battle. This was the central area where the defenders grouped for a last stand as the Indians swarmed around them. The monument consists of a large rock balanced on top of a column.

A path continues on from the monument to **Central Rock** on somewhat higher ground, a large boulder behind which the militiaman who held this all-important post was stationed until he fell, allowing the enemy to infiltrate and overwhelm his comrades. According to the plaque placed at the rock, Brant was about to give up the fight when he noticed this weakness in the militia line. The plaque further explains that the militia formed into a square as the Indians and Tories kept up a devasting fire.

Another path leads from Central Rock to **Hospital Rock**, the large overhanging rock under which Tusten placed his wounded for cover, and where he and they were put to the tomahawk and knife. The path then leads to Indian Rock, whose significance is not explained, and then back to the picnic area. Except for the more recent growth, the nature of the terrain has not much changed. The hill is intact; so are the rock outcroppings; and what was wooded then is wooded now. There is a pond off to one side about midway between the monument and the picnic area which looks like a regular feature of the area, though it may have overextended its banks after the rainy period that preceded my visit.

This is another site where you can plan to take a lunch or early evening meal break, cooking out or enjoying a sandwich and drinks. There were no refreshments available when I was there; so bring your own and plan to spend some time exploring the rocky, wooded slopes. It's a great place for the kids to climb around and explore. Situated as it is on high ground, it should be a comparatively cool spot even in the midst of the summer heat.

Drive back to Port Jervis and take 84 east to Newburgh for the beginning of a mopping-up operation that will take you up the Hudson Valley on the west side of the river and then across to the eastern shore for a swing south.

NEW WINDSOR CANTONMENT

Your next objective is the New Windsor Cantonment, the last winter campsite of the Continental Army. If you are still at Stony Point simply follow 9W north. If you are coming from farther south, take the Palisades Interstate Parkway to its northern terminus at the Bear Mountain traffic circle; then continue north along 9W. A few miles south of Newburgh, look for the signs for Route 94. Turn west onto 94 at the traffic light (a sign at the intersection points to Knox's Headquarters) and proceeding along that road keep a weather eye out for Temple Hill Road. Turn right (north) onto Temple Hill Road, which will take you to the cantonment. You will be guided along the way by "New Windsor Cantonment" signs. Should you come from the north, use the New York State Thruway to Exit 17, and take 17K east into Newburgh. Turn right or south at Route 9W and proceed south to the 94 turnoff.

The New Windsor Cantonment is open Wednesday through Sunday, 9:30 A.M. to 5:00 P.M. It is closed from the beginning of November until mid-April.

Leave your car in the parking area and walk up the hill to the cantonment area. The first building you come to is a **Museum of Free Masonry**, which should be of some interest to you whether or not you are a Mason since George Washington was a Mason of high degree. The Masons have contributed money and support to historical sites associated with Washington and sometimes carry out restoration and maintenance as is evident at the DeWint house in Tappan.

Near the museum is a large signboard which provides a description of the cantonment and a listing of current events there. The day I visited, for example, the Brigade of the American Revolution, a national historical society whose members dress in colonial military uniforms and drill with weapons of the period, was having one of its annual get-togethers. I watched them go through army drills of the eighteenth century, which included much firing of their weapons and a grand review at the end, all of it performed to field music of the period. They certainly could not have chosen a more appropriate setting.

It was here at New Windsor that the Continental Army endured its last winter encampment. Yorktown had been fought and won, and British and American representatives were meeting in Paris to hammer out the peace treaty. But with the British still in possession of New York City, Charleston, and Savannah, and with his French allies gone off to pull their own chestnuts out of the fire in the West Indies, Washington knew the army had to be kept intact. He ordered his men into camp at New Windsor in the fall of 1782. From 6,000 to 8,000 troops moved into the area and built about 700 huts under the supervision of the indefatigable Baron von Steuben. The huts, each housing two squads, were built out of wood cut from the forest that covered the area. The entire encampment was laid out in a regular pattern of streets with each regiment occupying its own neighborhood, very much as American army camps are laid out today. Separate huts were erected for the officers as well as a large public building, or Temple, for religious services and other meetings. This building gave its name to the area, **Temple Hill,** for it was built on the highest point of ground in the encampment. It measured about 110 feet by 30 and was surmounted by a cupola and a flagpole.

Most of the present cantonment, which represents only a small part of the original, is a reconstruction built and maintained by the National Temple Hill Association, which bought seventy acres of the original site to preserve its Revolutionary War character. Since the Continentals cut down most of the standing timber, today's growth is recent; the area immediately around the split-rail perimeter has been developed in typically modern rural-suburban style. As you stand on Temple Hill and look out over the countryside, keep in mind that in 1782, army huts filled all the fore and middle ground and much of the background as well, row upon row, regularly spaced with company streets running between. Imagine the pall of wood smoke that must have hung over the area during that winter of 1782–83 as the men tried to keep warm while sweating out the last eight months of their military service.

A prominent feature of today's cantonment is a large, rectangular *demonstration area* where I watched the brigade drill; it is bordered on the sides by reconstructed buildings, including the **Temple** which now houses display cases exhibiting artifacts found on the site and a collection of period weapons. One of the buildings is a camp store and refreshment stand; the site is under the administrative control of the Palisades Interstate Commission and camping is allowed. Another building is a reconstructed army *farrier's shop* in which a blacksmith in colonial garb demonstrates what an army farrier could turn out on an anvil.

The one other building of note is a Hudson Valley Dutch cottage with a high-peaked roof ending in a long overhang in front. At present it is furnished as a provost *officer's quarters* with rope beds, an army field desk, and period accouterments, including weapons, canteens, etc. On one wall hangs a map (drawn by geographer S. DeWitt, attached to the Continental Army) of the cantonment area that deserves careful study. It shows quite clearly the private homes and farms that were in the vicinity at the time, the nature of the terrain immediately surrounding the hill—there was low swampy ground at one spot—and how the cantonment was laid out. This is the only building in the cantonment which is not a reconstruction, though it has only been on its present site since 1934. On September 2, 1783, the day before the Treaty of Paris ended the war and Great Britain formally acknowledged United States independence, everything in the cantonment, including the buildings, was placed on the auction block. By that time most of the troops had been furloughed home. Most of the property went to one high bidder—he paid one dollar a hut—who immediately had the Temple pulled down. Another buyer, however, bought this officer's cottage, had it moved to his own land a few miles away, and refurnished it as a home. He lived in it for many years; and though we cannot trace all the events that finally brought it back to its original site, we do know it was returned to the cantonment after a career of 151 years as a private dwelling.

It was here at the New Windsor Cantonment that an event occurred which might have resulted in the establishment of a military dictatorship and bloody disorders. Discontented because the Continental Congress had not made provisions for their retirement pay and generally disgruntled with the cavalier way in which Congress usually sold the army short, some of the officers—among them McDougall, Alexander Hamilton, and Horatio Gates—authored and signed, in March, 1783, two highly inflammatory papers addressed to Congress. They threatened to retain their arms after the signing of the peace treaty or to leave the army for some "unsettled country" should the war continue. Washington denounced the Newburgh Addresses, as these papers were called, and summoned his officers to a meeting in the Temple. It had not been a year since Lewis Nicola, an able and influential Philadelphia merchant-politician, had written to Washington suggesting that he establish an American monarchy and assume a crown. Washington had rejected that offer out of hand. Now here he was faced with yet another movement that could, in its own way, negate everything for which the Revolution had been fought.

On Saturday, March 15, 1783, the officers gathered in the Temple. Washington read a long statement denouncing the movement and ended with a plea to his officers not to sully the honorable reputation they had earned in the service of their country during the long years of fighting. He then tried to read them a letter he had received from a Virginia congressional delegate bearing on the matter of officers' pay. Unable to follow the delegate's fine hand, Washington, for the first time in public, had to use his spectacles.

As he fumbled to put them on, he joked about his infirmity in a half-apologetic way, saying, "Gentlemen, you will permit me to put on my spectacles, for I have not only grown gray, but almost blind in the service of my country."

He read the letter and walked out, leaving behind a shocked company of old friends and comrades-in-arms, who had suddenly realized how much he had given to their cause and what it had cost him physically. A few hours later, Gates informed him the officers had regained their confidence in Congress and had rejected the Newburgh Addresses. Unfortunately, you cannot stand within the very walls where the scene was enacted, but you can stand in the reconstructed Temple, as bare of furnishings as the original, experiencing exactly the same high-ceilinged sound that catches and throws back a muted echo of that hesitating voice.

Not far from the Temple stands a *cenotaph* built of local stone and faced with commemorative plaques, which tell us this is the site upon which the original Temple building stood; that the Temple was known as "the birthplace of the republic"; and that it was also the birthplace of the Society of the Cincinnati, a fraternal organization whose membership was restricted to Continental Army officers and their eldest male descendants. General Henry Knox was its first president and Washington was elected its honorary president. During the politically formative years of the Republic, the society was attacked as a bastion of military aristocracy. In opposition to it, popular political organizations like Tammany societies were formed in New York, Philadelphia, and other cities. Cincinnati chapters were formed in many states, but the political furor aroused by its opponents sent it into eclipse. It was revived in 1893 and is still active in some states as a patriotic service organization.

Close by the cenotaph is a small *burial plot.* One of its stones marks the grave of an unknown soldier of the Revolutionary War, who died during the encampment, was buried at West Point, and then was returned to "rest among his comrades" in 1965. Among the other gravestones (all of them for men who died in the camp, probably of disease) is that of a James Hall, who died aged sixty-nine after "fighting his country's battles" at Long Island, Fort Montgomery, and Trenton. How ironic for James Hall who began his military service in at least 1776, served in some of the most important battles and campaigns, survived seven years of war, and then with victory achieved, peace secured, and his return to civilian life in a free and independent nation only months away, fell victim to disease. Smallpox, typhus, and mumps were constant companions of the men in the Continental Army as were malaria, measles, dysentery, and scurvy. Surgery was primitive, to say the least, and the battlefield was considered safer than any army hospital. Those who suffered severe wounds, such as skull fractures and amputations, and lived had to survive surgery without benefit of anesthesia, septic instruments and dressings, physicians who persisted in trying to cure their patients by bleeding them, and the generally unsanitary conditions of the hospitals and camps.

A short distance along Route 94, as you head back east from Temple Hill, you will see signs directing you to **Knox's Headquarters.** It is worthwhile to stop to visit this well-preserved stone house in which General Knox lived and entertained during the New Windsor encampment while he waited for the peace to be signed. It is set back from the road and has a small parking area to accommodate visitors' cars. Though the original construction was of fieldstone, a wooden wing was added some years later. Inside it is furnished with period furniture, none of it original to the house. Note in the downstairs hall the framed document hanging on one wall attesting to the exact length of time Knox occupied the house, thus giving the owner a specific claim on the national government for compensation. That should help to answer the question that hangs in the back of your mind every time you walk into one of these comfortable private homes used as headquarters and living quarters by Continental Army senior officers. Yes, the owners were compensated, unless of course they were Loyalists who had therefore forfeited their right to compensation.

Be sure to check out the two howitzers stationed in front of the house. They were captured by Wayne's Light Infantry at Stony Point.

Return along Route 94 to its intersection with 9W and turn left (north) toward Newburgh. In less than a mile you will come into Newburgh, passing a blinking caution light at a railroad crossing. The second traffic light after the caution light is companion to a black and white sign hung over the intersection saying "Visit Washington's Headquarters." The picture of a spontoon heads you into a right turn onto Washington Street, though there is no street sign at that point. Heading east on Washington Street, go downhill toward the river, and three traffic lights farther to an intersection with Liberty Street. On your left note a small blue and white sign attached to a lamppost with a pointing arrow which informs you that Washington's Life Guards camped on that spot during his Newburgh residence. The campsite is now occupied by a row of white, frame storefronts with apartments overhead. To your right front, diagonally opposite the campsite, is a parklike area surrounded by a metal picket fence, pierced by two gates which give access onto the grounds of what is probably the best known of all Washington's headquarters, the one in which he spent the most time—**Hasbrouck House.**

Hasbrouck House, when it was built in 1725, was the center of a ninety-nine-acre holding which had been part of a larger tract of land given by Queen Anne to a group of Palatine Germans who wished to settle in the New World. Like the DeWint House in Tappan, Hasbrouck House is an excellent example of the Hudson Valley Dutch farmhouse. You will have a good opportunity to admire it as you approach over the well-kept, shaded grounds. It was at first a small fieldstone house built by Jonathan Hasbrouck for his bride, to which additions were made extending both out and up. The roof is high peaked and shingled and overhangs the entire front. Inside the front door is a parlor to the left and a kitchen-dining room to the right. Washington lived here for a year and a half, much of the time with his wife, Martha. A few of the furnishings are original to the house, including the armchair in front of the fireplace in the parlor, a large, comb-back Windsor chair in the study near the window, a cradle, a milk yoke now hung on the wall in the kitchen-dining room, a fire bucket in the hall, and a set of andirons in the study. Since these items belonged to the Hasbroucks we may safely assume they were in the house during Washington's stay. The chest-on-chest in the parlor was used by Washington in the DeWint House in Tappan. Washington used the corner chair in the parlor when he visited sick and wounded soldiers in a Morristown, New Jersey, church serving as a hospital. There is a desk in the study that Washington used while he was headquartered in another Newburgh house before he moved here.

The central room on the ground floor was the main room of the original house. As the house was extended, each new addition was connected to the main room by a door. Today this room is called "the room with seven doors and one window." Notice the unusual fireplaces, unusual to modern eyes that is. During colonial times, the first part of the house to be built after the cellar and foundation wall was the fireplace, for this was usually of brick or stone and the center of family life. In Hasbrouck House the fireplaces are open; that is, they have huge, flagstone hearths and brick, back walls but no jambs or sidewalls. This made for warmer rooms, but much risk when doors and windows were allowed to remain open, particularly during windy weather. The huge flues overhead carried off the smoke and sparks. It was in this house that Washington received Lewis Nicola's letter suggesting he assume the kingship of the colonies, and here that he wrote his famous rejection.

Leaving the old house, turn left to get to the *museum,* a 1910 brick building which houses a treasure trove of odd and interesting Revolutionary War relics, many of them connected with some of the leading figures of the times. Just inside the main entrance, to the right, are a number of hinged wall-leaves or frames which contain several views of Hasbrouck House during its long career. To the left, a matching set of wall-leaves displays paintings, prints, and photographs of houses in the Newburgh area and elsewhere that were used by Washington and his general officers as headquarters.

The display rooms take up the ground floor, one on either side of the main lobby. To the right is the Washington Room, which contains exhibits connected with the New Windsor Cantonment. In a large glass case immediately to your right as you enter, notice first a long, framed, primitive view of the Massachusetts section of the encampment showing the Temple, huts, and company street plan. In this same case is a display concerning the Order of the Purple Heart which Washington inaugurated while staying in Hasbrouck House. It was in front of Hasbrouck House that the first presentations of this medal were made on May 3, 1783. In the same case is a bill of sale for some of the encampment huts and a facsimile of the auction notice at which the Temple was sold.

This case also displays the first printed edition of the Newburgh Addresses which were printed in New Haven; their authorship is here attributed to John Armstrong, Jr., son of an elderly militia general who was a close friend to Washington. Young Armstrong was the aide General Gates sent to recall Benedict Arnold at Saratoga when that gentleman galloped into battle against orders. After the war Armstrong became a member of the Senate, minister to France and President Madison's secretary of war, a post he was forced to resign after the British burned Washington. Just above this edition is a facsimile of the speech Washington made denouncing the Addresses.

The room to the left of the lobby, the Clinton Room, takes its name from items connected with the Clintons, the Americans George and James and the British Henry, who were distantly related. There are also cases of relics connected with Lafayette's last visit to the United States in 1824; a collection of money issued by the Continental Congress; a sword once carried by Lafayette, which he exchanged with an American officer at some sort of sword potlatch; and a christening robe made by Martha Washington for Mary Hasbrouck Smith, who was about to give birth in the summer of 1783. Mary Hasbrouck was married to Captain Israel Smith, an officer attached to Washington's staff.

Two of the most interesting Revolutionary War relics I have ever seen are on display in the basement room of this museum. One is a section of the log boom that was stretched across the Hudson just upstream of the West Point chain. It was dredged up out of the river near the old West Point dock in 1855. The logs measure about twenty feet in length and are held together by giant iron staples and links.

Directly in front of this exhibit, in a center floor case, is part of the chevaux-de-frise that was placed in the Hudson at Kingston at Polopel's Island, consisting of one of the wooden spikes sheathed in iron that protruded above water. There is an excellent sketch in this case showing how these points were placed in log cribs which were then loaded with rocks and sunk in the river.

Take a stroll over the grounds, which are quite extensive. The well with the bucket near the old house is not original to the property. An herb garden behind the house commemorates the garden Martha Washington busied herself with during her stay. The ground slopes eastward toward the Hudson about a half mile away. The mountains on the east bank, on whose tops beacon fires flared warnings of British approaches, loom over the scene. The little fieldstone building to the right behind the museum is modern though it looks old. The large, arched monument to the left commemorates the centennial of Washington's residency. Of all the guns that dot the lawns, only the huge, black gun behind Hasbrouck House is of interest. It was captured at Fort Ticonderoga, was part of Knox's Noble Train of Artillery, probably was on Dorchester Heights during the siege of Boston, and eventually wound up here via the old Watervliet arsenals north of Albany.

FISHKILL

Fishkill is one of the last stops on this mopping-up expedition and can be reached from Newburgh in a half hour by taking Interstate 84 east across the Hudson. The Fishkill exit signs take you out onto Route 9 north, which goes to the village. Route 9 north from points farther south on the east side of the river will also take you there, as will Interstate 84 west out of Connecticut via Danbury.

Fishkill was the center of a large military complex, which included a Continental Army supply depot, a headquarters center administering the troops on the east bank of the Hudson, a hospital, a prison, and an encampment of the Corps of Invalids which was on guard against any British moves in a northern direction. A village existed on this site before 1716. During the eighteenth century the immediate area came to be known as the Fishkills because of its numerous fish-filled creeks, or "kills" in Dutch. In those days what is now the town of Beacon was Fishkill Landing and served Fishkill and the surrounding area as a river port.

My first visit to Fishkill was in the summer of 1946. I remember it then as a pleasant little village whose tree-shaded streets dozed away the summer between the old frame and fieldstone colonial houses. There was a two-pump gas station at the intersection of 9 and 52, a summer theater on Main Street, and a wonderful feeling of other-timeliness. Today the intersection of 9 and 52 boasts two service stations; cars roar up and down both roads at all hours; and Main Street is crowded with morning and evening rush-hour traffic.

Begin your tour of Fishkill at the **Fishkill Reformed Church** on Main Street (Route 52) just south of the intersection with 9. Organized in 1716 by the descendants of local Dutch settlers, it was then known as the Dutch Reformed Church. The original building, completed in 1731, was built of fieldstone with a high roof and steeple and has been added onto since. From September, 1776, until February, 1777, the Provincial Congress of New York State met here, which made the village the state capital for that period. At that time the Congress began its deliberations on the state constitution, and the finished document was first printed in Fishkill.

When the Provincial Congress moved on to Kingston, the Continental Army took over the church and used it as a prison for local Loyalists, sympathizers and other suspicious characters. Enoch Crosby, a double agent working for Washington, was at one time confined in this church until secret orders from Washington allowed him to "escape" overnight into the swampy area that lay just to the west.

There are no Revolutionary War graves in the churchyard, but it is worthwhile to take a stroll between the tombstones, many of which predate the Revolution and bear the names of the old Dutch settlers.

Inside the church is a lectern made from a walnut tree that stood in front of the Van Wyck House. The tree was blown down in a wind storm in 1918, and when the local inhabitants gathered up the wood they found an iron ring that had been embedded in the trunk. It was believed to have been either a part of the tollgate that once hung across the road or part of a whipping post used to punish army miscreants. The ring is now in the possession of the Fishkill Historical Society, along with a number of other relics found in the area, all of which will be put on display during the years of the bicentennial. Also inside, note the framed flag hanging on the wall to your right as you face the pulpit. This was the guidon for the Washington Greys, Washington's personal bodyguard whenever he was in the state.

Now cross 9 at the light and go east along 52 for a short distance to **Trinity Church.** Built in 1760, Trinity has been restored to its original appearance. During the Revolution it served as a hospital, and many small-pox victims among the men stationed here were brought to Trinity. It was here that the state Provincial Congress sat during the first week they met in Fishkill after fleeing from White Plains. Unfortunately Trinity was not completely finished, and since birds kept flying in through the paneless windows, disrupting the proceedings, the body adjourned and reconvened in the Reformed Church down the road.

Continue east on 52, following roughly the same route Washington used to get to Connecticut and Rhode Island until you come to a church-yard on your left. Just beyond the churchyard a large, yellow house sits on a knoll overlooking the highway. This is the **Brinkerhoff House,** built about 1718 and lived in by the same family ever since. It was originally owned by Dirk Brinkerhoff and appears on maps of the area drawn by British spies conspicuously identified as the home of a "warm rebel" and an outspoken Whig. This is the house Washington stayed in whenever he was in the Fishkill area, and all of his correspondence headed "headquarters, Fishkill" was probably written here. The house has been somewhat altered over the years. It was originally all stone and had no veranda; the mansard roof was put on during the 1870s. Lafayette spent six weeks recovering from a bout with pneumonia in the room marked by the window farthest right on the second story.

We also know that the British troops captured at Saratoga, the Convention Army, marched by the house on their way to Cambridge. A letter from a young Prussian officer tells of his marching past the house and seeing Washington standing in front of it reviewing the prisoners. Since the house is privately owned, you may only be able to view it from the road. By the time the bicentennial is celebrated, however, chances are good that in a town like Fishkill, where sixty percent of the homes are of revolutionary vintage, those of particular interest may be opened to the public, at least on a visiting-day basis.

Return to Route 9 and turn south for a short distance until you go under the overpass for Interstate 84. Just beyond it, to your left, a white, frame house on a knoll is **Van Wyck House,** built by Cornelius Van Wyck in 1731; to be exact, that is the date for the east wing on your right as you face the house. The main section was built before 1756; by the Revolution Cornelius had died and the property had passed on to his son, Isaac, who was in residence when the Continental Army moved into the area in 1777 and built their encampment. This house was one of several requisitioned for army officers. It was used by General Israel Putnam for a time. Washington had dinner here on September 19, 1778, the one visit to the house by the commander in chief that has been authenticated. Other noteworthy people of the time who walked through its front door included Alexander Hamilton, John Jay, and the peripatetic Steuben. A number of courts-martial also sat in session here.

Directly opposite the house is a gas station which stands on the site where the encampment blacksmith shop was located. By the time you get here, however, the gas station may be gone and its place taken by a cloverleaf for Interstate 84, which may be the fate of Van Wyck House as well. This dastardly plot on the part of the state highway department has been foiled once, but whether the proponents of conservation, historical landmarks, and ecology will finally persevere against the spreaders of concrete remains to be seen.

The reason for an encampment in this area may be seen by facing south. Between the hills on the horizon, you will notice an indentation on the skyline, a pass through which the Albany Post Road, now Route 9, ran. The British would have marched north along that road had they attempted to move in force on Albany and New England; the army in the Fishkill encampment guarded that pass. The Van Wyck House and the blacksmith shop were on the northern fringe of the encampment and the area in the immediate vicinity of the house was the site of a supply depot.

The Van Wyck House is owned by the Fishkill Historical Society, which has restored it to its former condition. The house and the museum are open April through October, Wednesdays, Saturdays and Sundays from 1 P.M. to 5 P.M. Admission is $0.75 for adults; $0.25 for six- to sixteen-year-olds, and free for children under six.

About a half mile south along 9 is a marker placed by the D.A.R. supposedly on the site of a grave in which victims of smallpox were buried during the encampment. State archaeologists, however, have determined that the marker is misplaced. Local historians place the site farther back from the road, possibly in the vicinity of the hill to your left front that you see as you stand with your back to the front of the Van Wyck House. Letters from General McDougall found in General Putnam's papers complain about the inoculation of the men in the encampment against smallpox and ask that the practice be discontinued. This may seem very backward on McDougall's part until we remember that many people in those days of imperfect immunization contracted smallpox from the inoculations. Washington enthusiastically approved of immunization and had all his army inoculated during the Morristown encampment.

Proceed south along 9 for about a half mile from the Van Wyck House to a large, empty field on your right just beyond a sharp curve. A team of Temple University archaeologists dug into this field during the summer of 1971, hoping to find the foundations of ten encampment barracks that stood here during the Revolution. A previous team had uncovered five of the sites and then covered them up to protect them for some future dig. The Temple team turned up a lot of coins, buttons, button molds, and animal bones, indicating a kitchen area, but no foundations. There are tentative state plans to widen the highway and plans for a shopping center as well, so the future of the site is cloudy.

Stay for an hour or so in Fishkill for a quiet walk along its shaded streets, past the old homes and peaceful scenes. Despite the intrusion of the twentieth century, it is still a village of great charm and reminiscent in its appearance and atmosphere of the Hudson Valley during the halcyon days of the agricultural culture that once typified the region. Then, having had your fill of rural charm, travel south to cover the campaigns that marked the early days of the Revolution in and around New York City.

V.

THE NEW YORK CITY CAMPAIGNS

In 1775 the British had been content to remain in Boston awaiting reinforcements from the homeland before taking the field after the audacious rebels. However, when Washington occupied Dorchester Heights in March, 1776, and placed Knox's Noble Train of Artillery in position there overlooking the city, their position became untenable. The commander in chief of the British forces in America, General Thomas Gage, and his successor, General William Howe, both had planned to move eventually to New York City. It was a principal seaport with a population in excess of 25,000, and it commanded the mouth of the strategically important Hudson River. Washington forced them out of Boston and into New York ahead of schedule.

Aware of what the enemy's next move would be, Washington sent General Charles Lee to New York to arrange for its defense while preparing to move the army after him. The defense of the city was an almost hopeless task, for it was vulnerable to attack by water from all sides. The rebels had no fleet to oppose the British men-of-war which ruled the seas up and down the coast. The British fleet could move men and supplies onto Manhattan Island or bombard it practically at will from three sides.

Lee felt that though the city (which then occupied only the southern end of Manhattan) could not be held without naval support, the nature of the terrain north of the city gave the Continental Army a chance to fight delaying actions that would cost the British thousands of casualties, enough perhaps to discourage them from further attempts to crush the rebellion. Washington moved to New York in April, 1776. His army of

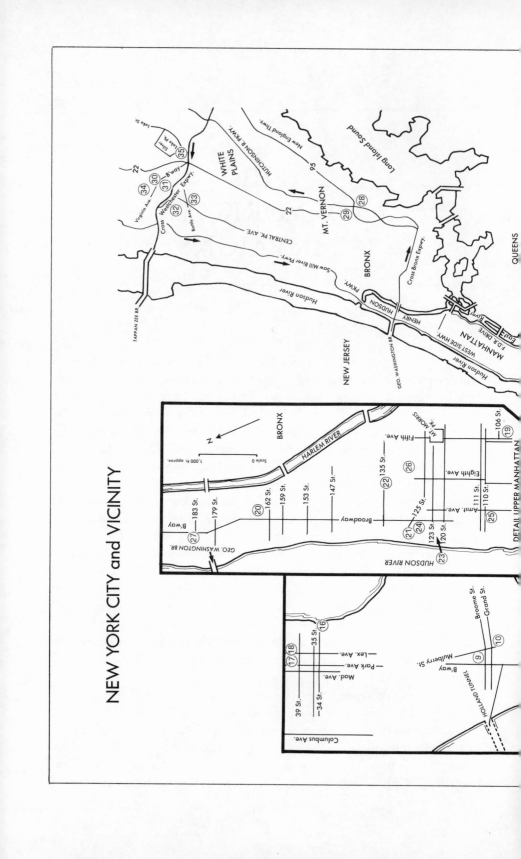

NEW YORK CITY and VICINITY

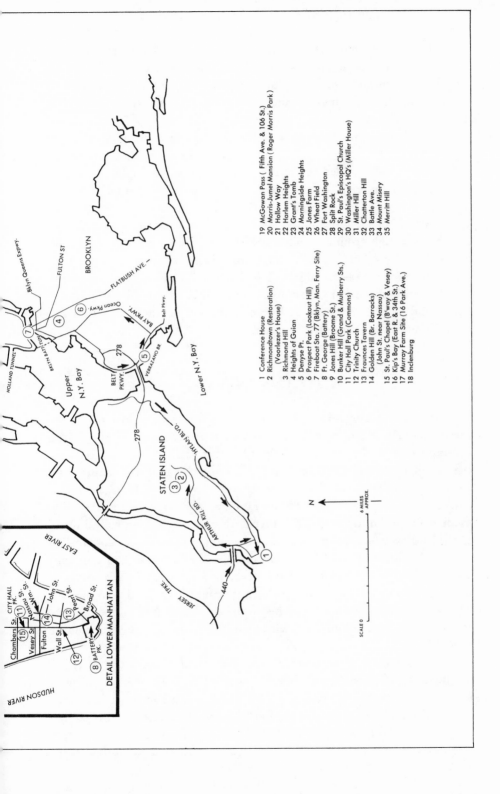

1 Conference House
2 Richmondtown (Restoration)
  (Voorlezer's House)
3 Richmond Hill
4 Heights of Guian
5 Denyse Pt.
6 Prospect Park (Lookout Hill)
7 Fireboat Sta. 77 (Bklyn, Man. Ferry Site)
8 Ft. George (Battery)
9 Jones Hill (Broome St.)
10 Bunker Hill (Grand & Mulberry Sts.)
11 City Hall Park (Commons)
12 Trinity Church
13 Fraunces Tavern
14 Golden Hill (Br. Barracks)
   (John St. near Nassau)
15 St. Paul's Chapel (B'way & Vesey)
16 Kip's Bay (East R. & 34th St.)
17 Murray Farm Site (16 Park Ave.)
18 Inclenburg

19 McGowan Pass (Fifth Ave. & 106 St.)
20 Morris-Jumel Mansion (Roger Morris Park)
21 Hollow Way
22 Harlem Heights
23 Grant's Tomb
24 Morningside Heights
25 Jones Farm
26 Wheat Field
27 Fort Washington
28 Split Rock
29 St. Paul's Episcopal Church
30 Washington's HQ's (Miller House)
31 Miller Hill
32 Chatterton Hill
33 Battle Ave.
34 Mount Misery
35 Merritt Hill

about 19,000 men, most of them untried in battle and supported by only a few guns, had begun moving there on March 18, the day after the British left Boston. The men dug fortifications and gun positions all around and through the city and waited for the British to make their move.

During June and July, 1776, General Howe brought 31,600 men to Staten Island. He was supported by Admiral Lord Richard Howe, his brother, who commanded about 280 ships in and around New York harbor. Faced by superior forces, forced to defend a highly vulnerable area, Washington spread his men all over the map. A force of about 4,000 on Long Island, in the area now called Brooklyn, was to hold Brooklyn Heights, the high ground which overlooked the East River on the Brooklyn side and thus dominated the city. Most of the rest were on Manhattan, with detachments at the northern end of the island at King's Bridge, which carried the Albany Post Road over Spuyten Duyvil Creek to the Bronx and Westchester, and at Fort Washington on the upper west side of the island overlooking the Hudson.

STATEN ISLAND

Before venturing into the wilds of Manhattan to follow the action there, take a side trip to Staten Island to visit the scene of the British encampment and the site of the first attempt to settle the dispute between the rebellious colonies and the mother country by peaceful means. This sixty-square-mile bit of land between New Jersey and New York was christened Statten Eylandt by Henry Hudson, who was, as far as we know, the first European to visit it. The first settlements were Dutch, and many of the landmarks and towns still carry the old Dutch names or corruptions thereof. For years Staten Island, the borough of Richmond, had the reputation of being the New York City Police Department's Siberia. According to popular belief, the worst thing that could happen to a cop on the beat was to incur the wrath of his superiors and so find himself transferred to a Staten Island beat where nothing ever happened, including promotions.

If this story is true, or ever was, then today there must be entire precincts of police officers in the ghettos of New York who would willingly trade their assignments for the relative peace and quiet of Staten Island. The building of the Verrazano Narrows Bridge between Brooklyn and Staten Island, however, putting midtown Manhattan within forty minutes of the center of the island, has mitigated that proverbial tranquillity. The borough is now undergoing a dramatic transformation, as highway builders and real estate developers, with potential home-buying commuters hot on their trail, convert what rural charm is left into suburban sprawl.

Getting there from Manhattan is a quick and simple matter of using the belt highways that ring the city. Take either the West Side Highway or the Franklin D. Roosevelt Drive on the east side to the Brooklyn Battery Tunnel. You will emerge on the Gowanus Parkway, an elevated highway that skirts the Brooklyn shore of the Upper Bay. Turn off onto Interstate 278, which will take you circuitously onto the Verrazano Narrows Bridge and so on to the island (at a cost of $0.75 each way). As you come off the bridge, 278 will take you clear across the island to New Jersey if you let it. Control your wanderlust; get off it at the Hylan Boulevard exit; and take Hylan Boulevard south to its very end. Just before it threatens to plunge into Raritan Bay, you will see the **Conference House** on the right on a knoll in the midst of a small park. This is your first and most important objective on Staten Island.

There is another way of getting to Staten Island from Manhattan, which takes more time but is twice as much fun. Instead of taking the Brooklyn Battery Tunnel when you get to the south end of Manhattan, follow the signs for the South Ferry. For a nominal fee—the price per passenger is still $0.05 but about to be revised upward drastically—you (and your car for $1.50) can enjoy one of the best boat rides in the world, a twenty-minute trip through New York's Upper Bay, one of the world's busiest harbors. Tugboats and barges, ocean-going freighters, cruise ships, the Statue of Liberty towering overhead, and the New York skyline will all be yours. George Wesley Bellows, the artist, Walt Whitman, and O. Henry all enjoyed the Staten Island Ferry in their time; enjoy it now in yours.

You will disembark from the ferry in St. George. As you come off the ferry slip, take the first left-hand turn and follow the road to Hylan Boulevard, which you take south as previously directed.

If you are coming from the north or from the west side of the Hudson, take the New Jersey Turnpike to either Exit 13 or 11. At Exit 13, follow the signs for Interstate 278 east and the Goethals Bridge onto the island. Follow 278, also called the Staten Island Expressway, toward the other side of the island; get off at Hylan Boulevard, and take that south to the Conference House.

If you come off the Jersey turnpike at Exit 11, as I did, take the second right turn after the tollbooth. Be careful not to go off to the left onto the Garden State Parkway, but stay right as though you were going onto U.S. 9. Follow a sign at that turnoff onto State Route 440 east for the Outerbridge Crossing. There is a $1.00 toll on this bridge, as there is on all bridges and tunnels leading into New York City, but the fee will cover your crossing in both directions. If you return over the same bridge or over any other bridge or through any tunnel heading out of the city you will not have to pay another toll. Take the first right after the tollbooth, and proceed to the second traffic light at Hylan Boulevard. Turn right and follow it to the dead end on the bay and Conference House.

When the brothers Howe arrived with their men and ships off Staten Island in the early summer of 1776, the total population of the island was about 2,000, according to modern demographers and available records. It consisted mostly of farmers living inland, seafarers such as fishermen and sea captains who lived along the shores close to their place of employment, and some merchants and tradesmen who were gathered together in several small settlements. Within a few weeks the population jumped to more than ten times 2,000 as 25,000 British and Hessian troops and Loyalist militia poured ashore. The island's inhabitants were probably neutral as many farmers were at the time, for they had hardly been affected by the Navigation Acts and other parliamentary devices aimed at restricting American trade and commerce. The centers of rebellion were located in the cities. One can surmise, however, that there must have been considerable resentment among Staten Islanders as the British forces cut down most of the island's trees to provide themselves with lumber for hutments. Forts and redoubts were built on all the strategic heights and shoreline points. Practically every house and tavern from the Kill van Kull at the north end of the island to Raritan Bay on the south had its complement of quartered officers. It was a complete occupation and gave the British an excellent base from which to launch attacks at any time they chose against the American positions on Long Island and Manhattan, or, as they did later, into New Jersey.

The Howes had come to America armed with something more than military might. At their insistence, they had been granted limited powers as "peace commissioners": that is, they could lift some of the trade restrictions and were empowered to grant pardons to the King's rebellious subjects if said subjects chose to take advantage of the opportunity. They could not do any of this, however, unless the colonists agreed to give up their rebellion. This was not to be the last effort by the British government to bring the Americans back into the fold by peaceful, if not completely honest, means. In 1778 they sent another commission to America under the Earl of Carlisle in an effort to head off the French-American alliance. The Earl and his compatriots became so embroiled in secret contacts and undercover negotiations, however, that they also made little headway.

In August, 1776, most of the troops on Staten Island were transferred to Brooklyn for the Battle of Long Island. Following the American defeat there, one of the rebel prisoners brought to the island was General John Sullivan who, through his conversations with Lord Howe, got the impression that His Lordship and brother had been granted considerable power by Parliament to negotiate with the Americans. Lord Howe allowed Sullivan to go to Philadelphia to sell Congress the idea of sending a delegation to negotiate a peace settlement. Congress, however, was not as easily taken in. They sent Benjamin Franklin, Edward Rutledge from South Carolina, and John Adams, not to make peace but to find out exactly what the Howes were capable of under the terms of their commission.

On Wednesday, September 11, 1776, a British barge put ashore at Perth Amboy and took on board the American delegation under the terms of a safe conduct pass. The three were landed at what is now called the Conference House, then known as the Manor of Bentley. Between two lines of redcoats extending from the landing to the house, the Americans walked up from the beach to meet with Lord Howe. General Howe was too busy with military matters to attend. (He was probably preparing for the invasion of Manhattan.)

Before you visit the house in which the conference took place, walk down to the beach where the three delegates landed. Essentially the beach is as it was then, with the exception of the landing which has long since disappeared. When I was there the beach and the immediate waters were swarming with horseshoe crabs. You are standing at the point where the Arthur Kill on your right empties into Raritan Bay on your left at the southwest corner of Staten Island. A kill is a narrow stream or creek; the Arthur Kill got its present name through a corruption of the Dutch name "Achter Kill," meaning the creek at the back or behind the island. All the land you see from here as you look to the left is New Jersey; those high, irregular hills on the horizon are the Atlantic Highlands. Except for the obviously modern buildings and facilities on the Jersey shore, the bay and kill and the area surrounding the house are also very similar to what they were in colonial times. The City Parks Department has purchased the land on the opposite side of Hylan Boulevard—flat woodland intersected here and there by dirt roads running through to the beaches on the east shore—with the intention of preserving it as park land. Therefore the likelihood that the area will remain essentially rural is very good, a prospect that enhances considerably the historic value of the site. The houses and other buildings showing through the trees on the Jersey shore to the right beyond the Arthur Kill are old Perth Amboy. The modern town is farther inland, but the section close to the water has been deliberately left as it was or reconstructed to retain something of its original appearance. The church steeple you can plainly see in old Perth Amboy was used as an observation post by the Americans, who kept the British on the island under constant surveillance. It was from the church that they spotted Christopher Billopp II as he moved about the house. Billopp was a Loyalist and fair game; and after determining that he was home, a party of raiders rowed across the kill one dark night and kidnapped him. He was eventually exchanged for an American prisoner.

Christopher Billopp II was the great-grandson of Christopher Billopp I, a British naval officer who was granted a land patent on Staten Island in the seventeenth century. One of the captain's daughters was married to a local farmer named Thomas Farmer. Since the captain had no male issue, he stipulated in his will that if his grandson was to inherit the Manor of Bentley, which then included some 1,600 acres, he would have to take the name of Billopp as well. Christopher II's father, Thomas, being sound of mind, changed his name to Billopp so Christopher II, we would like to think, lived happily ever after on his grandfather's patent. Unfortunately he chose to throw in his fortunes with the King during the Revolution, and so at the end of the war was forced to give up the manor for exile in Nova Scotia.

You can walk up to the house, which faces the beach, following roughly the same path Franklin and company took from the landing. The grounds around the house are a public park maintained by the city Parks Department. The house is maintained by the Conference House Association. The house is made of fieldstone and has a clapboard wing in the rear, which was added during the nineteenth century. It is two stories high, and when it was built around 1680, and for some time after, was the most imposing structure on the island. It is not at all like the Flemish cottages the Dutch settlers built along the Hudson Valley, but stands quite tall and large for a country house of that period with a steep, shingled roof and tall chimneys at either end. The original porch and/or steps are gone, as are the original windows, though the frames now in place are colonial. According to the soldier bricks over several windows, however, the original windows were probably somewhat larger and in somewhat different positions. In fact, if you walk around to the western end of the house and look to your left as you face the front door, two bricked-up windows are clearly evident. You will note by the comparatively fresh cement in many places that a certain amount of reconstructing has been done to preserve the exterior. The well behind the house is not authentic, but does mark the site of the original well.

The Conference House is open year-round, except Mondays, from 1 to 5 P.M. in the summer and spring and from 1 to 4 P.M. from October to April. Admission is $0.25 and children under twelve are admitted free. As you come into the house through the front door, the room in which the conference took place is immediately to your left. Centered in it is a scale-model impression of that meeting showing the American delegation sitting around a table with Lord Howe.

Howe opened the meeting by outlining the hopelessness of the rebel position. He made the only kind of offer he could: pardons and the lifting of some trade restrictions, provided the Americans gave up any idea of independence. The delegates first determined that Howe could not really agree to anything without first getting approval from London. Franklin is then reported to have informed the admiral that the Continental Congress had, not six weeks past, issued a Declaration of Independence and therefore had no intention of returning its constituents to British rule. Lord Howe had of course presented his proposal in the most favorable terms, but he had to admit that he could not engage in any negotiations predicated on American independence.

The conference broke up politely enough, but with nothing accomplished except for a conviction on the Americans' part that the Howe brothers had been commissioned to do very little. The three delegates returned to their barge and were rowed back to Perth Amboy.

None of the furnishings in the house are original Billopp furnishings, for that gentleman took most of his household effects with him when he emigrated. Most of the present furnishings are nineteenth century with a few colonial pieces as well, all donated by historical societies. The interior has been restored, according to the evidence of one's eyes, though the exposed ceiling beams and wide floorboards remain. There is some evidence in the upstairs rooms that partitions were put up or taken down at times to make additional or larger rooms. Busts and pictures of Franklin are much in evidence in an effort to make the house into a Franklin shrine, but none seem to be of any historic or artistic value. The fireplace mantels and walls have been covered with early nineteenth-century woodwork and moldings, and wood boxes have been built into the sides.

The basement, which is used as a meeting room by the Conference House Association, is interesting for its vaulted, brick vegetable cellar which has a low, arched ceiling. Another legend persists that a tunnel once connected the vegetable cellar with the landing on the beach, but the walls do not show any sign of having been disturbed since they were built three hundred years ago. At the time of my visit, several old tombstones were stored in this part of the basement. They were found in what was probably a family burial plot near the house, and one bears the name "Thomas Billopp," the same Thomas Billopp who sired Christopher II. The fancy bricks on the floor with the legend "V.L.C. Holland 1929" inscribed on them were part of a money-raising scheme for the house's reconstruction. Representative of the brick colonial sailing vessels sometimes carried as ballast, these bricks of red and blue clay were made by a brickworks in Holland, supposedly the same one that made the bricks that went into the original Conference House. Whether or not this is so, the story sold a lot of bricks and raised quite a bit of money. In the center of the basement floor is a single white brick, the most valuable and treasured of all, for it was bought and donated to the house by Queen Wilhelmina of Holland.

A fold-out pamphlet distributed by the Parks, Recreation, and Cultural Affairs Administration of the City of New York lists and describes many of the historic homes under the administration's care; but it inaccurately describes a large, heavy carved-walnut table, which was present in the basement when I was there, as the table at which the peace conference took place. That table is obviously Victorian and will probably have been removed by the time you visit the site. If it is still there, don't be fooled by it or the offending pamphlet.

The other notable feature in the basement, aside from excellent brick walls and huge, overhead beams, is the brick fireplace at one end. By its size and the marks in the bricks where the old Dutch oven was bricked over, it was a cooking fireplace marking this room as the original kitchen. Note the holes in the mantel brick, probably for hooks that held pots and pans and other utensils.

As you leave the house, stop to look at the small ship's gun mounted on a wooden carriage, which has been placed on a pedestal on the Hylan Boulevard side. An attached plaque explains that the gun was in position at Rossville (on the west side of Staten Island) when General John Sullivan, who had since been exchanged, led one of the many raids the Americans carried out on the island from New Jersey.

Raymond Safford, president of the Conference House Association, showed me through the house and invited me to attend a re-enactment of the conference in 1976. Through me, the invitation is extended to you. It will not take place at the Conference House itself, but at the Richmondtown Restoration, which you should visit while you are on Staten Island. To get there, take the first left-hand turn directly behind the house as you head back north on Hylan Boulevard, and find your way toward your left to Arthur Kill Road. Following this shore drive, you will be skirting the Arthur Kill and looking off at New Jersey beyond. As you pass the Outerbridge Crossing, make a mental note that near this spot Baron von Knyphausen embarked his men and rowed across to Elizabethtown for the beginning of the Springfield Raid which we will cover in New Jersey in Volume II.

Follow Arthur Kill Road to the **Richmondtown Restoration,** located at the geographic center of Staten Island. It recreates through buildings restored or in their original state the evolution of an American village through the seventeenth, eighteenth and nineteenth centuries. There is a large parking area around which the restoration is laid out in splendid and picturesque fashion. A millpond and a reconstructed gristmill should be in operation by the time you get there; there will eventually be a tidal mill at work as well. At present you can visit the Voorlezer's House, built in 1696, which was the country's first schoolhouse. There is also the Treasure House, so called for its tale of a hoard of gold coins found behind a fireplace in the eighteenth century; British officers were quartered in the house during the occupation. Many buildings were moved here from their original locations on other parts of the island.

There is also an excellent *museum* which contains two showcases, on the second floor, of artifacts found on the site of the fort and redoubt the British built on **Richmond Hill** just beyond the restoration. Take the road to the golf course to find it; leave your car by the side of the road, if you can, and climb up to explore the site. Nothing remains of the breastworks, but there are a number of potholes about to mark the efforts of local, amateur archaeologists. You might try your own hand here, for many of the artifacts were found only a few inches below the surface. Among the usual uniform buttons and clay pipes was enough to suggest that the fort was built and manned by a Loyalist unit known as the Queen's Rangers, the same unit that under John Grave Simcoe later earned a reputation for no-quarter and bloody raids, the infamous Simcoe Rangers.

There are a number of other British army sites on Staten Island, but little work has been done to identify them positively or to develop them. There is a period map hung on the wall of the second-floor landing of the Richmondtown museum which shows these sites and makes for some interesting browsing. This map might tease you into doing some exploring of the island on your own, if you are of the mind and have the time. Having seen the Conference House and Richmondtown, however, the time has come to return to the mainland and the action about to ensue there.

THE BATTLE OF LONG ISLAND

General Howe swung into action in July, 1776, by sending a small naval party up the Hudson past the American batteries, which did little to stop them, to the Tappan Zee off Tarrytown. This directed American attention to the north. Then on Thursday, August 22, British troops were ferried across the eastern end of the Narrows from Staten Island to Denyse Point, where the Staten Island–Long Island Ferry docked, to clear out an American detachment stationed there. Once that was accomplished, the rest of the British force began to land in Gravesend Bay immediately to the east. The Americans fell back toward the Heights of Guian, a line of hills that presented an escarpment on their southern side and heavily-wooded, tangled slopes on the north. The Heights of Guian ran across northern Brooklyn from Gowanus Bay to what is now Jamaica in the present borough of Queens. Three vital passes pierced these hills: Flatbush Pass, a mile or so from the village of Flatbush, Bedford Pass to the east, and Jamaica Pass to the east of that. The British drove on to take Flatbush, while Washington, not sure where the main attack was coming from, sent additional men from Manhattan to support his Long Island army, most of which was stationed along Brooklyn Heights.

The British extended their Gravesend bridgehead to include a good deal of south Brooklyn, taking over the villages of New Utrecht, Gravesend, and Flatlands, settlements which are now remembered in the names of neighborhoods in Brooklyn. The main body camped on what was then a wide plain, fringed on the north by the Heights of Guian and on the south by the bay and ocean.

Shortly after midnight August 26–27, General Howe opened a new attack. He sent a force of 5,000 men against the American right along a road that followed the shore of Gowanus Bay, thus drawing their reserves in that direction. At the same time, British warships tried unsuccessfully to beat up the Narrows against a strong wind to get into the East River and bombard the American line from the rear. The Americans did fairly well in the face of this attack, holding their ground and even repulsing the more experienced, better-trained British and Hessians.

The British at Flatbush began an artillery bombardment of the American lines in front of them while the main attack, under Howe's command—a column of about 10,000 men—marched east to Jamaica Pass. For some reason this pass had not been fortified or even kept under observation. Neither General Israel Putnam who was in overall command on Long Island, nor General John Sullivan who was Putnam's subordinate were familiar with the terrain, which probably accounted for the blunder. When the British column had marched through the pass to a point behind the American line and then had swung left to get into position, signal guns were fired. The British at Flatbush immediately opened a frontal assault while Howe's men closed in from the rear. The result was disaster for the Americans. Those who could escaped to Brooklyn Heights; at least 1,300 were either killed, wounded, or captured.

General Howe then made the first of what became his customary mistakes. Instead of following up with an immediate attack on the fortification on Brooklyn Heights, he was cautious and laid siege to the American positions. Had he moved resolutely forward, the Revolution might very well have ended then and there with the destruction of the rest of Washington's army. True the wind did not help the British, because it prevented the fleet from sailing up the East River to cut the Americans off from their base of supplies and reinforcements in New York City. Nevertheless, this hesitancy in the face of victory became part of a pattern of behavior that typified General Howe. Some historians blame the loss of the American colonies on the Howe brothers, arguing that had it not been for their unwillingness to press their military advantages during the first three years of the war, the American military effort would have been crushed.

William Howe was the product of an extra-marital arrangement between one of his grandmothers and George I. As a result, he and his brother were George III's illegitimate uncles. He had distinguished himself during the French and Indian War at Quebec under General Wolfe and elsewhere in Canada. He had also been a prominent Whig member of Parliament, in which capacity he displayed sympathy for the American colonists. He had also been in command of the British forces at Bunker Hill and had been made commander in chief of British forces in America, replacing General Gage while the army was still in Boston. He and his brother came under heavy criticism at home for their conduct of the war and were accused of wanting to see the Americans win. General

Howe became famous for his affair with Mrs. Loring, the wife of Joshua Loring, his commissary of prisoners, and for his style of living while in America.

Sir Henry Clinton accused him of losing the war for Great Britain by the actions he failed to take rather than by anything he did. Judging by the Battle of Long Island, however, he was a resourceful and enterprising military commander with a good eye for terrain, a perfect sense of timing, and a keen mind for planning battlefield strategy. He simply did not seem capable of taking proper advantage of his opportunities. Time and again Washington and his little army escaped the consequences of bad luck and bad planning because of General Howe's hesitancy to act at the decisive moment. All in all, General Howe remains something of a mystery. And incidentally, Sir Henry Clinton, then serving under Howe, claimed credit for the strategy of envelopment that surprised the Americans at the Battle of Long Island.

Fearful of what Howe's next move might be, Washington decided to evacuate Long Island. There followed the famous American withdrawal across the East River during the night of August 29–30. Ten to twelve thousand men were ferried across before the British realized what was going on. During that time, a small detachment left to cover the retreat abandoned the Brooklyn Heights defenses through an error and reported to the Brooklyn Ferry, where the rest of their comrades were debarking. Told of their mistake, they returned to their positions, which had been deserted for an hour, and waited until again told, this time correctly, to withdraw. By the time the British realized what had happened and entered the deserted American lines, this rear guard was still at the ferry on the Brooklyn side awaiting rescue. They were saved by a dense fog, which hid the withdrawal. Washington left Long Island in one of the last boats to make the crossing.

For the most part, Brooklyn and Manhattan are the history buff's despair. Like any other large city, New York's rapid rate of growth did not pause for historic landmarks or hallowed grounds, and with only a few exceptions, the sites connected with the Battle of Long Island lie under an endless panorama of streets, private homes on sixty-by-one-hundred plots, apartment buildings, shopping avenues, and Brooklyn's downtown area. As a Brooklynite born and bred—who grew up in Bensonhurst, not two miles from the site of the village of New Utrecht, played on the shores of Gravesend Bay, rode a bicycle times without number around Denyse Point and along the Narrows, and roamed the hills and valleys of Prospect Park—I can vouch for the fact that—

except for the old Dutch farmhouse that once stood on 18th Avenue and 84th Street, with its old milestone set in the front yard—there are few reminders of the events of two hundred years ago.

However, a few of the Brooklyn sites give you some feeling of atmosphere and sense of the battle. If you're coming from Manhattan, take the West Side Highway to the Brooklyn Battery Tunnel to the elevated Gowanus Parkway, past the Upper Bay of New York Harbor on your right—with Brooklyn Heights on your left, their tops long since bulldozed and leveled. Gowanus Creek, now a polluted inlet looking like a canal, shows up on your right as well. As you proceed east, note other high ground to your left—the **Heights of Guian,** once covered thickly with trees and underbrush, now covered thickly with row upon row of homes and apartment buildings.

Within a few minutes, the parkway will bring Staten Island into view across the Narrows and then at Sixty-ninth Street swings east to follow the Narrows on ground level. This is a pleasant drive, particularly in fine weather, with the hills of Richmond across the narrow stretch of water and a lovely park with walks and benches bordering the parkway. If you can pull off the road to park, you might take a walk on the paved path along the water, thinking of how the British frigates crowded the Narrows that August morning in 1776, their guns swung out to rake the meager American position at **Denyse Point.** You will know Denyse Point by Fort Hamilton which now occupies the site. You will also know it by the new Verrazano Narrows Bridge which now connects Brooklyn with Staten Island just at the point.

Driving farther east, swing around Fort Hamilton and pass over what was water when I was a boy and came here to climb the rocky breakwaters. It is now covered by thousands of square yards of fill with roads, private homes, and garden apartments surrounded by grassy plots. This is **Gravesend Bay**, where British boats once put redcoats and Hessians ashore. Take the Bay Parkway exit and follow that avenue into Ocean Parkway, where a left turn and a drive of ten or fifteen minutes will take you to **Prospect Park.** Drive or walk through the park for a good idea of what that part of Brooklyn was like at the time of the battle, for the park preserves the terrain as it was then: hilly, rocky, and covered by trees and shrubs. Following the park drive will take you to **Lookout Hill** from whose eminence you can look out over the park and the surrounding city in all directions to see what was once the battlefield. A monument on this hill commemorates the brave Maryland men of the Continental Line who made a stand here before they escaped across Gowanus Creek.

On the far side of the park, follow the Flatbush Avenue extension to Fulton Street. Though there is nothing at this busy, commercial intersection to remind you, some of the heaviest fighting of the battle took place here. Between this point and what was then the village of Brooklyn farther down Fulton Street, most of the American casualties were inflicted and hundreds of rebel men and officers, General Sullivan among them, fell into the hands of the British. Turn right off Fulton at Borough Hall (Court Street intersection); then turn left on Montague or Clark Street and follow it to the end to an overlook on the brow of **Brooklyn Heights** overlooking the East River. It is hard to believe that these heights could ever have been thought of as dominating the city across the river; today their positions are reversed. The towers of Manhattan completely overshadow and dominate the gracious homes and streets of the Heights, once the fashionable center of Brooklyn life during the nineteenth and early twentieth centuries. Continue on down Fulton Street until you can go no farther because of the river. Here at **Fireboat Station 77** was the Brooklyn terminus of the Brooklyn–Manhattan Ferry; it was here the beaten American army embarked under cover of night to live to fight another day.

EAST SIDE, WEST SIDE, 1776

Following the course of Revolutionary War events on Manhattan Island is a little easier than in Brooklyn, if only because there are markers here and there. As in Brooklyn there are also a few features of the terrain that are still distinguishable, even after two centuries. Of course, with the extensive building and renovation and the increased tearing-down and building-up in the modern city, markers that existed ten or twenty years ago are no longer to be found, and certain features of the terrain that were still to be seen fifty or sixty years ago have since been built over.

Nevertheless, it is possible to start at the southern tip of the island and, working your way north, cover the events as they took place from the time Washington evacuated Brooklyn until he retreated north from Manhattan. Make the tour easier and more enjoyable by doing it on a Sunday when traffic is at a minimum; parking is allowed almost everywhere then, and the only people on the island are those who live there and the few visitors who have taken advantage of the Sabbath calm. Keep in mind that in 1776 the city extended from the Battery, so named at the time for the battery of guns stationed there, only as far north as Chambers Street, which borders City Hall Park on the north. North of that were farms, some of them parts of larger holdings; a few villages; and a few roads, including Bloomingdale Road now known as Broadway, wandering through the bosky dells and over the wooded hills.

A history student at one of the city colleges recently completed, for his doctoral thesis, a study of sites on Manhattan Island fortified by the rebels before the British occupation. Though none of these sites now shows any evidence of its former military use you might want to check some of them out just to say you have been there.

Fort George at the southernmost tip of the island boasted a fort with six guns and a grand battery of twenty-three guns. This position on the Upper Bay was first fortified by the Dutch when they built the original city, New Amsterdam. It was here on what was once known as Bowling Green, for the Dutch burghers who played at bowls on the grass, that the statue of George III was pulled down by patriotic citizens in 1776 and melted down to make guns and bullets. Jones Hill near Broome Street in the City Hall area was crowned with a gun or two. On the east side, where Grand and Mulberry streets meet, was an elevation known as Bunker Hill on which was a very strong position featuring several batteries of guns. City Hall Park was enclosed by a barricade of logs, stones, boxes, and barrels which extended across Broadway from a point opposite St. Paul's Church. Trinity Church at the foot of Wall Street on Broadway marks the site of a battery situated on the high ground behind the church. There was a redoubt at Turtle Bay on the East River above east 44th Street, a breastwork somewhere on east 54th Street, a battery on the bluff overlooking the East River at east 74th Street, a battery at the foot of east 85th Street, and a strong battery called Thompson's Battery on the jutting promontory once known as Horn's Hook at the foot of east 89th Street, just below Gracie Mansion, the official residence of the mayor.

THE OLD SIDEWALKS OF NEW YORK

You can begin your Revolutionary War tour of the island by driving down either the West Side Highway or Franklin D. Roosevelt Drive on the east side to **Battery Park.** At this point, park and walk around the area from site to site or drive from one to the other, depending on the weather and your inclination. Driving can be quicker, but only if you know the area fairly well; every street is one-way, and you can spend more time finding your way about than looking at the sites. Since the sites are scattered throughout the district, I will not attempt to map out one definite route, but leave that to your own ingenuity.

Try to keep in mind that most of these streets were established thoroughfares in the seventeenth and eighteenth centuries, and that not a few of them, like Broad Street and Broadway, were laid out by the original Dutch settlers. Despite the modern, towering commercial structures that now line these streets, the area still retains something of its old character, perhaps because the streets wind about and so many of them are little more than narrow alleys, reminders of the cobblestone roads they once were, bordered by one- and two-story buildings, many of them private residences with kitchen and flower gardens out back and trees everywhere. Even during the business day, when these streets are so crowded with pedestrians that even the cabs cannot get through, something of that feeling hovers over the clerks and brokers and lawyers as they hurry to their desks or to luncheon appointments.

Just east of the Battery, at the foot of Broad Street where it meets Pearl Street, stands **Fraunces Tavern**, a four-story brick hostelry that still displays its original tavern sign and is still a restaurant. There is also a *museum* in the building (unfortunately closed on weekends, but open during the week from 10 A.M. to 4 P.M.) that houses a collection of Revolutionary War relics. The tavern was famous for the quality of its hospitality during the Revolution, and its proprietor, "Black Sam" Fraunces (so called because of his swarthy complexion), personally catered some of Washington's special dinners, including one at West Point during the fete staged in honor of the birth of the Dauphin. Fraunces Tavern is most famous for the touching scene that was enacted here on December 4, 1783, when Washington said good-bye to his officers before leaving for Philadelphia to give back his commission to Congress. Open to the public is the room itself where the commander in chief "with a heart full of love and gratitude" embraced each of his comrades-in-arms and revolution from senior officer Henry Knox, his commander of artillery, on down to the most junior officer present. All were in tears by the time he left. From here he went to the foot of nearby Whitehall Street, which at that time ended in a wharf, and left New York via barge.

A few blocks north of Pearl Street is John Street. At a point about midway between Nassau and William streets on John Street the ground slopes up, then down again to the east. This was once known as **Golden Hill** where a British army barracks stood. During the years preceding the Revolution, years marked by increasing discontent among the American city populations involved in trade and commerce and therefore affected by the Navigation and Stamp Acts, the populace of New York was often at odds with the British garrison stationed here. On several occasions British soldiers tore down and burned Liberty Poles, symbols of the colonists' opposition to the crown, and harassed known Whigs; on their part the local citizens responded with rocks and cudgels. In 1765 the Quartering Act required citizens to quarter British troops in their homes, an effort designed to ease the living conditions of the soldiers, which had brought on a number of mutinies in the ranks. The citizens of New York, backed by the state assembly, defied the law, which brought about the suspension of the assembly in 1767. In 1769 a new assembly knuckled under and voted funds for quartering, an action the people of New York considered a betrayal. Friction over the matter came to a clash between citizens and soldiers on January 19, 1770, in which the soldiers wielded bayonets against a mob armed with swords and clubs. The riot took place here on Golden Hill before the barracks to which the mob had driven the soldiers. Several people were bayoneted and seriously wounded. There is no record of military casualties.

City Hall Park on the east side of Broadway between Chambers and Fulton streets has managed to retain much of its original character. Still a park area, it was the city commons in revolutionary times and as such one of the main centers of civic activities.

Just to the west of the west wing of City Hall (the long, French classic building with the tower facing the open parking area at the park's center) is a tablet set into the lawn commemorating Lieutenant Colonel Isaac Barré who stood up in the British House of Commons in 1765 to oppose the Stamp Act. In the course of his speech he referred to Americans as "sons of liberty," an appellation that was taken to heart by certain public-minded citizens in the colonies who began erecting Liberty Poles forthwith. Five such poles were erected on New York Commons between 1766 and 1777. Beyond City Hall, but on the opposite side to the east, is another tablet marking the nearby site of the Provost Prison in which many Americans died between 1776, when the British marched in, and 1783, when they marched out for the last time. To the right of City Hall as you stand with your back to it facing south down Broadway is yet another tablet reminding us that on July 9, 1776, the Declaration of Independence was read on this spot to the American army in the presence of General George Washington. Just at the park entrance on Broadway, immediately west of the tablet, is a statue of Nathan Hale, though his capture and execution occurred farther uptown. A little north of this statue and easily read from the Broadway sidewalk is still another plaque commemorating the Liberty Poles erected on the commons.

Go south from City Hall Park to **Trinity Church** at the foot of Wall Street on the west side of Broadway. It is recognizable by its graceful, twin Gothic spires and the churchyard surrounding it on three sides, the tombstones and monuments crowding up to the iron picket fence along Broadway. Wall Street was named for the city wall that here marked the northern boundary of New Amsterdam. The first Trinity Church was destroyed in the fire that burned most of the city in 1776 soon after the British occupied it. The present structure was erected in 1846. Of particular interest to us is the *churchyard* where several men who were prominent in the Revolution are buried. For instance, note just off the entrance through the Broadway gate five large tablets laid on the ground, one marked by a small American flag. This is the final resting place of Charles McKnight, M.D., senior surgeon to the American army of the Revolution. Just beyond is a contemporary tablet marking the nearby grave of Francis Lewis, signer of the Declaration of Independence. Alexander Hamilton is buried in the southern section of the churchyard to the left of the main entrance of the church as you enter. Directly to the left of the entrance is a large stone erected by the Society of the Cincinnati in memory of Hamilton and other original members, all officers of the Continental Army and Navy, whose remains are interred in Trinity parish. The list correctly includes Horatio Gates and incorrectly Richard Montgomery, who, you will remember, died below the walls of Quebec in 1775 long before the Society was organized. Hamilton's grave is marked by a large monument close to the picket fence overlooking Rector Street. His widow Eliza, daughter of Philip Schuyler, is buried just in front of him. Nearby is a memorial to Robert Fulton, one of the inventors of the steamship.

A block or two north of Trinity, at Broadway and Vesey Street, is **St. Paul's,** built as a chapel for the first Trinity Church. It survived the fire of 1776 to receive within its pews at Sunday worship—regularly and otherwise—the officers of the occupying forces, including Sir William Howe and Major John André. Its design imitates London's St. Martin's-in-the-Field.

THE OPENING STRATEGY

While the Americans waited for the inevitable British attack, Washington and his staff debated the advisability of holding on to New York City. Of his 19,000 men about 5,000 were sick; militiamen were going home in droves as their enlistments ran out, and morale was at an all-time low. Suggestions were put forward that the town be burned, but Congress vetoed that idea. Congress wanted the city to remain intact in hopes of future American occupation.

Washington decided to divide his men into three divisions. Five thousand men under Putnam were stationed in the city for its defense; 9,000 under General William Heath were supposed to defend the northern part of the island from Harlem to King's Bridge; and the rest were deployed along the East River to stave off British attacks from Long Island. When Washington informed Congress that he had split up his army because he believed that Congress wanted the city defended, he was informed he was to hold these positions only as long as he thought it necessary or wise. In other words, the onus for defending the city was placed squarely on his shoulders.

Washington and his advisors held another council of war on September 12 and decided that it might be wiser to abandon all of Manhattan below Fort Washington as soon as the army's supplies and equipment could be moved. It was already too late for second thoughts. Two days before, on Tuesday, September 10, the British had occupied Montresor's Island, now known as Randall's Island, at the mouth of the Harlem River where it meets the East River, thus placing themselves in position to land either at Harlem or farther north for a march on King's Bridge that could cut off the entire American force on Manhattan. On the thirteenth, several men-of-war and a number of transports sailed up the East River and took positions opposite Kips Bay, while another small force of ships sailed up the Hudson to drop anchor above Fort Washington, preventing any movement between Manhattan and New Jersey.

Take the F.D.R. Drive north to the 34th Street exit where the street ends at the East River. Here at **Kips Bay** on Sunday, September 15, 1776, five British ships lay offshore, bow to stern, sheltering eighty-odd flatboats on the far shore loaded with about 4,000 redcoats and Hessians under the command of General Sir Henry Clinton. The bay was defended by some Connecticut militiamen crouched in a ditch above the rocky beach. They faced eighty-six ships' guns swung out and loaded, ready for action. At eleven in the morning, the ships opened a two-hour bombardment of the militia position with everything they had. At 1 P.M. the invaders came ashore. The rebels in the ditch had long since left; now other militia units stationed along the river south of Kips Bay retreated, offering only slight resistance and leaving the landing virtually unopposed. Washington, Putnam, and others tried to rally the fleeing men, but it was impossible to organize a defense line, and Putnam galloped for the city to get his men out before they were cut off. The British landing force moved inland to occupy Murray Hill, part of the extensive farm holdings of Robert Murray, while 9,000 more British came ashore. One detachment of Hessians marched to the neighborhood of what is now Park Avenue and east 23rd Street where they captured 300 Americans. The rest of Putnam's men hurrying north along the Post Road, now Lexington Avenue, would have run smack into the British had not Aaron Burr, Putnam's aide-de-camp, warned him in time and led the army west to Bloomingdale Road, now Broadway, and so to the north.

You can reach Park and 23rd by driving west, away from the river, on 34th Street, then turning left (south) on Fourth Avenue. Turning right (west) on 23rd Street, proceed to Broadway and follow it west by north in the rebel army's footsteps. The British continued up the Post Road without realizing that the main American force was almost paralleling their line of march less than a mile away. The distance between the two forces increased until the width of what is now Central Park lay between them.

If you wish to stay with the British command, take 34th Street west from the river to Park Avenue; turn right and stop on the next corner at 35th Street. On the opposite side of the avenue, on the southwest corner, stands Number 16 Park Avenue. Its entrance is off the avenue a little way west on 35th Street. A plaque on the side of the building identifies this as the geographic center of the **Murray Farm.** According to legend it was here that Mrs. Robert Murray entertained General Howe and his staff so well with her fine, old Madeira, that he quite forgot what he was on Manhattan for and allowed the rebels to escape. It is undoubtedly true that Howe's first objective was the capture of Inclenburg (Murray Hill), but his failure to move across Manhattan to trap the American army in the city was probably due more to his cautious nature than to Mrs. Murray's wine. His officers were also under orders to wait on Inclenburg until the army had crossed the river.

Inclenburg is still there, as you can easily discover by walking east on any street between 35th and 38th streets from Madison Avenue. There is a noticeable slope to the ground, and though the hill is not as high as it was in 1776, it is still steep enough to make your breath come faster if you take it at a normal walking pace. According to historian Bruce Bliven, if the Murray house were still standing, it would extend across Park Avenue between 36th and 37th streets.

Howe got all his men ashore by five o'clock that afternoon and occupied the city without firing a shot, while some of his men moved across the island west to the Hudson River and north toward Harlem. Six days later on the night of September 20–21, the city caught fire and much of it burned to the ground, thus denying most of the British army the snug winter quarters they had been anticipating. The British accused the Americans of starting the fire, and though both redcoats and civilians fought the blaze, there are reports of British soldiers seizing suspected arsonists and throwing them into the flames. The city was never the same after that, quite literally. The pleasant, gracious atmosphere for which it had been noted went up in smoke and flame, and it became a city of shanties and makeshift shelters. Two years later yet another fire broke out, destroying much of what had escaped the first conflagration; within that short space of time, twenty-four months, colonial New York disappeared.

I tried to find the spot where Nathan Hale was supposed to have been executed at 46th Street and First Avenue. A tavern stood there at the time and a tablet once marked the spot. Today the spot where Hale gave up his one life for his country is fittingly a part of the plaza surrounding the headquarters of a world organization dedicated to life and the preservation of peace, the United Nations.

THE UPTOWN BATTLEFIELD

By the evening of the day of the Kips Bay landing, the British had established a line running from 90th Street and the East River—in fact, from Horn's Hook where Thompson's Battery had been stationed and which was then presumably in British hands—west across what is now Central Park to 91st Street and what is now West End Avenue overlooking the Hudson. Howe set up his headquarters in the old Beekman mansion which stood at the intersection of First Avenue and east 51st Street. Clinton and Lord Cornwallis, his second-in-command, shared quarters in the Apthorp House at what is now Columbus Avenue and 91st Street. The British line faced the American line which ran from the Harlem River at about 155th Street to 135th Street overlooking the Hudson. British advance posts were established from McGowan's Pass, the east side of Central Park at 106th Street, all the way west to about 105th Street on the Hudson River.

Washington's advance positions ran along the edge of the plateau overlooking 125th Street and a valley known as the Hollow Way that still bisects the island at that point. A half mile to the rear was yet another line of men. A half mile to the rear of that was the first of three fortified lines, several small redoubts connected by trenches. Almost a mile north of that, at about 153rd Street, was the main defense line; north of that at about 159th Street was the third defense line. Fort Washington was at 183rd on the west side and 5,000 additional troops were at King's Bridge at the northernmost tip of the island on guard against possible attack from that direction.

Drive north along First Avenue to 66th Street where the British established a gun park for their artillery. Then proceed west on 65th Street five blocks and turn right (north) on Madison Avenue to approximate the British line of march up the island. Actually they marched along what is now Fifth Avenue, but Fifth is one-way in the wrong direction, a traffic situation that might have saved Washington a headache or two in September, '76. Turn west again on 106th Street and proceed one block to Fifth Avenue. The park blocks any further movement west, forcing you to turn left onto Fifth. Directly opposite 106th Street, a park entrance marks the east end of **McGowan's Pass.** Leaving your car, enter the park; within fifty feet you will be walking between two hills. Climb the one to your right and at the top find a round paved area encircled by a breastwork of benches. Inside the circle an 1812 gun mounted on concrete marks the site of an American blockhouse and then a British position commanding the pass at this end. It was also the site of Fort Clinton which was built during the War of 1812.

You can find the sites of the three defense lines by going west to the other side of the park, either via intersecting roads south of 106th Street which are prominently marked "West side," or by taking the Central Park Drive and following it around the northern end of the park and south to the first exit onto Central Park West. Take Broadway (three blocks west) uptown to 153rd Street to find a marker set in a cemetery wall on the northwest corner of the intersection, marking the second line of American defenses. (The marker for the first line at 147th Street is no longer there.) A marker for the third line may be found on the side of a building on the southeast corner of the intersection at 159th Street.

Three blocks north, at 162nd Street, turn right (east) and go two blocks to Jumel Terrace. There in Roger Morris Park stands a handsome, Georgian colonial mansion, the **Morris-Jumel Mansion,** built by Roger Morris, a Loyalist who fled to England in 1775. Washington made this his headquarters from the night of September 15 until he left the island. The house has many mementoes connected with Washington, including a hat, coat, and purse which he is said to have left behind in haste when the British landed north of Harlem Heights, forcing the American withdrawal from Manhattan. The house was then occupied by the British until the end of the war when it became a tavern, the first stop for the New York–Boston stagecoach. It was subsequently bought by a dashing Haitian planter, Stephen Jumel, for his lovely blonde mistress, Elizabeth Bowen, who became his wife and who married Aaron Burr after Stephen's death. Jumel Mansion is open daily from 11 A.M. to 5 P.M., except Monday. There is no admission charge. It was from this house that Washington rode on the morning of September 16, 1776, to see what all the shooting was about.

THE BATTLE OF HARLEM HEIGHTS

The shooting began when a reconnaissance force under Lieutenant Colonel Thomas Knowlton, sent out by Washington to find the British lines, ran into pickets posted by the British Light Infantry at about 106th Street and Broadway, a place known then as Jones's Farm. During the ensuing skirmish, detachments from the Forty-second Highlanders, the famous Black Watch, tried to encircle Knowlton's men who retreated west toward the river, then back across the Hollow Way. The light infantry chased them as far as the present site of Grant's Tomb. Washington, who had ridden out to see what was going on, heard a British bugler play a fox hunting tune, meaning that the fox had gone to ground. Anxious for some sort of victory to lift the morale of his men, he ordered a party of about a hundred volunteers under Lieutenant Colonel Archibald Crary to draw the British down into the Hollow Way. Knowlton's men, augmented by other detachments, were ordered to work their way around the British right.

As the British fell for the bait and pursued Crary's men down into the valley, Knowlton's encircling movement was proceeding well until some of his men opened fire prematurely and the British, becoming aware of their danger, fell back. Seeing a chance to get some of their own back after the ignoble retreat of the previous day, the Americans moved forward in hot pursuit. The fighting intensified as the British took shelter behind a split-rail fence; Knowlton and another American officer were mortally wounded. Washington threw in more reinforcements and the flank attack was driven home at about 123rd Street and Broadway. The British then withdrew to the edge of a buckwheat field at about 119th Street between Broadway and Riverside Drive, where they drew up in a line. The Americans formed a line facing them on 120th Street and the two forces stood there practically toe-to-toe, throwing hot lead at each other for some time, until the British line began to fall back. They retreated into an orchard at about 111th Street and then back to Jones's Farm where the affair had begun. By this time about 5,000 British and Germans were engaged against 2,000 Americans, who were spoiling to show the enemy that the foxes had become the hunters, but Washington decided to call them off rather than risk a general engagement. The Americans lost about 30 killed and 100 wounded; the British about 14 killed and 154 wounded. Though not a major battle, it forced Howe to become more cautious than ever in his pursuit of the rebels. For the next month he had his men building fortifications to protect his position in New York City from any possible counterattacks from the north. The Americans, on their part, had enjoyed the sight of British and German regulars running, and many of the green militiamen had learned that they too could stand and make the enemy give ground. It helped to take some of the taste of Kips Bay out of their mouths for the time being.

Covering the sites of this engagement requires some moving back and forth if you want to follow the action in sequence. Begin by going west to Riverside Drive north of 125th Street and then follow the drive south until it is carried over a valley below you on a viaduct or bridge connecting two high points of ground. The viaduct bridges the **Hollow Way**, a fact you can ascertain by finding a bronze plaque at the south end of the viaduct set into the southernmost of two cement pillars which flank the entrance to a small, flagstone overlook. Turning your back on the river, cross the drive to the east side and look out over the low ground that lies between **Harlem Heights** to the north and east on your left, and the high ground to the south on your right on which you can see Grant's Tomb and the Gothic revival towers of the Riverside Church. In front of you, where the new apartment building built by Columbia University for its faculty towers over the viaduct, is the now built-up slope of **Morningside Heights**, up which Knowlton and his men climbed toward their meeting with the British.

Continue south on Riverside Drive to Grant's Tomb at about 120th Street, where a wide parking area allows you to leave your car for a climb up to the monument and a look around. At approximately this spot the British trumpeter stood and played his merrie hunting tune toward the backs of the retreating Americans. You get a fine view from here of the high ground on the other side of the Hollow Way. Now proceed east on 120th Street to Broadway where you will see the buildings of Columbia University on both sides of the avenue. As you turn left, or north, the buildings of the Union Theological Seminary on the left side of Broadway mark the location of the wheatfield where the heaviest fighting of September 16, 1776, took place. Three blocks uptown at 123rd Street is the site where the Americans under Knowlton hit the British right flank and sent them scurrying for shelter. There is nothing at 111th Street or at 106th

Street to remind you of the orchard or of Jones's Farm where the fight began and ended.

Inspiring though it was, the Battle of Harlem Heights was no answer to Washington's dilemma: how to keep the British from cutting his army off from the only escape route open to him, King's Bridge, the Spuyten Duyvil crossing at the north end of Manhattan. He held a strong position on the Harlem Heights line, and Fort Washington on the Hudson was well manned, but he had no way of preventing General Howe from carrying out an end run around his line.

Outflanking movements were Howe's favorite tactic, and since he had the advantage over the Continentals of a virtually uncontested fleet and numerical superiority, he put them to use. Despite a log boom stretched across the Hudson from Fort Washington to Fort Constitution (later called Fort Lee) on the Jersey side and other obstacles like the sunken hulls of ships, he had already sent several ships north to the Tappan Zee and other points well above the rebels' positions on Manhattan. On Saturday, October 12, a strong British fleet, which had sailed up the East River from Kips Bay the night before, began putting ashore 4,000 men at Throg's Point, close to what is now known as Throg's Neck, where the Throg's Neck Bridge connects the Bronx with Queens. A small but well-placed force of Americans on the opposite side of a creek, however, held the British advance until reinforcements arrived and the invaders were successfully stopped. For six days Howe was forced to keep his 4,000 men idle on Throg's Point, with King's Bridge only eight miles away, while he prepared to try the same maneuver at another and, hopefully, more favorable spot—Pell's Point three miles to the north in Westchester. The cat was out of the bag, however, and deciding at a council of war held on the night of the sixteenth not to give Howe a second crack at envelopment, Washington gave the order to abandon Harlem, and move the army and its supplies across King's Bridge up to White Plains, where he felt reasonably sure he could form another effective defense line. Behind him he would leave 3,000 men to hold Fort Washington and 2,000 men to hold Fort Constitution on the Jersey side, both under the command of General Greene who was given instructions to hold the positions only as long as he thought possible.

DELAY AT SPLIT ROCK

On Friday, October 18, Howe shifted his forces from their stalemated position on Throg's Point to Pell's Point on Eastchester Bay. That same day the rebels began to evacuate Manhattan, their supplies moving at an agonizingly slow pace behind them because of the lack of horse-drawn wagons. A mile away from Eastchester Bay, Colonel John Glover, whose Marblehead regiment had ferried the Continental Army across the East River after the debacle on Long Island, watched from a hill near the Eastchester village green as the British came ashore. Including a number of elements from other Massachusetts regiments, Glover had about 750 men under his command and three guns. With this small force he decided to do what he could to hold up the British advance, which had to use Split Rock Road to reach the Post Road, the only road available.

The rock the road was named for, an ancient Indian landmark, is still there—a huge boulder with a crack or split probably caused by frost action. You can get to it from Manhattan by taking the Henry Hudson Parkway up the west side of Manhattan to the first turnoff for the George Washington Bridge. But instead of getting onto the bridge, bear right and follow the signs for the Cross Bronx Expressway. The Expressway will take you to the Hutchinson River Parkway, which you take north to the second exit for the New England Thruway north (after the parkway crosses a narrow body of water). The *rock* is on a grassy island between the north and southbound lanes of the thruway about where the Hutchinson River Parkway meets it. It is not easy to get to and seeing it is not all that rewarding, perhaps because the area has changed so completely. I have seen photographs of the rock taken sixty or seventy years ago when Split Rock Road was still a country lane, wooded on both sides, and the rock could still evoke the action that took place there.

Block out the landscaped parkways, if you can, and the surrounding apartment buildings and other structures, and try to see a clear view of Eastchester Bay to the east, filled with the British ships and the line of barges and other small craft taking the troops ashore. To the west, the rolling, wooded countryside stretches off to the Hudson and north into Westchester County, broken by pasturelands and croplands, bare and brown as fall wears on toward winter.

Glover's small advance unit met the British advance not far from the rock. A low, stone wall gave the Americans additional cover; and as their advance unit fell back before the British advance, the rest of the 750, sheltered behind the wall on both sides of the road, fired the first of many volleys that were to keep the Hessians under the redoubtable Knyphausen from making any appreciable headway. All afternoon the battle went on with the Americans falling back in good order, holding the British down to a snail's pace, despite the seven heavy guns they had brought ashore. After dark Glover broke off the engagement and withdrew slowly as the British licked their wounds. American casualties were about eight killed and thirteen wounded, and though Howe only reported three killed and twenty wounded, his figures may have only reflected British losses. The Hessians, who had borne the brunt of the fighting, made no report of casualties, but St. Paul's Episcopal Church, a mile or so away, was crowded that night and for days after with Hessian wounded.

By October 21, the British had occupied New Rochelle; on the twenty-second they entered Mamaroneck, but by then Washington was at White Plains with his rear guard holding a line along the Tuckahoe Hills awaiting Howe's advance. Before you join him there, however, return to the Hutchinson River Parkway and take it to the next exit north, U.S. 1 or the Boston Post Road. Go left or south on the Post Road; then make a right on east 233rd Street and proceed to Columbus Avenue (or South Columbus Avenue) which is also State Route 22. Turn right (north) on Columbus Avenue and watch for **St. Paul's Episcopal Church** on your right. Set back off the road, the pre-Revolution fieldstone building has a tower at one end surmounted by a steeple.

At the time of the Split Rock battle, this building was still under construction. The original church on this site, a wooden structure erected about 1700, stood where the flagpole is now in front of the present church. Knyphausen left his wounded and dying here under the protection of a detachment while he hurried on after the Americans. The wounded were moved into the half-finished structure, but since it still lacked windows and a floor, the old church was knocked down to provide shelter and firewood.

As time went on the church continued to serve as a hospital and at one time was crowded with Hessian victims of an epidemic, probably smallpox. Behind the church in the graveyard is a white marker close to the back wall, erected by the D.A.R. to mark the site of a sand pit where the bodies of the dead Hessians were buried. The tombstones here date back to 1704. A plaque on the church identifies at least thirteen known and a number of unknown Revolutionary War dead who are buried here, including three members of the Pell family which owned the original land grant in these parts and for whom Pelham Manor is named.

Beyond the back wall the cluster of oil-storage tanks in the middle distance are on the bank of Eastchester Creek. The creek is not visible from the church grounds, but from the steeple, which is reached by a rickety wooden ladder, I got as good a view as you might expect of the general area, including the Split Rock battleground which today is indistinguishable from the rest of the industrial and suburban sprawl.

The church originally stood at the edge of a village green where an election was held in 1735, which Peter Zenger reported in his newspaper; he was subsequently tried for libel and acquitted, an event that laid the groundwork for our traditional principles of freedom of the press. Until recently a Revolutionary War tavern stood on the other side of Columbus Avenue directly opposite the church, for the road was a well-traveled route to New England and stagecoaches made this their first stop out of New York on the way to Boston. At the time of my visit, the site was marked by two stone entrance-pillars and a pile of rubble, the remains of the tavern which had not yet been removed. There is a state historical marker at the curb. At that time the area was typically rural with farms and large estates around the church. Many of the larger establishments had their own landings on Eastchester Creek which gave them access to Long Island Sound. Today the church is in an industrial section known as Oil Town because of the oil-storage tanks which have proliferated.

As you stand facing the church, walk around to the right to find the old stile in the wall, stone blocks forming steps which allowed one to get over the wall. The custom was to drive up to the church in a carriage and stop in front of the stile. This permitted the passengers to step out onto the stile directly from the carriage and thus over the wall and into the church.

At that end of the church a white door admits one into the base of the tower. Over the door is a stone inscribed with the date 1765. This is the *tower stone*, which is to the tower what the cornerstone is to the entire building and marks the year when construction of the tower was begun. Actually it took a year to build the wall up to that level. The initials "R.P." scratched into the tower stone stand for Richard Pell, a friend of Lafayette buried in this churchyard. As you look farther up the tower, you will note square holes in the stone work at regular intervals. Each of the intervals between the holes marks one day's work. As the workers reached the end of the day, they would leave spaces along the top row into which the supports for the next day's scaffolding would be fitted.

The interior of the church has been restored with great devotion to detail, such as the foot warmers in the pews and the pews themselves which are completely enclosed to keep out the drafts that must have plagued the congregation on wintry Sundays. The *bell* now hanging in the belfry is a sister to the Liberty Bell in Philadelphia; it was cast at about the same time in the same foundry by the same workmen. As the British approached in October, 1776, it was hurriedly taken down, packed with the church silver, buried in a nearby swamp, then exhumed and rehung after the war. None the worse for the experience, it has served the church ever since and on the Fourth of July is rung thirteen times in memory of the original thirteen states.

By the bicentennial, it may be possible to see the bell close up, for plans are afoot to furnish the tower with a proper flight of stairs so that visitors may get into the belfry, not only to see the bell but to have a look around. The rickety ladder serves the purpose, but does not look half as sturdy as a ladder made in the revolutionary period that stands in the room below the bell room. It is made entirely of wood, with pegs instead of nails holding the rungs in place.

THE BATTLE OF WHITE PLAINS

Washington had retreated to White Plains in an effort to keep his army intact and prevent it from meeting the British in a direct confrontation, which would surely destroy it. Though some individual units had proved themselves battle-worthy, most of his men were still green and untrained and showed a disposition to run at the first sound of a shot, as they had on Long Island and at Kips Bay. What the Continental Army needed was time to rest and organize, time to train, and a chance to fight on ground of their own choosing; but Howe, even in his half-hearted way, was denying them all that.

Washington had at one time considered retreating to Norwalk, Connecticut, but the thought of placing his army close to Long Island Sound with no naval protection against the British fleet made him decide to chance Westchester instead. There was a fairly good defensive position on the hills of White Plains, and if he had to retreat from there he could go either north into the Hudson Highlands or west to New Jersey. Besides, his supplies were moving slowly, and he had to wait until they caught up with him to keep them from falling into British hands.

To join the Continentals at White Plains, return to the Hutchinson River Parkway and continue north to the White Plains exit onto the Cross Westchester Expressway west. Leave the expressway at the North White Plains exit and turn right (north) onto what is both Route 22 and North Broadway. At the third traffic light, you see on your left an A & P shopping center and Virginia Road leading off at an angle, marked by a sign reading, "Washington's Headquarters—Miller Hill." Follow this road past the turnoff for Miller Hill and on to the **Miller House**, a white, frame building on your right set off from the road by a fence, with a small parking area cut into the side of the hill.

The village of White Plains took its name from the name given to it by the earliest residents in the area, the Weckquaeskeck Indians, a Mohican tribe that paid tribute to the Mohawks. They called it Quaroppas, their word for the marshes and swamps that covered most of what is today the city of White Plains. So extensive were these flat wetlands that a white mist or fog seemed to hang over them perpetually, hence "white plains."

The entrance to the house is reached through a gate leading from the parking lot and you will find the gate open from February 22, Washington's Birthday, until December 15 for no charge. Inside the enclosure the mood is eighteenth-century rural, with the charming, two-story farmhouse taking up most of the area, an ancient root cellar off to the right, and around the left side of the house, an enormous syca-more tree which may have seen as many as 500 summers and is easily 250 years old. A member in good standing of the American Forestry Association's Hall of Fame for Trees, the sycamore is the last, living witness to the people who went in and out of this house 200 years ago and the events that brought them here. Though the trunk is largely hollow, the tree leafs fully every year and produces seedballs in season.

Washington put up at the home of Jacob Purdy when he first came to White Plains, but since it was in the path of the British advance, he moved his headquarters north of the village where the recently widowed Mrs. Elijah Miller offered him the use of two of her rooms. Charles Lee, who was Washington's second-in-command and actually in command on the field here, also used this house, and it became the general head-quarters building during the battle.

The house was built in 1738 by John Miller, a local farmer, when the prospect from this site must have been a most pleasant one with a gentle slope of open land ending at the Bronx River at the foot of Chatterton Hill and the low ridgeline that runs along the river. Today a sand and gravel company has placed its elevators on the opposite side of busy Virginia Road; beyond, the valley is filled with the local trainyards of the New York Central Railroad and other modern commercial and residential properties. Behind the house Miller Hill rises steeply with suburban homes showing through the trees.

You enter into what must have been the principal room, a large room with a life-sized figure seated at a table representing John Miller. To the left off this is the room Washington used for meetings, as illustrated by the three life-sized figures standing around the table used for these conferences. They represent Washington; Jacob Purdy, a local resident who was under Washington's command at the time; and Isaac van Wart, one of the three men who captured Major André. Why Van Wart is included in this group is obscure, but it is interesting to note that all these figures, including Miller, are dressed in authentic period costume. In fact, the Purdy figure wears part of the uniform worn by Purdy himself.

Beyond the main room is the kitchen, which displays a number of colonial domestic items including a large cooking pot described as a "colonial pressure cooker" and a colonial version of a washing machine, a large box set on rockers. A flight of steps leads up to the attic which exhibits period farm implements; off the kitchen beyond the stairs is a diorama with another life-sized figure, that of a drummer boy in the Continental Army.

At the foot of the steps on a kitchen wall I found a framed print of an old map of the village of White Plains as it appeared at the time of the battle, with the British and American positions clearly marked. The house is sparsely furnished and does not have the usual period antiques you have come to expect in the colonial homes you visit. In the conference room, however, beside the conference table are three chairs which, according to the plaques on them, were used by Washington at one time or another.

Leaving the Miller House, return along Virginia Road in the direction of North Broadway, watching for the sign for **Miller Hill** on your left. The sign has an arrow pointing up the hill at the intersection of General Heath Avenue. At the top is a large, open area with a stone marker on McDougall Drive, the street bordering it. When I was there the site was also marked by a large sign which identified it as the "Miller Hill restoration where the last shots of the Battle of White Plains on November 1, 1776, were fired."

Walk across the open area to the brow of the hill overlooking Virginia Road to one side and North White Plains to your left and right front. A long embankment with a trench at its foot runs along the hill from where a private home fronts McDougall Drive to the farthest point you can walk to overlooking North Broadway and the town. There, a bronze *map* of the battle area shows the main topographical features and several pertinent and visible contemporary landmarks. The embankment is the remains of the breastwork the Americans threw up on this spot (or perhaps the remains of its reconstruction); the hollow

ground behind it is what is left of the trench. At one time a row of
period guns was positioned here to give some idea of what the position
looked like during the battle, but they have all been misappropriated by
unknown parties.

This is a good spot to recapitulate the battle before you descend into
the town to visit individual sites. Although this was a decisive battle, it
was a comparatively small engagement of short duration. Facing the relief
map, look for North Broadway snaking away from the foot of the hill
toward the city of White Plains which spreads across the hills on the
skyline. To your right and behind you are other hills which you cannot
see. The Bronx River, which is also hidden from your view by trees and
buildings, runs along the foot of the line of hills to your right. The
American line spread across your line of vision from the hills on the
right, across North Broadway, and up and over the hills to your left.
Its right flank rested on **Chatterton Hill** on your right; the left flank
was anchored on a millpond to your left near what is now Silver Lake.
On the day the British came on the scene, however, Sunday, October 27,
Washington had not yet fortified Chatterton Hill. The next day when
the British engaged his advance units, forcing them to fall back, Washington had second thoughts. He decided that since the hill overlooked
his right flank, it was too vital a feature to leave unmanned. He sent
1,600 men to dig in on the top with two guns, all he could spare, for
support. Captain Alexander Hamilton was in command of the guns.

Spot the tower on the skyline off in the distance in White Plains; it
also appears on the relief map. Howe had his headquarters somewhat to
the left of that tower. His men approached the American lines from that
general direction, deploying on the plain below Chatterton Hill in view
of the Americans who, from your present viewpoint, were in the middle
distance. Washington had over 25,000 men in White Plains, but more
than half were ill and otherwise unfit for duty. Howe had delayed in
New Rochelle, waiting for his 4,000 Germans under Rall and Knyphausen to catch up. When he moved on White Plains he mustered 13,000
men, about half of Washington's force, but they were 13,000 trained and
tested troops and also included a force of mounted dragoons.

Howe had spotted the significance of Chatterton Hill almost at once
the first time he surveyed the field. On the day of the attack, he positioned his artillery about where the White Plains railroad station is now
and opened a bombardment of the American positions on the hill. The
top of the hill was open farmland divided into lots by stone walls, the
rebels' favorite form of cover, but the slopes were heavily wooded and

quite steep. While a force of Hessians began an attempt to cross the Bronx River at the foot of the hills, other detachments moved around Chatterton Hill and into the ridges to the west to enfilade the Americans, thus putting the men on Chatterton under fire from two directions. The troops crossing the river spread out around the foot of the hill as far as they could before they started up. They moved to the assault twice and twice were driven back down, until the dragoons hit a Massachusetts militia unit on one flank and forced them into panic-stricken flight. This exposed the rest of the position and the Americans on the hill were forced to withdraw. Again the Americans had been caught in one of Howe's enveloping movements.

Washington now pulled his right back and sent guns up onto Miller Hill under the command of Colonel Glover. Glover held his fire until the British had gone to the trouble of dragging a number of cannon to the top of nearby Travis Hill, a summit considerably below Miller Hill's height, and then peppered away at them. The British, caught flatfooted for once, managed to get off four return shots before they concluded that their position was too exposed and withdrew.

Unsure of the new American positions and still unwilling to risk a direct, frontal assault, Howe stalled while he waited for reinforcements for a general attack, which he planned for October 31. A heavy rainstorm broke over the scene, however, and for more than twenty hours the heavens poured down a deluge that delayed the attack and gave Washington a chance to withdraw to stronger positions at North Castle. The Americans had lost about 150 men, 50 of them killed, and Howe 313. By the time Howe got reinforcements he had increased his force to 20,000 effectives, but instead of advancing and forcing the issue—a battle he surely would have won, thus ending the war—he turned back to the south to focus on Fort Washington, which had prevented him from getting supplies overland and forced him to depend on ships getting up and down Long Island Sound and the Harlem River. Once again, General William Howe saved the Revolution.

THE HERITAGE TRAIL

The Battle of White Plains Monument Committee, which maintains the Miller House and Miller Hill, has laid out a driving and walking tour called the Heritage Trail which covers twenty-two historical sites, most of them in North White Plains. All of these date from the colonial period, but only a few are connected with the Revolution. A map of the trail, with descriptions of each site, is available at the Miller House. The map is not detailed, however, and gives you only the most general idea of where to go; it does not include directions from one site to another. There are distinctive Heritage Trail markers at points along the way; where the trail leads through woodlands colored blazes on the trees keep you from wandering. But most of the sites are located in what are now built-up areas or down country roads, and the markers and blazes are not sufficient. The committee plans to issue new maps with full instructions by the bicentennial of the battle, if not before. If you visit White Plains after they are issued, you will have no problems; otherwise, you must ask directions unless you know the town.

It is possible to walk the trail if you can devote most of a day to it; though the distance between any two consecutive sites is not more than a mile or two at most, the total distance adds up to a good hike. Most of the sites can be visited by car; those that must be reached on foot, including several connected with the Revolution, call for pleasant walks of not more than half an hour through wooded park areas.

I covered the sites in North White Plains proper by car, then walked the better part of the trail accompanied by a guide, eleven-year-old Scott Robeson who is one of several young guides and hosts at the Miller House and along the trail. Going up Mount Misery was a steep climb, and parts of the trail took us out of White Plains into Harrison and North Castle, but most of it was a delightful excursion along backcountry roads. We made frequent stops to explore the remains of old houses, a colonial cemetery where black slaves who were freed by their Quaker masters and settled on nearby land are buried, ancient Indian trails which became white man's roads, scattered tombstones of Revolutionary War soldiers buried along the trail, and in Silver Lake Park, the remains of the chimneys and foundation walls of some colonial homes. Only three of the sites we visited are connected with the Battle of White Plains, in addition to Miller Hill.

To see the revolutionary sites, begin by returning to North Broadway and go back toward the city of White Plains. About a quarter of a mile after the road passes over the Cross Westchester Expressway, look for a large, granite pillar on the right side of the road, just off the curb, flanked by yews. Mounted on it is a British *mortar* found nearby after the battle. A plaque informs you that the mortar and the pillar are remnants of the entrenchments which marked the center of the Continental line from October 28 to October 31.

Chatterton Hill on which Washington anchored his right flank is now directly to your right. If you go on just a little farther, you come to the intersection of Rockledge Avenue on your right. Rockledge Avenue was White Plains' main street during the colonial period. Turn onto Rockledge and follow it to the intersection with Spring Street. Stop at the corner and notice to your right on the opposite side of Spring Street an old, white, frame farmhouse, the **Jacob Purdy House** where Washington stayed before moving to the Miller Farm. The Purdy House is closed at this time, but the Monument Committee is working on its restoration and it should be open to visitors by the bicentennial.

Turn left onto Spring Street which will take you to Water Street, one block farther, where you make a right at the light. Water Street in turn takes you to Lexington Avenue where you make a left. All this part of town, now homes and storefronts, was originally part of the Purdy Farm. Lexington Avenue intersects Hamilton Avenue at a traffic light where you turn right, taking Hamilton to Bronx Street. Make a left onto Bronx Street and proceed to Battle Avenue where a right turn will take you under a railroad underpass. It was down **Battle Avenue** the frightened militia ran as they deserted their positions on Chatterton Hill. You are now at the foot of the hill. To your left are the New York Central tracks and station and a park through which the Bronx River meanders. The tracks and the station are built on the approximate site of the British lines, possibly the point from which the redcoats and Hessians started crossing the river. Ahead of you up Battle Avenue is the steep slope of Chatterton Hill, now thickly settled with homes, then thickly wooded. The attacking troops must have come up the hill on an opposite slope; otherwise the retreating militia would have run smack into them.

Proceed up Battle Avenue to Whitney, where a left turn will take you to an intersection with Wayne Avenue. On your right on a higher piece of ground, a breech-loading artillery piece, circa Spanish-American War, sits on a private front lawn with a commemorative boulder in front of it and a flagpole. The **gun** marks the American line of defenses. Turn your back on the gun and look down the slope of the hill in the direction from which the three assaults came. The final assault was made by British troops who had spread out around the foot of the hill and advanced on the Americans from every direction except the one from which you came.

Retracing your way down the hill, return to North Broadway and turn left (west); go back to Virginia Road and beyond to an intersection where a prominent sign welcomes you to North Castle. Turn onto Reservoir Road which goes down a small slope to Rockledge Road. Make a left onto Rockledge Road and bear right following the road as it goes up **Mount Misery.** The first turn to your right is Grove Road which takes you on up to Nethermont Avenue where you turn left. Like Chatterton

Hill, Misery Hill is covered with homes and private gardens. Nethermont Avenue takes you to the top where you will see a walkway between what seems to be two hurricane fences, but is actually one continuous enclosure. A sign announces that you have arrived on top of Mount Misery, so called because the American soldiers stationed here, though they saw no action and suffered no wounds, had to endure a bitter cold snap.

The enclosed walkway leads into a wooded area which is private property on the left and reservoir property on the right. At the end of the walkway, where your way is blocked by the fence, a sign informs you that during the battle American troops camped here from October 28 to November 15 and that the site was probably reoccupied by them in 1778, from July to September. A brochure put out by the Monument Committee describing White Plains landmarks and the Heritage Trail map-leaflet both mention trenches on Mount Misery which should be visible to you; but though I poked around all over the top of the hill (the fence was down in one spot and I was able to get over it), I found nothing remotely resembling a trench. Off to the left, however, just beyond the fence, you will see in front of a large boulder a square depression lined with the remains of stone walls. Up against the boulder, two large, flat stones have been set with a space between them suggesting a fireplace. The site is reminiscent of the hutment remains on Constitution Island and suggests that the soldiers stationed here built similar structures, using what material they had to hand, mostly rocks and trees, and using the large boulder as the backing for a fireplace. This area is marked for future archaeological work and by the time you get here, much more of the story of Misery Hill may have been revealed.

The third site you should visit is in Silver Lake Park. Return to North Broadway; drive back along it until you reach Lake Street or Road, which intersects only on your left. Turn left and follow it until you see a broad meadow, a pond, and a park area on your left. Lake Road was laid out in 1762 for stagecoaches traveling to Connecticut. The field off it is known as **Merritt Hill** and is the site of a skirmish during the battle. A re-enactment of the battle is staged on Merritt Hill every October with local residents in British and Continental uniforms and much firing of cannon and ancient weapons.

On the night of November 4–5 Howe quietly withdrew and headed south. The next day a detachment of Americans from a Massachusetts regiment under the command of a Major John Austin entered White Plains and, acting perhaps through excessive zeal or the influence of alcohol, turned out the occupants, looted their homes, and then proceeded to burn most of the village to the ground. The excuse Austin gave at his court-martial was that the village was a nest of Tory sentiment, a fact well known to Washington who had specifically ordered that the residents be left unharmed. Austin's action perhaps explains better than anything else why more of the original village is not in evidence today.

THE FALL OF FORT WASHINGTON

As soon as he learned Howe was moving south, Washington surmised quite correctly that the British general was intent on eliminating Fort Washington and perhaps invading New Jersey. Congress had insisted on keeping the Hudson closed to the British as much as possible, and, being situated in Philadelphia, was also anxious about what might happen should the enemy enter New Jersey, as he could at will, and proceed to Pennsylvania. Faced with having to defend a number of different localities all over the map, Washington divided his forces again. He had already split them before leaving Manhattan, leaving about 5,000 men in Forts Washington and Lee. He now left General Charles Lee in North Castle with 7,000 men, in case Howe pulled a switch and headed north again, and sent General William Heath with 4,000 men to Peekskill to guard the Hudson Highlands and keep the lines of communication open between New England, New York, and New Jersey. With 2,000 men he himself marched to Verplanck's Point, crossed the Hudson to Stony Point, and proceeded south to Fort Lee.

You can get to Fort Washington by taking the Cross Westchester Expressway west to the Saw Mill River Parkway, the parkway south to New York City and onto the Henry Hudson Parkway, and then leaving the parkway at the 178th Street exit to Fort Washington Avenue. Turn left or uptown on Fort Washington Avenue to find the site of the fort at 183rd Street. Now a small neighborhod *park* surrounded by middle-class apartment buildings, it is set on a hill whose sides are lined with fieldstone retaining walls. On the Fort Washington Avenue side a tablet in the wall identifies the site. In the park at the flagpole amidst the benches and playground equipment, the name of the fort and the date of its defense are inscribed in the pavement. A large outcropping of rock breaking the pavement at this point is all that is left to give you some idea of what the terrain was like at the time of the fighting. Less than forty years ago, this park did not exist and the site was just open, rocky land with cliff sides. The river is beyond the buildings that cut off the view on the west side; otherwise you might see what Colonel Robert Magaw and his men saw on that Saturday, November 16: the river and the Jersey Palisades with Fort Lee and its flag clearly visible.

When Washington got to Fort Lee he debated with himself and his advisors, including General Nathanael Greene who was in charge of both forts, whether to abandon the two positions. He also visited Fort Washington commanded by Colonel Robert Magaw to inspect its defenses which then consisted of a number of outerworks, including part of the old Harlem Heights line along the northern edge of the Hollow Way, a smaller fort close to the northern tip of the island, and several small redoubts stretching from the Hudson to the Harlem River. The optimism of the men and their commanders swayed him and he allowed them to remain, having been assured by Magaw he could hold his position until the end of the year if he had to and could safely evacuate his 3,000 troops whenever necessary.

This optimism was unwarranted. The fort was located on what was then called Mount Washington, 230 feet high, still the highest natural point on Manhattan. It dominated a heavily wooded, flat upland area that stretched right up to the northern tip of the island, with straight cliffs forming its sides along both the Hudson and the Harlem rivers. The Hudson cliffs remain to this day, and you can get some idea of what the eastern or Harlem River side looked like by driving up the Harlem River Drive from the northern terminus of the Franklin D. Roosevelt Drive, along the Harlem River, and on to the Dyckman Street exit.

The fort itself was nothing more than a huge five-sided earthworks, which could not possibly have withstood a siege or determined attack; for it had no outside ditch, no palisades, no food or water, and no interior buildings for shelter. Furthermore, since the interior was too small to contain the full complement of troops, most of the men were stationed at the outer positions.

The British began to get into position for the attack by sending a fleet of thirty boats up the Hudson through the Spuyten Duyvil and into the Harlem River under cover of night. The movement was undetected by the Americans. On November 15, Howe demanded the fort's surrender and was turned down. On the sixteenth, just as Washington was being rowed across the river for another visit, the British opened a bombardment of the fort and the other American positions from across the Harlem River to the east and the Hollow Way to the south. At the same time General Knyphausen moved against King's Bridge from the north with 3,000 German soldiers, crossed the bridge, and began to drive in the American forces north of the fort, while another force crossed the Harlem on small boats and advanced westward through McGowan's Pass. Altogether, Howe had committed 8,000 men to the fort's capture.

Washington and his party reached the fort, but seeing there was no way he could help—short of taking over the command from Magaw, which he was reluctant to do—he returned to Fort Lee. The British, who had opened fire at 7 A.M., pressed the attack steadily from all directions. The Americans in the outer defenses fought savagely and well, inflicting severe casualties on the attackers. The Germans coming down from the north had a particularly difficult time fighting their way across the rocky terrain of what is now Washington Heights; but by three in the afternoon all the outer positions had been overrun and the fort was crowded with the survivors. Magaw might have held out, but the fort was so crowded that had the British subjected it to an artillery bombardment, most of his men would have been killed or wounded. Faced with no choice but surrender, Magaw decided to give up the fort to Knyphausen. In the meantime, Washington had sent him a message ordering him to hold on until nightfall and then to evacuate across the river using boats he and Greene had begun to round up. The order came too late. Magaw sent word to Washington that he could not with honor go back on his word. The fort surrendered.

The defenders lost about 53 killed and more than 2,800 men were taken prisoner, including almost 100 wounded. The attackers lost 458 killed and wounded, about three-quarters of them Germans. As mercenary troops they seem, at least during this period, to have been used wherever the going was toughest, to the great benefit of their British employers.

Also lost to the rebel cause were a great many weapons and supplies, none of which could be spared, including forty-odd artillery pieces. The prisoners were marched south to New York City where they made good sport for British camp followers as they were paraded down Broadway on their way to the prison ships in the bay.

The loss of Fort Washington was a severe blow. As you sit in what is now a park, with children playing on the swings and their parents sitting around on benches talking and exchanging gossip, you might reflect on how black that November day was for Washington and the Revolution. The Continental Army had been beaten on Long Island, chased off Manhattan, then forced to move out of White Plains. They had done well at Harlem Heights, and the withdrawal at White Plains was well executed; but on Long Island, at Kips Bay, and again on Chatterton Hill many of the men had run instead of standing up to the enemy. New York City, Manhattan, Long Island, and Staten Island were lost; Westchester, the Hudson River and the Highlands, and now New Jersey were threatened; and 3,000 men and all their guns and ammunition were irretrievably lost. Perhaps worst of all was the evidence of bad leadership on the part of the American commanders. There had been a crisis of confidence in their leaders among the men in the ranks after the Battle of Long Island, a crisis that had been abated by Harlem Heights and White Plains. But now Washington could not make up his mind without leaning on advisors who were demonstrating bad judgment. The future of the Revolution looked dark indeed.

The coming winter whistled down the Hudson Valley and across the Jersey hills. Ahead of Washington and his ill-clothed, poorly fed men lay weeks of marching and fighting and months in winter camps that would claim more victims than ever fell to British bullets. The war in New York was over for the time being. Ahead lay times that would try men's souls, a phrase soon to be composed by the light of a campfire on a drumhead desk.

VI.

PENOBSCOT BAY
TO
THE CANADIAN BORDER

Come into Maine on Interstate 95, which you can pick up in New Hampshire, if you're coming from the south; it becomes the Maine Turnpike just beyond Kittery.

Your first site in Maine is in the town of Castine at the mouth of the Penobscot River. Most of the way, you travel north on the turnpike. The speed limit is 70 miles an hour. Along the way you will pass exits for all the Maine resort lakes (ponds they call them) and ski areas in the southern part of the state. Actually 95 runs north-south along a line just a few miles east of the midline of the state. You won't see any of the rock-ribbed coast on 95 or any of the lakes but you will make excellent time. If you have time for a more leisurely drive and you want to see the coast and sample the superb Maine lobster, take U.S. 1, which hugs the coast all the way north to the Maine–New Brunswick border. On this trip, you don't have to take it any farther than Bucksport to get to Castine.

CASTINE AND THE SIEGE OF FORT GEORGE

To get there via the turnpike, turn off 95 just north of Portland onto a branch that goes to Brunswick and Bath. The exit sign is so marked. Take U.S. 1 out of Bath and follow it as it cuts across the broken coast and up the west side of Penobscot Bay to Bucksport at the head of the bay. About 3 miles east of Bucksport, turn south onto Route 175 and take it to a fork in the road where Routes 166 and 166A

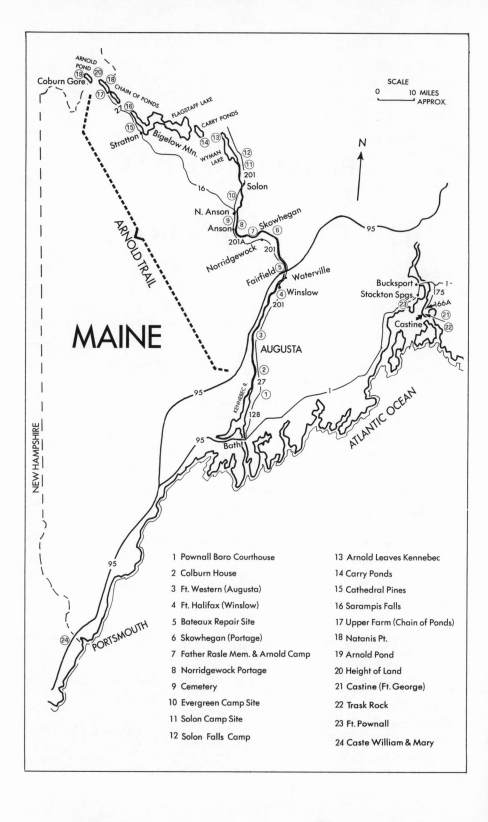

SCALE

0   10 MILES
     APPROX.

N

MAINE

ARNOLD TRAIL

NEW HAMPSHIRE

ARNOLD POND
19 20 18
Coburn Gore
17 CHAIN OF PONDS
21 16
15 FLAGSTAFF LAKE
Stratton CARRY PONDS
Bigelow Mtn. 14 13
WYMAN LAKE 12
11
201
16 Solon
10
N. Anson
9 8 Skowhegan
Anson 7 6
201A
Norridgewock 201
Fairfield
Waterville
4 Winslow
201
3 AUGUSTA
2
27
1
KENNEBEC R.
128
95 Bath

95

95

95

PORTSMOUTH
24

Bucksport
Stockton Spgs. 1
23 175
166A
Castine 21
22

ATLANTIC OCEAN

1   Pownall Boro Courthouse
2   Colburn House
3   Ft. Western (Augusta)
4   Ft. Halifax (Winslow)
5   Bateaux Repair Site
6   Skowhegan (Portage)
7   Father Rasle Mem. & Arnold Camp
8   Norridgewock Portage
9   Cemetery
10 Evergreen Camp Site
11 Solon Camp Site
12 Solon Falls Camp

13 Arnold Leaves Kennebec
14 Carry Ponds
15 Cathedral Pines
16 Sarampis Falls
17 Upper Farm (Chain of Ponds)
18 Natanis Pt.
19 Arnold Pond
20 Height of Land
21 Castine (Ft. George)
22 Trask Rock
23 Ft. Pownall
24 Caste William & Mary

go off in different directions. Take 166A to a dead end in Castine. Turn left onto Perkins Street and follow it past a number of modern, one-family homes with the bay on your right. Look for the **Wilson Museum,** a large, one-story, brick building with a peaked roof and a white, marble entrance with the date "1921" inscribed over it. A sign in front identifies it. Just beside it is the **Perkins House,** a two-story, clapboard house which was moved from its original site and restored. When we were there the restoration was still going on, and visitors were invited to walk through to see how the house was constructed and how it was being put back together. Built in 1765, it belonged to a local Tory and was used by some of the British officers stationed at Fort George.

The museum houses a mixed collection of anthropological exhibits from Europe and Central America and a lot of Americana, both Indian and colonial. Both the museum and the Perkins House back onto Penobscot Bay. Directly behind them out in the bay is Nautilus Island, which was called Bank Island when the fort was attacked. The Bagaduce and Penobscot rivers meet at this point, forming the peninsula on which Castine stands. Bank Island was taken by the Americans and used as an artillery position to bombard the British ships in the bay.

Continue along Perkins Street; take the first left turn; go up to Battle Avenue and turn right. At the top of a hill, you will find a maritime academy and opposite it, to the left, the remains of **Fort George.** Turn left onto a street that takes you in that direction and find immediately to your left a dirt road leading to the fort's entrance.

There was some stonework to the right as I drove in, suggesting that it was part of the walls of the fort. The fort was largely earthen breastworks, however, possibly with fascines placed on top, reinforced by logs. The stones came from an underground powder magazine and were placed here in haphazard fashion by a former caretaker who started to restore the fort. There is a small parking area beside a cannon mounted on a wooden ship's mount. A flagpole marks the highest point on the breastworks. You may walk right in and explore.

The fort was begun in June, 1779, by a party of 800 British troops under the command of Colonel Francis MacLean, a veteran of the French and Indian War and of the Portuguese struggle against the French and Spanish. They sailed from Halifax in a convoy. When the rest of the ships returned to Halifax three sloops of war remained. The British purpose was to establish a fort that would be a place of refuge for New England Loyalists and that could be used to raid the home ports of New England privateers who were harassing British shipping along the coast and in the Atlantic. At least, those were the military motives for the fort. There were political motives as well which looked to the future for their vindication.

The British were planning to hold onto as much as they could should the colonies succeed in gaining their independence. They expected that the boundary line between the new country and Canada would be west of the Penobscot; therefore a British fort already on Penobscot Bay would be in a most advantageous position. His Majesty's government supposed that in this way a new province would be added to Canada which would encompass the lands between the Penobscot and Saint Croix rivers. It would be called New Ireland; Castine would be the provincial capital, and land grants were to go to Americans who had lost their lands and property as a result of their loyalty to the crown. The planning for New Ireland had progressed so far that its officials had already been selected. They included Dr. John Calef, who was to be clerk of the council. Dr. Calef was a physician who, because of his Tory sympathies, had been forced to flee from his home in Massachusetts to Nova Scotia. He came to Fort George as its surgeon and chaplain and kept a journal of the siege.

When word of the British post arrived in Boston, action was taken immediately. At the time, Maine was Massachusetts territory. The Provincial Congress of Massachusetts saw fit to take action in defense of its land without waiting for the support of the Continental Army or Congress. Within a month of the British landing, 1,000 militia under the command of Generals Solomon Lovell and Peleg Wadsworth (Henry Wadsworth Longfellow's maternal grandfather) and a fleet of forty ships, including twenty transports, several privateers and three ships from the Continental Navy (with about 2,000 men aboard) set sail and reached Penobscot Bay on July 25. The British had been warned of their coming, but though they had labored mightily, they were far from ready to withstand an attack from a determined and aggressive enemy.

The British officer in command of the ships—Captain Henry Mowat, who had been responsible for the devastation of Falmouth, Maine, in 1775 —called off his scheduled departure with the convoy and sent many of his sailors and marines ashore to join more than 100 local Loyalists who had been helping the garrison. Nevertheless, by the time the Americans arrived, the two bastions being constructed to face the harbor were not completed and the breastworks were barely high enough to give shelter.

Eventually, when the fort was completed, it consisted of a twenty-foot embankment secured by fraising at the top (a palisade of pointed logs usually pointed outward to face attackers) and a chevaux-de-frise in the ditch at the bottom. There were two redoubts or bastions and barracks inside the fort as well as officers' quarters and underground powder magazines.

The grassy ramparts, the ditch, and the clearly distinguishable redoubts to the right and left are the remains of the fort as it was when it was completed during and after the American siege. It remained a British post until 1784, was the last British fort to be evacuated after the Treaty of Paris was signed, and was retaken and held by the British during the War of 1812. There is some archaeological work going on at this site which is uncovering rock and brick, possibly remains from the second British occupation.

As you walk along the top of the breastworks, you get an excellent view over the surrounding area and down into the bay on one side where the American and British ships dueled ineffectually. The American attempt to capture this position was an absolute fiasco. The fort would have fallen to an experienced commander, probably within a day or two. Command was divided, however, between Captain Dudley Saltonstall of the navy and Lovell and Wadsworth of the militia, none of whom had a soupçon of combat experience between them. The artillery was commanded by Colonel Paul Revere who was more at home on a horse or at his workbench. The militiamen were green but willing, but for that matter so were the men in the British garrison, none of whom had ever been in combat before. The British, however, had the advantage of experienced commanders of both ships and men, and therein lay the difference.

The Americans began well enough, landing a detachment on Bank Island to displace a company of British marines and a battery of guns. This gave Revere a chance to set up a gun position overlooking the bay, causing Mowat to pull his sloops back out of range. In the meantime, Saltonstall was busy exhibiting his inexperience to the British by the clumsy manner in which he maneuvered as he attempted to put up a show of force against Mowat's three sloops. An ambitious operation was decided on. On Wednesday, July 28, a storming party of marines, militiamen, and sailors went ashore against a high, rocky bluff along the west side of the peninsula supported by the guns of the fleet, which was the largest American fleet assembled up to that time. You will be able to find the landing beach and experience for yourself the difficulty of that climb.

The Americans succeeded in getting a toehold, moved to the top of the plateau on which the fort stood, and drove the British back to the fort. Instead of charging forward, however, and taking the fort, they stopped. Saltonstall refused to allow the shore commanders to send forward a flag demanding the fort's surrender. He also refused to land any more marines to reinforce the shore party in preparation for an assault on the fort. And in the days that followed, he refused to enter the harbor with his superior forces and engage the three British sloops. Instead, he sent whaleboats down the coast to Boston asking for more ships. MacLean, who stood ready to lower his flag, later said, "I was in no situation to defend myself, I meant only to give them one or two guns so as not to be called a coward and then to have struck my colors, which I stood by for some time to do, as I did not wish to throw away the lives of my men for nothing."

Seizing defeat out of the jaws of victory, the inexperienced Americans proceeded to go through all the motions of a siege. Useless naval exercises were carried out; roads were cut through the dense forest and underbrush; guns were manhandled into position; batteries were established; sorties were made, and attempts got underway to cut off the fort from the mainland. While all this was going on, the British worked away building up their defenses, making their position stronger by the hour. MacLean later said that every day the Americans stalled around was as good as a thousand men to him.

The witless exercises were matched by the witless exchanges between the American commanders. Lovell and Wadsworth demanded that Saltonstall destroy the British ships so they could not assist the fort's defenders with their guns. Saltonstall insisted that the fort be reduced first so its guns could not fire on his ships. The siege dragged on from July 28 to August 13 when the inevitable happened. Help for the fort arrived in the shape of seven British men-of-war which blocked the exit from the bay. That night the American cannon were hastily removed from their positions—some had to be spiked and left—and placed back on board the ships. On the fourteenth, the American ships tried to escape. Not one of them succeeded. There were seventeen left by then; many of the privateers had left for more profitable ventures on the high seas. They were either driven on shore, blown up, or set afire by their crews. The survivors had to make their way back to Boston on foot through the forests without provisions or water. The cost to the patriots was 474 men and to the state of Massachusetts about $8,500,000 worth of ships, supplies, and equipment for which it was eventually reimbursed $2,000,000 by Congress.

To get there, return along Battle Avenue to Perkins Street. Ahead of you is a plainly marked dead-end road. Proceed along that road out onto

Dice Point. The road brings you to some one-family homes and a light-house, then curves to the right and turns into a dirt road marked private. A wooden sign indicates an Indian trail. The dirt road leads to a small blacktop parking area at the foot of a rather steep drive to the left, which is there for the benefit of a summer colony. From the head of the drive, a foot trail leads on into the tangled woods that cover the top of the bluff which overlooks Penobscot Bay.

Ahead of you lies a hike of between a quarter and a half of a mile. The woods are mossy and overgrown and on a cloudy day quite shadowy and dim. In places fallen tree trunks lie across the trail. Outcroppings of rock and fallen boulders break through the underbrush. To your right, the slope of the bluff goes up steeply to the top of the plateau. On your left a steep incline leads to the water's edge. Sometimes you can see the shore below; at other times the trail goes up or the trees become too thick and your view is shut off. Then all you hear is the sound of the waves breaking on the unseen shore and occasionally the far-off put-put of a lobster boat.

Eventually, the trail dips to the left and peters out in a rock-strewn watercourse which probably gushes a flood during a heavy rain. Scramble down the wash until you reach the shore about twenty feet below. You will find yourself on a shingle facing an immense boulder perched just at the water's edge. When the tide is in, the rock is sur-rounded by water, but at low tide it is completely exposed. This stretch where you are standing, to your left and right, is where the Americans landed. The boulder, according to local tradition, is called **Trask Rock.**

Israel Trask was a fifer with the American landing party. The men came ashore at low tide. Before the landing, the ships of the fleet bom-barded the slope and the top of the bluff, doing their best to annihilate the defense forces. Once the landing party reached the shore, however, the guns fell silent and the British waiting at the top of the bluff, who had spent an hour or so dodging falling trees, branches, and cannonballs, opened up on the assault force. Trask headed for this huge boulder and took shelter behind it, from which he fifed away to encourage his com-rades. According to local tradition, Captain Hinkley, in command of the forlorn hopes who preceded the main landing party, jumped up on top of the rock to cheer his men on and was shot and killed for his pains. I find this a little hard to swallow, though in view of the inexperi-ence of all hands on the scene, it is possible an officer would deliberately place himself where he made so conspicuous a target, instead of cheer-ing his men on from the beach where he had the advantage of the natural cover of trees. For years after, the rock was known as Hinkley's rock until it was renamed for the fifer.

This site is as it was two hundred years ago. Though the trees have long since been replaced by more recent growth, in 1779 the bluff and the slope below it were covered by as dense a growth as what you walked through along the old Indian trail. The men in the assault force had to claw their way up that slope in the face of enemy fire, holding onto bushes and tree branches and scrambling over and between rocks, just as you will when you climb back up. According to an eyewitness account, added to the musket fire was that of the British ships. From a position on the other side of the bluff, they fired across the peninsula at the landing party. Out of the 400 men who landed in the first wave, 100 did not make it to the top of the bluff.

You cannot miss Trask Rock. There isn't another that size along the shore in either direction. From bottom to top it stands about eight feet high; its girth is enormous. You can also get to this point by following the shoreline. Near the lighthouse a path leads down the bluff to Dice Park, a local bathing spot. At low tide it is possible to walk from Dice Park around Dice Point to Trask Rock. If you cannot use the Indian trail to get there, you may have to go along the shore. Be sure that you know what time the tide comes in, however, before you start out, or wear your bathing suit.

As you face Trask Rock, the Bagaduce River is to your left; the Penobscot River comes in from the right, and the two meet off Dice Point to the left. The naval action all took place on the other side of Dice Point.

Before you leave Castine, you might want to take a look around the town. It is a lovely, typical Maine coastal town with many fine old homes. The people at the Wilson Museum can probably fill you in further on the town and its history and guide you to other points of local interest.

FORT POWNALL

Leaving Castine, return to U.S. 1 at Bucksport and take it back down the west side of the bay for two or three miles to a sign for Stockton Springs. Turn left at the sign. A quarter of a mile farther, a sign for the Fort Pownall Memorial will appear on your left, but facing away from you. Turn left again and follow the signs for Fort Pownall. They will take you through a number of turns to a Coast Guard station on the Penobscot River. Near the station are the remains of the fort, as much of it as the British left. Built of wood in 1759 and named for the royal governor of

Massachusetts, Thomas Pownall, it was burned by the British twice, in 1775 and in 1779, to prevent its falling into American hands. What is left is the outer ditch and the breastworks. Wooden bridges lead over the ditch into the fort's interior. Some archaeological work has been done on this site and some restoration has been attempted.

There is a parking area but no picnic facilities, though it is a lovely spot for a lunch alfresco on grassy slopes overlooking the river with the working lighthouse nearby.

THE ARNOLD TRAIL

Return to U.S. 1; take it into Belfast; then take Route 3 west to Augusta. Here you are on the Kennebec River at the start of the trail Benedict Arnold and his men followed on their epic march to Quebec in 1775. You have already covered the other half of that expedition with General Richard Montgomery to Montreal and up the Saint Lawrence Valley, the siege and battle of Quebec, and the retreat that followed (Book II). Now you are about to follow Arnold through Maine as far as the Canadian border.

Of all the roads and trails along which the armies of the Revolution marched, the Arnold Trail is probably the most completely defined. The Arnold Expedition Historical Society, which is devoted to its maintenance and interpretation, carries on archaeological surveys of the sites and conducts tours along sections of the trail. In the spring of 1971 the society conducted one such tour over the Quebec sites and the following September chartered a boat for a tour of the lower Kennebec River, retracing Arnold's route to a point just below Fort Western in Augusta. My wife, my son, and I were on that September excursion. It was a delightful day's outing and a most instructive experience. If you are interested, write to the Arnold Expedition Historical Society, P.O. Box 1775, Gardiner, Maine 04345. Ask for details concerning their plans for the bicentennial, which are still being prepared. Aside from the tours, the society schedules regular working-camping trips on some of the least accessible parts of the trail. Members are invited to a weekend or a week of camping. Campers help clear trails, hunt for landmarks and relics connected with the expedition, and take part in the archaeological work at known sites.

The entire trail has been declared a National Historic Place by the U.S. Department of the Interior and plans are being considered for building roads to those sections that are difficult to get to as well as parks and interpretative areas and displays. Arnold intended to cover the 180 miles from Augusta to Quebec in twenty days. Because of the faulty maps the expedition had, it took forty-five days for the exhausted survivors, 675 out of 1,100, to cover 350 miles of uncharted wilderness. About 300 men turned back, 70 sick were returned from the Dead River, and about 55 died or deserted. Of the entire route, 194 miles lie within the state of Maine between Fort Western at Augusta and Height of Land on the Canadian border near the present town of Coburn Gore. Below Augusta is the lower Kennebec, virtually unchanged since the expedition sailed up the river from its mouth, and one building which played a role in that part of the expedition.

The land along the Kennebec above Augusta and along the Dead River, which the expedition followed to reach the Canadian border, and the land between the two rivers is virtually unchanged. First-growth trees are gone, but the swamps, bogs, ponds, and wooded sections that were wilderness then are wilderness today. Parts of the Dead River are identical with the falls and rapids Arnold's men had to struggle against, but other sections of it are now under Flagstaff Lake. The upper Kennebec River has also changed. Around industrial areas at Skowhegan and Augusta, for instance, and at other places where the river once fell sharply or went through rapids, it has been altered by dams. It is no longer the rushing, white-water river it was in 1775. Where once the river ran free and clear and swift, pulp logs by the hundreds block the current, the bark that falls off drifts to the bottom to pile up many feet thick, choking the channel and killing the bottom plants that supply oxygen.

In Augusta, you can either begin at once to follow the Arnold Trail or take a side trip south to visit Pownalborough Courthouse and the Colburn House. If you decide on the latter, take State Highway 9 south to Randolph, sister town to Gardiner on the other side of the Kennebec. From Randolph, take State Highway 27 south through Pittston to Route 128. Continue south on 128 keeping your eye open for the sign for the **Pownalborough Courthouse.** The building stands on the right side of the road as you come south, a three-story, clapboard structure with a hip roof and two chimneys. It was built in 1761 and is the oldest courthouse extant in Maine. John Adams and Robert Treat Paine brought cases before the bench here. It stood on the site of the parade ground of Fort Shirley as the ships carrying Arnold and his men passed up the river just below. The old stocks, or a facsimile thereof, in which felons and others guilty of mis-demeanors were placed, are near the flagpole.

Go back north on Route 128 into Route 27 with the Kennebec River on your left. Watch for Arnold Drive which comes in at an acute angle from the left. Turn onto it and look for a two-story dark brown, clapboard house on the right with a peaked roof. This is the **Colburn House.** A bronze marker on a boulder in front of the house identifies it as Arnold's headquarters from September 21 to 23, 1775, when he was the guest of Major Reuben Colburn, the original owner. At this point the expedition, which had sailed from Newburyport on September 19, transferred to 200 bateaux. Colburn had had them built in a shipyard that stood to the left of the house as you face it, down close to the river which is just below the bluff where the house stands.

The Colburn House was a private residence when I visited it in 1971, but the following year it was bought by the Maine Department of Parks and Recreation and leased to the Arnold Expedition Society to serve as its headquarters and museum-library. The exterior is almost entirely original, but the interior has been remodeled by modern residents to provide modern conveniences. The original furnishings have long since disappeared. At this writing the society plans to fill the house with period antiques, artifacts, and other memorabilia recalling Major Colburn, Arnold, and the army. The society plans to have scuba divers explore the riverbank below the house to locate the site of the boatyard where Arnold's bateaux were built. By the time you visit the place, you should also be able to view full-scale replicas of the bateaux built by society members, and if you get there for the bicentennial reenactment planned for 1975, you may see a fleet of bateaux reproducing the expedition. A short distance back along Arnold Drive is a clump of trees on the same side as the Colburn House. Back in those woods in a recently discovered *graveyard* is the grave of Samuel Agry who milled the lumber for the bateaux. The discovery was made by White Nichols, president of the Arnold Expedition Historical Society. If you take the society's trip up the Kennebec, he will point it out to you. There was a *tavern* next to Colburn's house which stands there today out of sight from the road and close to the river. Now a private home, it has been remodeled over the years. Part of its foundation, however, is the original tavern foundation.

Return to Route 27 and continue north to Augusta to visit Fort Western, Arnold's headquarters from September 23 to 29 until the expedition pushed off. On the way, about six miles below Augusta, 27 crosses the Kennebec. Though Route 9 continues along the east bank to Augusta, take 27 and follow it along the west bank to the town of Hallowell where you will spot a marker on the right side of the road saying "Historic Site 1,500 ft." At the indicated spot you will find a turnoff overlooking the river and three large explanatory *panels.* There are supposed to be nine sets of these panels at key points along the trail, but we were able to find only two or three. Their purpose is to explain in a general way the historical significance of the surrounding area. By the time you follow the trail, they may all be back in place. If so, you will find them at Fort Popham (at the mouth of the Kennebec), Hallowell, Skowhegan, Solon, Moscow, Stratton, Sarampus, Chain of Ponds, and Coburn Gore.

The panels at Hallowell show a map of the Arnold Trail with explanatory text, Arnold's men leaving the ships for the bateaux, and three quotes from journals that were kept by members of the expedition. These panels are not located on the actual sites, but in their vicinity. They are visually interesting, however, and contain important information. They also serve to relate the expedition to the country you are passing through as you go along.

When you get into Augusta, you will reach a traffic circle which spins off just about every road coming into and going out of the city. Go around the circle to the street directly opposite your entrance into the circle. Look for a filling station on your left. The street should lead down into a business section. At the first traffic light, turn right onto a bridge that takes you over the Kennebec. As you come off the bridge, you will see a road immediately to the right. On it you will find **Fort Western** immediately to your right opposite a shoe factory. The fort was built in 1754 during the French and Indian War. What you see now is the original log barracks building, restored in 1921, and two reconstructed blockhouses connected by a palisade. According to one of the plaques at the fort, this was the site of the Indian village, Cushnoc. Pilgrims from the original Plymouth colony came here in 1625 to trade with the Indians, and an important trading post developed on the site. The road you turned onto to reach the site is actually the entrance to the factory. The parking lot farther along the road and around a bend was the fort's parade ground. Another plaque to the left of the blockhouse marks this as the spot from which the Arnold expedition began its march up the Kennebec. The fort is closed after Labor Day.

Now take U.S. 201 north out of Augusta to follow the expedition's route to **Fort Halifax** in Winslow with the Kennebec on your left. Some of Arnold's men went up the river in the bateaux, fighting the current as they went; others followed the stream on foot. About eighteen miles north of Augusta, 201 crosses the Sebasticook River where it joins the Kennebec just as you come into the town of Winslow. A sign reading "Fort Halifax State Memorial" shows up on your right as soon as you come over the Sebasticook. The sign has an arrow which points to the

left, indicating a road going off in that direction. Beyond a railroad crossing, surrounded by small factories and garages, is a **blockhouse** with a
fence around it and a flag post. Two panels placed in front present you
with a history of the fort, since its construction in 1754, and a pictorial
representation. I assume that the blockhouse now before you, the only
extant part of the fort, is the one shown at the lower left-hand corner of
the stockade, closest to the river. By looking at the picture, you can
determine how the fort was laid out and where other structures stood in
relation to the blockhouse and to the buildings that now surround the
site. You can enter the blockhouse and look it over. At the time we were
there, it was quite bare.

Walk around and notice how flat the area is and how close to the
river it comes. The Sebasticook is at the left as you face the blockhouse
with your back to 201. The brush and trees along the riverbank were
undoubtedly not there when the fort was garrisoned. Since it was built to
control the movement of the neighboring Indian tribes along the two
rivers, the garrison would have needed a clear field of fire. We drove
around the area for some time, but could find nothing to indicate where
the two blockhouses shown in the picture on high ground above the fort
stood.

Proceed north along U.S. 201 through Winslow and Waterville and
then into Fairfield. About a quarter of a mile past the Fairfield entrance
to Interstate 95, 201 curves and a road comes in from the right almost
directly ahead. Go off onto that road and look for a granite marker on
the right. The **memorial** marks the site where the bateaux were dragged
up onto the bank, repaired by a local man, and then replaced in the water.
This is the first of eleven markers erected along the trail by the D.A.R.

Return to 201 and continue north to Skowhegan. You will reach a
blinker light as you come into town. Turn right at the light, cross an iron
bridge over the Kennebec, and look for the local power company plant
on the right. There is a parking area you can enter and beyond it a hurricane fence. Leave your car and walk to the fence. You are directly over a
point where the river originally fell over a rocky ledge. A dam has tamed
the wild plunge, but the rocks are still there over which the expedition
dragged the bateaux up onto the **island** on which you are now standing
to get around the waterfall. They carried them across the island, including
the space you are standing on, and put them down in the water again at
the other end about where Dairy Treat now stands. The bronze marker
on the small boulder off the sidewalk at the edge of the parking area is
the second D.A.R. marker.

Walk away from the power company site, crossing the street as you do so, to enter a small, parklike area. You are now walking the length of the island. Notice ahead of you a stand of white pine, very tall and obviously old. Each is easily over a hundred feet high. They are believed to have been here in 1775.

Just beyond the pines, the ground slopes down to a creek which runs into the river to the left. On the high bank on the other side is where the expedition camped after the portage before continuing up the Kennebec. The camping area is built up now with private homes; a footbridge crosses the creek.

Return to the blinker light and turn right onto U.S. 201A in the direction of Norridgewock. As you cross the river, look right for a good view of the white pine area with the little footbridge and the camping grounds up on the bank. Norridgewock is a ten-minute drive from Skowhegan with the river almost constantly in sight off to your right. Be on guard for a very sharp right turn 201A takes as you come into Norridgewock, following the turn in the river. The road makes another right turn at a granite cenotaph placed in a triangle out in the middle of the road, crosses a railroad spur, and then crosses the river again. The roads you travel in Maine are two-lane with speed limits of 60 miles an hour between towns. There are motels here and there, but not side by side in rows, at least not in this part of the state.

You are now traveling along the east bank of the river which is often out of your line of vision at the bottom of an incline to your left. Those of Arnold's men who were not working the bateaux marched along the opposite or west bank. Notice now the mountains off to your left front to the northwest. It was toward those mountains and through them that the expedition marched, using rivers and ponds along the way for their supply-laden bateaux.

Coming out of Norridgewock, keep a lookout for a blacktop road going off to your left which is not marked on current Maine road maps. Take it. It is the old 201A; it parallels the new 201A, but goes closer to the river. As it comes around a bend, you can see the mouth of another river, the Sandy River, coming in to join the Kennebec. Arnold's men who were still marching along the west bank of the Kennebec had to cross the mouth of the Sandy when they came to it.

This area on the east bank of the Kennebec was the site of a large settlement of Norridgewock Indians. You will pass a cemetery on your left, then after a short distance come to a boulder with a plaque on it describing the site. A road goes through the middle of the cemetery. Park on the road and walk between the graves to a tall granite shaft at the far end with a cross on the top. This is the **monument to Father Rasle**, a French Jesuit who first evangelized the Hurons in Illinois, then became the apostle of the Abenakis for thirty-four years. He died in the slaughter that took place when the village was wiped out by the British in 1724. It was on this spot that Arnold and his men camped for three days while they carried their bateaux around Norridgewock Falls and rapids, which stretched upstream from here to where the modern town stands today.

You can walk through the woods behind the monument to the river's edge. Be careful that you do not fall into the holes left by amateur archaeologists and souvenir hunters. There are still rapids along the river and white water out in the middle indicating partially submerged rocks and sandbars. I remember being here for the first time in 1958 before the granite monument replaced the old wooden cross that originally stood in its place. At that time, the river was filled with logs floating down to the mills.

Continue north on old 201A for a good look at the rapids which were more severe in Arnold's time when the river was less deep. Eventually, old 201A takes you back onto new 201A and after a left turn continues north. You will again cross the Kennebec going from Madison to Anson. On the other side of the river, in Anson, make a sharp left onto Routes 43 and 148 west. As the road comes around a turn, look for a post office building on the left side. Close to the post office, also on the left, is a bronze *plaque* set into a boulder. It marks the road the expedition cut through the forest in October, 1775, over which they dragged their bateaux past the Norridgewock Falls.

Return to the bridge between Anson and Madison but don't go back over it. Instead, drive past it and take 201A north again. Notice the boom anchors in the river on your right, square platforms made of logs and filled with rocks. They were placed there by the pulp companies for boom drivers to stand on; from there they separated the logs coming downstream with their peaveys according to their company markings. Pass a lumber company on the left, a dairy farm on the right, and then a little way beyond, on the right, you will see a small cemetery with an arch over the entrance and a rail fence around it. Among the stones are a number that are unmarked or in pieces. They were moved here from Bingham when the Wyman Lake Dam was built in 1928 and the area around it was flooded. They are believed by local historians to mark the *graves* of members of the expedition who became separated from their comrades, died, were buried at Bingham, and then were moved here.

A short way on, you will come into North Anson, crossing a bridge over the Carrabassett River which feeds into the Kennebec just to the right. Look to your left to see a stretch of some really rugged rapids. The rocks are so profuse and obstruct the stream so much that they are really a natural dam rather than a set of rapids.

About eight miles farther, turn right to cross the Kennebec yet again on the Solon-Embden Bridge. As soon as you come off the bridge, turn right onto a dirt road that runs between log fences. A sign welcomes you to the Evergreens Vacation Center. At a split in the road, bear left; on this site, now a vacation spot with campsites and cabins, the Third Division of the Arnold expedition made *camp* during one of the stops along the trail. The Arnold Society, which discovered the site in 1968, also determined that this is the site of one of the oldest and probably the largest Indian settlements in the state of Maine. Members of the society have uncovered thousands of Indian artifacts here, mostly of the Abenaki tribe. Directly across the river, a thirty-foot ledge of rock protruding into the river is inscribed with more than 100 Indian pictographs believed to be 450 years old.

Ruth and Bill Perry, who run this commercial campground, maintain a small *museum* in the main lodge that exhibits a collection of remarkable artifacts found on this site. This is a delightful spot, shaded by pines, right on the bank of the river in the midst of one of the prettiest parts of the state.

Return to 201A, but instead of going back over the bridge, turn right and head for Bingham. At the stop sign in the town of Solon, make a left turn onto 201; take your first left turn onto Falls Road and continue to Solon Falls. The road swings around here and on the left side is a plaque mounted on a boulder, another D.A.R. marker at a *portage site* where the expedition dragged its bateaux out of the river and around the falls. The river here is now blocked by a power station dam. The flow of water is limited, and the rocks thrust up from the river bed like so many exposed bones. In 1775 the flow was probably greater and the partially submerged rocks presented a formidable obstacle to be bypassed. The Indian settlement extended to this point. In fact, these falls were the first jumping place for salmon along the Kennebec and, therefore, a favorite fishing spot of the Indians.

Continue for a short distance to an open area on the river near railroad tracks which permits you to turn around and head back for 201. Turn left onto 201 and proceed north through thirty-one miles of beautiful, scenic Maine with the Kennebec on the left. About a mile north of the Solon Falls dam, look for a small marshy area cut off from the river by a neck of land, actually the railroad embankment. This is about where

the expedition camped after the Solon Falls portage. About a half mile
farther is a rest area with picnic tables where during the spring and summer months another set of explanatory *panels* about the Arnold expedition is erected.

Continue north to Bingham which is a good place to stop for lunch
if you're doing this as a one-day drive. Leave Bingham still heading north
on 201 with the river on your left and into and through the town of
Moscow. The Kennebec, which is dammed in this area, widens into
Wyman Lake at this point. Now the road is climbing. To your left are
the hills over which the expedition built a road to get into Carry Ponds.

After passing a state picnic and park area on the left along the river,
a quarter of a mile beyond is a scenic turnoff where, during the summer,
three more of the explanatory *panels* are located. A plaque explains that
this is the site where Arnold's men left the Kennebec and marched northwest to Carry Ponds where they portaged to Dead River. Look across to
the opposite bank for a log slide and landing a hundred yards or so farther
upstream. To the right of that you can see the mouth of a stream entering
the Kennebec. That stream leads to Carry Ponds and some historians believe the expedition followed it. Notice the high, wooded ridge directly
opposite on the other side of the river where the Arnold Society has put
in a trail that follows the original trail.

When some additional work has been done on access roads, it will be
possible to go in to Carry Ponds from here to see the site of the stone
house and log hospital which Arnold had built for those members of the
expedition who were beginning to cave in from exposure and sickness.
The society has found several relics on the site. At this point, weather and
trail conditions not permitting, we had to turn around and return to
Bingham. From there we went around the Bigelow Range to pick up the
trail again on the Dead River.

In Bingham, pick up State Route 16 and take it across the Concord-
Bingham Bridge to the west bank of the Kennebec, then south to North
Anson where a right turn in the center of town takes you west on 16
along the Carrabassett River. Follow 16 through New Portland and then
through the mountains with Sugarloaf Mountain on the left and Bigelow
Mountain on the right. Members of the expedition who kept journals,
including Arnold, saw Mount Bigelow from the other side as they strug-
gled west over Carry Ponds and the bogs and swamps that lay between.
They wrote that the sight of the mountain looming over them day after
day sickened them, for they never seemed to be able to get beyond it.

Route 16 takes you into Stratton where the north and south branches of the Dead River meet and you pick up the Arnold Trail again. Take Route 27 northwest out of Stratton. Flagstaff Lake is off to your right and so is Mount Bigelow and the other hills of the Bigelow Range. Flagstaff Lake was enlarged to form a reservoir and in so doing was allowed to cover part of the Arnold Trail, including the campsite at which he erected a flagstaff giving the lake and the town its name.

You are now following Dead River along which the expedition continued after getting out of the Great Carrying Place, the terrible bog area around Carry Ponds. Eventually you will come to a stretch of cathedral pines along the road with a number of modern, one-family homes sheltered under them. A little, gray garage standing at the left side of the road is the landmark for a dirt road which leads into the pine woods to the right, on the south side of the Cathedral Pine Camp Grounds. Turn into the dirt road and where it forks, bear left. Park and walk to a spot overlooking what is now Flagstaff Lake. When we visited this spot, the water in the lake had been allowed to fall and the original river bed was back in sight as well as a vast, desolate area beyond it dotted with drowned trees, with Mount Bigelow off on the skyline. The Carry Ponds are in the woods you can clearly see to the left of the hills. Flagstaff Mountain is the hill far to the left showing beyond the trees. The Arnold campsite where the flagstaff was put up and where the old town of Flagstaff once stood is a few miles away between where you are standing and Flagstaff Mountain. The area here under the cathedral pines was another of the expedition's *campsites* established on October 11.

Continue along 27 through an area covered with cathedral pines which shelter a number of campgrounds. A sign marks the entrance to the Cathedral Pine Camp Grounds. Turn in at the sign for the office and picnic grounds. On the left you will find an *overlook* with plaques set into two of three granite stones. This is another spot where panels are erected during the summer and where you can overlook the Dead River–Flagstaff Lake area. You get a good idea of the extent to which the Dead River meanders, a fact that did not show up on the maps Arnold used. In actuality, if you were to follow the river as he did, you would travel almost twenty miles to cover ten miles on a straight line. A short distance farther along 27, you will see the Flagstaff Memorial Chapel on the left, a little, white church with two memorial plaques in front. One of them was obviously moved here from the old town of Flagstaff, for it states that near this spot Arnold and his men camped and erected a flagstaff.

Travel north toward the Canadian border with the Dead River on your right looking wider than it was in the winter of 1775, for dams have backed up the water in several places. It was along this stretch of the river that the expedition endured some of its most harrowing experiences. They were hit by a terrific storm that raised the level of the river eight feet, and they lost a number of boats as they negotiated falls and rapids; several also turned over spilling precious supplies into the water. The men who worked on the dams along the river in this region found relics of the expedition. White Nichols was given three musket balls by a lady whose father put a pole down into the water and struck an object which turned out to be a keg filled with musket balls. Undoubtedly the keg had fallen into the river when one of the bateaux turned over.

You are now traveling through the beautiful, wild, mountain country of western Maine in a region empty of towns and showing few signs of human habitation. Look for a place to stop on the right with picnic tables that overlook a small waterfall. This is **Sarampis Falls**, another portage site along the trail. When Arnold and his men were here, the river was up and the volume of water going over these falls was many times greater.

Going on from Sarampis Falls through the heavily wooded hills, look for water on your left, the first of the ponds that make up **Chain of Ponds.** By this time you have left the Dead River behind, probably without your noticing a small bridge that carried you over it as it turned and went off to the left. The expedition left the Dead River near here to portage to the first of the ponds, then proceeded to the border along these ponds which are connected by shallow creeks, portaging from one to the other.

When you come to a fairly open area to the left with a high ridge to the right, you are at what is known as the **Upper Farm** where a farm settlement was at one time. Look for a dirt road going off into a field to your left. Drive onto it as far as you can, then walk in to the edge of the pond. This was another site where the expedition made camp, but the blackened remains of fires that you may find here are more recent; this is a camping area, wild and lonely as it is. Look to your left to find a tremendous old pine trunk still standing in a small inlet. Nothing was left but the stump when we were there. If there's anything left when you visit the spot you will know that, judging from the size of the trunk, seven and a half feet in diameter, it was here when the expedition passed this way. It was known to have been capped 125 years ago; it was then 450 years old. In other words, it was well over 200 years old when Arnold's men camped under its branches. We found moose tracks here and a young tree pulled almost to the ground with the bark stripped off, indicating that a bear had visited the site not long before we did. Some old foundation walls are all that is left of one of the first farming settlements in Maine.

Two miles farther north on Route 27, the road moves closer to the pond with a beautiful vista of the mountains over the border to your left. After going around a sharp curve, you will find another set of the explanatory *panels* at a turnoff at Natanis Point. Around another curve, look for a dirt road leading off 27 to your left to a commercial campsite, the Natanis Campsite. This is a hard-packed road leading to a gravel section that takes you over a causeway only eight feet or so wide. Stop and look back along the pond to the south to see Mount Bigelow on the skyline with Little Bigelow on the right of it. The bateaux passed over where the causeway is now. Had you been standing on the shore of the pond at the time, you could have reached out and touched them as they went by.

Farther along on 27, look for a township marker for Coburn Gore on the right side of the road. Shortly after on the right after a couple of curves, look for a hill, Arnold Mountain, then for Arnold Pond on the left. Arnold Pond is a large lake. Directly opposite it, on the other side of the road is a small pond. A mile ahead is the little hamlet of Coburn Gore and the customs station at the U.S.–Canada border. To the right, beyond the small pond, that ridge on the skyline is **Height of Land.**

Pull in off the side of the road to take a good look around. At this point, the men pulled the bateaux out of the water and camped there on your left. Off to the right on the skyline, a gap shows through the hills through which the expedition continued after resting here. They left all the bateaux on the shore of Arnold Pond except for one per company in which the sick were carried. On the other side of the border, they camped again on Height of Land overlooking Lake Megantic before continuing on toward Quebec.

There is a fence made of split logs along the left side of the road. Just on the other side, between the fence and Arnold Pond, an old dirt *road* shows through the underbrush. This is the road that originally ran through this area and was actually part of the Arnold Trail. The Arnold Society owns a 600-foot-wide belt of land extending from this point up to Height of Land. Eventually visitors to Maine and history buffs will be able to walk the last three and a half miles of the Arnold Trail in Maine up to Height of Land.

You can go on from here for another mile into Coburn Gore to view the last set of *panels* covering the Arnold expedition.

When we visited this spot at five in the afternoon on a day in mid-October, the only sign of life aside from an occasional lumber truck passing on the road was a beaver in the little pond on the right who slapped his tail at us repeatedly. We stood in the gathering twilight enjoying the mountains and the lake and the quiet and especially the slap of that broad tail.

You will go through a number of small towns between Augusta and Bingham, which is a good thing to know, because you will not find many eating places in between. The towns are close enough together, however, that should you notice the tank is getting low and there isn't a filling station in sight, you really have nothing to worry about. From Bingham west on 16 to Stratton, however, towns are farther apart and so are filling stations. Between Stratton and Coburn Gore there is only the town of Eustis. The distance is comparatively short, but there isn't a filling station or restaurant to be seen until you get to Coburn Gore at the border, just all that wonderful, lonely scenery.

It should take you two or two and a half days to cover the entire Maine section of the Arnold Trail from the mouth of the Kennebec to Coburn Gore. Covering the route that I have described, however, from Augusta, where the march actually began, to Arnold Pond should not take you more than one day. If you do Pownalborough Courthouse and Colburn House, add another half day and a similar period to cover Carry Ponds and the Great Carrying Place if you can get in to them. The Arnold Trail should be one of the highspots in your tour of Revolutionary War sites.

VII.

NEW HAMPSHIRE
AND
VERMONT

Either going or coming to or from Maine, stop over in Portsmouth, New Hampshire, for a site connected with one of the many confrontations between colonists and British authorities that preceded the Revolution.

CASTLE WILLIAM AND MARY

Whether you're going north or south, Interstate 95 takes you into the traffic circle at Portsmouth. As you go around the circle, look for the big blue and white sign indicating the road to the New Hampshire beach resorts. Take that road and at the fourth traffic light after leaving the circle, with Yoken's "Thar She Blows" restaurant clearly visible on the right, turn left and drive down a long, winding road through a residential area to an intersection with State Route 1A. Turn left onto 1A and take it to the intersection with 1B which comes in from the right. Turn right onto 1B and take it down to the bay area with the bay and ocean off to the right.

After you cross a bridge over a river, notice the sign for New Castle followed by the Wentworth Hotel on your left, a big, old-fashioned seaside resort. As you continue, follow signs to the Coast Guard station in Portsmouth Harbor. When you get there, you will spot a large historical *marker* that tells you about the raid on Castle William and Mary. In December, 1774, General Thomas Gage in Boston ordered the military supplies in the castle (actually a fort) made secure against any possible move by rebel forces. When the order became known in Boston, Paul

Revere, the official courier of the Massachusetts Provincial Congress to the Continental Congress, took what was only one of a number of rides which culminated in the famous one to Lexington and Concord. On December 13, he rode to Durham to pass the news on to General John Sullivan and then to Portsmouth to warn the Patriots of the town. On December 14, the six British soldiers stationed in the fort were overpowered by several hundred men who took the supplies away for their own use, the Patriot cause.

At the Coast Guard station you will probably see Coast Guard ships tied up at the pier to the left. A brick structure that is obviously a fort is on the right, but it is not the fort of revolutionary days. That is Fort Constitution, erected on its site in 1808. All that we could see of it were the outer brick walls and a padlocked gate. According to the Coast Guard, no one is ever allowed in because of the crumbling condition of the walls. Of Castle William and Mary, we found not a trace.

ARNOLD'S COVE

Arnold's Cove is connected with the Battle of Valcour Island (Book I). It rounds out the story of Arnold's escape after the battle. To get there from the battle site near Plattsburgh, New York, take the ferry across Lake Champlain out of Port Kent, New York, to Burlington, Vermont; then take U.S. 7 south to Vergennes. Another ferry goes across the lake from Essex, New York, to Cedar Beach, Vermont, where you pick up Route F5 east to U.S. 7. Other routes to Vergennes include U.S. 7 north out of Massachusetts and 22A north out of New York.

From Vergennes, take 22A a little farther south and look for a road going west, to your right, to the village of Panton. The road to Panton is not easy to follow. First you will come to Panton Corners, a hamlet consisting of a general store, a couple of houses, and a post office. Notice a dirt road going off to the right, marked by a sign for Button Bay State Park. Follow that road until just before it curves sharply to the right. The lake is visible ahead of you. On the left sits a farmhouse. When we were there, there was a roadside fruit and vegetable stand in front of the house.

Instead of following the road around the curve (to the state park), look for a narrow dirt road going to the left just past the farmhouse. Take it until you see a farm silo on the left and a large, white farmhouse on the right. At that point, the road you are following intersects another dirt road. Turn right at the intersection and follow the road until you come to a marker set into a stone on the right opposite a fishing shack. The road goes on for another hundred yards or so before it curves toward the lake, which is immediately on your left, and ends on a little promontory featuring a prominent No Parking sign and numerous signs of picnickers who ignore it. If you want to play it safe, park along the road.

Opposite the marker is a path that leads through the underbrush down to the shore of the lake. This charming spot is Arnold's Cove and in it three of Arnold's boats lie on the bottom only a few yards in front of you. One has been marked by the scuba diving archaeologists of Plattsburgh and someday may be recovered. Arnold fled to this cove with the British ships pursuing and burned and scuttled his ships. From here he escaped on foot across country to Crown Point.

Button Bay State Park is a lovely state camping ground on the east shore of Lake Champlain. You can get to it by returning to the fruit stand–farmhouse and continuing straight ahead along the shore of the bay. The park entrance is marked by a booth at the gate and a long road which crosses a wide expanse of grassy ground to the campsites on the lake.

HUBBARDTON

Hubbardton battlefield is best reached from Castleton which is on Route 4 at its intersection with Route 30. From Arnold's Cove, you can reach Castleton by coming south on 22A. You can also get there on Route 30 from the south which comes off Route 7 in Manchester Center. From the east, take Route 4 west from Rutland.

Before leaving Castleton for the battleground, check the *house* where Arnold first met up with Ethan Allen before the attack on Fort Ticonderoga. It is located in town on the north side of Route 4, a little east of the post office, and is marked by a plaque set into a boulder in front.

To reach the battlefield, take Route 30 north from Route 4. A sign at the intersection indicates the direction. After driving about seven miles, you will see a granite shaft on the left marking the site of the only Revolutionary War battle to take place in the state of Vermont. A new *museum* right off the road was not yet open when we visited the site. At that time the museum was a small building on the top of a hill overlooking the scene of action three or four hundred yards from the rest rooms. Inside was a map and a diorama of the battlefield. Both have been drawn in perspective in relation to the battlefield just outside. It is a rather clumsy arrangement, but you can pinpoint the battle's landmarks by referring to the map, then going outside to take a bearing, returning to the map and so on. It is illuminated to show the main events of the battle.

Behind the museum is a low, stone wall. Beyond it the ground slopes down gradually over a broad, grassy expanse toward a row of trees which border a road. Beyond the road is a cleared field. A farmhouse and its outbuildings sit to the right on another road that runs away from the battle site to the west. The view to the west is magnificent. Green Vermont stretches away to the horizon which is dominated by the distant Adirondack Mountains. Somewhere off there is the Hudson River and somewhere off to the right beyond the nearer hills is Fort Ticonderoga and Lake Champlain.

On and near this spot, General Arthur St. Clair left 150 Green Mountain Boys under the command of Seth Warner while retreating from Ticonderoga, which had fallen to Burgoyne's army in July, 1777. Warner's orders were to wait until the rear guard caught up and then to lead them south to Castleton to rejoin St. Clair. Instead, after the rear guard arrived, Warner decided to spend the night here. By that time his command numbered about 1,000 men.

In the meantime, General Simon Fraser was in hot pursuit of the fleeing Americans, followed at a slower pace by Baron Friedrich Adolphus Riedesel with several regiments of Hessians and British grenadiers. Warner's camp was discovered by Fraser's scouts on the night of July 6. The next morning, Monday, July 7, Fraser attacked with his 750 men. Surprised, the Americans formed a line of battle with their left on the slopes of a hill now called Mount Zion. They killed a number of their attackers with their first volley, including one of the British commanders. Fraser's men attacked the slope on the other side of the road and through the woods off on your left in an effort to turn the American left flank. Fraser weakened his left to support this move, which resulted in his left flank being pushed back. Warner pulled his flank back, but kept it intact and facing the enemy. The movement brought the American line into the shape of a semicircle. The museum and the summit of the hill it stands on are at about the midpoint of that semicircle.

What was happening was almost a repetition of Bunker Hill with the British attacking up a hill in open formation and the Americans defending their position from behind cover. Just when it looked as though the British might take a beating, Riedesel arrived with his column, hit the American right, and at the same time threw some of his men against the main American position adding to the weight of the British pressing on it. As the Americans fell back and their front began to collapse, Warner ordered his men to scatter and make their way to Manchester.

The action lasted for two hours and ended with American losses of about twelve officers and 312 men killed and captured. The British and Hessians lost about thirty-five killed and 148 wounded. Historians are somewhat divided as to whether this was an American defeat or a successful delaying action. The pamphlet handed out on the battlefield says that the losses the British suffered caused Fraser to call off his pursuit of St. Clair and that the fight was the beginning of the end for Burgoyne.

Mount Zion is just to the left. It can be identified by outcroppings of rock which are clearly visible. The American left extended up onto its slopes. The British advanced up those slopes as they tried their flanking movement.

The first line was held by the New Hampshire regiment down at the foot of the hill before you, perhaps about where the farmhouse stands to the right. When they withdrew in the face of the attack, they came up here and re-formed behind the stone wall.

The stone wall now on this hill is not the original wall which stood in front of it. If you walk to the right end of the present stone wall, you will find parts of the old *wall* sticking up out of the ground. It was behind this wall that Colonel Ebenezer Francis of the Massachusetts militia was killed as the British came up the slope. The spot is marked by an X on the map in the museum. Looking down the hill to the left as you walk down the field, you can see where the American left was formed. The diorama in the museum shows that the field was heavily wooded except for the field you are walking over which was cleared ground. The main action of the battle took place right on this spot. The British advance came up the slope in front of the present stone wall and the two flanking movements occurred immediately to your left and right as you face the slope. All of it is within a few hundred yards and you can easily walk from one end of the line to the other in a few minutes. The granite monument is supposed to mark the spot on which Francis's body was found.

Sucker Brook, where Colonel Nathan Hale (no connection with the executed American spy) and his New Hampshire men were surprised by Fraser's men in the opening moments of the battle, is off to the right down the hill and is on land belonging to the farm. Upon inquiring at the farm, I was told that the stream has been dry for some years. There is a marker a hundred yards or so before the entrance to the battlefield, on the left side of Route 30, marking the old military road that cut across the battlefield. At that spot, behind a barbed-wire fence, are the remains of an old cabin which was the only building in the vicinity.

There are modern rest rooms here, good parking facilities and picnic tables. If the new museum is open when you get here, it will probably exhibit artifacts found on the site; the caretaker told me there are plans for state archaeologists to go over it with their expert eyes and, probably, a metal detector. The area around the remains of the original stone wall should be most productive.

VIII.

MASSACHUSETTS—
WHERE
IT ALL BEGAN

Massachusetts, the state in which the first shots of the American Revolution were fired, has the additional distinction of being the state in which shots that might have preceded Lexington and Concord were almost fired. The incident, which occurred in Salem, once the scene of witch trials, was only one of a series of acts of confrontation against British authority that began with the unruly mobs of Boston in 1770 and included the Tea Party of 1773, the general arming of the local militia, the secret accumulation of ammunition and supplies, Lexington and Concord, and, finally, a call for all the colonies to take up arms.

Begin your tour of the Massachusetts sites in Salem; then go south to Boston to cover those sites that stretch in time from the massacre of 1770 to the British evacuation of the city in 1776. Include in your Boston tour Bunker Hill in Charlestown and Cambridge before you go west to cover Paul Revere's ride, the events at Lexington and Concord, and the retreat of the British army from Concord back to Boston. Since all these sites lie within a radius of twenty miles from the city, you might make Boston your base of operations in view of the number of motels, hotels, and restaurants available in the area.

SALEM—WHERE IT ALMOST BEGAN

Take Interstate 95 north out of Boston toward Charlestown, over the Mystic River Bridge into Chelsea. Go off onto the Revere Beach Parkway and take it to State Route 107. Also called the Salem Turnpike, 107 will take you into Salem.

Salem is a fascinating old town. Once a major New England seaport, it is chock full of old houses, some of which date to the seventeenth century, including the House of the Seven Gables from which Nathaniel Hawthorne got the inspiration for his celebrated novel. Seven Gables is open to visitors and so is the Witch House, the restored home of Jonathan Corwin, the judge who presided over many of the witchcraft trials. It was in this house that he held preliminary examinations of those poor men and women who were accused of being witches. In Salem you will also find the Salem Maritime National Historic Site, **Derby Wharf**, in old Salem Harbor where the sailing ships of the town's heyday berthed. The old wharf is still there and so is the Customhouse facing onto it, in which Hawthorne worked for a while. Salem was also a privateering center during the Revolution and it was here in the old harbor that American seafaring guerrillas brought the British prizes they captured.

There are also several excellent museums in town, including the **Peabody Museum** on Essex Street which is devoted to the days of "wooden ships and iron men" and where you can pick up a copy of the tour map of the town. Parking is available in the big parking lots near the Peabody. Walking can beat driving in Salem if you follow the tours on the map which take you to the old houses and the harbor. However, if you do park on Essex Street, it might be best to drive to the **North River Bridge,** the principal reason for your being in Salem, for it is some distance from Essex Street.

General Thomas Gage, the military governor of Massachusetts, knew that the people of the province were arming themselves against possible encounters with His Majesty's troops. Against his express orders, the Massachusetts Provincial Congress established itself in Salem and proceeded to set up an ordnance depot at which nineteen cannon were stored while carriages were being made for them. When Gage learned about the depot and the guns, he ordered Colonel Alexander Leslie with 250 men from Castle William in Boston Harbor to Salem. Their mission was to seize the guns and the stores.

The detachment left secretly on the night of February 25, 1775, a Saturday. Gage had planned the entire operation under tight security, for he knew that Boston crawled with rebel spies who watched every move his troops made. The ship carrying Leslie and his men dropped anchor at Marblehead the following day on Sunday, the Sabbath, not unintention-

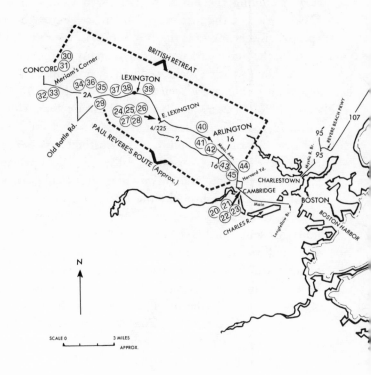

BOSTON and VICINITY

BRITISH RETREAT

CONCORD ⟨30⟩⟨31⟩ Meriam's Corner

LEXINGTON

⟨34⟩⟨36⟩⟨35⟩ ⟨37⟩⟨38⟩ ⟨39⟩

⟨32⟩⟨33⟩ 2A

⟨29⟩

⟨24⟩⟨25⟩⟨26⟩ E. LEXINGTON

⟨27⟩⟨28⟩ 4/225 ⟨40⟩ ARLINGTON

Old Battle Rd. PAUL REVERE'S ROUTE (Approx.) 2 ⟨41⟩⟨42⟩ 16

16 ⟨43⟩⟨44⟩ Harvard Yd.

⟨45⟩ CHARLESTOWN

CAMBRIDGE

CHARLES R. ⟨20⟩⟨21⟩⟨22⟩⟨23⟩ Main

107

95

95

REVERE BEACH PKWY

Mystic R. Br.

Longfellow Br.

BOSTON

BOSTON HARBOR

N

SCALE 0   3 MILES
                       APPROX.

1 Boston Common
2 Beacon Hill
3 Embarkation Point
4 Liberty Tree
5 Old Granary Burying Ground
6 King's Chapel
7 Old So. Meet. House
8 Franklin Birthpl.
9 Old State House
10 Boston Massacre Site
11 Faneuil Hall
12 Hancock House

13 Revere House
14 Old North Church
15 Copp's Hill
16 Tea Party (approx.)
17 Bunker Hill (Breed's Hill)
18 Revere's Landing (approx.)
19 Dorchester Hgts.
20 Cambridge Common—Army Camp
21 Christ Church
22 Longfellow House
23 Mass. Hall
24 Lexington Green
25 Buckman Tavern
26 Harrington House
27 Old Burying Ground

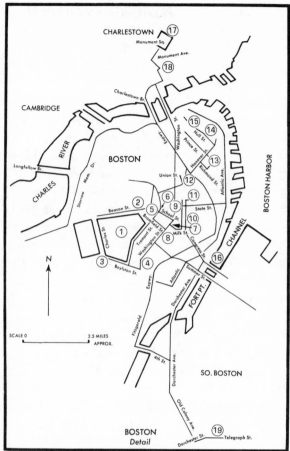

107

ally. You can see the approximate spot from Derby Wharf in Salem; Marblehead is just across the bay. Leslie waited until the Marbleheaders were in church for the afternoon service before debarking his men and starting the five-mile march to Salem. However, ever-watchful eyes, Sabbath or no Sabbath, saw the landing and the word was spread. Major John Pedrick, a locally prominent citizen, set off on horseback from Marblehead to warn the people of Salem. Along the way he had to pass the British column. Pedrick had entertained Leslie at his home and Leslie believed him to be loyal to the crown. When Pedrick overtook the troops, he appeared to be out for an afternoon's ride. Leslie allowed him to pass after a friendly exchange of greetings. As soon as he was out of Leslie's sight, Pedrick clapped spurs to his horse and rode hell for leather into Salem, bursting into the meetinghouse during the Reverend Thomas Barnard's sermon and sounding the alarm. Within minutes, messengers were riding to warn the militia in neighboring towns while Captain David Mason, a friend of Benjamin Franklin and an early experimenter with electricity, supervised the concealment of the guns.

The guns were being kept in a livery stable near a forge just the other side of the North River Bridge, which at that time was a drawbridge to allow ships to pass. Mason's men thoughtfully raised the bridge and hid most of the cannon under leaves in a nearby grove of trees while others were taken elsewhere for safekeeping. When Leslie and his redcoats came marching through the town with most of the inhabitants tagging along to watch the fun and appeared at the bridge, he found it impossible to cross the river. What's more, there was the local militia drawn up on the other side.

Leslie demanded that the bridge be lowered, but he was informed that it was private property and the owners, as was their right, refused. When he tried to use two boats drawn up on his side of the river, their owners had the bottoms stove in before his soldiers could get to them. One of the boat wreckers, Joseph Whicher, a distillery worker, bared his chest to the nearest British soldier and dared him to stab. The soldier obliged him and Whicher received a small but bloody wound. He later claimed that his was the first American blood shed in the Revolution.

Leslie was now preparing to fire on the men and militia across the river when the Reverend Barnard, though Loyalist by sympathy, suggested a compromise. The day was rapidly fading and Leslie had a long march ahead of him back to Marblehead which could be far from pleasant if he shed local blood; by now he was aware that other militia units were hurrying to Salem. Leslie agreed. The bridge was lowered;

Leslie marched his men across to a predetermined point; then, his honor saved, turned and marched back and on to Marblehead.

Take Summer Street which goes into North Street toward the present bridge into North Salem. This is the route the British marched along through the town. A marker midway across commemorates the old bridge and what happened around it. Nothing, however, remains of it or of the buildings that once occupied the land on both sides of the river. The bridge was the moveable part of a causeway that extended out from both banks. Where the livery stable and forge once stood is now a complex of filling stations, snack bars, and the like. The road Leslie marched his men across and back again is now Route 114, a very busy highway. Somewhere along that road was the house of Sarah Tarrant who, from an upstairs window, berated Leslie and his men loudly, accusing them of breaking the Sabbath and telling them to go back where they had come from. It must have been a delicious moment for the onlookers and a bitter one for Leslie. For a full and highly entertaining account of this incident that preceded Lexington and Concord by two months, look up Eric Barnes's article in the October, 1960, issue of *American Heritage*.

BOSTON—MASSACRE, TEA, AND BATTLE

As in New York and Philadelphia, Boston's Revolutionary War sites are in the midst of a modern city that has grown up around and sometimes over them. Like Philadelphia, there is little physical evidence left of the eighteenth century, except for some single buildings, burial grounds, and identified geographical locations.

FREEDOM TRAIL

A Freedom Trail, marked by lines of red brick set into the sidewalk, begins at the Boston Common and takes you to fifteen sites. Included are a number of sites not connected with the Revolution which you can cover or pass by, depending on your time and interest. The trail leads through the heart of downtown Boston, including the market area around Faneuil Hall and the Italian district, a colorful and interesting neighborhood with lots of pastry shops and restaurants that will brighten your progress. Notice that many of the old street names have been preserved; they appear above the modern street names on corner signposts.

The Freedom Trail is a walking tour, though there are special tour buses which begin at the Visitors Information Bureau on the Common on Tremont Street, a little way from Park Street at the Park Street subway station. There you can pick up pamphlets and street maps as well as a guide to the trail. A map you should supply yourself with, as an adjunct to a modern street map, is the Picture Map of Boston, Ancient and Modern. On one side the central city is depicted from 1630 on, showing the original boundaries and how the city was extended. On the other side, a map traces the routes followed by Paul Revere and William Dawes, Jr., who spread the alarm of the British raid to every Middlesex village and farm. There is a public garage under the Common and some parking on a street running between the Common and the public gardens just across Charles Street. There are also a number of commercial garages along Tremont Street.

Before you start off on the Freedom Trail, take a look around the **Common.** It has been here since the founding of the city. At one time it was the site of the stocks, ducking stool, pillory, whipping posts, and gallows on which the city's condemned paid for their misdeeds, alleged and actual, until public outcry finally brought a halt to public punishments and executions.

Towering over the Common is the gilt dome of the "new" Statehouse, built in 1795. It stands at the top of a flight of stone steps leading up from Beacon Street. This is **Beacon Hill** which in colonial days was surmounted by a tall pole from which an iron cage was suspended. A tar barrel in the cage was lit to warn the city of danger. The top of Beacon Hill was diminished by 110 feet to provide fill for the old millpond behind it. Before that the hill was almost as high as the state building, reaching to about the base of the dome. The Common is dotted with markers, memorials, and statues around the big fountain and wading pond in the center.

The Army and Navy Monument stands on the site of a British artillery battery which was stationed there during the siege of 1776. The most important site on the Common connected with the Revolution is at the corner of **Boylston and Charles streets,** just off Park Square with its statue of Abraham Lincoln. To get there from the Visitor's Center, walk down Tremont Street to the far end of the Common; turn right onto Boylston and walk to Charles Street. In 1775, the waters of the Charles River reached this far. All that built-up downtown area beyond Charles Street was under water until it was filled in over the years. On the Common the night of April 18, 1775, sixteen companies of British soldiers numbering about 700 men were encamped. It was to this spot, at Boylston and Charles, that they marched, embarked in small boats, and rowed across the river, then a mile and a quarter wide at this point, on their way to Lexington.

Retrace your steps along Boylston Street, noticing on your left an old cemetery, the **Central Burial Ground.** In it lie the remains of Gilbert Stuart, the portrait painter. Continue along Boylston back to Tremont Street; cross it and walk on, leaving the Common behind you.

At the intersection of Boylston and Washington streets, look up at the buildings around you to find a large stone marker with a tree on it, set into the side of one of the buildings at the third-floor level. It commemorates the **Boston Liberty Tree** which stood on this site until it was chopped down by the British in 1775.

The first Revolutionary War site on the trail is the **Granary Burying Ground** in which a number of revolutionary figures are buried, including the victims of the Boston Massacre, Paul Revere, John Hancock, and Samuel Adams. Take your time exploring the tombstones for other luminaries of the period and a few who were not so famous like Mary Goose, believed to have been the original "Mother Goose." Keep in mind that the original cemetery covered much more ground. As the city grew up around it and threatened to cover the grave sites, many of the remains and tombs were moved to their present sites. However, the prominent revolutionary figures buried here lie in their original graves.

King's Chapel is the next site on the trail, the burial place of William Dawes, Jr., Paul Revere's partner on his midnight ride. Many officers of the British garrison worshiped here during the occupation of the city. In the tower hangs a bell cast by Paul Revere in 1816, the sweetest he ever made, according to the bill of sale. Revere went into the business of casting bells and cannon some time after the war. His foundry at Canton turned out a lot of the hardware used on the U.S.S. *Constitution*. He also developed a way to roll copper into sheets and used the process to make the boilers for Robert Fulton's steamship.

The interior of the **Old South Meetinghouse** is now a museum. The pews that furnished it originally were broken up by the British for fuel during the occupation and the place was used as an indoor riding school. When Washington entered the city in triumph in 1776, he stood on the balcony that still runs around the room and looked down upon the damage wrought by the enemy. Among the meetings held here was the one that set up the Boston Tea Party. At another, the Boston Massacre was commemorated by Sam Adams, Joseph Warren, and other rebel leaders to the great rage of an assemblage of British officers who very nearly lynched them.

Among the exhibits in the showcases are letters written by George Washington (including one to his dentist and another to the man who made his false teeth), broadsides that were sold on the street after his death, tea leaves left over from the well-known party, relics dug up on Bunker Hill including skulls and cannonballs (one skull contains the fatal musket ball), and a number of pictures of the old meetinghouse over the years. A framed legend in one window directs your attention to **Franklin's birthplace** which originally stood across the street. Look through the window to the modern, commercial building opposite. A bust of Franklin sits on the second-floor ledge with the words "Birthplace of Franklin" near it. A framed lithograph of the house, which was destroyed in a fire in 1910, is on display here. One of the best exhibits in this museum is a scale model of Boston in 1775, showing all the buildings and streets with the well-known landmarks identified.

The **Old Statehouse** is a short distance farther along the trail. You will recognize it immediately, for though it is surrounded on three sides by modern office buildings, it sits at the head of a widening area that leads to the Boston Massacre site. Inside, among other items, in a safe-like showcase are a tankard and spoon made by Paul Revere in 1793 and a bottle containing tea found the morning after in the shoes of one of the partygoers. In another room on the ground floor is an excellent collection of items connected with the era of sailing ships and seafaring. Upstairs is an old cradle in which ten generations of the Minot family were rocked. It was brought from England in 1630. The main exhibit room is the Council Chamber in which James Otis's arguments against the Writs of Assistance were heard before the Massachusetts Supreme Court. From the balcony outside the east window the Declaration of Independence was read to the people of Boston gathered in the street below. John Hancock was inaugurated in this room as the first governor of the state of Massachusetts. His waistcoat and coat are exhibited in a showcase. Incidentally, on the walls of the hall leading into the chamber are several framed views of the reduction of Beacon Hill, showing what the hill was like before it was "urbanized" and how it was taken down a peg or two. Another exhibit room has relics connected with people who fought on Bunker Hill.

From the outside take a good look at the Old Statehouse. The original weather vane on top is a grasshopper; the figures of the lion and unicorn were copies from the British coat of arms. From their high perch the members of this little menagerie have looked down on a lot of history, including the tragedy you are about to remember.

☆

The trail now leads to the site of the **Boston Massacre** at the corners of Congress and State streets. There you will find a circle of cobblestones set into the paving in the middle of the intersection. None of the buildings that lined the street on that Monday night, March 5, 1770, are extant, with the exception of the Old Statehouse (then called Town House) at the head of what was then King Street. King Street led from Town House to Long Wharf at its foot, a pier that jutted out into Boston Harbor. Looking down State Street away from the statehouse you can still see the river. A sketch of the area and of the massacre attributed to Paul Revere and supposed to have been rendered for use at the trial of the soldiers, shows a number of streets coming in from right and left that are not there today or that had other names. The Customhouse stood on King Street a little way down from what was the intersection of King Street and Exchange Lane. At the time I was there the Customhouse site was empty, but construction had begun on 60 State Street, a forty-story office tower.

The Boston Massacre was one of those incidents between American civilians and British soldiers that plagued the peace of both Boston and New York. On this occasion the preceding Saturday and Sunday, March 3 and 4, had seen considerable brawling between redcoats and citizens, particularly in the vicinity of Grey's Ropeyard, then located between the present Pearl and Congress streets. Off-duty soldiers looking for after-hours work to supplement the pittance the Crown paid them had clashed with the ropeyard workers in a running battle, using clubs and fists.

On the evening of March 5, the streets were patrolled by bands of soldiers and civilians who were out for trouble. A wigmaker's apprentice taunted a British officer, wrongly it turned out, for not paying his hair-dresser's bill. Private Hugh White, on duty at the sentry box near the Customhouse, answered the insults with the butt of his musket. A crowd formed around White and some of the more openly belligerent threatened him with bodily harm. As the crowd grew to about 300 or 400, many drawn there through curiosity, White began to shout for the main guard to turn out. Eventually Captain Thomas Preston, in command of the guard, appeared on the scene, but for a half hour or so he was reluctant to do anything. The military were not supposed to take action against the civilian population unless ordered to do so by the civil authorities. Since the authorities usually stayed indoors whenever trouble developed, Preston was caught in an unusual dilemma.

Preston finally ordered seven members of the guard out and marched them through the crowd with fixed bayonets, but with unloaded muskets.

When the detail reached White, the captain ordered the hapless sentry to fall in. The detail, without orders to do so, then loaded their weapons. Numerous people in the crowd dared them to shoot; others egged their bellicose fellow citizens on; some moved up to the soldiers with clubs in hand to taunt and provoke them, and finally someone from the back of the crowd threw a club which struck a soldier and knocked him down. The soldier, Private Hugh Montgomery, got to his feet and fired his gun, hitting one of the civilians.

As the crowd began to give way, the rest of the guard fired at them, though not by Preston's orders, and others were hit. As the crowd began to regroup around the bodies, the guard reloaded and prepared to fire again, but were stopped by Preston who pushed up their gun barrels. The affair became a cause célèbre and was used as propanganda by the more radical Whigs to stir up the citizenry still further against the garrison and the crown.

As you face the Old Statehouse, standing in the middle of the cobblestone circle, the Customhouse was behind you to your right. At the intersection of King and Exchange Lane was a hitching post. Private White was stationed in a sentry box outside the Customhouse a short distance down King Street around the corner from Exchange Lane. The seven other soldiers who came to his rescue formed a semicircle with their right flank anchored on the hitching post and their left on the sentry box. After the shooting, according to Revere's drawing, two bodies lay directly in front of them; a third lay on its back out in the intersection just before a street which came in from the left called Quaker Lane; and a fourth was on its stomach facing King Street a short distance down Quaker Lane from the intersection. Actually five people lay on the street that night but Revere shows only four. He also left one of the soldiers out of the drawing.

King Street was then lined with private homes and small shops. Faneuil Hall, behind you and off to the right, stood on what was called Dock Square. Nothing is as it was except for the Old Statehouse, State Street, and Faneuil Hall. For an excellent account based on extensive research, read *The Boston Massacre* by Hiller B. Zobel, published by W. W. Norton in 1970. Most fascinating is his account of the trial that followed in which the soldiers were defended by Josiah Quincy and John Adams, second cousin of Samuel Adams. A lawyer by profession, Zobel paid particular attention to the evidence brought forth at the trial, which accounts for the precise detail in which his story is told. It differs at a number of points from the account jointly published by the Revolutionary War Bicentennial Commission and the Boston Public Library in 1970, entitled *Blood in the Streets: The Boston Massacre.*

Faneuil Hall, the next stop on the Freedom Trail, still has its commercial uses. The ground floor is taken up with stores and a food market in the midst of a larger market area. The meeting room upstairs is open to the public. The original seats are no longer there, but it is still a meeting hall with its benches and seats and is in essential respects as it was in 1775. You should remember, however, that the original building was enlarged to its present size early in the nineteenth century. The windows of the pharmacy on the ground floor display a set of copper scales made by Paul Revere in 1800.

Continue along the trail, crossing the square in front of Faneuil Hall, and around the corner onto Union Street. You are now walking through one of Boston's oldest sections. Past the Union Oyster House, check out the **Ebenezer Hancock House** on Marshall Street, the only building left in Boston that was owned by John Hancock. One assumes from this that Hancock owned a good deal of real estate in this city during his lifetime. It is also the oldest brick building in Boston. It stands by itself just off the dock-market area; Boston's belt of freeways goes by on overhead ramps nearby.

The trail now leads through an open-air street market, a break for you if it's a hot day, because you can buy Italian ices from the stands along the way.

Next on the trail is the **Paul Revere House** which is a bad reproduction of the original which was destroyed some time ago, with too much nineteenth century and not enough of the eighteenth, according to an informant. A guide within will answer your questions. The gentleman who was on duty when I visited said the house was 80 percent original. The furnishings are period pieces, but not original to the house.

When you get to the **Old North Church,** keep in mind that the famous steeple in which the lanterns were lit to warn the watchers in Charlestown that the British were on their way to Lexington was blown down in a gale in 1804, rebuilt in 1806, repaired in 1834 and 1847 and replaced on the brick tower, restored to its original lines by descendants of Paul Revere in 1912, repaired in 1934, and finally and irretrievably blown down again by Hurricane Carol in August, 1954. The new steeple put up in 1955 faithfully follows the lines and 190-foot height of the original.

The trail to the church takes you along the recently built Paul Revere Mall which is lined with commemorative plaques, benches, and local residents playing bocci. In the church the pews are marked by brass plaques with the names of the original owners. The first at the top of the left aisle was used by General Thomas Gage, military governor of the province who watched the battle on Bunker Hill from the steeple. In the crypt underneath the church is buried Major John Pitcairn who was in command of the British troops at Lexington and Concord and was killed on the slopes of Bunker Hill. Westminster Abbey asked that his body be sent to England for burial, but somehow the wrong body was sent and Pitcairn is still down there. This is a lovely church, inside and out, and well worth a half hour or so of your time. The gift shop sells a little booklet about the church for $0.50 which describes it very well.

The Freedom Trail ends at the Old North Church, leaving several other sites in Boston proper still to be found and explored. One or two, like the site of the Boston Tea Party and the place where Paul Revere began his midnight ride, have fallen victim to urbanization. That shouldn't stop you from taking a look at them, but don't expect too much. Even Bunker Hill has not escaped.

If you walk up the hill facing you along Hull Street as you come out of the Old North Church you will find **Copp's Hill Burying Ground** at the top. This has been a cemetery since 1660, but the British had another use for it. They placed a gun battery in it from which they bombarded Charlestown across the harbor. The view is of the river below, part of the Boston navy yard and Charlestown, the other side of the harbor. Among the people buried here are Cotton Mather and Edmund Hart, the builder of the U.S.S. *Constitution*, which is permanently moored in Boston.

To find the site of the **Boston Tea Party**, drive to Congress Street at the Boston Massacre site; then proceed on across State Street going away from Faneuil Hall. Continue through downtown Boston to Atlantic Avenue; cross Atlantic Avenue and continue until you see ahead a bridge going across a body of water, Fort Point Channel. Turn right onto Dorchester Avenue, which parallels the channel, and go one block to Summer Street. According to one source, the Boston Tea Party took place here between Congress and Summer streets. According to the map of Boston, Ancient and Modern, it took place at Griffin's Wharf at the foot of Pearl Street, which is to the left along Dorchester Street from Congress Street. According to the Boston Redevelopment Authority, the site is an abandoned garbage transfer pier somewhere in this vicinity. It did take place around here somewhere and the chances of your finding any of the spilled tea leaves are absolutely nil.

The Boston Redevelopment Authority was planning at this writing to do a lot of prettying up around Boston's Revolutionary War sites. They also plan to complement the Freedom Trail by establishing a number of other trails and parks which will center around historic sites, including those of the tea party and Revere's landing. By the time you tour the Boston sites, these plans may have been put into effect and the urban blight around them will have been transformed into pleasant park areas with interpretative material.

On your way to Bunker Hill, you will be able to see the site where Paul Revere landed on the Charlestown side after rowing over from Boston. To get there, take the Charlestown Bridge. As you get to the other side of the river, look to your left toward the bridge that carries the Fitzgerald Expressway across the Charles. Somewhere on the empty, desolate plot of ground between the two bridges is where Revere landed before finding himself a horse in Charlestown. As you come off this bridge, a right turn will take you to the U.S.S. *Constitution*, "Old Ironsides," lying at anchor in the Boston Naval Shipyard. Just follow the signs. Admission is free; there is parking within two blocks, and one of the sailors stationed on board will take you on a half-hour tour that is worth every minute. You can also wander on your own to your heart's content over this great old relic from the age of sail.

BUNKER HILL

Ever since the incidents on the Lexington Green and at Concord, the rebel militia had been gathering at Cambridge and the British had not dared venture out of Boston again in force. A full-scale siege was in the making; rebellion was openly on the march; and sooner or later General Gage would have to do something to reassert the power and control of his sovereign. In the meantime, the strategic heights in Charlestown and Dorchester had not been occupied by either side, a situation that had to be rectified if the British were either to remain in Boston or be forced out. When the rebels learned that Gage intended to occupy Dorchester Heights, they decided to fortify the hills above the town of Charlestown on the peninsula.

If you proceeded ahead as you came off the bridge following the signs for Bunker Hill, you should find yourself going up Monument Avenue to the top of **Breed's Hill.** You saw the *monument* as you came over the bridge. Once you get to the top, you will see it in front of you surrounded by a small park. The park is bounded on all sides by old townhouses and small apartment buildings built wall-to-wall. Parking will be along the neighborhood streets.

If you approach the monument up the steps to the statue of Prescott, you will find a nearby plaque explaining that the monument stands on the site of the southeast corner of the redoubt built by the Americans on the night of June 16, 1775.

At that time, Breed's Hill was a pasture. Militia forces 1,200 strong under the command of William Prescott left Cambridge the evening of June 16 under orders from the committee of safety to fortify Bunker Hill, which is much higher. Instead, they decided to fortify Breed's Hill and build a secondary position on Bunker Hill to which they could fall back should they be forced off Breed's Hill. The redoubt they threw up in four hours was about forty-five yards square and stood up well against the bombardment that followed as soon as daylight revealed it to the British.

Standing before the entrance to the monument looking down the hill toward Boston Harbor with Boston across the way, the Mystic River is to your left, the Charles River to your right. The redoubt extended to your right across its widest part; at this point it was built to present one angle of a square to the harbor, the direction the British were expected from. Several British men-of-war shelled the rebel position and the narrow neck of land that connects this peninsula with the mainland.

To your left front was another smaller hill called Moulton's Hill. Bunker Hill was behind you and to the left. Whatever is left of it cannot be seen now from Breed's Hill. The pasture extended down the slope of the hill toward Charlestown, which extended along the shore from a point just in front of you on the river and around the peninsula to your right. The town was completely exposed to the British ships and to artillery batteries in Boston, including the one on Copp's Hill. During the fighting Charlestown was shelled and set afire, since it was being used as cover for American snipers. Luckily the inhabitants had had the foresight to leave as soon as the rebels laid siege to Boston.

General Gage decided to land on the beach near Moulton's Hill and turn the American left while frontally assaulting the redoubt. His object was to destroy the position before the Americans could extend and strengthen it. At about noon on Saturday, June 17, 1,500 troops, including light infantry, grenadiers, marines, and twelve artillery pieces, under the command of General William Howe, left Boston on barges, landed on the Charlestown peninsula, and formed up on Moulton's Hill. One part of this force moved to the bottom of Breed's Hill, somewhere in front of you.

The Americans had not been idle. Besides the redoubt they also threw up 100 yards of breastwork extending from your present position off to your left and three, small V-shaped positions called flèches at right angles to the breastwork, which filled in the gap between the redoubt and a rail fence that covered their left flank. The fence was actually made of stone posts or pillars with rails laid across them, and it extended from a point behind and to the left of the redoubt to the edge of a bluff overlooking the beach. In the meantime Israel Putnam, a brigadier general in the Connecticut militia and a veteran of the French and Indian wars, had been fortifying Bunker Hill and trying to get reinforcements to the defenses on Breed's Hill. Many of the militiamen were afraid to leave Bunker Hill and face the fire of British ships out in the Mystic and Charles rivers as they crossed the exposed area between the two hills. Finally, Colonel John Stark of New Hampshire, who was later to be in command of victorious American forces at Bennington, led his militia through enemy fire to reinforce Connecticut militia Captain Thomas Knowlton's men behind the rail fence. Stark also threw up a breastwork of stones that stretched across the beach from the foot of the bluff where the rail fence ended.

For $0.10 you may climb the 294 steps it takes to get to the top of the monument where four windows give you a wide-ranging view over Breed's Hill, Charlestown, the harbor, and Boston beyond. As you probably expected, Breed's Hill is completely built up. Streets and buildings cover what was once pasture. The beaches on which the British landed and advanced toward Stark and Knowlton are covered with industrial structures. Piers jut out into the Mystic River and the harbor. What looks like a large garbage dump or a site for the disposal of industrial wastes at the foot of the hill marks what were once the outer limits of Charlestown. The narrow neck of land that made this area a peninsula has been extended by fill over the years. Charlestown still stands on a peninsula, but the neck is considerably thicker.

If you can, shut out temporarily the smog and haze, rub out the railroad yards and gas storage tanks, erase the tangle of buildings on the hill in front of you. Instead, see the spire of the Old North Church in Boston off to your left front (you can make it out still); then spot Copp's Hill, looking somewhat flattened out from this elevation, from which the guns threw carcasses (incendiary projectiles) and shells into Charlestown. Now look down to your left front. There in the hollow between Breed's and Moulton's hills the redcoated soldiers are spreading out in well-ordered ranks, fanning out to the left and marching along the beach while the rest of the line begins to climb the hill toward you.

The British left under General Robert Pigot advanced up the hill toward the redoubt while the right under Howe advanced along the beach toward Stark and Knowlton behind the rail fence and stone breastwork. The cannon the redcoats had with them were brought up to soften the rebel positions. Luckily for the rebels, they had carried the wrong size of ammunition.

When Howe's men advancing along the beach off to your left were about fifty yards from the rebels, they prepared to charge with the bayonet. Stark ordered his men to fire. The British attackers went down in heaps. The companies coming up behind charged in their turn expecting to get at the rebels before they could reload. Stark had his men arranged in three ranks, however, one behind the other. As one rank fired and reloaded, the rank behind fired and so on. The British attack was stopped in its tracks. The grenadiers who charged the rail fence under Howe's personal command had no better luck and Pigot's men met similar resistance from the redoubt. The first attack failed.

Howe took just enough time to reorganize his troops before attacking again. This time the primary attack was directed against the redoubt while a secondary thrust tried to turn the American left on the beach. The men going up the hill against the redoubt had to negotiate fences and stone walls as they moved through the tall pasture grass. They went down like mown wheat before the American fire. The attack on the beach positions fared no better. American officers who had seen service during the French and Indian wars had such good control over their green militia they could get them to hold their fire until the British were well within range and then keep them standing their ground to follow up with continuous fire.

The second attack failed, but the Americans were running out of ammunition. Reinforced by fresh troops, Howe prepared to try a third time. He also tried to lessen the odds. His men had been advancing in the face of enemy fire uphill under a blazing June midday sun carrying packs that weighed over a hundred pounds as well as their muskets and bayonets. He permitted them to put down their packs and anything else that might be a hindrance before they attacked again. This time the weight of the attack was directed against the redoubt with only a diversionary tactic in front of the rail fence. The right ammunition for the guns had finally arrived from Boston and the Americans were forced to abandon the breastwork and take shelter in the redoubt. Again the British infantry advanced and again they were stopped, but the fire from the redoubt was weak and they went forward again. It was at this point that Major Pitcairn, who is buried under the Old North Church, was mortally wounded by Peter Salem, a black militiaman. He was carried from the field by his son who was serving with the marines.

The third attack carried over the wall of the redoubt. Hand-to-hand combat followed, British bayonets against muskets, rocks, and fists. About thirty of the rebels were killed in the redoubt. Prescott, using his sword furiously against the bayonets, managed to get out. Among the dead was Joseph Warren, president of the Massachusetts Provincial Congress and a general of militia. Warren was one of the most active Patriots in the state. He came to Bunker Hill as a volunteer, refused offers of command twice, and fought in the ranks. His body was later identified by two false teeth Paul Revere had made for him.

British eyewitnesses to the battle said later that the Americans were not routed from the field, but fell back in good order, fighting from fence to wall to tree until they were driven back to the Bunker Hill defenses. Their losses were about 441 killed and wounded; thirty of the wounded were captured. The British, who had been reinforced up to 2,500 from the 1,500 who originally left Boston, lost 1,150 men. Ninety-six redcoats died on the beach under the guns of Stark's men in the first attack made on that position. According to Boatner, the fight on Breed's Hill accounts for one-eighth of all British officers killed in the twenty battles of the Revolution and one-sixth of all those wounded.

This battle had one other result. It really shook up Sir William Howe and may account for the caution he exercised when he subsequently confronted the Continental Army, particularly when he had them in a difficult position. He is supposed never to have forgotten the dead as they lay in the blood-stained grass on Breed's Hill.

There is a small *museum* on the ground floor of the monument. In the exhibit cases are Israel Putnam's sword and the musket used by Peter Salem. There is also an illuminated map of the site showing the battle and moves that led up to it.

You can walk over the site of the redoubt, pacing it out and noting that it covered most of the top of the hill. An earlier monument made of wood supposedly stood on the spot where Warren was killed. You can find the site as you face the statue of Prescott from the street. It's at the intersection of Concord Street and Monument Square just to your right.

DORCHESTER HEIGHTS

The battle on Breed's Hill was for control of high ground dominating Boston. Since Bunker Hill was higher than Breed's, however, the decision to fortify and hold Breed's was an obvious mistake. In fact, there was another hill to the south which overlooked the city in what is now South Boston, but the Americans did not decide to occupy it until ten months after Breed's Hill. In March, 1776, having laid siege to the city for eleven months, Washington had to make a move before the British garrison was reinforced from the sea, which he could not prevent. Since he and his generals agreed that the Continental Army was not strong enough to take the city by storm, some stratagem had to be devised to force the British out. Dorchester Heights seemed to be the answer.

Take the Fitzgerald Expressway south from Boston center (there is an entrance ramp behind City Hall). Look for the exit onto the Massachusetts Turnpike extension. It should alert you to the next exit, which is yours. Come down the exit ramp onto a street that parallels the expressway overhead for a short distance. At the first intersection, Fourth Street, turn left; go under the expressway, and continue into South Boston just over a small bridge. The first large cross street you come to is Dorchester Avenue. Turn right onto it and where the road forks to the left, turn onto the left fork, Old Colony Avenue. Continue for several blocks to a traffic light and turn left onto Dorchester Street. Keep your eyes open for Telegraph Street on your right, which comes in at a gradual angle. Take Telegraph Street right up to Thomas Park and the **Dorchester Heights National Historic Site.** A continuous street surrounds the park. Parking is curbside, wherever you can find a space.

At the highest point in the park is a granite tower with a spire on top and a smaller monument or marker at its base. Both bear plaques explaining that here on March 4, 1776, the men of the Continental Army built two redoubts in which they placed the guns that forced the British to evacuate Boston. There is a little more to the story than that. The entire operation was made possible by Knox's Noble Train of Artillery, the cannon captured at Fort Ticonderoga that General Henry Knox dragged through the snows of the previous winter all the way from the southern end of Lake Champlain to Framingham, Massachusetts, where they had been stored for just such an occasion. Since the ground was frozen, the breastworks had to be prefabricated and carried to the site.

On the night of March 4, 2,000 men and 360 oxcarts under the command of General John Thomas climbed quietly to the top of Dorchester Heights and went to work. The noise of the construction was drowned out by an American artillery bombardment that had been in progress since March 2. At daybreak, the British awoke to find the newly emplaced batteries pointed down their throats. Howe planned an attack to capture the position, but just before the attack was to take place on the night of March 5–6, he called it off. He blamed it on a storm that began a few hours after the hour of attack had already passed. It is possible that the ghosts of Breed's Hill had more to do with his decision than the weather. By March 7, he had decided to pull his army out of Boston.

There is nothing left of the Dorchester Heights redoubts and not a cannon in sight. The large monument was erected on the site of the redoubts. Boston is clearly visible in the distance over the roofs of the houses that surround the park. The harbor is just below. The American guns on Dorchester Heights caused the British naval officer in charge of His Majesty's ships to declare that he would have to move if the position was not taken. Undoubtedly, had push come to shove, the American guns would have made Boston untenable for the British army as well as the navy.

CAMBRIDGE

Cambridge, just across the Charles River from Boston, was the site of the rebel encampment following the retreat of the British from Concord in 1775. It was here that the militia gathered from all over New England, here that the first muster of the Continental Army was held, and here that headquarters were established that directed the siege of Boston. That muster and Washington's acceptance of command were held on the old Common, and the Cambridge sites connected with the Revolution are all on or in its vicinity.

Longfellow Bridge over the Charles coming off the James J. Storrow Memorial Drive is the best way of getting to Cambridge from Boston. As you come off the bridge, continue straight ahead onto Main Street; take it into Massachusetts Avenue; bear right onto the Avenue, and take that to the Common which you cannot miss. There is parking on the Harvard campus side, if you're lucky, at one of the meters in a parking island in the midst of all the traffic. Otherwise, I am afraid it will be something of a scramble finding a spot. A block or two farther past the Common brings you into the heart of Cambridge where there are several commercial garages. This is a highly congested business and shopping area, however, and difficult to get around in by car.

Christ Church should be your first stop, the colonial, gray and white spired church in which George and Martha Washington worshiped. In the outer vestibule is a bullet hole put there by a British soldier as he marched by on the way to Lexington.

The church faces onto the *Common*, a square park area criss-crossed by paths with benches and shrubs. In 1775 it was a camping ground on which hundreds of tents and hutments sheltered the gathering rebel army. Turn left as you leave the church and walk down the street for about a hundred yards. On your right, on the Common is the memorial marking the site where Washington took command of the army July 3, 1775. The elm tree under which he stood during the ceremony is no longer there. A granite marker commemorates the occasion with an interesting plaque that shows the steeple of Christ Church in the background. To the right are three cannon which were abandoned by the British on Castle Island when they evacuated Boston. Close by is a memorial to Thaddeus Kosciuszko.

Continue along the street bordering the Common to the intersection of Brattle Street. Turn left at the traffic light and follow the street as it curves around; after a block or two you find yourself in front of a handsome, three-story, yellow clapboard house. This is **Longfellow House**, the former home of the poet Henry Wadsworth Longfellow. In 1775–76, it was Washington's home and headquarters during his stay in Cambridge. The house is furnished in the style of the nineteenth century and contains nothing connected with the Washington residency.

Retrace your steps to Christ Church; continue on past it to the end of the Common, and cross into Harvard Yard. The three-story brick buildings facing the Common on that side are Harvard University buildings. The rightmost of them with the clock on the side facing the Common is **Massachusetts Hall**. A gate admits you into the yard allowing you to inspect the building at close range. It was occupied by American soldiers in 1775–76. At the present time it is a university administration building.

THE SHOT(S) HEARD 'ROUND THE WORLD

All through the winter of 1774–75, militia units had been drilling and training throughout New England, particularly in the crown colony of Massachusetts. London intended to assert British control of the colony and was prepared to use military power to do so. Aware of this, or suspecting as much, the colonists were not only drilling, but also storing up powder and ball for any move the British commander, General Gage, might make.

Pushed by his superiors in London to take some definitive action, Gage finally decided to send a punitive force out into the surrounding countryside. Its aims would be to find and seize whatever warlike supplies it could lay its hands on and to arrest known rebel leaders. Determined to move quickly and take the rebels by surprise, Gage clamped what he thought were tough security measures on his Boston garrison and on the city and its surroundings. Despite his patrols and secrecy, by the time he was ready to move, in April, 1775, his every move inside the city had been seen and reported.

Now it is time to cover those overt acts of resistance that finally led to armed confrontation and the first shots exchanged between American rebels and the forces of His Majesty's government. From Cambridge you can follow what is known as the **Paul Revere Route**; continue along Massachusetts Avenue west out of Cambridge all the way to the Lexington Green. The route leads from one urban area to another. Busy shopping centers, filling stations, commercial buildings, and private residences line the road where Middlesex villages and farms once stood. There are extant houses and sites along the way, particularly as you come into Lexington. Most of them, however, are connected with the British advance and retreat, not with Revere's ride.

You can save time by taking Massachusetts Avenue from Harvard Yard to Route 16. Turn left onto 16 and take it a short distance to Route 2, an expressway. Get off at the exit for East Lexington and go back onto Massachusetts Avenue and so into Lexington.

LEXINGTON

The British marched along Massachusetts Avenue early on the morning of Wednesday, April 19, 1775, approaching the village before dawn. General Gage was determined to seize the arms and supplies he knew were stored at Concord. The moment Gage's troops fell in on Boston Common and marched to the boats, the word was out. Paul Revere and William Dawes, Jr., set off on horseback, Dawes an hour before Revere, along different routes to warn the militia and to alert John Hancock and Samuel Adams, who were staying in Lexington while attending sessions of the provincial congress in Concord. The British force numbered about 700 men and was under the command of Colonel Francis Smith. His second-in-command was Major John Pitcairn of the Marines, who was possibly picked for the job because he was known by many of the colonists and was generally well liked.

The British march to Lexington was heralded by church bells and signal guns. Realizing that the countryside was alerted, Smith sent Pitcairn ahead with an advance party and sent back to Boston for reinforcements. Revere was captured between Lexington and Concord, but not before he had warned Hancock and Adams and alerted the militia. The Lexington

Minutemen fell in on the green, but after waiting around without a sign of the British, they were dismissed and told to stand by. Scouts were sent out of Lexington, some along Massachusetts Avenue. As Pitcairn came into town, he found and captured three of them. The fourth, however, spotted the approaching column and carried the news back to Lexington that the British were less than half a mile away. Once more the drums beat assembly and the Minutemen again assembled on the green.

East of the center of town, Massachusetts Avenue is lined with private homes, a number of which date back to the Revolution and before. Most have markers or signs posted on them or are identified by curbside markers. If you drive slowly along this stretch, you can trace out the story of Lexington and Concord and then of the British retreat by hitting the sites in sequence.

Number 561 Massachusetts Avenue, on the right side, is supposed to be the site of the home of Solomon Brown who was the first to detect that the British were out that night. A party of about ten officers had been sent ahead to intercept anyone who might spread the alarm. Brown probably ran into or saw them as they passed. The house is no longer standing; there is only an empty field beyond a sidewalk hedge and a stanchion that might have held a sign or marker at one time.

A short distance farther you will come to a three-way intersection with two roads coming in at the left to form a triangle. A modern church stands nearby with a statue on its lawn. A *marker* identifies this as the site where Benjamin Wallington, one of the scouts, was captured and disarmed by Pitcairn's men. When he was released, Wallington got himself another gun and joined his friends on the green in time to stand up to the British. **Number 955** is the next stop; it's an old clapboard building on the right that was the home of Jonathan Harrington, a fifer in the militia who survived the Lexington encounter and died in 1854 at the ripe old age of ninety-six, probably one of the last veterans of the Revolution.

Look next for the **Russell House** at 1505 on the right side next to a school. The building now on the site was built about 1779, but incorporated into the frame is an earlier house, the home of Matthew Mead. According to local tradition, on the evening of April 18 three British officers, part of those Gage sent ahead, came in and helped themselves to food without a by-your-leave.

A short distance farther, Massachusetts Avenue blossoms into Lexington's town center with shops and commercial buildings on both sides. Then the road widens and forks around **Lexington Green**, which you will know by the *statue* of the minuteman facing you as you drive toward it. Behind it is a triangular area of grass shaded by trees and dotted with memorials where the fateful encounter took place.

You can park along the streets bordering the green. The Visitor's Center, a modern, white building with a gambrel roof and three dormers, is on your right fronted by a wide lawn. Inside is a very good diorama showing the battle in great detail with the figures of the participants and the landmarks numbered and named. A printed account describes what happened. Also on display are relics dug up when the foundations of the Hancock-Clarke House were uncovered. Admission is charged to enter Buckman Tavern, the Hancock-Clarke House, and the Munroe Tavern, which are visited as part of a tour. A combination ticket for all three is $1.25 for adults. Children under fourteen are charged $0.15 a house.

Before you visit the scene of action, go next door to **Buckman Tavern** which faces onto the green. It was in this tavern, in the taproom, that the minutemen gathered before the British troops made their appearance. Paul Revere (who had been captured and then released) witnessed the approach through a window upstairs; two wounded British soldiers were carried into the tavern after the shooting. One died two days later. The tavern has been in continual use ever since.

The interior was recently restored to its original condition. Some of its furnishings were in use in 1775, including the two tables in the taproom and many of the utensils in the kitchen. Everything else is of the period. The tavern is open year-round from 10 A.M. to 5 P.M. on weekdays and from 1 to 5 P.M. on Sundays. A guide will take you through, explaining the furnishings and the history of the building. One of the muskets hung on the wall of the taproom was fired by a minuteman during the battle. The original door of the tavern is marked by a bullet hole from a British musket.

When you leave Buckman Tavern, you are behind where the British advance party was drawn up when they faced the minutemen. The statue of the minuteman at the end of the green stands approximately on the site of the meetinghouse. Pitcairn had led the men up what is now Massachusetts Avenue, around the meetinghouse, and was in front of them as the two forces faced each other. Pitcairn called on the minutemen to lay down their arms. Some accounts say there were seventy-seven of them standing in two lines under the command of Captain John Parker. One witness said he counted forty and that they were drawn up in a single line.

Accounts of what happened differ. According to one, the minutemen stood fast when Pitcairn ordered them three times to lay down their arms. Another account says that Parker, seeing the number of soldiers opposing his little force, told his men to disperse, and that they were actually doing so when the shooting began.

Revere had returned to the tavern to carry away a trunk filled with papers belonging to Hancock. He said that he passed through the ranks of the minutemen and that he thought there were about fifty. He and a Mr. Lowell, who was helping him, were about a hundred yards from the meetinghouse on their way to the Hancock-Clarke House and saw the face-off. Revere said he saw what looked like the flash of a pistol followed by two shots and then "a continuous roar of musketry." Pitcairn, who had not given an order to fire, later said that he saw powder flash in the pan of a gun, ostensibly held by one of the minutemen, without going off. At any rate, the British units fired volley after volley, then charged with the bayonet, killing eight minutemen and wounding ten others. Some of the wounded were bayoneted where they lay. Jonathan Harrington, Jr. (not the fifer) was shot in the chest and died on the doorstep of his home on the green.

The Massachusetts Provincial Congress carried out an investigation of the affair and concluded that the Patriots had not fired the first shot and had not even fired back, despite the fact that two soldiers were wounded and Pitcairn's horse was hit twice. The report prompted the citizens of Concord to claim that the first bullet fired in defense of the Patriot cause was in Concord at the North Bridge and not at Lexington. This brought on a feud between the two towns that lasted until well after the centennial and still evokes an echo or two today.

There is a tablet near the minuteman statue marking the site of the **meetinghouse**. There is also a marker for the site of the belfry from which the alarm was rung announcing the redcoats' approach. A flagpole on the green flies the flag every day of the year. As you face it you will see a **boulder** on your right which marks the line along which the minutemen were drawn up. Stand next to the boulder facing the statue at the east end of the green to get the full picture of what happened. The streets around you are as they were then. The road along which the British approached the green is Massachusetts Avenue; the fork in the road was there and so were the two streets which border the green on either side. Buckman Tavern is on your left; to your front is the site of the meetinghouse; beyond is Lexington village. As the minutemen fell into line on either side of you, the first British troops appeared around the meetinghouse led by Major Pitcairn on a horse. Marching toward the green off in the distance was the rest of the British column. To your right rear is the Harrington House.

The two groups faced each other only about 150 feet apart. As the British deployed, which they did cheering according to their custom, they overlapped the minutemen. One account says that as they were deploying the firing began.

Today the green is surrounded by a number of houses that were there two hundred years ago. You can find the **Harrington House** by facing the boulder marking the line of minutemen. Walk across the street to a wide, two-story white house with two tall, brick chimneys and a white plaque fastened to the right front. Harrington, whose wife witnessed his shooting through a window, dragged himself across the road to his home and expired at her feet as she ran to help him.

Walk along the green toward the west end until you come to a *monument* covered with ivy and encircled by an iron picket fence. Erected in 1799, this was the first Revolutionary War monument. Those who died on the green were first buried in the Old Burying Ground and then in 1835 reinterred in the rear of this monument. The **Old Burying Ground** is indicated by a sign at the far end of the green. Walk beyond it to a boulder which seems to be located on a driveway between two houses. The driveway is actually an old road which leads in to the burial ground. In it you will find a number of graves marked by flags indicating Revolutionary War veterans. Buried here under a white cenotaph is William Eustis who served in the Revolution and then was secretary of war and ambassador to the Netherlands. A stone marks the grave of the British soldier who died in Buckman Tavern. Captain John Parker, who commanded the minutemen, is buried at the rear of the cemetery beneath an imposing memorial.

Walk along Hancock Street, which runs in front of Buckman Tavern and the Visitor's Center, to the **Hancock-Clarke House.** This is the house in which Hancock and Adams were staying when Revere found them. A guided tour takes you through it. Originally the house stood on a site across the street; it was moved here in 1896 and restored. The original foundations were still visible on the old site when I visited. In the Hancock-Clarke House, look for another musket used by a minuteman, the drum that beat the alarm, and Major Pitcairn's pistols, which he dropped at the Fiske farm during the retreat from Concord. They were worn by Israel Putnam throughout the rest of the war. If the account of a pistol shot preceding the general firing on the green is true, and since only officers carried pistols, one of the two may have fired the first shot of the Revolution.

CONCORD

Continue to follow the British advance by taking Massachusetts Avenue out of Lexington at the far end of the green. It will lead to 2A which will take you into Concord. Along the way you will pass a number of sites which have to do with the British retreat, for you are now driving along Battle Road. Pass them by for the time being and proceed to the site of **Paul Revere's capture.** A short distance past the sign for Lincoln, look for Buttrick's, an ice cream parlor off the road to the right in a cleared area. A flagpole and a large plaque mark the spot where Revere was caught.

He was accompanied by William Dawes, Jr., and young Dr. Samuel Prescott, who had been visiting his fiancée in Lexington and was on his way home to Concord. Revere was out in front when four British officers hiding at this spot surprised him. Dawes turned and rode back to Lexington. Prescott rode to Revere's aid, but the British were too much for the two and forced them off the road and into a pasture. Prescott then jumped over a stone wall, escaped into a ravine, and galloped to the Hartwell House (which we will find along the retreat route) and so carried the alarm to Concord. Revere tried to get away through the pasture, but six other British raiders surrounded him. A pistol was pointed at his head and he was taken prisoner. Revere told his captors that the British column had been delayed and that 500 militia were on the march. He was eventually taken back into Lexington, relieved of his horse, and turned loose before the shots at Lexington.

As you continue into Concord you will pass on the left the **Wayside,** once the home of the Alcotts, Nathaniel Hawthorne, and a Captain Whitney who was a fifer in the Continental Army. Next to it is Orchard House, another Alcott Home, the one described in *Little Women.* Notice the high ground that borders the road on your right. As the British marched toward Concord along this road they had an escort. The Concord militia came out to intercept them, but when they saw the column advancing, they took to the high ground and, with fife and drum playing, flanked the British into town.

In Concord you will drive into Monument Square where a number of monuments set on an elongated grass strip form a traffic circle of sorts. Park along the street wherever you can. Concord is a busy and very pretty town. When Colonel Smith and Major Pitcairn led their men into Concord center, they were under orders to act with circumspection as they searched for the supplies and arms the local militia had hidden. Using Concord as a base, Smith sent detachments out in all directions, one of which made its way to the North Bridge.

The British officers set up headquarters in **Wright's Tavern** on your left as you entered town just before Monument Square. It is a two-story, clapboard building, now a souvenir shop and restaurant. About the only supplies the troops turned up were some musket balls which they dumped into a millpond that occupied a large part of what is now the business section. A short distance down the town's main street a plaque on the left describes the pond. The British also set fire to two buildings, but the town's inhabitants persuaded them to put out the flames.

There are a number of interesting sites in and around Concord; not all are connected with the Revolution, but you may want to visit them. They include the Hill Burying Ground on the steep slope just across the road opposite Wright's Tavern; Emerson House; the Sleepy Hollow Cemetery, in which a number of authors connected with Concord are buried; and Walden Pond.

While the British were busily searching, the Concord militia had already hidden their supplies and munitions and were gathering on the west side of the North Bridge. Militia units from neighboring locales had learned of the bloodshed on Lexington Green and were beginning to converge on Concord.

The next scene took place at the **North Bridge.** From the far end of Monument Square, take Monument Street to the right. You will reach the North Bridge site, which is well marked by signs, within a few minutes. On the right side of the road is a large parking area; directly opposite, a broad tree-shaded footpath leads to the bridge. To the left through the trees you will see the Old Manse which was owned by Ralph Waldo Emerson's grandfather, the Reverend William Emerson, who watched what was to follow from an upstairs window.

A Visitor's Center is located a short distance farther, just off Monument Road, with rest rooms, a souvenir shop, and exhibits interpreting the events of April 19. A Battle Road Automobile Tour begins there and, by means of a pamphlet, guides you back along Battle Road to Lexington; but though the directions are explicit, the text is brief to the point of skimpiness and leaves out much pertinent information.

The present North Bridge is a reconstruction of the original. There are a number of memorials at the west end, including one marking the grave of two British soldiers who were killed on this spot. It bears a

verse by James Russell Lowell which was written for the centennial cele-
bration. From June through September a national park ranger gives a talk
which explains what happened in excellent detail.

On the other side of the Concord River, the stream the bridge spans,
you can see the high ground on which the militiamen stood watching the
British companies who had crossed to the east end. Six companies had been
sent to the North Bridge; three had gone off to search Colonel James
Barrett's farm where the supplies had been hidden before their removal.
The three companies left at the bridge, under the command of Captain
Walter Laurie, watched anxiously as the number of militiamen on the
ridge grew to three or four hundred.

Near another bridge, called the South Bridge, one British detachment
found some wooden gun carriages which they set on fire. The militia at
the North Bridge saw the smoke and, deciding to investigate, moved
down the ridge toward the South Bridge. The British retreated to the
other side and began to remove the planks. The militia under the command of Barrett came down to the east end of the bridge. They were
under orders not to fire unless fired upon. Captain Laurie tried to arrange his men in a column of fours facing the bridge, the approved
British method of holding narrow streets and passages. The idea was for
the first four men to fire, file to the rear, the next four to fire, and so
on. Laurie's men fired two volleys. The first fell short, but the second
killed two militiamen.

Major John Buttrick, whose home was up on the ridge, was with
the militia and shouted for them to return the fire. The militiamen fired
into the closely-packed British ranks. Two redcoats fell, one dead, the
other badly wounded. Four of the eight officers present were wounded
and so were a number of other enlisted men, one of whom subsequently
died. When the militia started to cross the bridge, the British retreated
leaving two men on the ground. The militia followed them for a short
distance toward Concord until they met Colonel Smith coming up with
reinforcements. Militia and redcoats stared at each other for a while;
then Smith turned and led the way back into town. In the meantime, a
teen-age boy living in the vicinity came across the bridge carrying an
axe. One of the two fallen British soldiers, who was only wounded, tried
to get up. For some reason the boy struck him on the head with the
business end of the axe and killed him. The detachment at the South
Bridge came on the scene a short time later, saw the disfigured body, and
carried the news back to their comrades that the Americans scalped their
victims.

Across the bridge, on the east side, stands the Daniel Chester French *statue* of the minuteman with the first verse of Ralph Waldo Emerson's "Concord Hymn" inscribed on the pedestal. Walk from here along the road the militia followed to the point where it forks. It leads up to the old Buttrick mansion to the right, and to the left, in the direction the British detachment took, to Barrett's farm. The left fork peters out before it goes very far, however. There is an *overlook* behind the Buttrick House which gives you a good view of the terrain around the east end of the bridge. At that point you are standing where the Concord and Lincoln militiamen stood watching the British down at the bridge. When you walk back to the bridge, you follow the path they used on their way to challenge the British.

THE LONG ROAD BACK

After returning to Concord, Smith delayed for an hour or so, then marched his men out of town and headed back for Lexington and Cambridge. By this time, local militia units were swarming around him, preparing a farewell party at **Meriam's Corner** a mile out of town. To get there, take 2A out of Concord back toward Lexington. Meriam's Corner is 0.4 mile past the Wayside at an intersection with Bedford Road, which comes in from the left, or north. A stone marker in a low, stone wall right at the intersection confirms the site.

Look to your left up Bedford Road and notice the old clapboard house, now called **Meriam House,** facing the intersection. Drive up Bedford Road to the house on your right and look back. About 1,100 militiamen from communities all over this part of the state had gathered here to await the British. The British column appeared with flankers out on either side. As the redcoats passed Bedford Road and the silent, watching militiamen, who were in plain sight, Smith called his flankers in. The militiamen took cover behind the stone walls around the house. The British continued over a little bridge across Mill Brook, only a few hundred feet past the intersection. Suddenly, the last unit to cross the bridge turned and fired a volley in the direction of Meriam House. The militia responded in kind. The American Revolution was in business.

Return to 2A and continue along the British route. The bridge over Mill Brook is no longer there, but the brook is still in evidence. On the other side of the bridge two British privates lay dead, and several more wounded were added to those the column was carrying away from Concord.

Now clock a half mile on your odometer to the top of **Hardy's Hill.** The Sudbury militia were under cover along the roadside here and opened fire and kept shooting as the British hurried down the other side of the hill. Brooks Tavern stood nearby, and though there is an old, clapboard building there with a central brick chimney, I have not been able to identify it as the tavern. At the bottom of the hill is Tanners Brook, which the British crossed. A short distance farther, one part of the old **Battle Road** curves off to the left. Two sections of the old road show up as detours of 2A, long semicircular side roads marked at their 2A entrances by low, wooden signs that say "Battle Road." Each is only a mile or so in length and they connect with other county roads that go off to the north or south.

You can taste their flavor completely by parking at one end or the other and walking along them at a leisurely pace, passing a number of buildings extant from the time of the battle. They lead through wooded, rural areas with occasional pastures and fields on either side, very like the area that bordered the road two hundred years ago. Turn left on this first detour as the British followed the road in that direction.

Scores of militiamen raced through the fields and woods on either side to get here before the British. Concealing themselves in the woods, they waited silently. The old Battle Road curves to the right soon after you get onto it, passing through an area that is wooded just as it was. As the column marched past the militia opened fire, killing eight soldiers and giving this curve in the road the name **"The Bloody Angle."** They paid for the privilege, however. A British flanking party came up behind them and shot or bayoneted Captain Jonathan Wilson of the Bedford militia and three others. Most of the American casualties along the sixteen-mile route into Cambridge were victims of these flanking parties with which the British tried to keep the sides of the road clear of attackers.

Ignore a road going off to the right; bear left and stay on the old Battle Road. A half mile farther, you will come across two ramshackle colonial houses quite close together. The first one was the **Hartwell Tavern.** The second was the *home* of Sergeant Samuel Hartwell of the Lincoln militia, the house Prescott came to when he escaped from the British. It was shut off from the public by the National Park Service when we were there. Only part of it was left with a sagging roof and a debris-strewn area just in front of it; most of it had been destroyed by fire in 1969. The old, brick chimney stuck up through the burned timbers at the rear of the building. The park service is planning to have it restored by the bicentennial.

Between the second Hartwell house and a third house, the home of Captain William Smith which is no longer there, were two bars of a split-rail fence. The bars, or their replacements, are visible in an 1899 photograph of the spot, but they are not there today. A British grenadier was shot and killed here. Another was mortally wounded near the Smith House and left by his fleeing comrades, for by now the retreat had become a rout. The wounded soldier was carried inside by members of the Smith family. He died several days later.

The old Battle Road will lead you back into 2A just before you come back to the site of Revere's capture. On the left of the marker, north of the road, were two fields with stone walls around their perimeters. Part of those fields have been built over by an apartment project. William Thorning of the Lincoln militia stationed himself here and fired at the British until they made the spot too hot for him and he had to leave. Continue along 2A until you see another detour of the old Battle Road going off to the left. Follow it to an area strewn with boulders. When we were there, a horse farm was on the right. Opposite the farm on the other side of the road is a small *park* set off by a rail fence. The remains of a brick chimney are visible, and behind it is a group of big boulders grouped around a huge stone that may be as big as the Trask Rock at Castine. There is a parking area on the right side of the road where you can leave the car while you explore the site.

The chimney and a mound of rubble and old foundation walls, enclosed by a chicken-wire fence, are the remains of either the Muzzy House or the Hasting House, both of which were here at the time of the retreat. William Thorning ran to this pasture from his sniper's nest and, hiding behind the big boulder, killed two soldiers as they passed on the road. The rock is known today as the **Minuteman Boulder.** The two soldiers are buried across the road in what was then an orchard.

As the other did, this stretch of the old Battle Road will lead back to 2A where you turn left and continue east toward Lexington. After recrossing the Lincoln town line, look for high ground on the left with a power line crossing it. It was on that bluff, known as **Fiske Hill**, that Smith organized a rear guard action while he attempted to get his disorganized column back into shape. Signs for **Minuteman National Park** will appear on the left to lead you into a paved parking area at the foot of the **Fiske Hill Trail.** Here you can leave your car and stretch your legs along the trail which takes you over the scene of this action in a half-hour hike. The trail is actually a restored section of the old Battle Road which led up and over Fiske Hill. Signs along the way point out such sites as the remains of a stone wall behind which the militiamen took cover and the spot at which Pitcairn was unhorsed and lost his pistols. You will also pass the site of the Fiske farmhouse and well. A plaque at the well tells the story of Thomas Heywood, a young minuteman who stopped for a drink and encountered a British soldier who was there for the same purpose. Both leveled their pieces at each other and fired. The soldier fell dead; Heywood was mortally wounded. Nearby, inside an enclosure, are the remains of the Fiske farm foundation walls and the front doorstep.

The Fiske Hill area is just as it was at the time of the battle, open fields with the road cutting across them, though the trees now in evidence were not there then. It was here that Captain Parker and the reassembled Lexington Minutemen got some of their own back. It was also here that the British began to run out of ammunition and that Colonel Smith was wounded in one leg. The attempt to bring order out of developing chaos failed. The redcoats broke rank and ran for the comparative safety of Lexington.

The trail leads in a circle back to the parking area where there are rest rooms and picnic facilities. There are also explanatory maps and diagrams accompanied by a recorded text under a shelter. From here return to Lexington, where snipers accounted for three additional soldiers in front of Buckman Tavern, which again played the role of hospital for wounded men.

By this time Earl Percy was on his way from Boston with a relief column and, in fact, was entering the eastern outskirts of Lexington. Continue through the center of town on Massachusetts Avenue to pick up the retreat sites in Lexington.

The corner of Winthrop Road and Massachusetts Avenue is the site of the Benjamin **Merriam House** which was pillaged by the British. From here on, the British pillaged, burned, and killed wherever they discovered snipers or those they suspected of firing at them. The Merriam House has been moved and is up Woburn Street, across Massachusetts Avenue. It is the first building on the right after you cross the railroad tracks.

Somewhere in this vicinity, Smith and his officers made a desperate attempt to stem the rout. Getting out ahead of their men, they pointed bayonets at them and threatened to kill any who tried to get by. By this time, the militia were around their ears in force again and they were under heavy fire. Nevertheless, the troops responded to their officers and formed a column. A short distance farther, about a half mile east of Lexington Green, they made contact with Percy's column of about 1,400 men. The relief force formed a square giving Smith's exhausted, frightened men some shelter while they faced the American militia.

Percy had brought along six cannon, and two of them now went into action. As you move on east, look for the Muzzie School on the left side of the avenue. In front of it is a stone *cannon* marking the spot where one of the guns was set up and opened fire. It caused no casualties among the militia, but did hit the meetinghouse. Another artillery site may be found near Bloomfield Street farther east on the right side. There is a marker on the avenue, but hidden behind boxwood in front of a contemporary home. The actual site is on a hill to the right.

Several homes in this area were burned by the British. Farther along is number 1377 which was built on the site of the Raymond Tavern. **Number 1361** is on the site of the Mulliken home where Dr. Samuel Prescott had kissed Elizabeth Mulliken good-bye during the early morning hours of April 19, before he fell in with Dawes and Revere. The Mulliken house was burned by the British and the family was forced to live in the Raymond Tavern until 1377 was built.

Number 1332 is your next stop, the **Munroe Tavern** which Earl Percy briefly made his headquarters while he organized the retreat to Boston. The house, a red clapboard, two-story building with a big brick chimney, sits off the road with a small parking area just to the left of the driveway. While Mrs. Munroe, the wife of Sergeant William Munroe who was fighting with the militia, and her children hid out in the woods behind the house, the British helped themselves to food and drink and took care of their wounded. John Raymond, who worked for the Munroes despite his crippled leg, served the drinks, but when he tried to slip out the back door, other soldiers shot and killed him.

Over one mantelpiece is the gun that was carried by another Munroe, John Munroe, on the green on April 19. Munroe had double-loaded it, and when he fired at the British the charge split the barrel for about a foot down from the muzzle. The room immediately to the left as you enter was where the British wounded were treated. Washington was entertained here during a visit in 1789. The chair, table, dishes, and hat rack used by him have been carefully preserved in the Washington Room upstairs. Many of the furnishings now in the house have been in the Munroe family and in the house for generations. One of the relics on display is a piece of the Washington Elm under which Washington stood when he took command of the Continental Army on Cambridge Commons.

Farther east along Massachusetts Avenue is the Sanderson House, at 1314 on the right side, where a wounded British soldier was left. As the retreat resumed in mid-afternoon, fresh militia forces kept entering the fight. Follow along east on Massachusetts Avenue into **Arlington**, which was called Menotomy in revolutionary times. Along the way you will see a number of homes that date from colonial days. The heaviest fighting of the retreat took place in the Menotomy area, particularly near a hill known as Pierce's Hill at the west end of the town, now called Arlington Heights. At that time the road led over Pierce's Hill and down to a rocky area known as Foot of the Rocks. Arlington Heights is on the high ground to the left or north as you come through Arlington, but though I explored the area carefully, I could find nothing to indicate the old road.

In the center of Arlington, turn right at the intersection of Jason Street and Massachusetts Avenue and look for the Jason **Russell House.** It stands a short distance up Jason Street from the intersection on the right, a gray, two-story, clapboard house behind a stone wall. Russell, who was fifty-eight years old and lame, had taken his family to safety and then returned to safeguard the house. About twenty minutemen took shelter in the house as the main British column came down the road. As they crowded in through the front door, Russell arrived on the scene and entered after them. At that moment the British fired at the house, wounding him. A detachment of soldiers entered the house, stabbing Russell with their bayonets as they entered, and killed twelve minutemen. About eight of the rebels hid in the basement and threatened to kill anyone who came down the stairs. One redcoat tested their word and found it to be good. The British left and Mrs. Russell returned to find her husband, eleven dead minutemen, and two British soldiers laid out on the floor of her home, the largest number of combatants killed in any one place at any time during that long, bloody day.

The route from the Russell House to the site of the Cooper Tavern, a half mile farther, marked the most desperate fighting of the day. This is in the heart of Arlington's business section and precious little is left to remind the passerby of the action. There is, however, a little sidewalk *park* on the left side of Massachusetts Avenue just off Arlington's busiest intersection, set off by a low, brick wall. A granite marker informs you that near this spot Samuel Whittmore, eighty years old, shot and killed three British soldiers. Caught by flankers, he was bayoneted and left for dead, but recovered to live to be ninety-eight.

The site of Cooper Tavern was not marked when I came along this route. Two local men who were drinking in the taproom were killed by the redcoats while the landlord and his wife hid in the cellar. More men were killed in old Menotomy than in any other town—forty British and twenty-five Americans. Some homes were burned, but the militia were pressing too hard to allow the British to tarry long enough to do any extensive damage.

About a mile and a quarter farther east, you will cross a bridge over what is now called Alewife Brook and was then known as Menotomy River and go into North Cambridge. By this time on April 19, 1775, darkness was coming on and the fighting was beginning to slack off. A mile ahead, another small band of militia lying in ambush behind some empty barrels was surprised by flankers and lost three men. Turn left at the traffic light at Beech Street, about a quarter of a mile past the unlucky ambush, just as Percy's men turned. A short block in this new direction and you are in modern **Somerville** at the corner of Beech and Elm streets. The British again came under attack here, this time from a small band of militia hiding in a grove of trees, perhaps somewhere ahead. Percy unlimbered one of his guns and drove them off with cannon fire.

Turn onto Elm Street, clocking a mile on your odometer. You are driving through a modern city; two hundred years ago this was a pleasant, rural area with open fields, wooded lots, and small ponds. One such pond was at what is now the foot of Laurel Street where it meets Elm Street. Here the exhausted redcoats threw themselves into the water and drank. The pond has not been here for many years.

Percy had originally intended to bivouac for the night on Cambridge Commons and then destroy the Harvard buildings. After what had transpired that afternoon he marched on to Charlestown instead, where he arrived after dark without further incident and rested his men, prophetically enough, behind Bunker Hill; there they waited for hours until boats came across the harbor to carry them to safety in Boston.

The momentous day ended with seventy-three British soldiers dead, 174 wounded (among the killed and wounded were nineteen officers), and twenty-six missing. Out of the estimated 3,700 Americans who took part in the day's fighting, forty-nine were killed, forty-one wounded, and five were missing. During the following days, word of what had happened spread throughout the colonies and to England. On April 23, the Massachusetts Provincial Congress called for an army of 30,000 to be raised throughout the colonies. All of New England responded, and by June 15,000 armed rebels were encamped around Boston. That one shot on the Lexington Green, wherever it came from, had struck a hornet's nest and the entire swarm was buzzing around the ears of the British.

It is possible to drive out from Boston and do Lexington, Concord, and the British retreat in one day if you start out early enough in the morning. If you want to split it up into two comfortable days, giving you plenty of time to poke around at a leisurely pace, there are motels in the Lexington-Concord area. There are also a number of small restaurants in both towns, but not very much along the road in between.

IX.

RHODE ISLAND

This collection of islands, harbors, rivers, and coves centered around Narragansett Bay was refused admittance to the New England Confederation during the seventeenth century because it allowed religious freedom within its boundaries. It had been a source of annoyance and irritation to the British ever since its inhabitants stubbornly refused to observe the Molasses and Navigation Acts. In December, 1776, 6,000 British troops and a fleet, both under the command of Sir Henry Clinton, occupied the city of Newport and the south end of the island of Rhode Island on which it is located. The last 3,000 of them did not leave until October, 1779, when Sir Henry, by then commander of British forces in America, decided they no longer served any useful purpose there.

In 1780 the city played host to a French expeditionary force commanded by the Comte de Rochambeau. The fleet that accompanied it, commanded by Admiral Charles Louis d'Arsac de Ternay, was promptly bottled up in the harbor at Newport by a British fleet. The French army, snug in the arms of Newport hospitality, was pleased to stay where it was until it marched out in June, 1781, to join Washington's Continentals for the Yorktown campaign.

Only one attempt was made to get the British out. During the summer of 1778, a joint American-French effort was launched to take the island of Rhode Island. The Battle of Rhode Island was the largest land action fought in the state. You can get to the scene by taking Interstate 95 north from Connecticut into Providence, then switching onto Interstate 195. At the North Swansea exit, take State Route 136 south into the town of Warren. From Warren south through the city of Bristol,

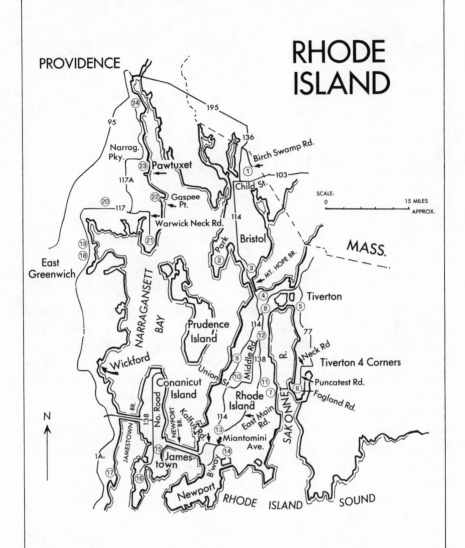

RHODE ISLAND

PROVIDENCE

1 Windmill Hill
2 Colt State Pk.—British Campsite
3 Bristol Neck Fort
4 Fort Site
5 Ft. Barton
6 Fogland Point
7 Sandy Point
8 Butts Hill Fort

9 Turkey Hill
10 Lawton Valley
11 First skirmish
    —Battle of Rhode Island
12 Quaker Hill
13 Olney House
14 Green End Fort
15 Jamestown Site
16 Beaver Tail Redoubt

17 Bonnet Pt. Battery
18 Varnum House
19 Ft. Daniel
20 David Arnold Tavern
21 Warwick Neck Ft.
22 Gaspee Site
23 Gaspee Landing Site—Ft. Hill Site
24 Ft. Independence

onto the island, and down into Newport, you can find a number of sites connected with the British and the French and with the battle.

THE BATTLE OF RHODE ISLAND

As you proceed along Route 136 through Warren, look for Schoolhouse Road going off to your left. If you come to a Big G shopping center, you will have gone too far. Schoolhouse Road winds its way over gently rolling hills and farmlands to the Warren School Administration Offices on your right at the intersection with Birch Swamp Road. You are in a farm area with some one-family homes here and there and signs of real-estate developers moving in. To your right is higher, wooded ground. This general area, originally called **Windmill Hill**, was the scene of a French army encampment prior to the long march to Yorktown in Virginia. Though the name is no longer in evidence on road signs in the neighborhood, it still rings a bell with local inhabitants who have always known there was an army camp of some sort here long ago. According to an entry made on December 16, 1777, in Frederick Mackenzie's diary (Mackenzie was an officer in the Royal Welsh Fusiliers), the British built a fortified barracks for 200 men on Windmill Hill.

Return to Route 136 and continue south to Route 103. Turn right (west) on 103, which becomes Child Street in Warren, and take it to Route 114. Turn left onto Route 114 and drive south toward Bristol. Just before you come into Bristol proper, you will see the waters of Bristol Harbor on your right.

Bristol was subjected to a British naval bombardment in October, 1775. In May, 1778, it was occupied and pillaged. At this point, Route 114 has become Hope Street. Turn right onto Poppasquash Road and follow it across a narrow causeway to **Colt State Park** on the right. The British camped in this area before investing the town. Beavertail Fort, built by the Americans in 1776, occupied the southern tip of this peninsula. We tried to reach the site, but Poppasquash Road becomes a private road with a fence across it, making access impossible.

Before you leave Bristol, you may want to wander around this quaint New England seaport. There are many old homes, including several that go back to the seventeenth century. The Reynolds House at 956 Hope Street, built in 1698, was occupied for a while by Lafayette. For a walking or driving tour from house to house, complete with map and booklet, get in touch with the Bristol Historical Society at 21 Constitution Street, Bristol 02809, or the Rhode Island Development Council, Tourist Promotion Division, Roger Williams Building, 49 Hayes Street, Providence, Rhode Island.

Continue south on 114 out of Bristol through a semirural area to the Mount Hope Bridge, which takes you into Portsmouth on the island of Rhode Island. Route 114 becomes a four-lane highway as it approaches the bridge. The buildings and campus of Roger Williams College appear on your left just before the bridge approach.

The land on this end of the bridge is **Bristol Neck.** In 1776 the rebels built a fort on it with three eighteen-pound cannon to guard the inlet. There was also a ferry, recently replaced by the bridge. Before you reach the bridge toll booth, a road leads off to the left down to the shore of Bristol Neck. There is a parking area where you can leave your car while you walk under the bridge and around the neck, noticing how effectively this fort and its sister on the other side of the inlet must have covered any vessel coming through the channel.

Take the bridge to the other side; go off on the first road on your right, and follow it around to the left to a dirt road which leads under railroad tracks and the bridge supports. There are some old ferry pilings at the water's edge and a broad expanse of grassy ground sloping down to the water. We found a long, high, grass-covered mound which set us wondering until we remembered the bulldozers that prepared this ground for the bridge supports. They must have destroyed whatever was left of the fort on this side.

Drive back up to the bridge approach where the road forks, with Boyd Lane going off to the right and 114 going left. Take Boyd Lane to Route 24 and 24 to Tiverton. You will cross the Sakonnet River with the East Passage to your right presenting a long, beautiful vista of water and low, wooded hills. Leave 24 at the exit for Route 138, which is also Highland Road, and follow it for a short distance to the sign for **Fort Barton.** A parking area is on the right with the Tiverton Town Hall just beyond it. The fort is on the left on a high bluff with a macadam footpath leading up to it.

Fort Barton was another of the many American defense works built in this area. Its purpose was to command the East Passage or Sakonnet River which it overlooks. General John Sullivan, sent by Washington early in 1778 to command American forces in the assault on Newport, made his headquarters in Tiverton just to the south of the fort. There are old breastworks here, the remains of star redoubts, and interior sites that may have been powder houses and bombproofs. A very good map of the area is mounted on a granite boulder identifying the principal points on the landscape spread out before you. You can improve your sight lines by climbing to the top of a wooden *tower* which stands on this site.

To your right, you can see where you crossed from Portsmouth and beyond it to the west, the Mount Hope Bridge and Bristol Neck. Directly in front of you, on the other side of Sakonnet River, is the north end of the island of Rhode Island. Somewhere on that high ridge of ground are the sites where the main actions of the battle were fought. To your left front is Gould Island, a small island with the piers of a nineteenth-century bridge that connected it with the mainland still showing. There was a small American redoubt of several guns on Gould Island, but there is nothing left to show where it stood. To your left, you look down the East Passage to Block Island Sound with the open ocean beyond it. The narrow neck of land sticking out into the water from your side some distance south is Fogland, the next site you visit. It was along the Sakonnet to your left, in the Fogland peninsula area, that the British ships trapped by the French fleet suffered severe losses.

In the summer of 1778, the French fleet under Admiral Charles Hector Theodat, Comte d'Estaing, had tried to get at the British fleet in New York Harbor. When that did not work, it was suggested in Philadelphia that an attack be made on the British garrison in Newport, which was under the command of the same general, Robert Pigot, who had commanded the British left at Breed's Hill. An army of 10,000 was assembled, mostly militia, with General Sullivan in command. Nathanael Greene, a native Rhode Islander, and the Marquis de Lafayette were Sullivan's seconds-in-command, and John Hancock, former president of the Continental Congress, was in command of part of the Massachusetts militia. D'Estaing sailed for Newport with his fifteen ships, including twelve battleships and three frigates, and got there on July 29.

Matters between Sullivan and the admiral did not go well. Sullivan had planned to attack the British in Newport with French naval support and with French soldiers landing on the west side of the island. On August 8, d'Estaing was to sail up Narragansett Bay past the British defenses to get into position. Sullivan was to land on the north end of Rhode Island on the night of August 9–10. On August 5, Pierre André de Suffren de Saint Tropez, a French admiral who later became a brilliant naval commander, sailed two frigates into the Sakonnet and threw the British fleet into a panic. Six British ships ran aground trying to get away, and two others were scuttled to block the entrance to Newport Harbor. The French then sailed the rest of the fleet to battle positions on August 8, as had been planned.

From your position on the watchtower at Fort Barton you are over-looking the scene of the August 5 action, to your left between Goat Island and Fogland peninsula to the south. For a closer look, drive south from Tiverton along Route 77 for five miles or so to Tiverton Four Corners. Turn right onto Neck Road, which makes a right-angle turn to the left and becomes Punkatest Road. To your left is Nonquit Pond; to your right, the Sakonnet River. At the intersection with Fogland Road, turn right on Fogland Road toward the water until you see a road going off to the right that looks as though it goes over a causeway. The road is marked by a small, white booth about thirty feet off Fogland Road. Take it as far as it goes, right to the edge of a stone-strewn shingle along the water. To your right is a low bluff crowned with a row of summer cottages and year-round residences.

This is **Fogland Point.** Look for an open grassy area on the west shore of the Sakonnet opposite your position. A number of contemporary one-family homes are clearly visible. That is Sandy Point. A little left of that, where the shoreline falls away into the river, is Black Point. There was a British redoubt on Sandy Point and an army barracks behind it, probably on that grassy slope. This redoubt is mentioned in Mackenzie's diary in a listing of the defenses around Newport built by the British. His reference is to a redoubt at "Fogland ferry," suggesting that in revolutionary days some boat crossed the Sakonnet at this point. Admiral Suffren sailed his two ships up the river from its mouth to your left. Three of the British ships were set afire immediately to the left and then drifted across the river where they ran aground and went up in smoke, flame, and exploding powder just below the British barracks on Sandy Point. The guns on one of the ships had been left loaded when the crew abandoned it. As the fire reached the touchholes they went off, and some of the shot landed uncomfortably close to the barracks. The French ships sailed up very close to this point, but saw the enemy ships in flame, trimmed sail, and stood off at a safe distance.

Local tradition says the British paymaster had his pay chest fastened to the keel of one of the ill-fated ships. The paymaster was visiting his mistress in Newport when the French ships moved up the river and could not get back to the ship with the key before the pay chest went down. Naturally this occurred just before payday. There is also a local tradition about Fogland Point. The local militia supposedly would bring out a gun on an oxcart under cover of the early morning fog, blast off a shot or two at the British position across the river once the fog had lifted, and be off before the British could return the fire. Considering the time it must have taken to lift the gun off the cart, limber it, fire it, unlimber it, and load it back onto the cart, you may swallow that one with a grain or two of salt.

Get back off Fogland Point and take 77 north through Tiverton to Route 24, which will take you west again across the Sakonnet to Portsmouth so you can cover the battle proper. The moves leading up to it began with Sullivan jumping the gun. The British, in the face of superior force, drew back from their outer defenses and concentrated their strength in Newport and the immediate vicinity. In the process, they abandoned Butts Hill Fort at the north end of Rhode Island just above the town of Portsmouth. Upon hearing of the British withdrawal, Sullivan crossed the Sakonnet from Tiverton and occupied the works on Butts Hill early on August 9 without telling d'Estaing beforehand. This disregard for the original plan probably did not matter much to the French commander, however, since the British fleet had just reappeared off Newport, catching him with his ships well inside Narragansett Bay and his sick sailors ashore on Conanicut Island. D'Estaing felt the need to pull himself together before the British could bottle him up inside the bay, robbing him of maneuverability.

The best way to get to the Butts Hill Fort, despite the maze of new highways, overpasses, and old roads that make a concrete tangle of the north end of the island, is to return to the vicinity of the Mount Hope Bridge. Make a turnaround there and come south again on Route 114. Look for the Anne Hutchinson School on your right. The next intersection, Sprague Street, is marked by a traffic light. Turn left onto Sprague and look for the American Legion Hall. It stands at the Dyer Street corner, and an old sign for the fort stands opposite. Around it are small, one-family homes, and behind it is Butts Hill. Dyer Street leads up to the main entrance of the **Butts Hill Fort.**

Some thirty or forty years ago, the Newport Historical Society erected a large, granite marker here. The road going up to the fort and what must have been a parking area just outside the entrance indicate this was a popular local attraction. It has since lost its popularity and is in need of rehabilitation. When we visited the dedication marker was on the ground and the stone walls and drive showed signs of abandonment and neglect. The old breastworks are still there, however, covered with grass and enclosing a large area several hundred feet long and about one hundred feet across. The star redoubts at the corners of the walls are well defined. A path leads around the fort's perimeter outside the remains of a ditch at the foot of the breastwork and the remains of a stone wall that once enclosed the entire area and was probably built when the tablet was erected. Though young trees block the view on some sides, the view toward the south, from which the British attack came, is still unobstructed. Narragansett Bay is off to the right; looking south, you can see the hills on which the British formed before moving north to retake the fort.

D'Estaing went out to meet the British fleet, leaving Sullivan facing the British along a siege line north of Newport. As the two fleets maneuvered to keep the weather gauge (the wind at their backs), they were struck by a ferocious gale on the night of August 11 and scattered to the four winds. By the time the French fleet reassembled, many of the ships had been so severely damaged that d'Estaing, mindful of his responsibility for Louis XVI's navy, decided to put into Boston for repairs. In vain did Sullivan send Lafayette galloping to Boston to persuade him to return. D'Estaing refused and Lafayette, who was to have commanded one wing of the American forces, returned in time to help what was left of the army withdraw from Rhode Island.

When they learned their French allies had withdrawn, Sullivan's 10,000 men began to melt away and Sullivan's siege of Newport was getting nowhere very fast. The British had surrounded the city with a cordon of forts and redoubts that were more than enough to hold the shrinking American forces at bay and refused to come out and fight.

Realizing that without naval support he would be vulnerable to enfilading fire from the waterway around him once the British fleet returned, Sullivan began to withdraw on August 28. Pigot came out after him to advance northward as he retreated.

The British moved along two main roads which ran north and south on either side of the island, just as they do today, West Main Road and East Main Road. Greene wanted to stop them before they reached Butts Hill, but instead they were allowed to come on practically unhindered until they had driven in the American outposts. When they stormed the Butts Hill Fort, however, they were repulsed and thrown back time and again despite naval guns from ships of the fleet that performed the same function for the British the French ships were to have performed for the Americans. Finally on the night of August 30–31, Sullivan withdrew his troops safely across the Sakonnet in boats rowed by Glover's Marbleheaders, who again were on hand to perform their specialty.

You can find the sites that mark the highlights of this battle, but you will have to do it piecemeal since they lay along two parallel routes.

Begin by returning to Route 114 and take it south past the tangle of ramps and roads where Route 24 comes down to join 114. Turn around as soon as you can, and going back in the opposite direction, take Route 24 north as though you were going back to Tiverton. As the road goes up a ramp, to the left on a grassy knoll lost between the high-speed roads is a *slab* of granite and a flagpole. Since there was no guard rail along the road, I pulled off onto the shoulder and walked to the pole.

The marker or plaque that had been attached to the granite was no longer there. It marked the area in which a Rhode Island militia regiment of freed slaves under Colonel Christopher Greene, that same Christopher Greene who served with distinction at Fort Mercer, fought desperately to repel successive assaults carried out by Hessian forces advancing on Butts Hill. This same regiment served in the Yorktown campaign. During the encampment in southern Westchester County where the French troops from Newport joined the Continental Army for the march to Virginia, French officers noticed them and remarked in their journals on the excellence of their uniforms and training.

You can continue up the ramp and find a turnaround which will take you back onto 24 south until it joins 114. Just before you reach that point, notice a county road parallel to 24 just to the right. Turn off onto it and stop to take a look at the rolling farmlands immediately to the west. This is the area along which a lot of the fighting on this side of the island took place as the Americans drove the British left flank back from Butts Hill to Turkey Hill. Farmers plowing in these fields still turn up musket balls and other trophies of the battle.

Clock about a mile and three quarters from this point as you drive south on 114. The road goes up a rise of ground until you are on a hill with the Latex Submarine Division plant on your right. This is **Turkey Hill,** one of the two hills (this is the west hill) on which the British captured American redoubts and formed for the attack on Butts Hill. They fell back to Turkey Hill when they were repulsed.

To find the remains of these redoubts, proceed south on 114 to an earth dike on your left with a reservoir visible on the other side. This is **Lawton's Valley** and you are at the Newport Waterworks. There is a small park on your left close to the Lawton Valley water treatment center with picnic tables under the trees. A road off to the left from 114 goes along the reservoir, which was originally a millpond for Lawton's Mill, and up to the treatment building. The remains of breastworks are in the woods surrounding the picnic area. A short distance farther along 114 you come to Union Street. Just off 114 to the left on Union in a white frame house on the left (on the property of the Narragansett

Builders Company) are the remains of the old mill itself. The road passes over a small stream that feeds into the reservoir. By looking to the left down that stream bed, you can see where it leads to the house and the remains.

Continue along Union Street to East Main Road. Look for a white marble *marker* on the right side identifying the site of the first skirmish that opened the battle. Turn left onto East Main Road and proceed north until you see Middle Road coming in on your left at an acute angle. Just at the juncture is a one-and-a-half-story house made of white, wooden shingles with brick chimneys at either end. Swing around and park in front. You can further identify the building by the police station diagonally opposite to it. This is the **Portsmouth Friends Church**, established in 1658. The area immediately around it is **Quaker Hill**, the east hill on which Pigot's right flank formed behind a redoubt for the attack on the American left and to which they were driven back. Quaker Hill was also the position held by the American rear guard on August 29 before they were ordered to retire. The order from General Sullivan to the commander of the rear guard, Colonel Edward Wigglesworth, was carried by Colonel John Trumbull, a volunteer serving as Sullivan's A.D.C. Trumbull was to become famous as a painter, particularly for his paintings of Revolutionary War scenes. In his reminiscences, Trumbull describes the scene on Quaker Hill:

"I had to mount the hill by a broad, smooth road, more than a mile in length from the foot to the summit [the road is still there and the slope is just as long] where was the scene of conflict . . . At first I saw a round shot or two drop near me and pass bounding on. I met poor Colonel Toussard, who had just lost one arm blown off by the discharge of a field piece, for the possession of which there was an ardent struggle. He was led off by a small party. Soon after, I saw Captain Walker of H. Jackson's regiment, who had received a musket ball through his body, mounted behind a person on horseback. He bid me a melancholy farewell and died before night. Next grapeshot began to sprinkle around me and soon after musket balls fell in my path like hailstones. This was not to be borne. I spurred on my horse to the summit of the hill and found myself in the midst of the melee. 'Don't say a word, Trumbull,' cried the gallant commander. 'I know your errand but don't speak; we will beat them in a moment.'

" 'Colonel Wigglesworth, do you see those troops crossing obliquely from the west road towards your rear?'

" 'Yes, they are Americans coming to our support.'

" 'No Sir, those are Germans; mark, their dress is blue and yellow not buff; they are moving to fall into your rear, and intercept your retreat. Retire instantly—don't lose a moment or you will be cut off.' The gallant man obeyed reluctantly and withdrew the guard in fine style slowly, but safely."

Trumbull goes on to describe how on his way back to Butts Hill he found a friend about to have a leg amputated. He was a volunteer serving on General Glover's staff who was quartered in a house at the foot of Quaker Hill to the east. While the general and his staff were enjoying their breakfast, the firing around them became heavy and Glover ordered an officer seated at the table to investigate. As the officer got up to carry out the order, Trumbull's friend took his seat in time to have his ankle crushed by a spent cannonball which bounced through an open window and rolled across the floor right at him.

"If this happened to me in the field in active duty the loss of a leg might be borne," the volunteer lamented to Trumbull. "But to be condemned through all future life to say I lost my leg under the breakfast table is too bad."

At the end of the fighting that day, the British remained on the two hills and formed a line from the east shore to Quaker Hill, across the crossroads just south of the meetinghouse, west along that road (now called Hedley Avenue) to Turkey Hill, and west from Turkey Hill down to the west shore. They were harassed during the night by rebel patrols trying to take shots at the sentries. This was probably just so much masking, however, to conceal the withdrawal out of the Butts Hill Fort down to the boats and across to Tiverton.

If you continue north along East Main Road, passing through another area of the fighting between Quaker and Butts hills, you will eventually come to 2851 East Main Road, the house in which Lafayette stayed before the battle.

Come back south again on East Main Road and, as soon as you can, take any road that goes to the right, or west, to Route 114, West Main Road. Turn left onto 114 and continue south along the west side of the island. Just above the Middletown County line, you will notice a reconstructed colonial village on the left side of the road. Next to it is a large, two-story colonial building, the **Olney House.** Colonel Richard Prescott, commander of the British garrison in Newport and highly unpopular with the local Whigs because he went out of his way to be unpleasant toward them, had made this his headquarters. On the night of July 9, 1777, Major William Barton with forty men came to this side of Rhode

Island by boat from Tiverton, sneaked up across the fields just across the road over a path that no longer exists, and captured the colonel and his first subordinate. Eventually Prescott was exchanged for Charles Lee and returned to Newport only to be succeeded by General Pigot.

NEWPORT

Newport, the well-known summer resort of the late nineteenth and early twentieth centuries, home of the Newport Cup Yacht Race, is a marvelous town for walking and exploring. Occupied by the British and then the headquarters for the French expeditionary force under Rochambeau, it is steeped in antiquity. Entire streets are lined with eighteenth- and nineteenth-century buildings that have been lovingly restored or preserved with signs noting the date of their construction and the well-known personages who resided there.

There is a large plaza in the heart of town called Washington Square with good parking facilities in and around it. The Preservation Society of Newport County, located on Washington Square, puts out a very good pamphlet with a map of the historic areas which outlines a walking tour. Newport is worth hours of your time, perhaps a day or two. Take your time and stroll through the town. Many of the houses are open daily, but a few must be seen by appointment. Don't miss the White Horse Tavern, the oldest tavern in America (built in 1673), which is still open for business at lunch and dinner times; the Old Stone Mill, that strange, stone tower some people believe was built by Norse settlers; Touro Synagogue, built in 1763, the oldest Jewish house of worship in the country and a masterpiece of architecture; the Newport Artillery Museum, headquarters of the Newport Artillery Company; the Lawn Tennis Hall of Fame; the Redwood Library; and scores of other landmarks.

Newport's Revolutionary War sites include, besides the site of at least one British fort, Vernon House which was Rochambeau's headquarters; the John Bannister House in which British General Prescott made his headquarters (he had been promoted after his capture and returned to Newport); Colony House on Washington Square, which still shows on the floor in the big downstairs room the marks made by the axes of British soldiers who were quartered there as they chopped wood for their fires; the William House where the French admiral de Ternay died; the Thomas Robinson House, the headquarters of the Vicomte de Noailles; Governor John Tillinghast House, used by a French regiment of engineers as its headquarters and in which that indefatigable traveler and observer of revolutionary America, the Marquis de Chastellux, wrote his impressions of Newport. The Tillinghast House was also rented at one time by General Greene and was visited by Lafayette, Kosciuszko, and Baron von Steuben. If you love old towns and enjoy soaking up their atmosphere, Newport is for you.

As they prepared for the American siege, the British built a number of redoubts and fortified sentry posts in and around the city, but we were able to find only one, the **Green End Fort.** The town and the surrounding highways have grown around and over the others. Take Broadway north; turn right onto Miantomini Avenue; take the second right off Miantomini Avenue, and you are in a residential area of one-family homes. The fort is off to your left overlooking Green Hill Pond, but out of sight. A number of streets go off to the left and one of them, probably the first or second, leads to it. It is just off the road, a semicircle of breastworks overgrown with grass. Behind the breastworks is a wide, open area which was the interior of the fort. There is a stone column in the middle commemorating the site. There is no marker on the road, but the area is surrounded by a low wooden fence with cement posts. A marker on the breastworks describes the fort as having been built in 1777 by the British for the defense of Newport.

The view from the top of the breastworks is across Green Hill Pond and Middletown beyond. Green End Avenue to your left goes over a bridge at the north end of the pond. Just beyond the breastworks, the ground falls away, then rises again into what may have been outer works. The view is generally to the east and north. The pond is created by a narrow causeway. A second pond, called Easton Pond, was created by another causeway which carries Memorial Boulevard from Newport into Middletown. Beyond both ponds is Block Island Sound and the open sea.

According to Mackenzie's diary, Green End Fort was part of the city's main defenses which consisted of four or five redoubts extending from Easton Beach, possibly on your right in the vicinity of Easton Pond, to the "North Battery" and connected by lines of redans in between. Mackenzie mentions three windmills in this vicinity and describes the line of fortifications as 3,000 yards long, between a mile and a half and two miles in length. On the other hand, Rhode Island at its southern tip ends in Easton Point. From where you are now at Green End Fort, Easton Point is off to your right beyond the ponds about two miles away. If the Easton Beach mentioned in Mackenzie is now called Easton Point, this line of fortifications may have extended along the far shore of the small but deep bay, now the shoreline of the ponds off to your right; if that was the case Green End Fort may have been the "North Battery" Mackenzie mentions.

Return to Miantomini Avenue; head back for Newport, but when you get to the turnoff for Broadway, continue straight ahead onto Admiral Kalfus Road. This is an elevated four-lane road which leads to a traffic circle. Go around the circle and take Connell Highway south, watching for the turnoff to the Newport Bridge to Jamestown on Conanicut Island. As you go over the bridge, you get an excellent view of the Newport Harbor area, including the naval base with Narragansett Bay extending north to your right and Block Island south to the left.

At the west end of the bridge you are on Conanicut Island where d'Estaing put his sick sailors ashore for treatment and rest. Coming off the bridge, follow the road to your left with the bay on your left. At the foot of the hill to your right, turn right onto Narragansett Avenue which leads up into the town. To your left you may have noticed a three-masted ship, a full-scale replica of the H.M.S. *Rose,* an authentic restoration which is open to the public.

Jamestown was burned by the British as an act of retaliation after the American forces withdrew from Rhode Island. The only building left standing is at 72 Narragansett Avenue, a two-story, red, clapboard house with a stone wall in front. Continue along the avenue to the intersection of North Main Road. To your right is a church graveyard used by the British as an artillery park. Turn left onto North Main Road and follow it as it curves to the right and crosses a causeway between Mackerel Cove on the left and Dutch Island Harbor on your right. In the distance you can see the towers of a navy communications center. The road is lined with garbage dumps on which flocks of gulls feed voraciously, marshlands, and open beach. A short distance off the causeway, look for a house with a peculiar shape on the right behind tall bushes. A short distance beyond on the left is an old, weatherbeaten shingled house with a gambrel roof. Opposite this second house a road leads off to the right. Take it.

Though it is paved, the surface has heaved in places and you will have to drive carefully between low, grassy dunes among which military defenses have been built from revolutionary times up to and including World War II. Along the way, you will come to what were probably turnoffs or wide places to allow military vehicles to pass each other. Keep going until you reach a dirt road going off to the right. Take it down to the shore. It will lead into a wide, grassy area in the midst of a semicircle of breastworks along the shore of Narragansett Bay. These are the grass-covered remains of a *redoubt,* one of a series built by the British and then taken over by the Americans when the British pulled in their outer lines. The first shots fired by British guns at d'Estaing's ships may have come from one of these redoubts. They guarded not only this narrow passage between Conanicut Island and the mainland, but also the entrance to Conanicut Harbor to your right, now known as Dutch Island Harbor. Another fort was located on Bonnet Point on the opposite shore to your left. The higher mounds behind the breastworks off to the right as you drive back out are the remains of fortifications built during World War II to guard Newport Harbor.

Retrace your route to North Main Road and head north past Narragansett Avenue. Make a left onto Eldred Avenue, which is also 138 west, and cross the Jamestown Bridge. On the other side at the traffic circle, take 1A south. In a short distance, you will see a sign on the right at Snuff Hill Road alerting you to the Gilbert Stuart birthplace one mile to the west. Follow 1A to Bonnet Shores. Take Bonnet Point Road to your left and follow it past Wesquage Pond to a beach club, a white, stone, circular structure which is a converted 1812 fort. On that site was located another battery of American guns guarding the passage between the mainland and the south end of Conanicut Island.

Return to 1A where you have a choice between two roads to Greenwich to the north, the site of Fort Daniel and other local landmarks. You can take 1A as far as Wickford where it curves west to U.S. Route 1; or, you can take 1A for a short distance north to Bridgetown Road going off to the left which will take you to U.S. 1 almost immediately. Route 1A stays close to the shore and is the scenic route, but you will make better time along U.S. 1.

U.S. 1 becomes East Greenwich's Main Street where you will spot the old courthouse on your left at the intersection of Main and Court streets. This is a bustling little town and you are right in the heart of its business and shopping district, so parking may be difficult at certain times of the day and on Saturdays. A sign at the intersection on the courthouse corner points up Court Street to the Varnum House. Walk up Court Street right out of the twentieth century and into the eighteenth. At the end of the street, a flight of steps carries you up to Pierce Street above and parallel to Main Street. On the other side is the **Varnum House**, a large, two-story, frame building, once the home of General James Mitchell Varnum. Varnum was one of Sullivan's commanders during the Battle of Rhode Island. He had been in command of the Delaware River forts, Mercer and Mifflin, had an active role at the Battle of Monmouth under Charles Lee, and served throughout the war, usually in command of Rhode Island militia units. As you turn back down Court Street, notice on your left at the head of the steps the home of a physician who served with the Continental Army.

Continue north along U.S. 1–Main Street for a few blocks to Division Street and turn right to Greenwich Cove. This is an area of marinas and boatyards where the Kentish Guards manned a redoubt. Just north of that, to the right off U.S. 1 as you proceed along it, a railroad embankment and other modern embellishments have effectively destroyed the site of **Fort Daniel,** another American fortified position which guarded Greenwich Bay.

Take U.S. 1 north to State Route 117, and turn right to go east on 117, also called West Shore Road. A short distance past the juncture with Route 113, 117 forks. Keep to the right fork, which is still West Shore Road. Look for 1836 West Shore Road, a one-story, dark red, clapboard house. Now a private residence, this was the **David Arnold Tavern.** To this tavern Colonel Prescott was taken after his abduction from Rhode Island. At the time we visited, the marker that had previously identified the house had been taken down so the owner could paint the exterior. Visitors are not allowed, but the inside of the house has been remodeled; the original beams and floorboards have been covered over with plasterboard and linoleum. Close by, in the direction from which you came, is a smaller house, also of dark red clapboard, which we believe to be the Thomas Wickes House, formerly the headquarters of Colonel Waterman and the guardhouse for the local militia unit.

Continue along 117 for a block or two to Warwick Neck Road and turn right. Follow it down through a lovely semirural, suburban area as far as the road goes. It will take you to a dead end at a hurricane fence, with handsome private homes on both sides, and a Coast Guard station and lighthouse directly ahead overlooking the north end of Narragansett Bay. The station is open to the public during normal weekday and weekend hours. As you enter, walk to your left across the grassy area that slopes down to the water. On the private property next door, notice a hump or hillock in the middle of the lawn. According to the Coast Guard man on duty here, the owners of that plot of land have uncovered other similar mounds closer to the water, suggesting that this may be the site of **Warwick Neck Fort,** which is known to have stood on this point of land. The fort contained a battery of guns with which the rebels covered this area of the bay. Directly opposite are Patience Island and the larger Prudence Island which narrow the passageway considerably, thus shortening the range of the guns stationed on this site.

Returning to Warwick Neck Road, take it north to 117; turn left onto 117, and in a block or two turn right onto 117A going north. Eventually, 117 comes in from the right and you will suddenly find yourself driving on 117 instead of 117A. Less than a mile from where 117 merged into 117A you will come to Narrangansett Parkway coming in from the right. Turn right onto the parkway and follow it east. When you get to Parkside Drive, turn right and follow Parkside down to a dead end on the waters of Passconkquit Cove. To your left is the Sakonnet River at a point north of Bristol and just below Providence. Ahead of you, on the other side of the cove, is **Gaspée Point.**

In 1772, the British armed schooner, the *Gaspée,* commanded by Lieutenant William Duddington, was making life miserable for all boats, large and small, sailing these waters. Duddington delighted in sending shots across the bows of his victims, forcing them to submit to search parties on slight pretexts, taking them into court on minor charges and in general making a nuisance of himself. Protests to Duddington and to the admiral above him from the royal governor on down did no good. Duddington went right on being his usual obnoxious, arrogant self.

On the afternoon of June 9, 1772, Captain Thomas Lindsay set sail in his packet from Newport for Providence. On the way he was hailed by the *Gaspée.* Lindsay decided to ignore the summons and the *Gaspée* gave chase. As he came around the point you are looking at, Lindsay, perhaps purposefully, cut a very wide arc presenting Duddington with an apparent chance to cut him off. Duddington took the bait which took him very close to the Point where he hit a sandbar and went aground. The tide was going out. The *Gaspée* began to heel over. There wasn't a thing Duddington and his crew could do to get the *Gaspée* afloat but wait for the tide to come in at three the following morning.

When Lindsay reached Providence about five in the afternoon and reported the *Gaspée*'s plight, certain interested parties, their sympathies aroused over the plight of the poor British tars stuck out in the river, got together and decided to offer Lieutenant Duddington the hospitality of the town. Slipping downriver in eight long boats, after providing themselves with whatever welcoming implements they could get their hands on, they approached the *Gaspée* where she lay heeled over on the sandbar. As soon as the deck watch announced them, the commander and his men tumbled out of their bunks. By that time, the welcoming committee was over the rail and on board. There followed a short but lively ceremony during which many expressions of mutual esteem were exchanged. After raising a number of genteel protestations, Lieutenant Duddington and his men graciously bowed to fate, accepted the generous offer of hospitality, and went ashore with the reception committee. The longboats then returned to the *Gaspée* to make sure she was safe and secure. Somehow flames spread over the now vacated ship, unfortunately reached the powder on board, and the ship blew up. The governor of Rhode Island offered a reward for the apprehension of those responsible and so did the king, but none of the members of the expedition were ever identified.

Gaspée Point from your viewpoint is a long stretch of brushy, sandy land pointed out into the Sakonnet River. Few houses show through the trees, and it seems a delightful idea to drive or walk out to the end of the point and try to spot the sandbar on which the *Gaspée* came to grief. Appearances are deceptive, however. Most of the point today is covered with a housing development. If you return to Narragansett Parkway and turn left, you will see the marker and memorial put up by the local chapter of the D.A.R. to the patriots who destroyed the *Gaspée*. I made a valiant effort during the better part of one afternoon to find a way out to the end of the point. The best I could do was to hit a private road that led into a beach colony, which did me no good at all. I did find two of three paths leading off into the brushy woods that cover the rest of the point, but none led into anything but the nastiest patches of brambles I have ever seen.

Continuing north on Narragansett Parkway, a beautiful drive along the river with delightful prospects of headlands and water on the right, and shortly after crossing the Pawtuxet River, look for Ocean Avenue going off to the right. Follow it east to the Rhode Island Yacht Club where a wide, paved parking area gives you a chance to spend a few minutes looking out over the water. At this point, the mate of the *Gaspée* was brought ashore by one of the longboats and taken into custody. Notice Fort Avenue which comes in from the right toward the yacht club. The name commemorates Fort Hill that stood on this long neck of land protecting the entrance to Providence Harbor during the Revolution. The actual site has been lost.

PROVIDENCE

Return to Narragansett Parkway; turn right, and go north to the junction with 1A. Follow 1A as it turns first right and then left again. You are now in Providence. All around you is a modern city with tenements, apartment buildings, industrial properties, and a new attractive downtown area. Turn right onto New York Avenue and follow it out into an industrial zone on the shores of Narragansett Bay called Field's Point. Somewhere in this area stood **Fort Independence,** later called Fort

Constitution, which was built by the Americans to protect the entrance to Providence Harbor. A photograph of this area circa 1890, before it became a home for sheet-metal factories, power plants, and garbage dumps, shows the old breastworks. Off to your right is a high bluff of land. The cliff is scooped out on the side facing the water, suggesting that at one time that high ground continued on to the water's edge or shelved down to a beach. According to the photograph and other evidence, the fort stood on that stretch of land between the present edge of the bluff and the beach. Fort Independence was part of a ring of fortifications that continued north from this point around the harbor, presenting unfriendly intruders with a horseshoe-shaped ring of guns and breastworks. Had the British ever attempted to take Providence, they would have been without naval support, for ships venturing into the harbor faced enemy fire from three directions.

Providence has, of course, overgrown many of its military sites dating from the Revolution, but some of its eighteenth-century buildings still stand, and the former locations of some of the military sites can be identified. What follows is a tour of as many of the Revolutionary War sites as I could find under Al Klyberg's expert guidance.

Begin at the corner of Rochambeau Avenue and North Main Street. North Main is U.S. 1 and this particular spot is north of the City Hall–Kennedy Plaza area. Take me literally when I tell you to look up Rochambeau Avenue, for you will be looking up a hill. On the ridge at the top of the *hill* is where the French army camped prior either to its march to Yorktown in 1780 or to its march in 1782 to Boston where it embarked for France. To your left at the foot of the hill is a red, clapboard, colonial dwelling, the old **Morris Homestead** which was here at the time. Opposite on North Main Street is the **North Burial Ground** where over a hundred French soldiers who died during the encampment lie buried. At the top of the hill is a marker on Summit Avenue and Brewster Street commemorating the French camp. A block up the hill is Camp Street which recalls the use this site was once put to. Looking down the hill you can see the Moshassuck River which runs into the Providence River.

Turn right onto Camp Street and follow it until it dead-ends in Olney Street. Turn right onto Olney and take it back to North Main Street. Turn right onto North Main and immediately look to your right for a low, brick wall built around a young tree. A granite marker identifies this as the site of the original **Liberty Tree** which was dedicated on July 25, 1768. A speech made on this occasion by Silas Downer was one of the earliest expressions of the desire for independence on the part of the colonists not for complete independence, but for autonomy under the crown. The speech was printed in a pamphlet which was widely distributed, and many of Silas Downer's sentiments were echoed again and again in subsequent speeches and written declarations as antagonism grew between the colonists and the mother country.

Turn around and head along North Main in the opposite direction looking for Benefit Street, which goes off to the left. Follow Benefit Street and turn left onto Jenckes Street, then right onto Prospect Street. You are driving through an old section of the city. The streets are lined with old homes, many from the early nineteenth century or the eighteenth. They have been well kept and are still residences. Take Prospect to the corner of Prospect and Meeting streets.

You are now on the highest point of land in the city, overlooking the dome of the state capitol, the city center, and one of the many Roger Williams parks in Providence, directly in front of you. Here in revolutionary times stood one of the alarm beacons that were erected throughout Rhode Island to warn of British troop movements. The beacon has been described as "a simple affair consisting of a spar or a mast some eighty-odd feet in height secured and based at the foundation. Wooden pegs for steps at regular intervals enabled those managing it to ascend to the kettle which hung from an iron crane or a mast arm. This kettle was filled with inflammable stuff so as to produce a brilliant light." A broadside published at the time warned the inhabitants of the city to look for the first lighting of this particular beacon. The broadside explains that it was only a test, that the firing of a cannon by itself was not an alarm, but that "the firing of the beacon itself even without cannon would be an alarm in all cases excepting on Thursday the 17th Instant [August 17] at sunset when the beacon will be fired not as an alarm but that all may ascertain its bearings and fix such ranges as may secure them from a false alarm and that they may know where to look for it hereafter." After the test, letters were received by the city's newspaper stating that the beacon had been seen from Cambridge Hall to New London and from Newport to Pomfret, which covers quite an area. Despite all these precautions, many people who saw the beacon assumed it was the real thing and flocked into Providence for protection, believing the British were about to attack.

Somewhere in this area was an arsenal and magazine in which arms and ammunition were stored for the local militia. Continue along Prospect Street to the campus of Brown University, marked by a tower with a clock to the left. **University Hall,** the original building built in 1770, is on your left, long, four-story, brick with an arched cupola surmounted by a weather vane. When the British occupied Newport and threatened Providence in 1776, the local militia flew to arms, marched up to University Hall, turned the students out, all forty of them, and turned the building into a barracks. From that time until 1782, it was used as a barracks and hospital by the militia and the Continental Army and the French army as well. Rhode Island declared itself an independent republic on May 4, 1776, beating the Continental Congress to the punch by two months. Every year on this anniversary, candles burn in the windows of many of the Brown University buildings.

Turn right onto College Street and take it to Benefit Street. Turn right again onto Benefit and go one block to the corner of Hopkins Street. Here stands the two-story, red, clapboard **Stephen Hopkins House,** home of Stephen Hopkins, a signer of the Declaration of Independence and ten times governor of Rhode Island. The house, which originally stood on another site and was moved here recently, has been partially restored and is open to the public in the afternoons.

Take the first intersection to the left to South Main Street; turn right, and go back to College Street. Make a left on College Street and find the old **Market House** on the right standing on Market Square. It is a typical market building of the period with arched openings along the ground floor where the merchants' stalls stood. It was used as a barracks by the American army during the Revolution.

Go back to South Main Street; turn left and follow it until it becomes North Main. After you pass Kennedy Plaza on your left with Providence's City Hall and other official buildings, look to the right for the **Old Statehouse,** a handsome brick edifice with a square steeple over the front entrance, faced with a clock on the Main Street side. This is the building in which that May fourth Declaration of Independence was passed. Built in 1760, it was in continuous use as a statehouse until 1900.

Now find the first street back to Benefit Street, which runs parallel to North Main behind the Old Statehouse. Turn right onto Benefit Street and follow it to its end at Fox Point at the mouth of the Providence River. As you face the water with Benefit Street behind you, the Washington Bridge to East Providence is to your left and the Point Street Bridge is behind you and to your right. The cement structure that looks like a dike is the Fox Point Hurricane Barrier. It protects Providence from hurricane-induced waves that in the past have rolled up the bay and into this part of the city. In Revolutionary War times, this was a large sandy hill called **Fox Hill.** On Fox Hill July 31, 1775, a town meeting convened and decided that a fort should be built here for the defense of the town, including trenches and breastworks. Interstate 95 runs over what was probably the site of the fort. There is a hurricane fence shutting you off from the highway, and though there may have been a historical marker at one time, the construction of the interstate has probably erased even that.

Now go back up Benefit Street to Wickenden Street just on the other side of the interstate; turn left; cross the Point Street Bridge, and take Point Street to Friendship Street. Turn left onto Friendship and take it to the intersection at Broad Street. Sullivan's men were encamped in a roughly square area bounded by Chestnut, Foster, Friendship, and Broad streets. Chestnut Street is some distance north of this point. You can reach the northern perimeter of the camp by going back up Friendship Street, following it under the overhead ramps that mark the juncture of Interstates 95 and 195 until you reach Chestnut Street. Incidentally, that area under the interstates marks the spot where a stream ran through the camp. It is believed that the French army camped there before they left for the Virginia campaign. Broad Street was the main route then between Providence and the Pawtuxet area to the south and still is today as State Route 117.

X.

CONNECTICUT

Connecticut was distinguished by having as its governor Jonathan Trumbull, the only royal governor to forswear his allegiance to the crown and support the Patriot cause. It contributed about 3,000 men to the provincial army that laid siege to Boston in 1775 and additional brigades and regiments in response to calls from the Continental Congress for men.

Connecticut also contributed Benedict Arnold, who was born in Norwich and became a successful New Haven merchant. Arnold honored the state of his birth by opposing the first of three major raids carried out by the British here, but then led the third, after his defection. These raids, though widely spaced over four years, shared a common objective: to put a stop to the steady stream of supplies Connecticut was sending to the Continental Army.

The Marquis de Chastellux, who traveled through the state on his way to and from Virginia, mentions the provisions Connecticut Patriots were preparing and shipping to Washington's men. According to what he understood of the system, each state or section of the country was called upon to provide certain items. For instance, the eastern states were to furnish cattle, rum, and salt. Boatner notes that Washington's first and second commissary generals were Joseph Trumbull (Jonathan's son) and Jeremiah Wadsworth, both natives of Connecticut; that they were highly instrumental in supplying the army with food, clothing, and munitions, of which Connecticut was the main source among the colonies. I have also found references, however, to the lower Hudson valley and the Schoharie Valley as major sources of flour, New Jersey and Pennsylvania for a variety of farm products, including beef, and repeated

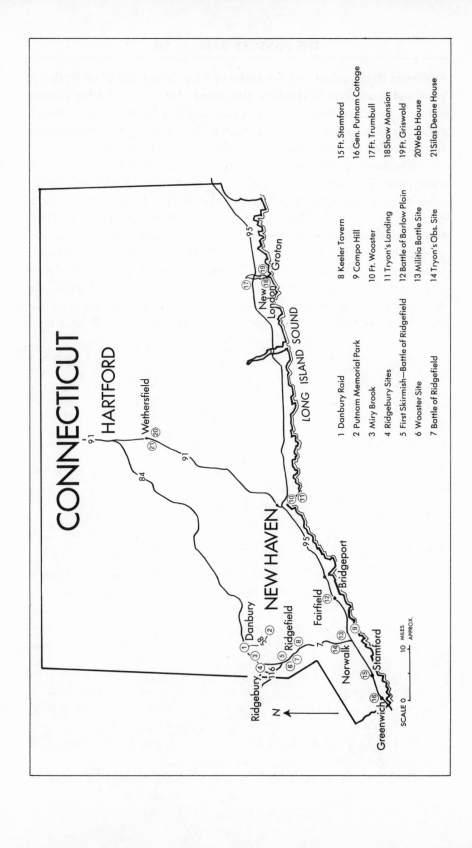

references to the mines and foundries of New Jersey and New York for guns and munitions. Chastellux also noted that a considerable cottage industry had developed in Connecticut, utilizing home looms on which entire families worked and made their livings weaving textiles intended for the collective backs and legs of the Continental Army.

Whether Connecticut was the main source of these supplies is a moot point. The fact is that it suffered at the hands of the British for its contributions. In April, 1777, General William Tryon, formerly royal governor of North Carolina and then of New York, led a raid on Danbury and the surrounding region where he encountered resistance organized by Arnold and General David Wooster. In July, 1779, General Clinton sent Tryon and General George Garth into the Havens (New and East Haven) to pillage and burn. In 1781 Benedict Arnold, the British army's "new broom," reportedly anxious to wreak vengeance for André's death, raided New London and Groton and brought on a massacre that is remembered in Connecticut to this day.

Since Connecticut is a comparatively small state and the distances involved are not great, I have arranged three tours to cover each raid in chronological order. The tours begin in the western part of the state, follow the Long Island Sound coast from Greenwich to New London, and make an excursion into the north central part to pick up other sites. Included along the way is part of the route the French army followed on its way from Newport to Yorktown.

Connecticut has a network of excellent roads, including two interstates: 84, which runs across the state from east to west; and 95, which is the Connecticut Turnpike and follows a northeast-southwest axis. Interstate 84 connects with New York state highways along the New York–Connecticut border; 95 connects with the New England Thruway at its southern terminus and continues north into Rhode Island and Massachusetts.

THE DANBURY RAID

On Wednesday, April 23, 1777, General Tryon sailed from New York City with about 2,000 men and disembarked two days later at Compo Beach near Fairfield. On Saturday, April 26, he marched overland to Danbury, a distance of about twenty-three miles. His objective was to destroy a supply depot located in the town. In the process, his men managed to destroy most of the town as well.

Danbury can be reached from the south by taking the Saw Mill

River Parkway north. Coming from New York City, you can get to the parkway by taking the Henry Hudson Parkway up the west side of Manhattan. Saw Mill will take you north through Westchester, eventually to a junction with Interstate 684 and then to Interstate 84 east, which in turn will take you to Danbury.

If you are coming from the north out of Massachusetts, take Interstate 91 to Hartford, where it meets 84, and take 84 west to Danbury. If you're coming south from upper New York State, Route 22 goes to a point close to the 684–84 junction where very large signs lead onto 84 east.

In Danbury leave 84 at Exit 5, which should take you onto Main Street. Main Street is also U.S. 202. Take it south until you notice that the street is divided by a long, parklike area. That planted divider is actually the remains of the old commons or green. You are now in the heart of what was colonial Danbury.

A short distance beyond where the commons ends, look for an old, gray, frame house on the left side of Main Street, the **David Taylor House**, part of the Danbury Scott-Fanton Museum. A driveway leads off Main Street. At the head of the driveway is a modern building which is Huntington Hall, a museum featuring exhibits of arts and crafts, industry and science. A smaller colonial house behind the Scott-Fanton Museum is the **Dodd House and Hat Shop.** Built in 1770, it belonged to John Dodd, a hatter. Danbury was a major hat manufacturing center. In 1957 the Dodd House was moved from its original site a short distance down Main Street to its present site and was restored in 1958.

The David Taylor House was built about 1750. Since Taylor was a Tory, it was spared during Tryon's raid. It and the Dodd House are old Danbury's only surviving buildings. The Taylor House and the Dodd House are open to the public Wednesday through Friday from 2 to 5 P.M.; on Saturdays from 10 A.M. to 5 P.M.; and on Sundays, 1–5 P.M. The Taylor House contains a collection of Americana, some of which dates to colonial times and is connected with the Revolution.

There is a very good diorama with scale-model homes in the basement of the house showing how this part of town was laid out and how the British did their fiery work. As you proceed along Main Street past the Taylor House in the direction you were going, you are still driving through old Danbury. The British were virtually unopposed during the raid. A small force in the area managed to remove some of the supplies stored here, but otherwise did nothing to hinder the raiders. Most of the destruction began late in the afternoon of Saturday, April 26, and was continued on Sunday, April 27, when forty-one homes, barns, and warehouses were burned along with the clothing, tents, and other provisions they contained.

By this time, Generals Arnold and Wooster were rallying Connecticut militia units and some Continental troops to contest the British return to their ships, but Tryon was a little too smart for them. Instead of retracing his steps through a swarm of angry countrymen, he decided to return by another route and headed west to Ridgebury, en route to Ridgefield. Since we are this far north and so close to Redding, however, it would be more convenient to detour for a visit to Connecticut's "Valley Forge" before following the redcoats.

Continuing down Main Street, with the Taylor House behind you on the left, you will come to a major intersection with South Street; on the opposite side is the Cephas B. Rogers Park which contains Danbury's war memorials. Continue ahead across the South Street intersection and through the park. The road swings left and becomes a very narrow road called Overlook Road, which soon dead-ends. Turn right and enter the town of Bethel. At the intersection of Fleetwood Avenue and Mansfield Street bear right, and at the intersection with Route 202, turn right and take 202 east toward Redding. Follow 202 to Route 58, and then take 58 south.

A mile or so along 58 you will see on the left the first of three entrances to **Israel Putnam Memorial Park.** This entrance goes into a very pretty, wooded camping and picnic area with a small lake close to the road. Though there were some encampments in this part of the park, they are not marked and have probably been lost. Continue on a short distance to the second entrance, this time on your right. It is prominently marked by two gateposts surmounted by representations of log blockhouses and an old cannon just beyond them. A road to your left beyond the gate leads up a hill to a small, fieldstone building housing a *museum.* A small parking area is nearby. As you walk up to the museum's entrance, look down the hill to your right and notice what seems to be a row of tumbled *rocks* on the other side of another road. They are the remains of some of the hutments Putnam's men lived in during the winter of 1778–79.

Israel Putnam, who had been one of the moving spirts of the Revolution during the opening years, was an old man by '78 and had proved himself unworthy of important commands and had been placed in charge of the forces stationed in the Redding area. They constituted the right wing of the American line extending from Redding to the Hudson.

According to the Redding Historical Society, it was in this area, now the memorial park, that Putnam quartered about 5,000 men, their wives, and other camp followers. Among them were 200 free, black men and some Indians who had joined up to fight the British. Records of the encampment show that 1,500 men had no shoes, and 400 had no coats, shoes, or blankets. A pamphlet put out by the Connecticut State Park and Forest Commission, which maintains the site, says that the exact number of men encamped here is unknown.

The museum contains a number of artifacts found in the area. It stands on the site of a picket post at which sentries were stationed. A dirt and gravel tour road takes you circling through the encampment areas. A tour map shows the numbered sites, which include the firebacks of the fireplaces that warmed the hutments, a reconstructed officer's hut, and a reconstructed guardhouse. One of the park's outstanding sites shows up shortly after the museum: a cave at the foot of a small, rocky hill known as **Phillips Cave.** According to local tradition, Phillips was a soldier who had served with Putnam and was at the encampment. After the war he returned to live in this cave, but made such a nuisance of himself "ripping off" the local farmers that a party of them visited him one night and hanged him.

If you do follow the tour map, you should begin at a third park entrance farther south along 58. Another set of blockhouse gateposts leads to a statue of Putnam, first on the tour map, then to the reconstructed guardhouse, a memorial to the men who served here, and around the road to the row of firebacks and the museum at the end of the tour.

There are picnic tables scattered through this area and on the opposite side of 58. The rest rooms are across the road, and there is a scout camping area just off the old encampment site.

The simplest way to get to Ridgefield and the scene of the Arnold-Wooster attempt to stop Tryon's raiding party is to retrace your steps to Danbury through Bethel; go back along Danbury's Main Street and look for the turnoff onto West Street to your left. Take West Street for a short distance to Park Avenue and turn left. Park Avenue eventually leads through an underpass beneath U.S. 7 and onto Backus Avenue. You are now on the route followed by Tryon and his raiders as they detoured through Ridgebury, then went south to Ridgefield and back to Compo Beach. You are also following the route the French army took in June, 1781, from Newport, Rhode Island, to meet the Continental Army for what became the Yorktown campaign. Backus Avenue will take you to the Danbury city line where Pine Mountain Road comes in from the left.

Notice the brook meandering through the immediate area. It is called **Miry Brook** because of an incident along the British line of march. The local militia had removed a bridge that crossed the brook. As the British tried to ford the stream, one of their guns became mired in the mud and so the brook was given its name.

Backus Avenue leads onto George Washington Highway on the other side of the brook. As you leave the stream and head around a winding bit of road, notice a large, white house with a central chimney on the right, formerly the **Norris homestead.** On the morning of the French army's arrival in this vicinity, Rochambeau and some of his officers stopped here for water and learned that a daughter had been born to John Norris. Local legend has it that the Norrises wanted to name the child after Rochambeau, but he declined and requested she be named after his cavalry officer, the Duc de Lauzun. The story may be true, for the name Lauzun was used repeatedly in the Norris family following the Revolution and is still in the family. You will meet Lauzun again at Gloucester Point opposite Yorktown.

As you go through Ridgebury visiting the French army campsites, keep in mind that they were not chosen haphazardly as the army marched along. Washington sent out his chief engineer, Robert Erskine, to map the route in advance and went over it himself with the French army engineer. Each site was chosen for its access to forage and water and because it occupied either a sheltered or strong position. Eventually Louis Alexandre Berthier, a famous French army cartographer, drew a map of the route, one of many excellent drawings the French produced of Revolutionary War sites and lines of march and left for modern historians to delight in.

Continue east along George Washington Highway into the historic town of **Ridgebury,** a charming hamlet whose few streets are lined with many residences dating back to the eighteenth century, some to the early 1700s. When George Washington Highway meets Ridgebury Road, turn left or south and proceed to the intersection with Old Stagecoach Road. My tour of the Ridgebury sites began here under the expert guidance of Daniel M. McKeon, a local historian who has been researching the area for many years.

On one side of the intersection is a large, yellow frame house built in 1782. A plaque describes it as the former home of David Hunt who operated a stagecoach to Norwalk via Ridgefield and Wilton. On the other side of the road, directly opposite and west of the **Hunt House,** is a field which was part of the camp of the advance units of the French army, several companies of chasseurs and grenadiers under the command of Berthier, the map maker. They camped here on the nights of July 1 and 2, 1781, and used the spring now located behind the house. They used so much water that they emptied the spring, revealing a large community of frogs which they speedily converted into a feast of legs. The *campsite* extended up the hill to a point opposite a small, white frame building at the summit that marks the site of a former school. The site and the region is very like what it was then, with its fields, stone walls, and orchards.

Return north along Ridgebury Road to pick up the sites you passed on your way. A short distance from the campsite, look on the left for a rectangular, stone-wall enclosure just off the road. It is the remains of a cow pound, or pen, built in 1737 for local farmers to keep their cattle in during the winter. From the cow pen clock one mile back into Ridgebury to find the main French campsite. As you go, note a riding academy with a driveway leading off to the right to the barn. This was where the French pay carts stood. They contained the gold bullion Rochambeau had brought to pay the expenses of both armies during the Yorktown campaign. Incidentally, this same route was used by Washington accompanied by Lafayette in 1780 when he was on his way to his first meeting with Rochambeau. About 0.6 mile from where you started to clock, a modern white house stands on the left, the home of a Thomas Belden. Built in 1939, it is on the *foundations* of the home of Dr. Burr who provided Washington and Lafayette with a night's lodging during their journey.

Shortly after, you will come to the intersection with George Washington Highway. If you continue along Ridgebury Road past the Ridgebury Congregational Church on the left (built in 1760 and the town's meetinghouse during the Revolution) and the Country Day School on your right, you will come to a white house with a porch and a brick chimney on the left. Now the home of P. W. Wilson, it stands on the probable site of the *tavern* Rochambeau stayed in while his army was camped in the town. A little farther is an old *cemetery* with many colonial tombstones, including some marking the graves of Revolutionary War soldiers. Beyond that at the foot of Shadow Lake Road, which comes in from the right, stands a pink saltbox on the left which was built in 1712 and is probably the oldest building in Ridgebury. It is still lived in by a descendant of the original family, N. Lyman Keeler. A short distance beyond on the right is an old yellow house which is almost as old as the **Keeler House.**

Since, however, you're running the clock for the French army campsite, make a mental note to follow Ridgebury Road later, and turn right onto George Washington Highway. Almost immediately, the road crests a ridge and you will have clocked one mile. To the left, where the ridge climbs still higher, is where the main French army was encamped on the night of July 2, 1781. Parking is impossible at this spot, but a little farther on I found room to pull off the road so we could climb to the *campsite.*

The ridge is now covered with pasture grass and a sparse growth of young trees and is likely to remain so, for the local historical society has managed to keep it out of the hands of real-estate investors and builders. Designated along the line of march as Camp II, the Ridgebury sites provided for 4,800 troops: 3,600 infantry, 600 cavalry, and 600 artillery from four regiments, the Bourbonnais, Royal Deux-Ponts, Soissonnais, and Saintonge. The officers were put up at Ensign Samuel Keeler's tavern, which was probably the scene of some festivities since the army was celebrating Rochambeau's fifty-sixth birthday.

Once you have had your fill of rural Ridgebury, return to Ridgebury Road; turn left, and go back south, concentrating on the Tryon raid as you follow the raiders' route to Ridgefield. Ridgebury Road meets North Salem Road which is also Route 116. A short distance before, however, Ridgebury Road forks. You should bear left. As you approach Titicus and then Ridgefield on 116, keep your eyes peeled for the sign on the left marking the first skirmish between the British and the militia and the opening shots of the Battle of Ridgefield.

When we visited the site, the marker was a hand-painted wooden sign with black lettering on a white background. By the time you visit, the wooden sign will probably have been replaced by something more substantial and more visible.

The sign says that General Wooster attacked the rear guard of General Tryon here and captured forty prisoners, the first engagement in the Battle of Ridgefield, April 27, 1777. Tryon's men had camped at what was then the intersection of North Salem Road and Barlow Mountain Road. The latter road is no longer in existence, though traces of it remain in Ridgefield as an overgrown woods road. Wooster and Arnold had mustered about 600 men between them and probably had followed Tryon by devious routes and moved around the British position. Leading 200 men, Wooster took the British by surprise as they were camped, throwing them into confusion. There is some difference about the time of this attack. It occurred either at 8 A.M. on a rainy Sunday morning or between 11 and 12 A.M. In any event, the British offered little resistance. Wooster captured forty and quickly withdrew. The British resumed their march toward the village with Wooster's men trailing along, skirmishing constantly and looking for another opportunity to strike.

Continue south toward Ridgefield. Route 116 will be joined by Route 35 from the left. Clock exactly one mile from the site of the first skirmish and watch for what looks like a tall, narrow *tombstone* off the right side of the road, probably with an American Legion flag marker in front of it. It was here that Wooster attacked again and was mortally wounded. This was the southern intersection of North Salem Road and Tackora Trail and was just over two miles from the center of Ridgefield. Most of the British column had already passed. Wooster's little force, which had been firing at the redcoats constantly for more than an hour, must have been so close and their fire so hot that the British rear guard felt compelled to turn on this high ground and await an attack. They had three cannon which were wheeled about and brought to bear on the militia.

Wooster thought he saw a chance to capture one of the guns and led his men forward. One horse was shot from under him, but the intrepid commander, who had been exposed to the enemy's fire all morning long, mounted another and went forward again, sword in hand, toward the British. A solid shot hit nearby, showering his men with sand and throwing them into disorder. He turned in the saddle to urge them on, spoke a few words of encouragement, and was struck in the spine by a musket ball. It was fired by a Loyalist who, according to contemporary accounts, carried a musket with an unusually long barrel. He had to persuade the British officer in command to allow him to fire, so the story goes. The officer doubted that the Loyalist could drop Wooster at 300 yards and felt the shot would bring unnecessary retaliatory fire. Since, according to this same account, the British were already firing their cannon at the attackers, it is difficult to understand how a single musket shot could have affected the situation. At any rate, the shot was fired and it dropped Wooster from his saddle, paralyzed. He was carried first to a nearby meetinghouse and then by litter to Danbury where he died six days later on May 2.

In the meantime, Arnold and General Gold Selleck Silliman of the Connecticut militia had arrived in Ridgefield after a forced march from Bethel, collecting about 400 militia along the way. By about eleven in the morning, they had organized a defense of the town. Clock 1.2 miles from the site of Wooster's wounding to find the Arnold-Silliman defense position and the third and final part of the Battle of Ridgefield. At that point, you will have come up to the top of a rise of ground where the road narrows considerably. The top of the *ridge* has been excavated to allow for the modern roadbed, constricting the sides of the road by embankments and eliminating the shoulders. Because of this and the traffic going by, you will have to find parking wherever you can pull out of the way.

In 1777 this was the narrowest part of Main Street. It was here that Arnold and Silliman had their men erect a barricade of farm carts, logs, and other impediments. On one side of the road was the home of Benjamin Stebbins, situated at the northern end of Main Street. If you face south in the direction of the town, the Stebbins house would have been on your left; beyond it was a steep slope where the ground fell away sharply. On the right side of the road was a rocky ledge forming a natural barrier and a good anchor for the left flank of the American line. South of the rocky ledge was a marshy area.

The militia waited behind their barricade for the British. Tryon reconnoitered the position and approached in three columns. At two in the afternoon, he reorganized his men into a line of battle with guard units of 200 men on each flank and three fieldpieces in the center. The entire British command then moved forward to the strains of field music, perhaps hoping to overawe the local yokels with this display of British pomp and martial array. While his cannon fired on the barricade, Tryon directed his attack against Arnold's left, which, despite the rocky ledge, he judged to be the weakest part of the American line. While the militia behind the barricade directed incessant musket fire against the British center, Tryon sent a platoon to work its way around the rocky ledge under cover of an orchard and turned the American flank by scaling the ledge.

As the Americans fell back toward the town, the British on the ledge fired at Arnold at a distance of less than thirty yards and succeeded in killing his horse. As the animal fell, Arnold's feet became entangled in the stirrups. A Tory named Coon rushed forward and demanded his surrender. Arnold, however, managed to free himself. Drawing his pistol, he shot Coon dead and escaped into the swamp with British balls flying thick around him. According to legend, Arnold remarked as he gained cover that one live man was worth more than ten dead ones; he was a master of logic. According to another account, Benjamin Stebbins remained stubbornly at home during the engagement, though numerous British bullets ripped their way through the walls. The house was torn down about a hundred years ago.

The site of the Stebbins house is now occupied by modern buildings off the road with a driveway and a large sign at the entrance reading "Casagmo," which may be a commercial enterprise. A low, fieldstone wall borders the Casagmo property about six or seven feet from the road. Set into it is a *tablet* commemorating the battle. In part it tells us that in April, 1777, at this spot eight Patriots died who were laid in the ground companioned by sixteen British soldiers, living, their enemies; dying, their guests.

Flagstones laid into the ground originally marked the grave, though they are not evident now. Another plaque a little north of the Casagmo entrance commemorates the battle itself. A large, frame house, probably built at a subsequent date since no other house is mentioned on the site, occupies the *rocky ledge.* The ridge is clearly discernible, for the same road the British used, still called North Salem Road, comes up and goes down quite a steep grade on either side. This is the spot where the barricade was built and where the fighting took place. The American line extended on either side of the road, but the marshy area below the rocky ledge is now just a wooded plot with growth considerably younger than two hundred years. The American right is now occupied by Casagmo, but the ground still slopes away steeply. The original top of the ridge has been somewhat reduced by the roadbed.

As the Arnold-Silliman force withdrew, the British occupied Ridgefield to the accompaniment of further skirmishing along the streets and lanes until the town was completely in their possession. There was some looting and burning of supplies and several homes were set on fire, but there was no wholesale destruction as in Danbury. The British lost about 155 men killed, wounded, and missing; the Patriots, about 100.

Continue south into and through Ridgefield until you reach the far end of town, where you should look for the **Keeler Tavern** on the left at a junction where Route 35 goes off to the right at a diagonal. This is the tavern French officers were quartered in when Rochambeau's army camped in Ridgefield. A fountain stands in the center of the intersection, making a most conspicuous landmark.

The present Route 35 was a stagecoach road from New York to Boston. Keeler Tavern was a favorite stop for lodgings and refreshments. As you come in through the gate, note the large, flat stones to the left, on which passengers dismounted, and the stone steps leading down to ground level.

Admission to the tavern, $1.00 for adults and $0.25 for children, entitles one to mulled cider and cookies. The old building is furnished with numerous antiques and displays a number of relics of the eighteenth century, including a double mammy bench and a child's chair and table that converts into a highchair. Part of the present building was added by Cass Gilbert, the architect for the Woolworth Building and the Supreme Court Building in Washington, D.C. Gilbert rescued the original tavern from decay and restored it as a dwelling which he occupied during the early 1900s. Also of interest is a cupboard of sorts which served as a post office. Still posted inside the cupboard is a list of prices left by a traveling dentist.

The tavern was the target of British guns during the Ridgefield battle, as it had been reported the rebels were making munitions there. Several cannonballs were sent in its direction, one of which struck and lodged in a side wall. You can see it by going around to the left side of the house (facing the present front door) and looking for the marker which points to it. Another ball, according to legend, passed between the legs of someone who was coming down the steps from the upper floors. After the British occupied the town they set the tavern afire, but a Tory gentleman living next door persuaded them to allow him to put it out, since his own home was too close for comfort.

From Ridgefield, Tryon led his men back to Compo Beach on Long Island Sound without further serious incident. You can find the beach site by taking Route 35 south out of Ridgefield to Route 102. Turn left onto 102 east and take it to U.S. 7. Then take 7 south into Norwalk and Interstate 95, the Connecticut Turnpike. Take the turnpike to Exit 18.

As you come off the turnpike at Exit 18, turn left and proceed to the second traffic light. Turn left again and you will be paralleling the turnpike, heading back toward Norwalk. You will come to an intersection with a stop sign. Continue across the intersection to the next one at Compo Road. Turn left onto Compo Road and head for the Sound. As you drive through an area of one-family homes, you will arrive at the *statue* of a Minuteman in the middle of an intersection. It is a memorial to the men who resisted Tryon's 1777 raid.

After the Ridgefield battle, Arnold withdrew his men toward the Sound and Tryon's embarkation point. He prepared another position supposedly athwart the British line of march, but Tryon avoided it and reached Compo Hill, in this vicinity, at a point behind Arnold. Undaunted, Arnold led his men toward the British position. Before they could attack, however, the British pulled a diversionary attack of their own that threw the militia off balance and allowed them to embark and head back to New York. There is high ground in this area not far from the memorial, but it is obviously private ground now.

Turn right at the statue and drive along Green Farms Road to Compo Beach where the road swings left and traces the perimeter of a beach recreation area. You will come to a large parking area where you can leave your car and walk to the beach at the end of the driveway where two mounted cannon will catch your eye. On the other side of a low, stone wall is a *tablet* set into a stone commemorating the Compo Hill action. Tryon disembarked his men near here at the start of his raid and then reembarked for the return voyage.

THE 1779 RAID

Return to the turnpike and take it east to New Haven to cover Tryon's next visit to Connecticut. Get off at Exit 50, the last New Haven exit, onto Main Street, which extends directly ahead. Follow Main Street in the direction you are facing to Townsend Avenue. Turn right onto Townsend and follow it through a completely urbanized area to the shore of Morris Cove, which is part of New Haven Harbor.

To your right along the water is a park with grassy areas, benches, and walks. Ahead to your right front, you will see a neck of land curving out into the harbor with a lighthouse at the end. The lighthouse is your destination, but getting to it is a little tricky; Townsend Avenue will not take you there. Turn right onto Lighthouse Road to a wide intersection with a triangular grassed plot in the middle, the site of a war memorial. On the opposite side of the intersection is the entrance to Lighthouse Park. Drive into the park and follow the road out as far as you can to the *lighthouse.* This is a beach area with picnic grounds, playground, bath house, and picnic pavilion.

At the abandoned lighthouse, where an old British gun was once mounted, is a tablet erected by the New Haven D.A.R. The tablet says the spot is close to where that portion of the British raiders commanded by Tryon landed on July 5, 1779. According to the marker, the opposing forces became so large that the raiders had to retreat to their boats by July 7 without burning New Haven. This date, however, is suspect, since most accounts of this action give July 6 as the date the British withdrew.

Clinton sent 2,600 troops from New York under the command of Brigadier General Garth and Tryon to raid New Haven, destroy supplies, and in general raise hell in retaliation for the rebel ships that regularly raided British shipping from the Connecticut shore. Part of the force, under Tryon, landed at what was then East Haven (there is an East Haven today, but whether the two are the same is not clear); the other division under Garth entered New Haven. Tryon met only slight resistance in East Haven, and eventually both forces joined up in New Haven which they plundered before reembarking on July 6. They proceeded down the coast to Fairfield, which they occupied, and went on to Norwalk, which they destroyed. The recreation park and beach area has obviously changed the nature of the shore. The city probably did not extend this far, but lay farther inland where the local militia did put up some resistance in a hilltop fort which you should visit next.

Return to Townsend Avenue and take it back toward Main Street. Once away from the harbor area, watch for a wooded hill on your right, and an entrance between fieldstone gateposts onto a winding, dirt road to the summit. This is **Fort Wooster Park** where the remains of the breastworks are clearly seen and can be explored. Not a very big fort, it commanded the approaches to the town and overlooked the route the British must have followed as they marched up from the beach.

The tablet on the spot tells you that a signal beacon was set up here in 1775 and that a local force, whose size is not mentioned, resisted the British invaders on July 5, 1779. You can climb into the center of the fort area where what may have been a powder magazine appears to have been bricked to preserve it. The view is out over New Haven Harbor and the surrounding area. For the most part the park does not look as though it is taken care of by the city fathers. There are benches and one or two picnic tables, but the prospect of picnicking is not very appetizing.

Continue along Townsend Avenue to the intersection with U.S. 1; turn left onto 1, and follow it past the New Haven Railroad Terminal on your left and then some tank farms. Eventually U.S. 1 becomes Columbus Avenue and takes you to a large cemetery on the left. Close to the farther end of the cemetery, look for a small park on the right side of the avenue. It contains a large, heroic statuary group poised on top of a mound that could be the remains of a breastwork. Dressed in colonial costume, the old bronze figures serve a cannon pointed in the general direction of the West River. The *statue* commemorates a small part of the New Haven action in which some Yale students took up the planks of a bridge Garth and his command might have used. As additional local militiamen turned out, two guns were placed to cover the river approach, but the British found a way around the bridge. There doesn't seem to have been any real action here.

Return to the Connecticut Turnpike and head west to pick up the trail of the raiders in Fairfield. Get off at Exit 22; coming off the exit, continue along the service road parallel to the turnpike. At North Benson Road turn north; go under the turnpike, and look for Workman Road coming in from the right at a diagonal. In a small, triangular plot of ground to the right look for a bronze *plaque* set into a boulder. The plaque is in memory of the Americans who were killed in a skirmish during the raid, the Battle of Barlow Plain. The British occupied Fairfield on July 8, 1779, two days after they left New Haven. Since this is the only site in Fairfield connected with the event, return to the turnpike and head west again to cover the destruction of Norwalk.

Leave the turnpike at Exit 15. The ramp leads to West Avenue. Bear right onto West Avenue and follow it into a business-residential area. After several traffic lights, West Avenue forks and becomes Wall Street to the right. Follow Wall Street up a hill and into a residential area. At the top of a hill, in a parklike area, you will see the General Putnam Inn on the left and opposite it, on the right, an old brick church which is now a local museum. At the very top of the hill is a confusing intersection where several roads come together. To the left is a long, narrow, park area. Bear right as you come through this maze and look for the Norwalk Motor Inn on your left. In front of the inn entrance is a historical marker for the spot on **Grumman's Hill** from which General Tryon watched the burning of Norwalk, Sunday, July 11.

Return to that intersection-maze, and, watching the street signs carefully, make a left onto Park Street. As you come across North Avenue, Park Street becomes France Street. Proceed along France, up a hill with a church on the left side and a parochial school and private homes on the right. The next intersection will be Adams Avenue, which comes in from the left. The intersection is marked by a triangular plot of grassy ground. In the center is a *plaque* set into a granite boulder. The plaque marks the site of part of the resistance offered the British by local militia. On Monday, July 12, while the town was still burning, refugees with their household possessions piled up on horse-drawn wagons passed this way to escape the British. If you continue along France Street, it eventually becomes West Rock Street, the route the refugees used to find a haven on Belden Hill in what is now the town of Wilton just north of Norwalk.

Retrace your route to West Avenue and follow it back to and beyond the Connecticut Turnpike, past Reed Street, Garner Street, and Pine Street, which comes in from the left, to where the avenue forks. Bear right onto Spring Street, and look for a sharp right turn onto Fairfield Avenue. Take that right, but almost immediately make a left onto Couch Street which goes up a fairly steep hill in a residential neighborhood. Two blocks up the hill you will come to Elmwood Avenue.

Near the intersection of Elmwood and Couch, to the right as you look up the hill, notice a contemporary, white cottage on top of a low bluff behind a cement retaining wall. Between the wall and the road is a large, flat *rock* surrounded by decorative plantings. Set into the rock is a small cannonball. The words inscribed on the rock inform you that on July 12, 1779, a battle took place here between the local militia and the British raiders. The cannonball was found on the site a hundred years later. According to Christopher Ward's *War of the Revolution,* about fifty militia were engaged against the invaders, who were held up by this resistance only a few hours. More than 250 buildings were destroyed in Norwalk, including homes, barns, shops, and warehouses; the loot carried away amounted to about $150,000.

STAMFORD

Return to the turnpike and take it west to Stamford to see some other sites while you are along the sound. Get off at Exit 6; continue along the service road for a short distance to West Street; turn right onto West Street, and take it to Stillwater Avenue. Bear left onto Stillwater; look for Connecticut Avenue coming in from the left, and proceed to a turnoff to the left onto Palmers Hill Road. There is a rehabilitation center to your left at this intersection. Turn left, but immediately bear right on Westover Road. The site you are going to is 2.1 miles from this point.

You will be driving through a wealthy residential area with many large estates and beautiful country homes on both sides of the road. Look for a huge sycamore tree, which is every bit of two hundred years old, standing at a fork in the road. The site is 0.8 mile from that tree. Immediately before the site, you will see Merry Brook Lane, a private road to the left. Just beyond, on the left side of the road, is a large, gray stone which may be partially obscured by high grass. It stands opposite a large, colonial frame house, No. 887 on the mailbox, once the home of Alan Bunce, the actor.

The stone is a D.A.R. marker for old **Fort Stamford** which lies off the road in the sparsely wooded fields beyond a low stone wall. A short distance farther are the intersections of a circular driveway which goes into the field. I drove into the entrance nearest the D.A.R. marker into a Stamford park area. If you leave your car and walk on ahead, you will come to the remains of what was once a marble grape arbor, pavilion, or lily ponds of some sort. If you go left, however, and walk parallel to the road, you will see a flagpole sticking up above a grove of trees. Inside the grove are the remains of a circular **breastwork** with the flagpole in the middle. Turn your back to the road; walking farther away for fifty or sixty feet, you will find the remains of another breastwork. These breastworks are the remains of Fort Stamford. Built early in the Revolution, it was part of the American defense line that stretched from Long Island Sound to Peekskill on the Hudson River. This is only one of several "lost" Revolutionary War sites we found, lost because there are no signs showing the way, inadequate markings, and no explanatory aids. The old fort is on Stamford parklands, however, and I understand the city fathers are planning to rehabilitate the site for the bicentennial.

Go back the way you came, and as you come down Stillwater Avenue, look for the intersection with West Broad Street. Turn left onto West Broad, which will take you to the center of Stamford, until it dead-ends at Grove Street. Turn onto Grove Street and follow it to Elm Street, where you must turn left. Take Elm Street through an underpass beneath the turnpike and then through another under the New Haven Railroad tracks until you reach Shippan Avenue. Turn right onto Shippan and head for a site on Shippan Point. Leaving Stamford's business center, drive through a residential neighborhood and turn onto Ocean Drive West, which comes in only from the right, follow it down a hill to a road that skirts the sound just beyond. Turn left and immediately look for the Stamford Yacht Club on your right.

Behind the clubhouse, on a lawn that slopes down to the edge of the water is a *marker* indicating that on the night of September 5, 1779, Major Benjamin Tallmadge embarked with 130 men here to cross the sound and raid Lloyd's Neck, Long Island, and returned with 115 prisoners. According to other sources, Tallmadge's force consisted of 150 men; they surprised 500 Tories and got back to Stamford with no losses and with most of the 500 as prisoners. The site is on private property, the yacht club grounds, but James L. Wood, the manager of the club at the time I visited, assured me the site may be viewed by groups who ask for permission beforehand; otherwise it is not ordinarily open to the public.

Since you have come this far, it would be wise and convenient to go just a few miles farther west to Greenwich and two sites connected with Israel Putnam.

GREENWICH

Retrace your route to the turnpike and take it west to Exit 4. Coming off the exit ramp, follow the signs for U.S. 1, the old Boston Post Road, and take it west. Look for Putnam Avenue in a section where the road seems to be lined with churches on both sides. The **General Putnam Cottage** will be on your right near there on U.S. 1. A sign identifies it as the place from which Putnam escaped the British by his famous ride down Put's Hill. The story of this legendary feat has been questioned by several historians who insist that Putnam was too old and too fat to have performed such a task of horsemanship. The following account is based on an article by Konstance Kirkpatrick in the D.A.R. magazine in May, 1965.

During the Revolution, Greenwich, then known as Horseneck, lay in a no-man's-land very like southern Westchester County. The town was filled with Tories. Plundering bands robbed and looted almost at will. It was also filled with ample supplies of food, ammunition, and salt. On Thursday, February 25, 1779, General Tryon led a force of 600 light infantry from King's Bridge, New York, to New Rochelle where they skirmished with a small Continental detachment. The leader of the detachment, Colonel Titus Wilson, escaped and rode to Horseneck to warn the 150 Continental soldiers stationed there. General Putnam, then in command of the forces encamped at Redding, was in Horseneck at the time. He had put up at an inn kept by Israel Knapp. Wilson got there at 8:30 A.M. on February 26 and warned the general the British were approaching. A half hour later, the enemy made its appearance.

By that time, Putnam was mounted and with his men on a hill near the Congregational Church. They pointed their two small cannon at the British, who were now approaching up the post road and preparing to charge. Seeing he was badly outnumbered, Putnam ordered a volley and then a retreat. The rebels escaped into nearby swamps where pursuit was difficult. Putnam headed down the post road toward Fort Stamford where he hoped to obtain reinforcements. Recognizing him, a detachment of British cavalry chased after him. Sixty-one years old and fat, Putnam could not hope to outride his pursuers. He came to the edge of a steep drop where stone steps had been cut into the sides for the convenience of people living in nearby Cos Cob who attended services in the Episcopal Church in Horseneck. With the British hot on his heels, Putnam rode his horse without hesitation down the steps. Afraid to follow, the redcoats reined in at the top of the hill and fired their guns after him. The old man gained the swamps below, turned in his saddle, and shaking his fist at the enemy swore that he'd hang them all if he ever caught them.

Putnam got away to Fort Stamford while the British occupied Horseneck and spent the rest of the day in "drunken debauchery, robbery, and murder." Came evening and they started back to King's Bridge. The reinforcements arrived and the retreating redcoats were harassed all the way back, losing many men killed or taken prisoner and all their plunder.

The old Knapp Inn is now the Israel Putnam Cottage. It is a two-story, frame building built sometime between 1692 and 1729, with a small, fieldstone wing to the right as you face it that was subsequently added on. It is open to the public, 10 A.M.–5 P.M., Mondays, Thursdays, Fridays, and Saturdays and is furnished with period antiques.

To find the hill down which Putnam escaped, turn left as you leave the cottage and walk along the sidewalk bordering the post road. After a block or two, U.S. 1 goes down a slope to your right and you will be walking along the top of a rising bluff. Shortly after you pass a sign for Old Church Road–1749, you will come to a wide, grassy plot of ground which overlooks U.S. 1 some twenty or thirty feet below. A large, oval block of granite surrounded by ornamental shrubs bears a plaque commemorating Putnam's escape. Walk behind the boulder and look down the precipitous side of the *bluff*. Outcroppings of rock thrust through from under the topsoil and vegetation to form what is actually a small cliff. The *steps* cut into the side for the Cos Cob parishioners are still there to climb down if you so desire. It was down this steep descent that Putnam rode or probably slid his horse, if the story is true. Down at the bottom is a stretch of woodland that looks rather wet and swampy and presumably marks the old wood into which he made his escape.

Having covered two of the three raids and several other sites as well, return to the turnpike and head east again, this time for a drive of over an hour to New London to attend the raid Arnold carried out against the citizens of his native state.

NEW LONDON—ARNOLD'S RAID, 1781

Get off the Connecticut Turnpike at any one of the New London exits and follow the signs for the Orient Point Ferry. As you do, you will pick up signs for the Naval Underwater Systems Center as well. Abandon the ferry signs for the navy signs, which will take you to Wallback Street and the main gate to the base which stands on the site of **Fort Trumbull**. By prearrangement, we were shown over the base by a representative from the public relations office. Similar arrangements can be made beforehand by anyone wishing to view the site. Actually there is nothing left of the Revolutionary War fort. The military structures now occupying the site, with the exception of one structure, were built between 1839 and 1850.

Before that, there were coastal gun emplacements here during the early years of the nineteenth century.

The eighteenth-century fort was built between 1775 and 1777 by order of the colonial assembly of Connecticut, as was Fort Griswold across the Thames River in Groton. Fort Trumbull was built on three acres on a rocky point called Mamacock. It consisted of earthen ramparts which, if they followed the plans laid down by the engineer who drew them up, Colonel Elderkin, consisted of three ramparts facing east, south, and north, each measuring eighty feet, with five gun embrasures in each rampart capable of mounting eighteen- or twenty-four-pounders. Both Forts Griswold and Trumbull were built by the citizens of New London and Groton working in relays. Work began in 1776 and was completed in the summer of 1777. In March, 1778, the works were repaired and additional guns were placed in position as directed by Lieutenant Colonel William Ledyard, whom we will meet again under tragic circumstances.

All that is left of the eighteenth-century buildings is a stone *blockhouse* dated 1794 when Congress enacted a law that required the fortification of all harbors along the coast. You will find the blockhouse on the highest point of land within the base, overlooking the Thames and giving you a fine view of this stretch of the river where it widens to form its mouth as it empties into the Sound. On the opposite bank, the tall, granite obelisk that marks the site of Fort Griswold stands out boldly on the skyline and the fort itself, surrounded by modern homes, can be clearly seen.

This was the last military action to take place in the North. Washington and Rochambeau had already made a feint toward New York with their combined armies and were on their way to Virginia. In fact, on September 6, the day of the New London battle, the allies had already reached Head of Elk in Maryland and Clinton was well aware of what Washington was up to. New London was a known repository for many of the supplies rebel privateers had seized from British ships and a center of privateer activity. When Clinton ordered this final Connecticut raid he had a dual purpose in mind: to seize the stores and lay waste this important base, and to cause a diversion which he hoped would distract Washington from his advance toward Cornwallis in the southern theater.

His choice of commander of the enterprise was a man who had been born and bred in nearby Norwich, Brigadier General Benedict Arnold who knew the area well. On the night of Wednesday, September 5, Arnold, with 1,700 men in thirty-five ships, hovered in the waters of Long Island Sound near the shore opposite New London awaiting a favorable wind for a night attack. With the wind against him, however, he was not able to approach the mouth of the Thames until the next morning at about 9 A.M.

An hour later he landed half of his force under Lieutenant Colonel Eyre on the east bank of the river near Groton Heights and the other half, under his command, on the west bank near New London. Fort Trumbull was not defended from the land side. Arnold sent a detachment to see to the fort. Captain Adam Shapley ordered his men there to fire their eight guns and muskets once, had the guns spiked, and evacuated his command in the face of superior forces. He and his men rowed across the river to reinforce Fort Griswold. Arnold continued on into New London which he virtually destroyed, burning about 143 buildings and leaving almost 100 families homeless. He also destroyed much of the shipping in the harbor. Later he said the fires that destroyed the homes were started accidentally and that his men made every effort to put them out.

Jonathan Rathbone, a member of the Colchester militia, was on the scene after the battle and sacking of the town on the morning of September 7, along with hundreds of other militiamen who poured into New London too late to do anything but pick up the pieces. These excerpts from his diary, published in the *Magazine of History,* give a graphic description of the aftermath of the raid.

"The city was in ashes. More than 130 naked chimneys were standing in the midst of the smoking ruins of stores and dwelling houses. Very little property had escaped the conflagration except for part of the shipping which on the first alarm was sent up the river. But though the city was destroyed it was far from being deserted. Numerous companies of militia from the neighborhood were pouring into the town; and the inhabitants, who had fled from their burning dwellings, were returning to gaze with anguish on the worthless remains of their property. Women were seen walking with consternation and despair depicted in their countenances, leading or carrying in their arms their fatherless and houseless babes, who in a few short hours had been bereaved of all that was dear on earth. Their homes, their provisions and even their apparel were the spoils for the enemy or lay in ashes at their feet. Some were inquiring with the deepest distress for the mangled bodies of their friends while others were seen following the carts which bore their murdered fathers, husbands or brothers to the grave. More than forty widows were made on that fatal day."

According to Rathbone, Arnold had a sister living in New London with whom he dined and whose home he then had set afire "as is supposed by his orders immediately afterwards. Perhaps he found her too much of a patriot for his taste and took this step in revenge." This should, most certainly, be taken with a grain or two of seasoning until some proof appears to either discredit or verify the story.

To continue the story of the raid, leave Fort Trumbull and returning to the Connecticut Turnpike, take it east across the Thames River to the first exit after the bridge, the Groton exit. Keep your eye on the Fort Griswold monument and you can't go wrong. As you come down the exit ramp you will see a sign for **Fort Griswold State Park** directing you along a street that skirts the Thames River on your right. Look for two fieldstone gateposts on either side of Fort Street where it intersects from the left. Turn left between the gateposts and drive up the hill to Slocum Terrace. A left onto Slocum Terrace will take you along the foot of the hill now on your right on which the fort stood. At the second stop sign you will be at the intersection of Slocum Terrace and School Street. Turn right onto School Street, which will take you to Monument Street, where another right turn will take you to the entrance to the park and the remains of the fort.

A low, stone wall and two imposing gateposts mark the entrance opposite the **Bill Memorial Library** which is housed in a Victorian structure. The library has accounts of the Fort Griswold affair that you may want to read before or after you go over the site. The *obelisk* is open to the public during the spring and summer for a climb to the top and a view out over the river and harbor. A small *museum* just beyond the monument has relics and artifacts of the battle and the history of the town. The two guns flanking the entrance to the fort look like naval or coastal guns of the post-revolution period.

The original fort, according to the diary of Stephen Hempstead who fought here, had stone walls ten or twelve feet high surrounded by a ditch. There was also a line of pickets or a palisades twelve feet high and a parapet with gun embrasures. Immediately behind the wall were platforms for cannon and a firing step. There was a flagstaff in the southwest bastion and a gate on one side with a triangular breastwork to protect it as well as a redoubt mounting a three-pounder. A bird's-eye view of the fort from the top of the monument shows a roughly star-shaped structure with protruding bastions at both of the two corners facing the river. Two long walls angle outward and extend inland. At the opposite side is a straight wall broken by two sides of a triangle coming to an apex. There was also a barracks, a long narrow structure. One diagram, which may be of the post-Revolution fort, shows the rampart between the two bastions facing the river mounting seven guns. The southwest bastion in which the flagpole stood mounted three guns facing the river; the other bastion mounted four guns, two facing the river and two facing the opposite direction to cover the gate, which was just beyond this bastion.

You will find intact the breastworks around the entire perimeter of the fort, the triangular rampart that protected the gate, the two bastions facing the river, and a ditch just beyond a sallyport in the wall opposite where you entered, the remains of a covered way that leads down a slope to a lower, outer defense work. You will also find the spots marked where Major Montgomery fell and where Ledyard, the fort's commander, died. Walk the ramparts, look out over the river, walk down the ditch to the lower works, but as you cross the parade grounds inside the fort, imagine if you can the cries of the wounded and dying that filled the air that September day as the victorious British troops put most of the garrison to the sword and bayonet.

As soon as the British fleet was discovered at daybreak, two of the fort's guns were loaded with heavy charges of powder and fired as a signal to militia units in the outlying districts that an attack was imminent. The British, however, had probably been tipped off and fired a third gun immediately after the two alarm guns, turning the alarm signal into a "good news" message that threw the Connecticut militia off guard and prevented reinforcements from arriving.

While Arnold's column was devastating New London, Lieutenant Colonel Eyre and his men were trying to invest the fort, which was manned by about 160 men under the command of Lieutenant Colonel William Ledyard. They began their attack about noon and were met by determined resistance.

Rufus Avery, a sergeant who was on guard duty the night of September 5–6 and gave the alarm that morning, described the ensuing action in his diary. He describes the landing of Eyre's force which, he says, was divided into two units, one led by Eyre, the other by Major Montgomery. Eyre's men were sheltered behind some rocky ledges 130 rods away (more than 2,000 feet). Montgomery's men were behind a high hill about 150 rods away. While this was going on, Arnold's command was investing New London and taking Fort Trumbull. According to Avery, seven of Captain Shapley's men were badly wounded while getting away from Fort Trumbull in the boats.

Before attacking, Eyre sent a flag of truce to the fort demanding its surrender. Ledyard refused and was then informed that by the rules of war, his garrison was subject to no quarter.

While the parlaying went on, shots were exchanged between the British detachment now in Fort Trumbull and the Americans in Fort Griswold. At about 11 A.M., Eyre's men advanced in columns and were met first by round shot and then by grape. The fort's cannon were aimed by a Captain Elias Henry Halsey, who had had much experience as a privateer and knew how to aim cannon with deadly effect.

"I was at the gun with others," wrote Avery, "when it was discharged into the British ranks and it cleared a very wide space in the solid columns. It has been reported by good authority that about twenty were killed and wounded by that one discharge of grapeshot. As soon as the column was broken by loss of men and officers they were seen to scatter and trail arms coming on with a quick step towards the fort and climbing to the west. [West would be before you as you stand on the ramparts of Griswold and face across the Thames toward Trumbull.] We continued firing but they advanced on the south and west side of the fort. Colonel Eyre was mortally wounded. Major Montgomery now advanced with his men coming on in solid columns bearing around to the north [to your right as you face Trumbull] until they got east of the . . . battery which was east of the fort [perhaps the lower works which are east of the fort proper. In view of where Montgomery was killed, this seems likely], then marching with a quick step into the battery. Here we sent among them large and repeated charges of grapeshot which destroyed a number as we could perceive them thinned and broken. Then they started for the fort a part of them in platoons discharging their guns; and some of the officers and men scattering they came around on the east and north side of the fort . . . Here Major Montgomery fell near the northeast part of the fort."

Despite the loss of their commanding officers, the British came on and could not be prevented from surrounding the fort. An attempt was made to open the gate, but was repulsed. "There was hard fighting and shocking slaughter and much blood spilled," continues Avery, "before another attempt was made to open the gates which was this time successful."

The garrison was then overpowered. Avery says that there was no blockhouse on the parade "as there is now so that the enemy had the chance to kill or wound every man."

At this point occurred the shocking murder of Ledyard. All accounts agree that when Ledyard saw that further resistance was useless, he offered his sword in surrender to a British officer who took it and stabbed him with it, after which Ledyard was bayoneted to death. Accounts differ, however, as to who that officer was. Boatner cites a Lieutenant Colonel Abram van Buskirk of the New Jersey Volunteers. Benson J. Lossing says it was a Major Bromfield, another Tory officer. Stephen Hempstead says that Colonel Beckwith, a New Jersey Tory, shouted, "Who commands this fort?" to which Ledyard replied, "I did, sir, but you do now," and handed over his sword, only to be stabbed by Beckwith.

Avery describes what he saw: "I noticed Colonel William Ledyard on the parade stepping toward the enemy and Bloomfield [probably Bromfield, the Tory officer] generally raising and lowering his sword in a token of bowing in submission. He was about six feet from them when I turned my eyes off from him and went up to the door of the barracks and looked at the enemy who were discharging their guns through the windows. It was but a moment that I had turned my eyes from Colonel L. and saw him alive and now I saw him weltering in his gore."

According to memoirs of the war written by Major General William Heath of the Continental Army, another American officer standing nearby saw Ledyard's murder and stabbed the officer who had stabbed Ledyard, whereupon the British troops began to bayonet the rest of the garrison.

Here is Avery's account of what followed Ledyard's death. "The column [Montgomery's division who had come through a gate] continued marching toward the south end of the parade and I could do no better than to go across the parade before them amid their fire. . . . They killed and wounded every man they possibly could and it was all done in less than two minutes. I had nothing to expect but to drop with the rest; one mad looking fellow put his bayonet to my side swearing, that by dash he would skiver me. I looked him earnestly in the face and eyes and begged him to have mercy and spare my life. I must say I believe God prevented him from killing me for he put his bayonet three times into me. . . . There were two large doors to the magazine which made a space wide enough to admit ten men to stand in one rank. There marched up a platoon of ten men just by where I stood [He stood after being bay-oneted three times!] and at once discharged their guns into the magazine among our killed and wounded and also among those who had escaped uninjured and as soon as these had fired and another platoon was ready yet immediately took their place when they fell back. At this moment Bloomfield came swiftly around the corner of the building and . . . exclaimed, 'Stop firing or you will send us all to hell together.' I was very near him when he spoke. He knew there must be much powder depos-ited and scattered about the magazine and that if they continued throw-ing in fire we should all be blown up. I think it must before this have been the case had not the ground and everything been wet with human blood."

Avery goes on to describe how the British put their own wounded in the shade and left the American wounded and dying out in the hot sun and refused to give them water. Reports of casualties vary. One source said that seventy to eighty of the fort's garrison were killed, all but three after the surrender. Arnold's report to Clinton says eighty-five were found dead in the fort and sixty wounded, many of them dying later. Altogether the Americans seemed to have lost about 240, with another seventy taken prisoner. British losses were forty-eight killed and 145 wounded. Other accounts, Avery's included, tell how the wounded were loaded onto an ammunition wagon which some redcoats pulled up to the brow of the hill preparatory to taking them to the ships below. The men pulling the cart lost control and the load of wounded men rolled down the hill and collided with a tree, which added to their suffering. Avery himself was taken to New York as a prisoner and was exchanged not long after.

The site must have been continuously fortified after the Revolution; besides the blockhouse mentioned by Avery, a monument on the present site is dedicated to Civil War soldiers who served here. It is interesting to note that the rampart on which Montgomery was killed was the object of one of the heaviest assaults of the battle and marks the spot where many of the British casualties occurred. According to one account I found in the library, the British buried their dead in a mass grave in the ditch of the triangular work that protected the gate, but there is no marker to indicate the spot. According to the narrative of an eyewitness, George Middleton, the enemy attacked the fort on three sides at once and, getting into the ditch outside the ramparts, cut away the palisades. Using scaling ladders, they got into the fort and tore away the gate from the inside. Middleton's account says that Montgomery's last words were an order to put the garrison to death and that he was buried in a grave within the parapet of the fort in front of the gates.

Arnold is supposed to have viewed the battle from an old burial ground near the rocky ledge behind which Eyre grouped his unit for the attack. We drove down the street bordering the fort away from the library, turned right at the first big intersection, and found the only burial ground in the vicinity, a large cemetery in which Colonel William Ledyard is buried. At the far end of the cemetery, which contains a number of colonial tombstones predating the Revolution, is indeed a bluff with rock ledges protruding that may identify this as Eyre's jumping-off place and **Arnold's vantage point.**

You may want to visit one additional site in New London before you leave the area, the **Shaw Mansion** on Bank Street, which was the naval war office during the Revolution. It is open to the public, Tuesdays–Saturdays, 1–4 P.M. In it you will find a sword carried by one of the officers at Fort Griswold in a showcase on the ground floor off the main entrance. The mansion marked the southern boundary of the destroyed area during the Arnold raid. The rebels' first naval expedition, authorized by the Continental Congress in 1776, was organized and fitted out in this house; and it was here that Commodore Esek Hopkins, first commander in chief of the Continental navy, met with Washington in April, 1776. Washington spent the night here and his room has been preserved as a memorial. You can visit the Shaw Mansion before you go on to Fort Griswold from Trumbull. Go back the way you came toward the Connecticut Turnpike to Bank Street and turn right onto Bank Street. A few blocks from the statue, you will see the Shaw Mansion on the left on a little street that comes off Bank Street. It is set off from the sidewalk on a rise of ground, a fine, handsome old colonial structure. It has a number of furnishings original to the house and family.

WETHERSFIELD

Before you leave Connecticut, visit Wethersfield, a lovely, old town filled with a hundred or more old homes, many of them dating from the eighteenth century. Take Interstate 91 (from Interstate 95) to the exit for the Berlin Turnpike just south of Hartford, and then the Berlin Turnpike to the exit marked Wethersfield–99. Follow Route 99 south to Church Street. Make a left on Church which will lead you into Main Street. Notice the signs for the Joseph Webb House and the Buttolph-Williams House along the way. Turn right onto Main Street and look for three old colonial houses standing in a row on your right a short distance from the intersection.

These venerable and well-preserved relics are the Isaac Stevens House, the Joseph Webb House, and the Silas Deane House. All three are open to the public, Tuesdays through Saturdays year-round from 10 A.M. until 4 P.M. They are also open on Sundays, May 15–November 1, from 1 to 4 P.M. Admission to each is $1.00; a combined admission to all three is $2.50.

The **Webb House**, built in 1752, is where Washington met with Rochambeau to plan the strategy that took the French-American army to Yorktown. The room in which the conference took place is the first room to your left as you enter through the front door. Though the house underwent some restoration, all the paneling and moldings are original, as are the treads on the stairs. The furnishings are period antiques, but none of the furniture is original to the house, with the exception of a chest on loan from Yale University which stands next to the stairway in the downstairs hall. There is also a Charles Willson Peale portrait of Joseph Webb, the builder and original occupant.

Upstairs on the second floor to the left as you come off the staircase is the room Washington slept in during the period of the conference, May 21–22, 1781. On the walls is the original wallpaper which was placed there especially for his visit. Rochambeau's room was the one directly opposite. The reconstructed garden behind the house was built according to an approximate idea of what the original garden may have been like.

This is a fine, old house and well worth an hour or so of your time. So is the **Silas Deane House** next door, built in 1766. Deane was a member of the Continental Congress and the first American diplomat to carry out foreign assignments for the new government. It was Deane who in 1776 was sent by Congress to France to explore the possibilities of French assistance. Deane compromised his mission by indulging in profiteering in partnership with a British double agent, but he was also instrumental in arranging for French money and supplies to reach the rebellious colonists through Beaumarchais, Louis XVI's unofficial agent in the matter.

Many of Wethersfield's old homes bear identifying plaques. As you leave the Webb House, look to your left diagonally across what was a town green and notice the fine, old, colonial church with a spire designed in the manner of Christopher Wren.

BIBLIOGRAPHY

GENERAL

ADAMS, JAMES TRUSLOW, ed. *Atlas of American History.* 2d rev. ed. New York, 1943.

————. *Dictionary of American History.* 5 vols. 2d ed., rev. New York, 1942.

The American Heritage Book of the Revolution. The Editors of American Heritage. New York, 1958.

American Heritage Pictorial Atlas of United States History. The Editors of American Heritage. New York, 1966.

BEARD, CHARLES A. and MARY R. *A Basic History of the United States.* New York, 1944.

BOATNER, MARK M., III. *Encyclopedia of the American Revolution.* New York, 1966.

CARRINGTON, HENRY B. *Battles of the American Revolution.* New York, 1877.

CHASTELLUX, MARQUIS DE. *Travels in North America* . . . Translated and Edited by Howard C. Rice, Jr. 2 vols. Chapel Hill, N.C., 1963.

COMMAGER, HENRY STEELE and MORRIS, RICHARD B., eds. *The Spirit of 'Seventy-Six* . . . 2 vols. Indianapolis and New York, 1958.

DUPUY, R. ERNEST and TREVOR N. *The Compact History of the Revolutionary War.* New York, 1963.

FLEXNER, JAMES T. *George Washington: The Forge of Experience* (*1732–1775*). Boston, 1965.

————. *George Washington in the American Revolution* (*1775–1783*). Boston, 1967.

FORD, COREY. *A Peculiar Service.* Boston, 1965.

FREEMAN, DOUGLAS S., et al. *George Washington: A Biography.* 7 vols. New York, 1948–57.

GREENE, EVARTS B. *The Revolutionary Generation 1763–1790.* New York, 1943.

HICKS, JOHN D. *The Federal Union.* Boston and New York, 1937.

HIGGINBOTHAM, DON. *The War of American Independence.* New York, 1971.

HUNT, GAILLARD. *Fragments of Revolutionary History.* Brooklyn, N.Y., 1892.

LANCASTER, BRUCE. *From Lexington to Liberty.* Garden City, N.Y., 1955.

LOSSING, BENSON J. *The Pictorial Field Book of the American Revolution.* 2 vols. New York, 1850–52.

MILLER, JOHN C. *Origins of the American Revolution.* Boston, 1943.

MONTROSS, LYNN. *Rag, Tag and Bobtail* . . . New York, 1952.

NATIONAL PARK SERVICE. *National Register of Historic Places.* Washington, D.C., 1969.

SARLES, FRANK B., JR. and SHEDD, CHARLES E. *Colonials and Patriots.* Vol. 6. National Survey of Historic Sites and Buildings. Washington, D.C., 1964.

SCHEER, GEORGE F. and RANKIN, HUGH F. *Rebels and Redcoats.* Cleveland and New York, 1957.

TALLMADGE, BENJAMIN. *Memoir of* . . . Boston, 1876.

TREVELYAN, GEORGE M. *History of England.* New York, 1953.

TUNIS, EDWIN. *Colonial Living.* New York, 1957.

VAN DOREN, CARL. *Secret History of the American Revolution.* New York, 1941.

WARD, CHRISTOPHER. *The War of the Revolution.* Edited by John R. Alden. 2 vols. New York, 1952.

WASHINGTON, GEORGE. *Affectionately Yours, George Washington.* Edited by Thomas J. Fleming. New York, 1967.

THE WAR IN THE NORTH

BARNES, ERIC W. "All the King's Horses and All the King's Men," *American Heritage.* October, 1960.

BECKER, CARL L. *History of Political Parties in the Province of New York 1760–76.* Madison, Wis., 1960.

BEDINI, SILVIO A. *Ridgefield in Review.* Ridgefield, Conn., 1958.

BLIVEN, BRUCE, JR. *Battle for Manhattan.* New York, 1956.

CARR, WILLIAM H. and KOKE, RICHARD J. *Twin Forts of the Popolopen—Forts Clinton and Montgomery, N.Y. 1775–77.* Bear Mountain, N.Y., 1937.

CASTONGUAY, JACQUES. *The Unknown Fort.* Montreal, 1965.

CLARK, DONALD F. *Fort Montgomery and Fort Clinton; Several Contemporary Accounts of the Battle* . . . New York, 1952.

DIVERS EMINENT HANDS. *The Cambridge of 1776* . . . Boston, 1876.

EVELYN, W. GLANVILLE. *Memoirs and Letters* . . . *1774–76.* Oxford, 1879.

FOCHT, JACK and WATTS, JOSEPHINE. *Trail of Intrigue.* New City, N.Y., Undated.

FRANKO, ALFRED M. *The Place of Mount Vernon's Village Green and St. Paul's Church in American History.* Mount Vernon, N.Y., Undated.

HENRY, JOHN J. *Account of Arnold's Campaign Against Quebec.* Albany, N.Y., 1877.

HERON, LOUISE. *Historic Kingston, New York.* New York, 1969.

HUFELAND, OTTO. *Westchester County During the American Revolution, 1775–83.* New York, 1926.

HULTON, ANN. *Letters of a Loyalist Lady.* Cambridge, Mass., 1927.

MACKENZIE, FREDERICK. *Diary of* . . . 2 vols. Cambridge, Mass., 1930.

RATHBONE, JONATHAN. *Narrative of* . . . Arno Press Eyewitness of the American Revolution Series. New York, 1911.

SAWYER, JOHN. *History of Cherry Valley from 1740 to 1898.* Cherry Valley, N.Y., 1968.

SIMMS, JEPHTHA. *History of Schoharie County.* Albany, N.Y., 1845.

SNELL, CHARLES W. and WILSHIN, FRANCIS F. *Saratoga National Historic Park.* National Park Service Publication. Washington, D.C., 1950.

STONE, EDWIN MARTIN. *Our French Allies.* Providence, R.I., 1884.

ZOBEL, HILLER B. *The Boston Massacre.* New York, 1970.

INDEX